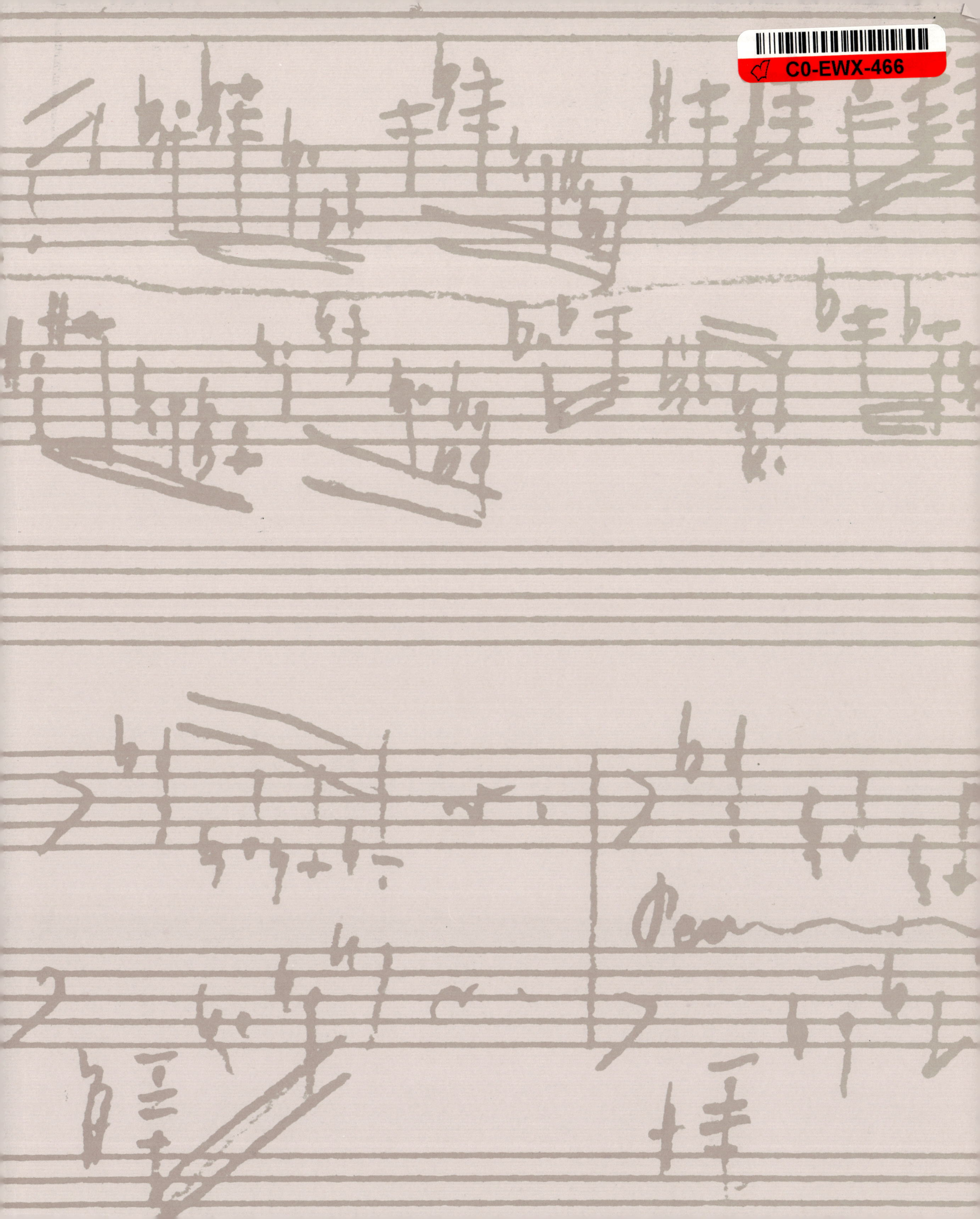
Ped

Schoenberg, Kandinsky, and the Blue Rider

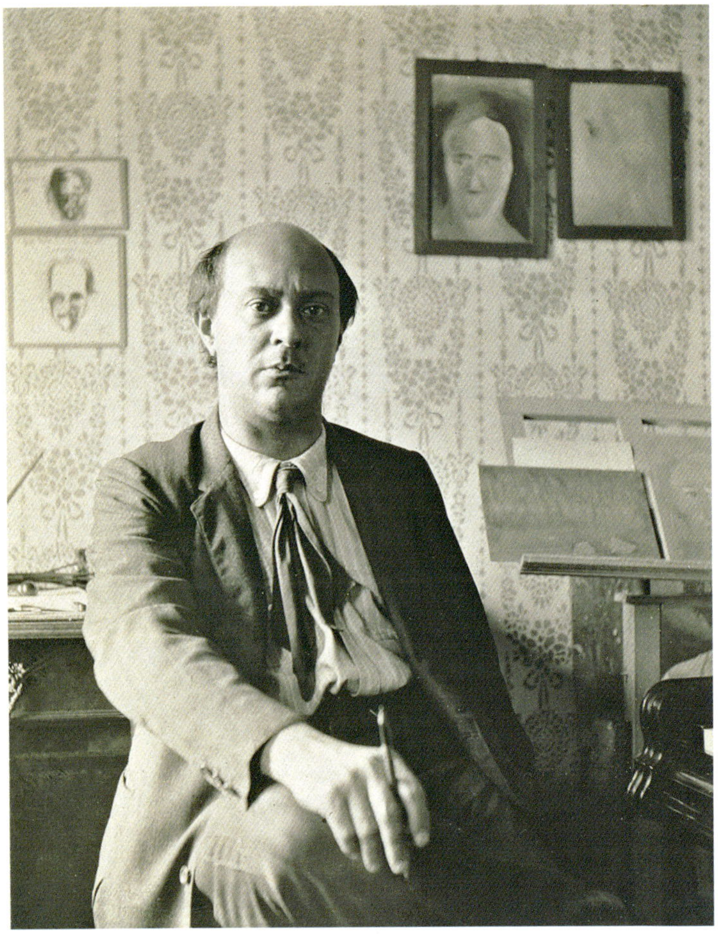

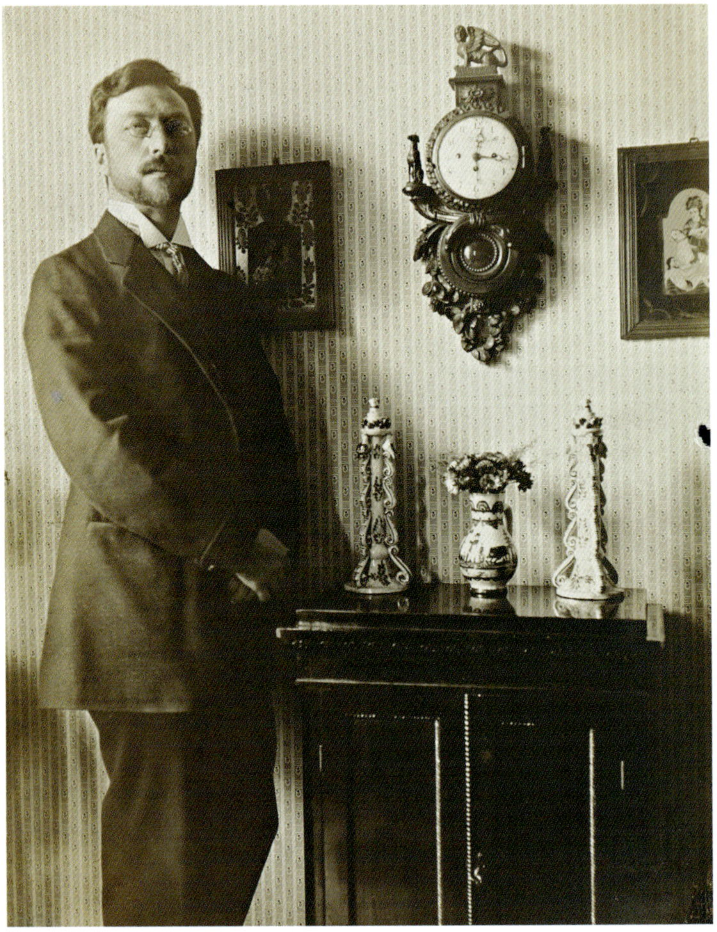

Schoenberg, Kandinsky, and the Blue Rider

Edited by

Esther da Costa Meyer

Fred Wasserman

With essays by

Magdalena Dabrowski

Esther da Costa Meyer

Christopher Hailey

Reinhold Heller

Fred Wasserman

The Jewish Museum, New York

Under the auspices of
The Jewish Theological Seminary of America

Scala Publishers

London, New York, and Paris

Published by The Jewish Museum, New York, in association with Scala Publishers on the occasion of the exhibition ***Schoenberg, Kandinsky, and the Blue Rider***, presented at The Jewish Museum from October 24, 2003, to February 12, 2004.

The Jewish Museum
1109 Fifth Avenue
New York, New York 10128
www.thejewishmuseum.org

Scala Publishers Ltd
Gloucester Mansions
140a Shaftesbury Avenue
London WC2H 8HD

Exhibition Curators: Esther da Costa Meyer and Fred Wasserman
Manager of Curatorial Publications: Michael Sittenfeld
Project Assistant: Gabriel de Guzman
Manuscript Editor: Alexandra Bonfante-Warren
Copyeditor: Ellen R. Feldman
Exhibition Design: Tsao & McKown

Director of Publications, Scala: Jennifer Wright

Designed by Steven Schoenfelder
Production by Margaret Staker
Printed in Italy by Conti Tipocolor

Credits for all illustrations appear on page 198.

ISBN 1-85759-312-X

Library of Congress Control Number: 2003108881

FRONT COVER: Wassily Kandinsky, *Impression III (Concert)* (detail), 1911
ENDPAPERS: Arnold Schoenberg, Sketch for Three Piano Pieces, op. 11 (detail), 1909
FRONTISPIECE: Arnold Schoenberg and Wassily Kandinsky, 1911
BACK COVER: Arnold Schoenberg, *Blue Self-Portrait*, 1910

Contents

Donors to the Exhibition

Our thanks to **The Peter Jay Sharp Foundation** for its leadership grant in support of *Schoenberg, Kandinsky, and the Blue Rider*. Major support is also provided by The Starr Foundation, The Andrea & Charles Bronfman Philanthropies, Anne and Bernard Spitzer, Arnhold and S. Bleichroeder Holdings, Inc., and the Department of Cultural Affairs of the City of Vienna.

Additional support is provided by Mr. and Mrs. Henry R. Kravis, Austrian Cultural Forum, Joseph Alexander Foundation, Robert Lehman Foundation, New York Council for the Humanities, a state program of the National Endowment for the Humanities, and other generous donors.

Exhibition audio guides are sponsored by **Bloomberg**

This exhibition is supported by an indemnity from the Federal Council on the Arts and the Humanities.

This catalogue was made possible by the Dorot Foundation publication endowment.

Schoenberg, Kandinsky, and the Blue Rider is based on an exhibition organized by the Arnold Schoenberg Center, Vienna.

Lenders to the Exhibition

Albright-Knox Art Gallery, Buffalo, New York

The Albert Bloch Foundation, Lawrence, Kansas

Collection Deutsche Bank

Estate of Heinrich Jalowetz

Solomon R. Guggenheim Museum, New York

The Israel Museum, Jerusalem

Library of Congress, Washington, D.C.

Milwaukee Art Museum

Gabriele Münter und Johannes Eichner Stiftung, Munich

Musée National d'Art Moderne, Centre Georges Pompidou, Paris

Museen der Stadt Wien

National Gallery of Art, Washington, D.C.

Philadelphia Museum of Art

Hanna Bekker vom Rath Collection

The Saint Louis Art Museum

Arnold Schoenberg Center, Vienna

Städtische Galerie im Lenbachhaus, Munich

State Hermitage Museum, St. Petersburg, Russia

Sylvia and Ulrich Ströher Collection, Germany

University of Applied Arts Vienna

Westfälisches Landesmuseum für Kunst und Kulturgeschichte, Münster, Germany

Yale University Art Gallery, New Haven, Connecticut

Private collections

Foreword

It is a testament to the artistry of Arnold Schoenberg that a concert of his music—presented in Munich in January 1911—could change the course of modernism. In attendance at that fateful performance was Wassily Kandinsky, who was electrified by Schoenberg's atonal compositions. Kandinsky at once saw Schoenberg as a kindred spirit, seeking to push beyond the conventions of art, even in the face of public disapproval. The two men struck up a friendship that reflected the artistic triumphs and political tensions of their time.

That concert represented a remarkable confluence of aesthetic ideas, as did the first exhibition later in 1911 by a group of artists known collectively as the Blue Rider. Spearheaded by Kandinsky and Franz Marc, the group sought to "demonstrate through the diversity of the represented forms how the *inner desire* of the artists manifests itself multifariously." The first Blue Rider exhibition included paintings by, among others, Kandinsky, Schoenberg, Franz Marc, Gabriele Münter, and Albert Bloch (some of which appear in these pages and in our exhibition). At Kandinsky's request, Schoenberg published his essay "The Relationship to the Text" and the score of his composition *Herzgewächse* in the *Blue Rider Almanac.*

The world in which the Blue Rider artists explored the possibilities of abstraction in art was shattered by the upheavals of World War I. Several years after the war, Schoenberg's relationship with Kandinsky foundered on a charge of anti-Semitism. As a Jew who converted to Protestantism, and later converted back to Judaism, Schoenberg had a complex relationship with his religious background. During the Nazis' rise to power in the 1920s, Schoenberg was forthright both in his dedication to his Jewish heritage and his revulsion over the spread of anti-Semitism in Germany. In 1923, when Schoenberg heard from his friend Alma Mahler that Kandinsky had made anti-Semitic remarks, the composer abruptly cut off his friendship with the painter. (They did, however, renew their friendship several years later.)

One of many fascinating themes in *Schoenberg, Kandinsky, and the Blue Rider* is Schoenberg's heightened consciousness of his Judaism and its effect on his association with Kandinsky. Other essential themes are the historical context for the meeting of the two artists, and the relationship between painting and music at a time when aesthetic and political boundaries were being radically redrawn.

Schoenberg, Kandinsky, and the Blue Rider is based on an exhibition shown at the Arnold Schoenberg Center in Vienna in 2000. That show was seen by Jewish Museum curators, who felt that its subject would be extremely compelling for New York audiences. The assistance and support of the Arnold Schoenberg Center were essential in creating our own version of the exhibition, and we are indebted to the center's director, Christian Meyer, for his commitment to this project.

There are many other individuals and institutions to thank for their participation in *Schoenberg, Kandinsky, and the Blue Rider*. First and foremost are the exhibition's curators, Esther da Costa Meyer and Fred Wasserman, whose expertise and creativity shine through in every aspect of the exhibition and catalogue. They were ably assisted by Gabriel de Guzman, who worked tirelessly on this project. Michael Sittenfeld, Manager of Curatorial Publications, collaborated closely with the curators to create this excellent catalogue. Steven Schoenfelder brought a fresh and innovative approach to the design of this book and the exhibition graphics, and Calvin Tsao of Tsao & McKown conceived a superb exhibition design.

My great appreciation next goes to the very gracious public and private lenders to the exhibition (listed on page 7), whose spectacular works make this an enormously vibrant show, and to the tremendously generous and enthusiastic donors, whose financial contributions made the exhibition possible. I especially wish to thank The Peter Jay Sharp Foundation for its leadership grant in support of this project. Major support was also provided by The Starr Foundation, The Andrea & Charles Bronfman Philanthropies, Anne and Bernard Spitzer, Arnhold and S. Bleichroeder Holdings, Inc., and the Department of Cultural Affairs of the City of Vienna. I also want to acknowledge Mr. and Mrs. Henry R. Kravis, the Austrian Cultural Forum, the Joseph Alexander Foundation, the Robert Lehman Foundation, the New York Council for the Humanities—a state program of the National Endowment for the Humanities—and other generous donors for their additional support. As with many other exhibitions at The Jewish Museum, exhibition audio guides for *Schoenberg, Kandinsky, and the Blue Rider* were sponsored by Bloomberg. The exhibition was supported by an indemnity from the Federal Council on the Arts and Humanities. In addition, this catalogue was made possible by the Dorot Foundation publication endowment.

Every department of The Jewish Museum is involved in creating an exhibition and I thank everyone who played a role, with particular appreciation for the time and attention of the Collections and Exhibitions Department and the Development Department. In singling out one person among the many who were engaged in bringing the exhibition, catalogue, and related education programs to fruition, I thank Ruth Beesch, Deputy Director for Program, who guided the project from the initial concept to its final realization.

Finally, it is a pleasure to acknowledge The Jewish Museum Board of Trustees. More than ever, it has been my pleasure and privilege to receive their support and counsel, and I wish to express my deep appreciation to the members of the Board for their role in creating this wonderful publication and exhibition.

Joan Rosenbaum
Helen Goldsmith Menschel Director
The Jewish Museum, New York

Preface

The paintings of Arnold Schoenberg have attracted growing attention over the last decade. In the early 1990s, a remarkable series of Schoenberg exhibitions throughout Europe presented the complex visual work of a man widely known as the inventor of twelve-tone music. Several exhibitions followed, all of which had to cope with the difficulty of bringing the paintings, watercolors, and drawings to Europe from Los Angeles, where the collection of more than 160 pieces was kept by Arnold Schoenberg's family. With the transfer of Schoenberg's legacy from the Arnold Schoenberg Institute in Los Angeles to the Arnold Schoenberg Center in Vienna, which opened in early 1998, Schoenberg's artworks found a new home in Austria. The manifold activities of the Schoenberg Center are evident in the inclusion of Schoenberg's artworks in exhibitions about Vienna in 1900, the relationship of Schoenberg and Kandinsky, and Schoenberg and the Austrian Expressionist painters Egon Schiele, Oskar Kokoschka, and Richard Gerstl. Schoenberg's paintings have also been featured in monographic exhibitions. The four paintings the composer exhibited in the Blue Rider exhibition in 1911 in Munich are highlights of the Schoenberg collection and are often sought for exhibitions all over the world.

Despite his close relationship with Kandinsky, Schoenberg vehemently denied the purported influence on his own artworks of the Russian painter and his Austrian compatriots Gerstl and Kokoschka. Schoenberg admitted, however, that he was inspired by others, presumably Gustav Klimt, Edvard Munch, and Vincent van Gogh, whose works he had the opportunity to view at exhibitions in the Vienna Secession after 1900. "As a painter I was absolutely an amateur and had no theoretical training," Schoenberg recalled at an event hosted in the 1940s by the Los Angeles County Museum, which had rejected a proposal to exhibit Schoenberg's paintings and opted instead to organize a concert and radio discussion with the composer. This remark applies to the composer Schoenberg as well, who, apart from several months of instruction from his future brother-in-law, Alexander Zemlinsky, learned everything he knew about music on his own. Schoenberg cited German composers from Bach to Wagner and Brahms as his teachers. He was thoroughly familiar with their oeuvres, which accounted for a significant portion of his reference library.

Although most of Schoenberg's paintings and drawings were created within a brief period before World War I, the most complete catalogue to date includes 268 works, indicating that Schoenberg also produced drawings and watercolors sporadically in later years. The Schoenberg Center has begun work on a new catalogue raisonné, which will contain additional artworks recently discovered on the back of paintings, in manuscripts, and in the background of archival photographs (such as paintings hanging on the wall of Schoenberg's apartment). The largest group of Schoenberg's works consists of self-portraits and Gazes/Visions, which he created throughout his life as a kind of diary of self-questioning and which are more often dated than his other works. In the early years, there were often colored oils. Later, there were intimate studies in ink and pencil.

The extent to which Schoenberg's aesthetics are based on the principle of the subconscious, even as they foreswear formal conventions, is evident in his essay on Franz Liszt published on October 20, 1911, in the *Allgemeine Musikzeitung*: "Genuine feeling cannot be prevented from repeatedly descending into the dark realms of the subconscious to bring back content and form as a unit." What Kandinsky had noted with a sure instinct in the work of Schoenberg was precisely this creative principle, the "inner necessity," the immediacy and unconditionality, the sobriety and concentration on the essence that informed Schoenberg's attempts at painting. Both in his portraits and in his Visions, the eyes play a dominant role. As Schoenberg himself was later to admit, when he met people, he did not see their faces, but perceived only their gaze. This explains the intensity of his pictures: eyes that dominate a face, that seem to have a life of their own, that even seem to emerge out of nothing.

The first decade of the twentieth century saw an almost simultaneous musical and visual revolution. Because of Schoenberg's innovations, musicians were freed from the system of tempered tonality. At the same time, painters, especially Kandinsky, broke away from the system of central perspective and figural representation. These traditions had been legitimated for centuries by an overwhelming number of masterpieces and were so universally sanctioned that they had come to be regarded as the unquestioned essence of both arts. This explains the anarchist energy that had to be unleashed to liberate music and painting from the bonds of tradition, and at the same time it illuminates the "atonal character" of pre-World War I painting in Europe, which reflects this revolution. While Schoenberg's music was an inspiration to Kandinsky as he explored abstraction, today Kandinsky's paintings function as ambassadors for Schoenberg's musical works. The strong, colorful essence of Kandinsky's prewar works has the same richness of sound colors in Schoenberg's compositions. And even his own paintings reveal much to those searching for a musical understanding of the works by the composers of the Second Viennese School. It seems that in today's visual world the fine arts are still required to understand music, the most abstract of all arts.

It is with great pleasure that the Arnold Schoenberg Center is collaborating with The Jewish Museum for the first time. I wish to give our sincere thanks to the museum's director and staff, and to the supporters, sponsors, and international lenders involved in making this venture a reality. May the exhibition and accompanying catalogue and concerts lead to a deeper understanding of artistic developments in Vienna and Munich after 1900, a period often described as an explosion of the arts.

Christian Meyer
Director
Arnold Schoenberg Center, Vienna

Introduction & Acknowledgments

On January 2, 1911, Wassily Kandinsky attended a concert of the music of the revolutionary Viennese composer Arnold Schoenberg in Munich. Deeply struck by what he heard, the artist depicted the performance in a remarkable oil painting, *Impression III (Concert)*. Sensing an affinity between his own work and the composer's ideas, Kandinsky wrote Schoenberg shortly thereafter, initiating an extraordinary epistolary exchange between two artists and two fields—music and painting—that is at the heart of *Schoenberg, Kandinsky, and the Blue Rider*.

With their fascinating relationship and intellectual dialogue as a starting point, *Schoenberg, Kandinsky, and the Blue Rider* illuminates a pivotal moment in the early twentieth century when artists and musicians embraced radical ideas and created new modes of expression. In bold, colorful paintings that depart from traditional perspective, Kandinsky began to free art from the restraints of representation as he developed an increasingly abstract vocabulary. Meanwhile, Kandinsky learned that Schoenberg had also turned to painting to express things he felt he could not convey in his music. His involvement with issues of color and composition drew him near to Kandinsky, whose own work often evoked music. The painter was impressed with the composer's artworks, and invited him to take part in the Blue Rider (*Blaue Reiter*) exhibition that he organized with Franz Marc in Munich in December 1911. This celebrated show presented groundbreaking work by an international group of artists. At the core of the exhibition were paintings by Kandinsky and Marc as well as a small circle of their associates—among them Gabriele Münter, August Macke, and Albert Bloch—that reveal their interest in the symbolic and psychological effects of color.

The work of these artists, as well as that of Alexei von Jawlensky, who was closely associated with the Blue Rider group, is represented in our own exhibition, which includes more than sixty paintings and forty archival documents from museums and private collections in Austria, Germany, Russia, Israel, and the United States, that capture the excitement and broad spectrum of interests that characterized this group of artists. Though not conceived from a historicist perspective, the show brings together a number of paintings that have not been shown side by side since that first legendary exhibition. It also constitutes the first major showing of Schoenberg's paintings in an American museum—half a century after his death.

Music also plays an integral part in the exhibition. Visitors hear pioneering works by Schoenberg and the other great exponents of Viennese musical modernism—Gustav Mahler, Alexander Zemlinsky, and Franz Schreker (all of whom, like Schoenberg, were Jewish) as well his students Alban Berg and Anton Webern. Readers of this book can listen to the companion CD that features a selection of Schoenberg's compositions that Kandinsky heard at the Munich concert as well as a performance of Schoenberg's *Herzgewächse*, which appeared as a musical score in the *Blue Rider Almanac*.

The essays in this catalogue explore the relationship between Schoenberg, Kandinsky, and the Blue Rider from a variety of perspectives. Fred Wasserman examines the significance of the Schoenberg concert that Kandinsky heard on January 2, 1911, his painting inspired by this performance, and the ensuing correspondence and friendship between the two artists. Esther da Costa Meyer analyzes Schoenberg's paintings, a body of work that offers illuminating insights into the man, his music, his intellectual concerns, and his identity as a Jew. Reinhold Heller investigates the Munich avant-garde in the first decade of the twentieth century and the emergence of the Blue Rider, a forum for many of the artistic and musical issues that concerned both Kandinsky and Schoenberg in the prewar years. Magdalena Dabrowski addresses Kandinsky's aesthetic theories and his development of abstraction in light of Schoenberg's music. Finally, Christopher Hailey discusses Schoenberg's revolutionary musical innovations—atonality and serialism—in the context of his relationship to the Viennese classical tradition. Not surprisingly, all of the authors touch on the 1911 concert, a singularly resonant event that runs as a leitmotif through this volume.

Organizing an exhibition and catalogue of this magnitude involves the participation of a great number of people and institutions. First, we owe our deepest debt of gratitude to the Arnold Schoenberg Center, Vienna, and its director, Christian Meyer, who organized an exhibition in 2000 that was the inspiration for our own exploration of Schoenberg and Kandinsky in the context of the Blue Rider. He and his staff have been remarkably generous with their collection and expertise. The members of the Schoenberg family have also graciously cooperated with The Jewish Museum in realizing this exhibition. We especially appreciate the kind assistance of Lawrence Schoenberg and E. Randol Schoenberg, who helped us with many matters related to the composer's music and his legacy.

We are greatly indebted to the private collectors and staffs of the many institutions that have kindly lent their works to the exhibition. We especially wish to thank Helmut Friedel, director of the Städtische Galerie im Lenbachhaus, Munich, for his interest and participation in the project and his generosity in lending Kandinsky's *Impression III (Concert)*. This painting is the central work in the exhibition and we are delighted to be showing it in the United States for the first time. For their efforts on our behalf, special thanks are also due to Douglas G. Schultz, former Director, Albright-Knox Art Gallery; Lisa Dennison, Deputy Director and Chief Curator, Solomon R. Guggenheim Museum, New York; and Jock Reynolds, the Henry J. Heinz II Director, Yale University Art Gallery; as well as Jeffrey Weiss, Associate Curator, Twentieth-Century Art, National Gallery of Art, Washington, D.C.; Michael R. Taylor, Associate Curator, Modern and Contemporary Art, Philadelphia Museum of Art; and Boris Asvarich, Senior Curator of the Department of Western European Art, The State Hermitage Museum, St. Petersburg, Russia.

We are indebted to a number of other colleagues who generously facilitated loan requests and assisted in other ways: Annegret Hoberg, Curator, Städtische Galerie im Lenbachhaus; Didier Schulmann, Curator and Head of Collections Management, Musée National d'Art Moderne, Centre Georges Pompidou; Angelica Jawlensky Bianconi, Alexej von Jawlensky-Archiv S.A.; Magdalena Dabrowski, Research Curator, The Metropolitan Museum of Art; Renée Price, Director, and Sefa Saglam, Registrar, Neue Galerie New York; Nicolas Iljine, Representative for the Solomon R. Guggenheim Foundation; Seth Fogelman, Assistant Registrar, The Museum of Modern Art, New York; Blaženka Perica, Curator, Schirn Kunsthalle Frankfurt; Helena Newman, Head of Impressionist and Modern Art, London, and Senior Director, Sotheby's Europe; Elizabeth Gorayeb, Cataloguer/Researcher, Impressionist and Modern Art, Sotheby's, New York; Eva Avloniti, Archivist, Impressionist and Modern Art, Sotheby's, London; Allison Whiting, Vice President and Director, Museum Services, Christie's, New York; Jane Kallir, Director, Galerie St. Etienne; and Lucy Dew, Mitchell-Innes & Nash Gallery.

We could not have organized the exhibition and catalogue without the extraordinary cooperation of Therese Muxeneder, archivist at the Arnold Schoenberg Center, whose assistance was invaluable. We also wish to thank Susanne Böller and Karola Rattner, Registrars, and Daniela Müller, rights and reproductions, Städtische Galerie im Lenbachhaus; Margaret Brown, Exhibitions Registrar, and Bonnie Coles and Margaret Kieckhefer, photoduplication services, the Library of Congress; and Milan Hughston, Chief of Library and Museum Archives, and Jenny Tobias, Associate Librarian, The Museum of Modern Art.

Calvin Tsao of Tsao & McKown created a masterful exhibition design that sensitively responded to the art and the story at the heart of the show. His colleague, Elvis Wells, carefully attended to the many details of the exhibition design process. We would also like to express our appreciation to Steven Schoenfelder, who designed the handsome exhibition graphics, and to Sandy Goldberg and Julie Twitmyer of Antenna Audio for producing the audioguide. And a special thanks to Christopher Hailey for writing the audioguide script as well as for sharing his expertise and serving as our musical advisor.

We are sincerely grateful to the other authors of the essays in this catalogue—Magdalena Dabrowski, Christopher Hailey, and Reinhold Heller—who creatively drew on their vast knowledge to illuminate the subjects and themes of the exhibition. We extend our heartfelt appreciation to Steven Schoenfelder who created the elegant design for this volume. Alexandra Bonfante-Warren edited the manuscript with great care and helped us shape the essays into a cohesive book. Ellen R. Feldman capably copyedited the manuscript. It has been a pleasure to work with our colleagues at Scala, especially Jennifer Wright, Director of Publications, and Margaret Staker, Production Manager. We also thank David Somlyo of Museum Music for his assistance with the production of the companion CD of Schoenberg's music.

Many individuals at The Jewish Museum were critical in bringing *Schoenberg, Kandinsky, and the Blue Rider* to fruition. Joan Rosenbaum, Helen Goldsmith Menschel Director, was an enthusiastic supporter of the exhibition and championed it from the outset. Ruth Beesch, Deputy Director for Program, played a crucial role in dealing with the complexities of realizing an exhibition of this scope. Her thoughtful comments, constant encouragement, and unwavering belief in the exhibition were invaluable. Norman L. Kleeblatt, Susan and Elihu Rose Curator of Fine Arts, expressed a keen interest in the project and was extremely generous with his insights at key moments in the development of the exhibition. Michael Sittenfeld, Manager of Curatorial Publications, guided the creation of this volume with great professional expertise and a deft touch. Gabriel de Guzman, project assistant, was indispensable; he expertly handled myriad aspects of the exhibition and catalogue, with remarkable skill and enormous grace under pressure. We also appreciate the informative chronologies of Schoenberg and Kandinsky that he contributed to this volume. Katharina Garrelt was helpful in dealing with German lenders and translations. Ivy Epstein ably assisted on photograph requests as well as numerous other aspects of catalogue production. We would also like to thank Jennifer Goldstein for her work on the initial loan requests as well as Abigail Deutsch and Marcus Patka for their assistance with final catalogue production.

Organizing an international loan exhibition could not have been accomplished without our talented and dedicated Head Registrar, Jane Rubin, who was assisted by Sarah Fogel, Guest Registrar, Lauren Smith, Registration Assistant, and Jody Heher, Coordinator of Exhibitions. Al Lazarte, Director of Operations, skillfully turned our exhibition design into a reality in the galleries. Aviva Weintraub, Director of Media and Public Programs, organized a thoughtful and exciting group of related concerts, films, and programs. Carole Zawatsky, Director of Education, and her staff developed innovative ways to present art and music to visitors. Susan Goodman, Senior Curator-at-Large, and Mason Klein, Assistant Curator of Fine Arts, generously offered collegial support and advice. Gregory Fienhold, Director of Development, and his staff were creative and successful in their fundraising efforts. Grace Rapkin, Director of Marketing, and Anne Scher, Director of Communications, developed effective strategies to reach a wide audience for the exhibition. Emily Hartzell, Assistant Curator for Web Projects, created an innovative online presentation of the exhibition.

Finally, on a personal note, we would like to thank our friends and loved ones for their enthusiasm and support throughout the course of what has been a wonderfully challenging and exciting project.

Esther da Costa Meyer
Fred Wasserman

Konzert-Bureau Emil Gutmann

Jahreszeitensaal

Montag, den 2. Januar 1911, abends 7½ Uhr

Kompositions-Konzert

Arnold Schönberg

Ausführende:

Marie Gutheil-Schoder
K. u. k. Kammersängerin (Gesang)

Etta Werndorff
(Klavier)

Das Rosé-Quartett

Prof. **Arnold Rosé,** 1. Violine — **Paul Fischer,** 2. Violine
Ant. Ruzitska, Viola — Prof. **Friedr. Buxbaum,** Violoncell

Programm:

ARNOLD SCHÖNBERG (geb. 1874 in Wien)

Werke: op. 1, 2, 3 und 6 Lieder; op. 4 Sextett „Verklärte Nacht" (komp. 1899); op. 5 „Pelleas und Melisande" (1902); op. 7 I. Streichquartett (1905); op. 8 Orchesterlieder; op. 9 Kammersinfonie; op. 10 II. Streichquartett (1907/8); op. 11 Klavierstücke (1908); außerdem „Gurre-Lieder" (1900); Stefan George-Lieder (1908); Orchesterstücke, Monodrama „Erwartung" (1909); „Glückliche Hand" (1910) und einige kleinere Werke.

1. **Zweites Streich-Quartett** op. 10 (mit Gesang im 3. und 4. Satz)
   1. Satz: Mäßig
   2. Satz: Sehr rasch
   3. Satz: „Litanei" } Gedichte von Stefan George
   4. Satz: „Entrückung" } Gedichte von Stefan George
2. **Drei Klavierstücke** op. 11
3. **Fünf Lieder**
   1. Erwartung
   2. Verlassen
   3. Am Wegrand
   4. Mädchenlied
   5. Der Wanderer
4. **Erstes Streich-Quartett** op. 7 (in einem Satz)

Sämtliche Kompositionen werden in München zum ersten Mal aufgeführt.

Konzertflügel: BLÜTHNER,
beigestellt von **J. Reißmann,** Hoflieferant, Wittelsbacherplatz 2.

Texte 20 Pfennig

Schoenberg & Kandinsky in Concert

Fred Wasserman

"Something special awaits me tomorrow (I think)," wrote the artist Franz Marc to his future wife, Maria Franck, on January 1, 1911. "I'm going to a concert of Arnold Schönberg; you know, that most modern of Vienna composers whose artistic program could be printed in its entirety at the front of the catalogue of the Neue Vereinigung," the latter a reference to the Neue Künstlervereinigung München (NKVM), an artists' group that Marc had publicly defended and that he would officially join the following month. "The uncanny thing about him," Marc continued, "seems to be his complete abandonment of tonality—he no longer works crosswise through the keys but does so longitudinally—which seems to be related to Kandinsky's ideas. In any case, I'm terribly excited and I'm already thinking about it."[1]

On the previous evening, Marc had attended a New Year's Eve party at the home of the NKVM artists Alexei von Jawlensky and Marianne von Werefkin at which he had actually met Wassily Kandinsky for the first time. In fact, Marc spent the whole evening talking with him and his partner, the artist Gabriele Münter, and the following day wrote Franck that they were wonderful people, that he was looking forward to her meeting them, and that he found Kandinsky particularly enchanting.[2] Thus began an important artistic friendship between Marc and Kandinsky, who, after leaving the NKVM, would go on to organize jointly the two landmark Blue Rider (*Blaue Reiter*) exhibitions in late 1911 and early 1912, and to publish the *Blue Rider Almanac* (1912).

Another singular meeting of artistic minds would occur the following evening, Monday, January 2, 1911, when Marc, Kandinsky, Münter, Jawlensky, and Werefkin attended the concert of Schoenberg's music at the Jahreszeitensaal in Munich (fig. 1). Marc had suggested the outing based on suspicions that something was up, and the other artists too had "sensed that something was cooking," for the controversial Viennese composer's reputation preceded him.[3] During the past several years, Schoenberg and his music had prompted audience uproars and critical outrage. Notably, at the premiere of *Pelleas und Melisande* on January 26, 1905, the crowd had hissed and walked out in the middle, banging the

Fig. 1. Program for the concert of Arnold Schoenberg's music in Munich, January 2, 1911.

doors as they exited.[4] The scenes at the Vienna premieres of the composer's two string quartets had been even more tumultuous. At the February 5, 1907, debut of the First String Quartet, op. 7 (1905), Gustav Mahler angrily reprimanded a noisy audience member, and they almost came to blows.[5] But the biggest scene was at the December 21, 1908, premiere of the Second String Quartet, op. 10, (1907–8), which abandoned tonality in the last movement; a near-riot occurred when a critic stood up and ordered the performers to stop playing, another critic screamed for them to go on playing, and the soprano continued singing in tears.[6]

Schoenberg, then thirty-six, had not yet had a major performance of his work in Munich and he wanted to introduce it there. The concert agent Emil Gutmann was receptive to the idea of a Schoenberg evening and thought there would be a good deal of interest in the composer's music in the Bavarian capital, though he favored a somewhat more traditional program for the conservative Munich audience than the composer envisioned. For the January 2 concert, Schoenberg quite intentionally placed the controversial Second String Quartet at the top of the program, followed by the more completely atonal Three Piano Pieces, op. 11 (1909) (fig. 2). The evening would be rounded out by five lieder from op. 2 (1899) and op. 6 (1903–5), and the First String Quartet.[7]

In promoting the concert, Gutmann played up Schoenberg's controversial musical theories by including on the poster an excerpt from "On Parallel Octaves and Fifths," a section of his forthcoming treatise, *Theory of Harmony* (*Harmonielehre*). Challenging musical orthodoxy with a revolutionary new concept of harmony, Schoenberg had written: "Dissonances are only different from consonances in degree; they are nothing more than remoter consonances. Today we have already reached the point where we no longer make the distinction between consonances and dissonances."[8] It is this "emancipation of the dissonance," so at odds with traditional harmony, that led the composer to create compositions in which, as Schoenberg himself put it, he "renounced a tonal center."[9] These ideas, which were printed in the concert program as well, made a major impression on both Kandinsky and Marc.

Gutmann enlisted outstanding Viennese musicians for the Schoenberg concert: the distinguished Rosé Quartet (fig. 3), the soprano Marie Gutheil-Schoder (fig. 4), and the pianist Etta Werndorff, all of them well versed in the Schoenbergian idiom. Indeed, the Rosé Quartet and Gutheil-Schoder had performed the Second String Quartet at its stormy December 1908 premiere in Vienna, and again in October 1910 at the opening of Schoenberg's solo painting exhibition at Hugo Heller's Vienna bookshop, while Werndorff had premiered the Three Piano Pieces in Vienna in January 1910. Gutmann also wanted to reprise Heller's exhibition of Schoenberg's paintings at the Munich concert hall, but the composer decided to send just one of his self-portraits to hang in the box office lobby.[10]

As Franz Marc had expected, the Schoenberg evening did indeed turn out to be "something special." This is evident in the reviews—a veritable anthology of critical response to Schoenberg's music—which, curiously, have not been explored despite all the scholarly attention paid to the January 2, 1911, concert.

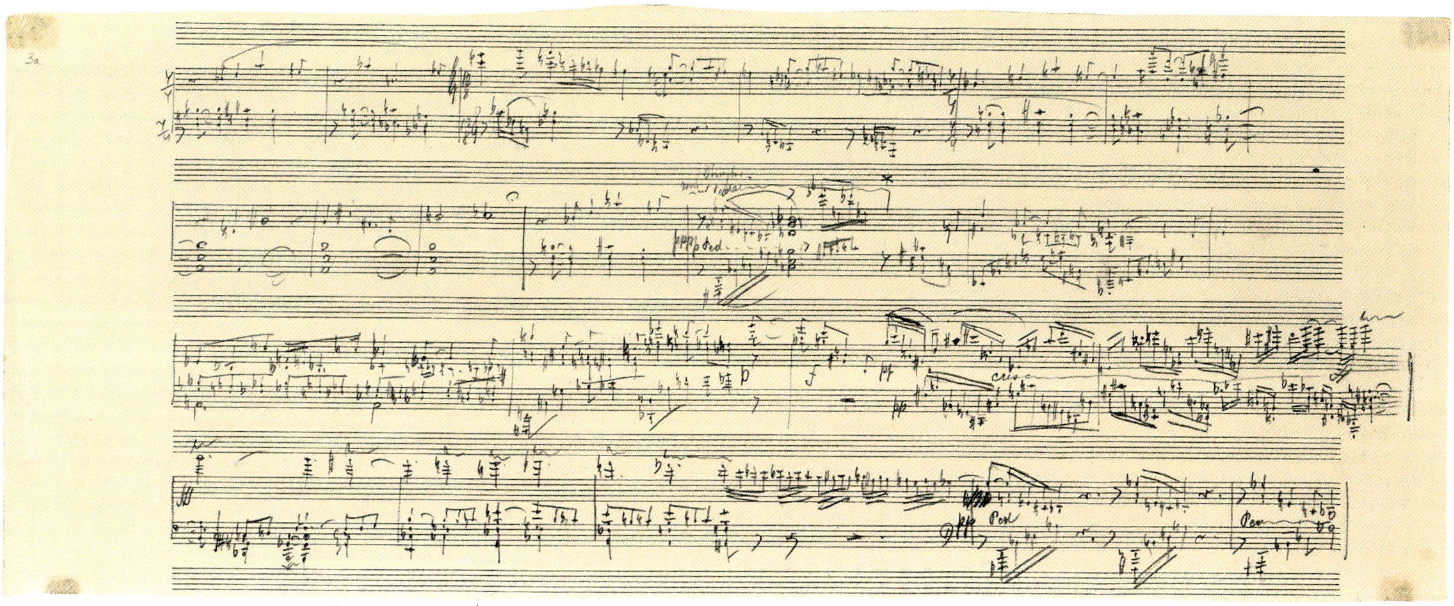

Fig. 2. Schoenberg's sketch for Three Piano Pieces, op. 11 (1909).

"The most sensational event of the past week was a concert by the well-known Vienna cacophonist Arnold Schönberg," declared the *Allgemeine Musik-Zeitung*,[11] while the critic Arthur Hahn snidely complained, "A full cornucopia of Arnold Schönberg compositions was dumped on our heads!"[12] The *Münchener Post* echoed this tone, announcing, "A rather horrible 'Happy New Year' was what came of the Arnold Schönberg evening in Munich." The same writer, however, also cautioned that the composer could not be dismissed: "Arnold Schönberg, the wildest of the moderns, is too much of a genius, albeit of an unconventional sort, to be relegated to the realm of musical impossibility; there is method to even the most extreme madness. . . . One must, therefore, reckon with him as a composer who is here to stay."[13]

All in all, the Munich performance prompted less scandal than the Vienna premieres. In a letter to Schoenberg the next day, Gutmann characterized the concert as "a great and a loud success," but went on to detail the conflicting reactions of the audience. The lieder and the First String Quartet, op. 7, were well received. But the piano pieces provoked "some opposition" and "after the [Second] String Quartet, op. 10, loud attempts at hissing were countered by extraordinarily loud applause."[14] Gutmann was being diplomatic, as we can see from Marc's far more colorful description of the crowd: "The public behaved vulgarly like schoolboys, sneezed and cleared their throats with titters and moving their chairs about, so that it was very difficult to follow the music at all."[15]

The critics, too, focused on the tensions in the concert hall. As the *Münchener Post* reported, "The Munich audience, at least those still there by the middle of the concert, did not hurl rotten eggs and apples at the 'Professor of Remote Consonance' but instead broke into calls of bravo without applause that sounded like stifled laughter; people were dumbfounded."[16] The *Allgemeine Musik-Zeitung* critic dismally observed that the concert left "no impression but of—to put it mildly—pointless experimentation. There was no shortage of applause, but there was plenty of laughter and cursing as well."[17]

The critics themselves were similarly uneasy, if not distraught. Otto Keller's remarks about the Second String Quartet in the *Chemnitzer Tageblatt* were typical: "It is thoroughly modern to the last detail. We detect no treatment of thoughts or motifs, one patch follows another without rules, and we certainly don't get a sense of a beginning, middle, or end; and the whole thing stops suddenly, with only God or the composer knowing why."[18] Keller lambasted the Stefan George poems that Schoenberg introduced in the third and fourth movements, calling them "horrors of thought and language,"[19] while another reviewer dismissed them as "insane lyrics in the style of a telegram" that were mismatched with the music.[20] However, the critic Arthur Hahn found something to appreciate in, as he put it, "the infamous String Quartet, op. 10": "Surprisingly, there is even a specific key indicated, and what's more, it begins, outrageously enough, in this key, and with a completely simple F-sharp minor chord! What follows is, in any case, often of a seriously muddled nature. But even so, there are moments not lacking in pronounced idiosyncratic color and mood, and such vividness can be riveting. The treatment of the vocal line in the last two movements, however, defies description. Mrs. Gutheil-Schoder's eminent artistry achieved something unbelievable in the task set before her."[21]

For all the consternation over the partially atonal Second String Quartet, it was the completely atonal Three Piano Pieces that prompted the most vociferous reaction, as Hahn observed:

> The almost hair-raising cacophonies seemed almost too much even for those who up until now had followed the musical revelations of Schönberg's weltschmerz with a straight face. One can only shake one's head in astonishment at the cheek of this sort of thing being taken for what has always been understood as music. These same "sound effects" gave rise to an accidental convergence of completely random notes. At times coincidence itself might lead to tonal combinations that could sound harmonic to our ears. Schönberg however—and this remains the only continuity in his compositions including the piano pieces—deliberately selects only the opposite of what sounds "right" to our ears.[22]

Even more emphatically, Keller reported, "The craziest things in modern music, however, are the Piano Pieces, op. 11. . . . aimless wanderings on the keys with nothing to connect them." And then, in an indictment that was fairly typical of the contemporary response to the composer, he continued, "I believe that Arnold Schönberg has deliberately produced mischief. He uses these compositions to trick his audience; they can't be taken seriously. An artist, however, who has recently been appointed Professor at the Imperial Academy of Music in Vienna should abstain from such frivolity. [Still,] it would be foolish to deny Arnold Schönberg's ability."[23]

While the critics generally panned the music, they universally praised the quality of the musicians, crediting them with saving Schoenberg from complete ignominy. For example, Friedrich Keyfel wrote in the *Signale für die musikalische Welt*: "Arnold Schönberg would have been a lost man, were it not for such excellent artists as Gutheil-Schoder and the Rosé Quartet taking pity on his work; Etta Wernsdorf [*sic*], a casualty of Schönberg's piano pieces (op. 11), performed a feat

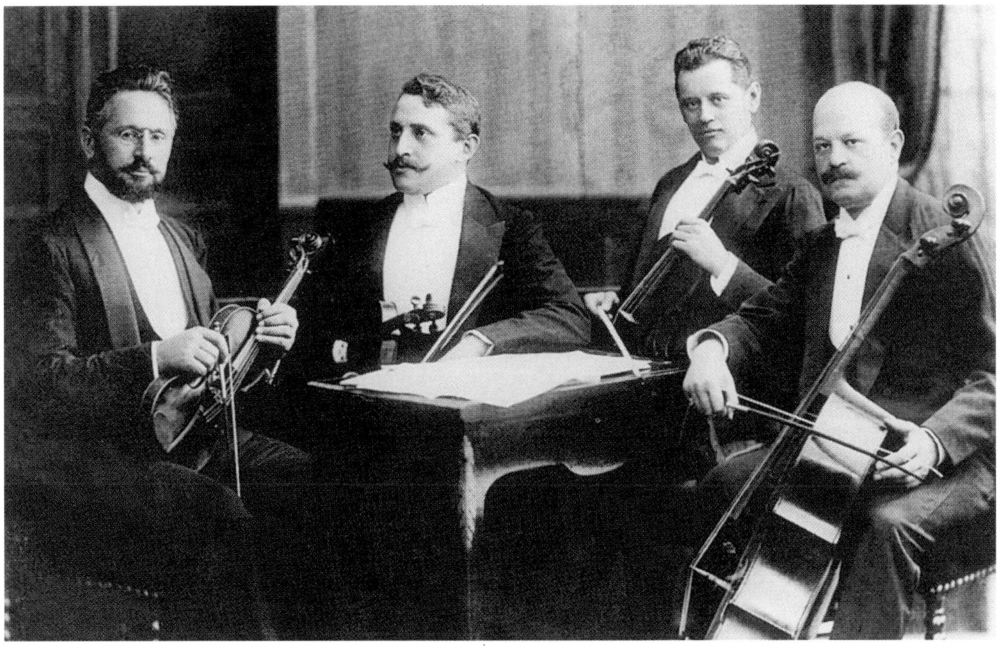

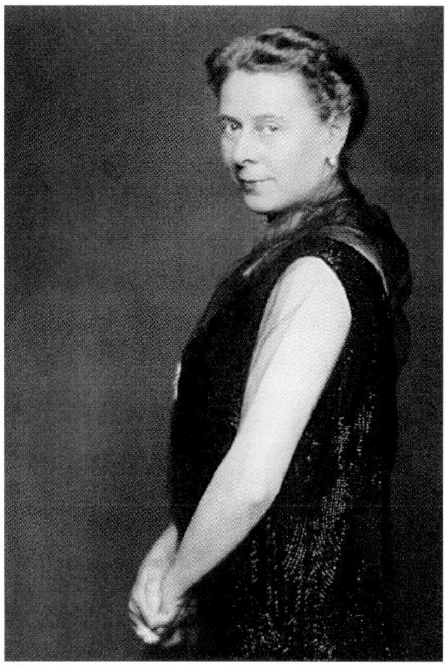

Fig. 3. The Rosé Quartet.

Fig. 4. Marie Gutheil-Schoder.

of heroism by coaxing a certain degree of music from her piano as if by magic."[24]

Despite the mixed response of the audience and the critics, "at the close of the evening," Gutmann wrote Schoenberg the next day, "there was much applause and many calls for you to come forward, as some of the audience had assumed that you would be in Munich."[25] Following the concert, Kandinsky, Münter, Marc, Jawlensky, and Werefkin repaired to a rathskeller, where they drank "a few bottles." They were dazzled by their first encounter with Schoenberg's music, as well as by his theories, which they had read in the program. Marc told Maria Franck that the concert had fulfilled all his expectations.[26] As he wrote August Macke on January 14, 1911:

> Can you imagine a music in which tonality (that is, the adherence to any key) is completely suspended? I was constantly reminded of Kandinsky's large *Composition*, which also permits no trace of tonality . . . and also of Kandinsky's "jumping spots" in hearing this music, which allows each tone sounded to stand on its own (a kind of *white canvas* between the spots of color!). Schoenberg proceeds from the principle that the concepts of consonance and dissonance do not exist at all. A so-called dissonance is only a more remote consonance—an idea which now occupies me constantly while painting.[27]

Kandinsky, too, took the Schoenberg concert very much to heart—and soul. He drew two quick sketches of the performance and the following day made a large painting in oil.[28] It is unknown whether the artist sketched during the concert (the small scale of the drawings makes this at least a physical possibility) or made the sketches later that evening or the next day. In any case, these three works offer in microcosm an extraordinary illustration of Kandinsky's working method: he began with the representational object and progressively pared it down so that only traces of the original references remain in the final work.[29] Rather than trying to depict the performance literally, the artist was striving for a deeper, more emotive rendering of the event. In keeping with his artistic theories, Kandinsky was trying to capture the inner essence or spirit of the concert, rather than its external appearance.

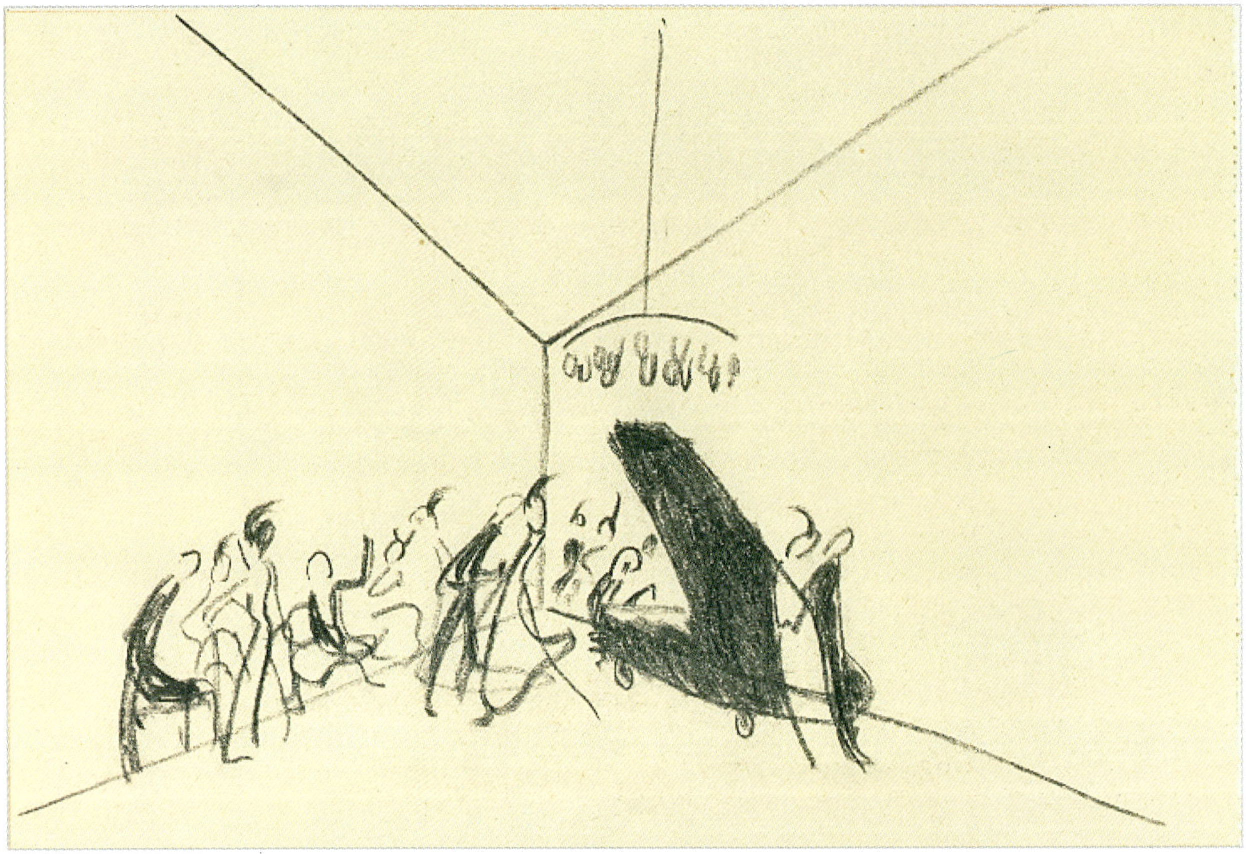

Fig. 5. Wassily Kandinsky (Russian, 1866-1944). *Sketch for Impression III (Concert)*, 1911. Crayon on paper, 3¹⁵⁄₁₆ x 5⅞ in. (10 x 14.9 cm). Musée National d'Art Moderne, Centre Georges Pompidou, Paris.

In the first drawing, *Sketch for Impression III (Concert)* (fig. 5), the artist quickly drew the concert hall in a perspectival space with the performance in the center. The piano is at right center illuminated by a chandelier, and we can even identify the pianist playing on the left side of the piano while a singer stands at the right. A group of cartoonlike figures at the far left might be the audience, although they could also be the string quartet, since several of them seem to have their feet or chair legs on the stage.[30] Curiously, the standing figure in the center could perhaps be playing a bass, although this would not jibe with the Rosé Quartet's two violins, viola, and cello. So, while at first glance this drawing appears to be a realistic depiction of the concert, closer scrutiny reveals that even in his first sketch Kandinsky took artistic license: the converging lines are artificially constructing a space that is unlike a stage or concert hall; the vantage point is ambiguous—it could be from the audience or from the wings; and there is a conflation of musicians, all of whom would not actually have been onstage at the same time—which is in effect also a melding of the different pieces on the program.

The second drawing, *Sketch for Impression III (Concert)* (fig. 6), is considerably more abstract, because Kandinsky eliminated the perspective and reduced the representational elements to schematic forms. Unlike the first sketch, which could stand alone as an independent work, the second is clearly a study for the painting, indicating only the outlines of the forms afloat against a flat surface, and annotated with words or letters to indicate color. Kandinsky made the piano

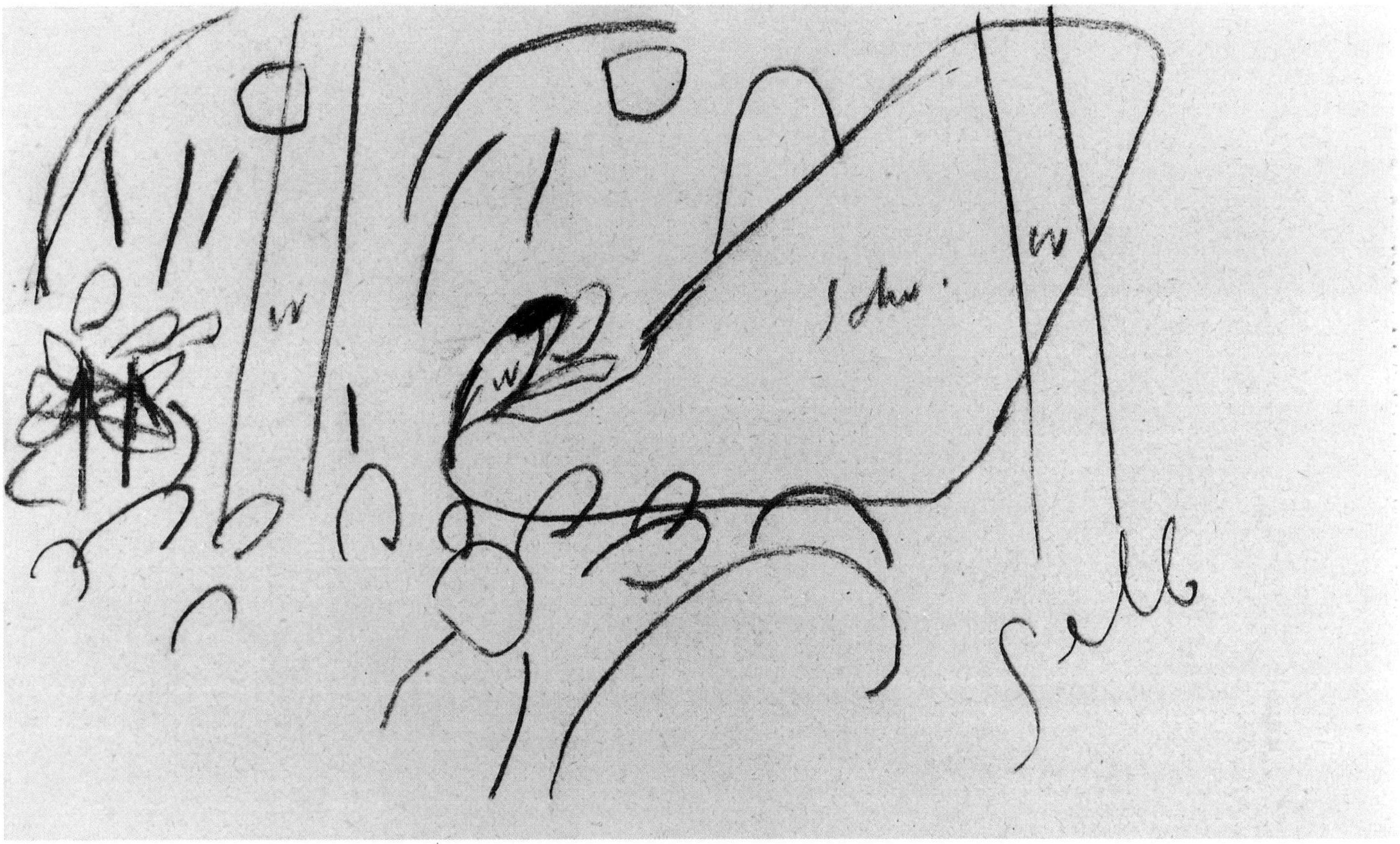

Fig. 6. Wassily Kandinsky. *Sketch for Impression III (Concert)*, 1911. Crayon on paper, $3\frac{15}{16} \times 5\frac{7}{8}$ in. (10 × 14.8 cm). Musée National d'Art Moderne, Centre Georges Pompidou, Paris.

considerably larger and changed its orientation. The audience is now indicated by cursory circles and curves. Two wide "pillars" may refer to the architecture of the concert hall.

In the final painting, *Impression III (Concert)* (pl. 1), Kandinsky retained the overall composition of the second sketch, infusing it with color, which becomes the key element of the work. The lack of perspective flattens the image, but at the same time effectively enlarges or opens up the sense of spatial—even musical—breadth in the picture. The singer and other performers are gone, with the exception of a circle that may still be the pianist's head. The piano has become a dominant mass of black (bisected by a white band), smashing up against and vibrating with the overwhelming intensity of the yellow that envelops most of the painting—including the audience, now reduced to curved black lines and spots of cadmium and ultramarine with dabs of alizarin, and various blues and greens. Kandinsky made the black piano more curved at the top and gave it a strong diagonal thrust toward the upper right corner in an arc upward from the audience, which is grouped to the lower left of center. The black piano, now seemingly aloft in the air and so compositionally powerful, has morphed from the instrument that created the sound into the embodiment of the sound itself.

Impression III (Concert) reflects Kandinsky's exploration of synaesthesia, the idea (popular at the time) that the senses were interrelated and that stimulating one sense would simultaneously trigger the others.[31] In particular, Kandinsky equated sounds with color tones. Colors, Kandinsky believed, have an "inner sound" that has a "profound effect, which occasions a deep emotional response . . . calling forth a vibration from the soul."[32] Kandinsky saw yellow as a particularly musical color and, in fact, gave the title *Der gelbe Klang* (The yellow sound) to his opera, which appeared in the *Blue Rider Almanac*. In his treatise *On the Spiritual in Art* (1912), Kandinsky wrote:

> Yellow . . . is disquieting to the spectator, pricking him, stimulating him, revealing the nature of the power expressed in this color, which has an effect upon our sensibilities at once impudent and importunate. This property of yellow, a color that inclines considerably toward the brighter tones, can be raised to a pitch of intensity unbearable to the eye and to the spirit. Upon such intensification, it affects us like the shrill sound of a trumpet being played louder and louder, or the sound of a high-pitched fanfare.[33]

"Black," in contrast, "has an inner sound of nothingness bereft of possibilities, a dead nothingness as if the sun had become extinct, an eternal silence without future, without hope. Musically, it is represented by a general pause. . . . Black is externally the most toneless color, against which all other colors, even the weakest, sound stronger and more precise."[34] Thus, when an intensely strong color such as yellow is juxtaposed with black, it creates a particularly resounding effect.

In *Impression III (Concert)*, we see Kandinsky's theories—and Schoenberg's—come to life. Just as the composer wanted to emancipate dissonances to create a new kind of musical harmony, Kandinsky propounded a theory of artistic harmony based on "clashing discords, loss of equilibrium, 'principles' overthrown, unexpected drumbeats, great questionings, . . . opposites and contradictions."[35] Kandinsky's painting of the concert embodies the artist's notion of a harmony based on (often disharmonious) color juxtapositions. In this way, the artist captured his experience of Schoenberg's music, which he tellingly referred to years later in his only written description of the January 2 concert: "I also happened to observe the audience during one of Schoenberg's quartets, in which the manipulation of the line of the instruments, and, in particular, the incorporation of the voice, produced the impression of the lash of a whip. It is interesting to note that Arnold Schoenberg introduced the flow of parallel lines into some of his compositions with (at least for musicians) virtually the same revolutionary effect."[36]

The intense vibration of the black and yellow, the dynamism of the spots of color that define the audience, and the disorienting picture space are Kandinsky's visual analogue of the lashing whip. Furthermore, the discord Kandinsky created with the jolting black and yellow embodies not just the unresolved dissonance of the Second String Quartet, but also the discordance of the Three Piano Pieces and the agitation of the audience. For, as Kandinsky himself noted, while music has the advantage of "duration of time," painting's unique strength is that it "can in an instant present the spectator with the entire content of the work, which music is unable to do."[37] In *Impression III (Concert)*, Kandinsky distilled the temporal experience of Schoenberg's music into a single essential and resonant visual image.

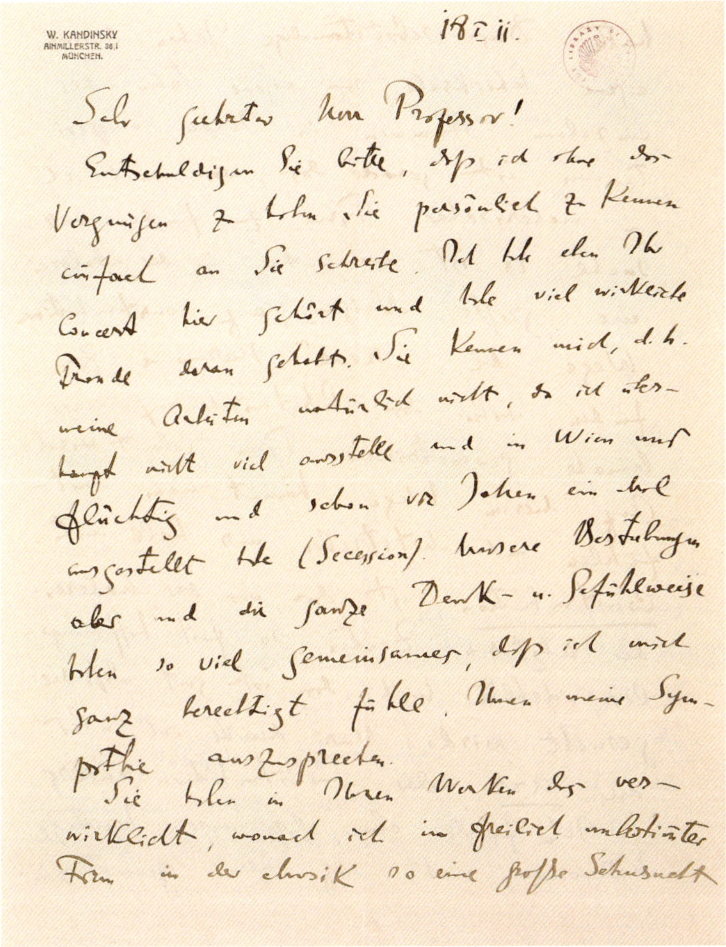

W. KANDINSKY
AINMILLERSTR. 36.I
MÜNCHEN.

18.I.11.

Sehr geehrter Herr Professor!
Entschuldigen Sie bitte, dass ich ohne das Vergnügen zu haben Sie persönlich zu kennen einfach an Sie schreibe. Ich habe eben Ihr Concert hier gehört und habe viel wirkliche Freude daran gehabt. Sie kennen mich, d.h. meine Arbeiten natürlich nicht, da ich überhaupt nicht viel ausstelle und in Wien nur flüchtig und schon vor Jahren ein Mal ausgestellt habe (Secession). Unsere Bestrebungen aber und die ganze Denk- u. Gefühlsweise haben so viel Gemeinsames, dass ich mich ganz berechtigt fühle, Ihnen meine Sympathie auszusprechen.
Sie haben in Ihren Werken das verwirklicht, wonach ich in freilich unbestimmter Form in der Musik so eine grosse Sehnsucht

Fig. 7. Kandinsky's first letter to Schoenberg, January 18, 1911.

Two weeks after finishing this extraordinary painting, Kandinsky wrote the composer on January 18, 1911 (fig. 7).[38] "Dear Professor," his letter began, "Please excuse me for simply writing to you without having the pleasure of knowing you personally. I have just heard your concert here and it has given me real pleasure." He continued:

You do not know me, of course—that is, my works—since I do not exhibit much in general, and have exhibited in Vienna only briefly once and that was years ago (at the Secession). However, what we are striving for and our whole manner of thought and feeling have so much in common that I feel completely justified in expressing my empathy.

In your works, you have realized what I, albeit in uncertain form, have so greatly longed for in music. The independent progress through their own destinies, the independent life of the individual voices in your compositions, is exactly what I am trying to find in my paintings. At the moment there is a great tendency in painting to discover the "new" harmony by constructive means, whereby the rhythmic is built on an almost geometric form. My own instinct and striving can support these tendencies only half-way. *Construction* is what has been so woefully lacking in the painting of recent times, and it is good that it is now being sought. But I think differently about the *type* of construction.

I am certain that our own modern harmony is not to be found in the "geometric" way, but rather in the anti-geometric, antilogical [*antilogischen*] way. And this way is that of "dissonances in *art*," in painting, therefore, just as much as in music. And "today's" dissonance in painting and music is merely the consonance of "tomorrow."[39]

In order to introduce his own work, Kandinsky enclosed a portfolio of woodcuts, *Xylographies* (figs. 8–13), created some years earlier, as well as two photographs of more recent works, *Improvisation 7* and *Improvisation 16*, both painted in 1910 (figs. 14–15).[40]

Kandinsky found a sympathetic artist in Schoenberg, who responded just a few days later (fig. 16). "I am particularly happy when it is an artist creating in another art from mine who finds points of contact with me," responded the composer, noting that he appreciated the portfolio and understood it completely (though he was less certain about the paintings). He continued:

I am sure that our work has much in common—and indeed in the most important respects: In what you call the "unlogical" [*Unlogische*] and I call the "elimination of the conscious will in art." I also agree with what you write about the constructive element. Every formal procedure which aspires to traditional effects is not completely free from conscious motivation. But art belongs to the *unconscious*! One must express *oneself*! Express oneself *directly*! Not one's taste, or one's upbringing, or one's intelligence, knowledge or skill. Not all these *acquired* characteristics, but that which is *inborn, instinctive*.

In this first letter, Schoenberg also mentioned that he painted and offered to send

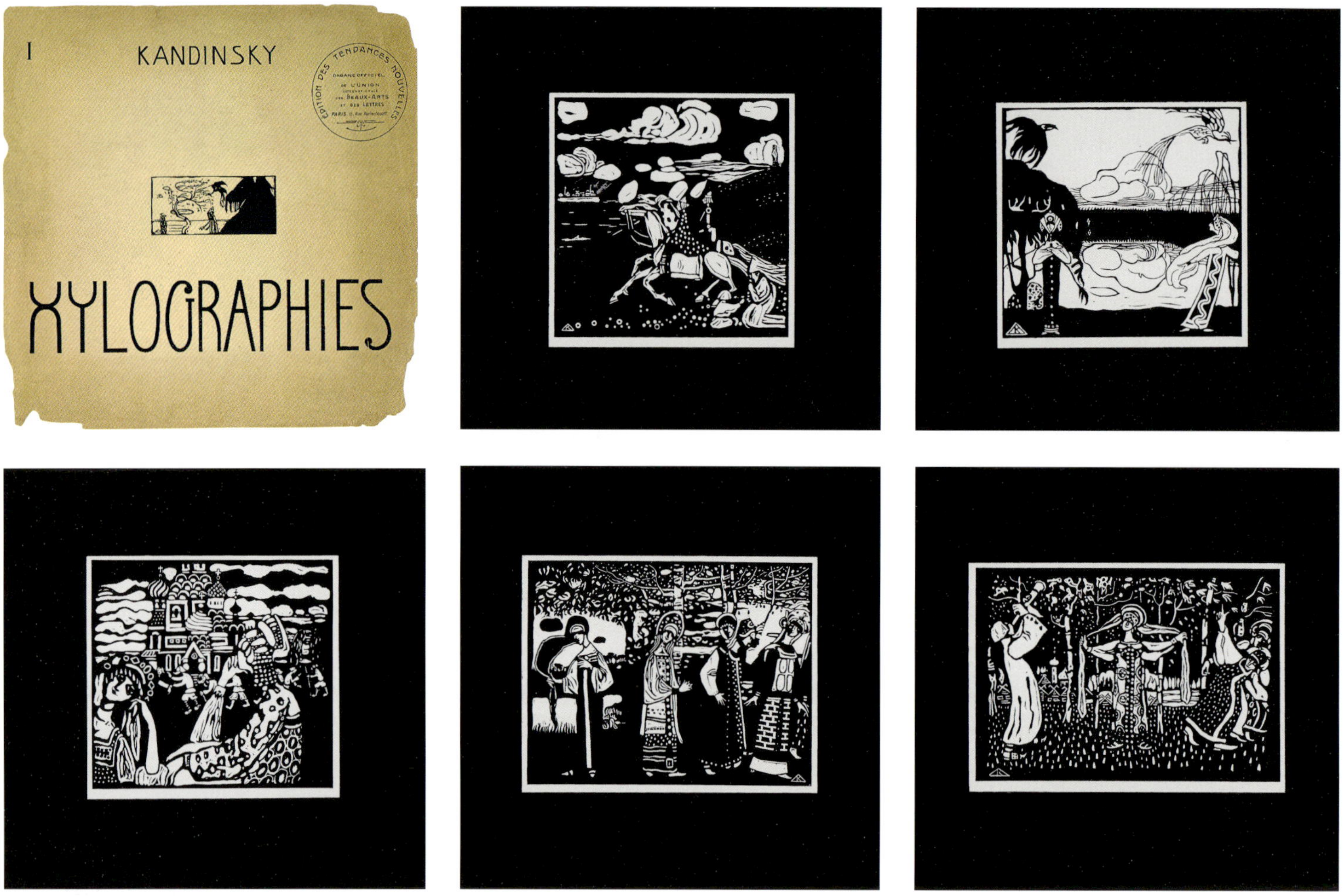

Figs. 8–13. Wassily Kandinsky, *Xylographies*, 1909. Woodcuts, photo engraving, each $12\frac{5}{8} \times 12\frac{5}{8}$ in. (32 x 32 cm). Arnold Schoenberg Center. Top row: title page, *Rider*, and *Birds*; bottom row: *Church*, *Birches*, and *Women in the Woods.* Kandinsky included this portfolio of woodcuts as a gift with his first letter to Schoenberg on January 18, 1911. He inscribed it, "Prof. Arnold Schönberg, with affinity, Kandinsky, Munich, 18 January 1911."

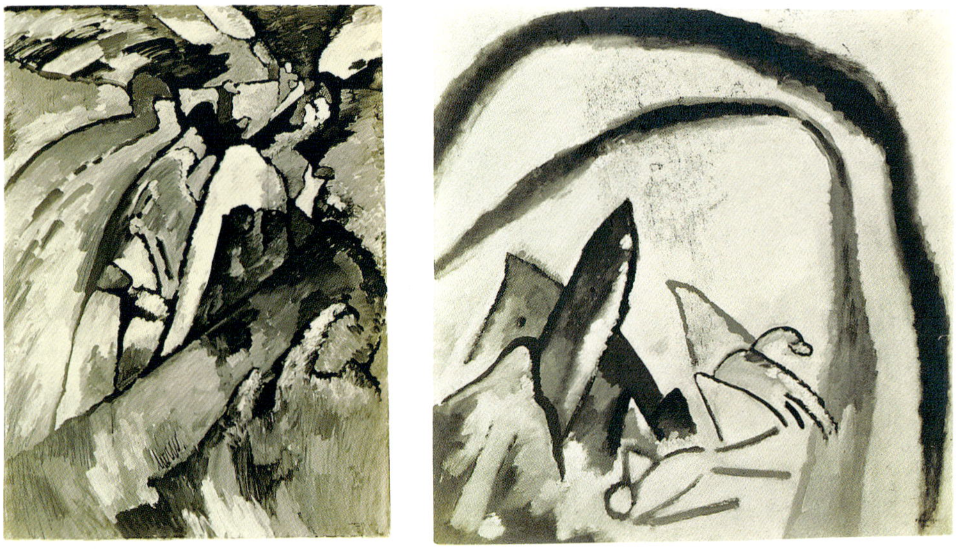

Figs. 14–15. Kandinsky enclosed these photographs of *Improvisation 7* and *Improvisation 16*, both painted in 1910, with his first letter to Schoenberg.

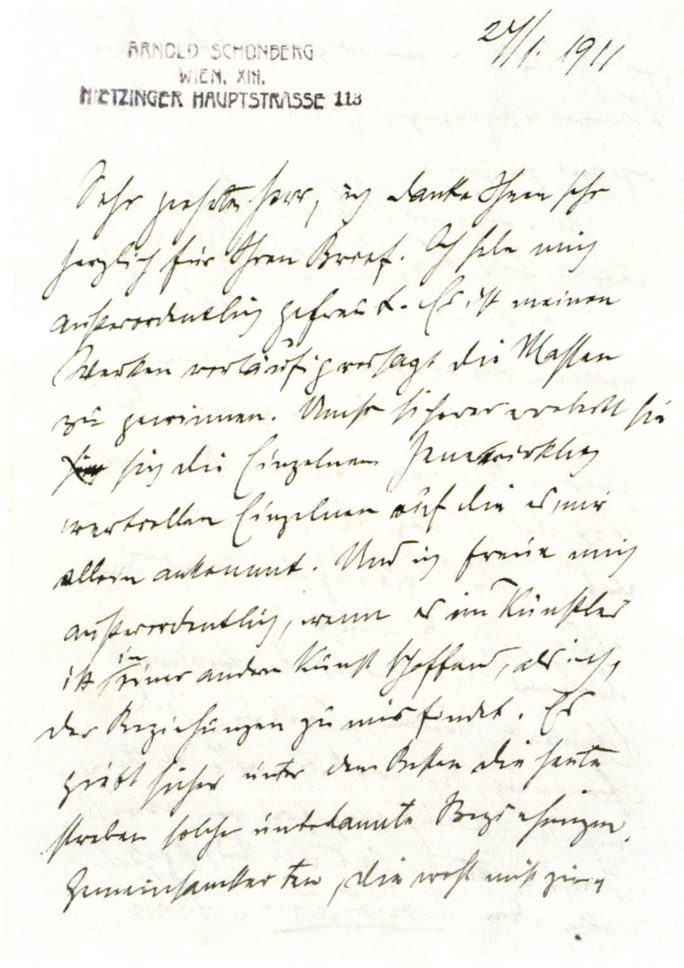

ARNOLD SCHÖNBERG
WIEN, XIII.
HIETZINGER HAUPTSTRASSE 113

24/1. 1911

Sehr geehrter Herr, ich danke Ihnen sehr herzlich für Ihren Brief. Er hat mich außerordentlich gefreut. Es ist meinen Werken vorläufig versagt, die Massen zu gewinnen. Umso sicherer erobern sie sich die Einzelnen. Jene wirklich wertvollen Einzelnen, auf die es mir allein ankommt. Und ich freue mich außerordentlich, wenn ein Künstler, der in einer anderen Kunst schafft, als ich, Beziehungen zu mir findet. Es gibt sicher unter den Besten der Jetztzeit solche unbekannte Beziehungen. Gemeinsamkeiten, die wohl nicht zu

Fig. 16. Schoenberg's first letter to Kandinsky, January 24, 1911.

photographs of his works to Kandinsky if he was interested. He apologized for his absence in Munich during the January 2 concert but trusted that they would meet sometime in Vienna or Munich, and warmly concluded, "I think we would have a lot to say to each other. This thought gives me pleasure, and I hope to hear from you soon."[41]

The correspondence between the two new friends would continue with intermittent frequency, sometimes almost daily, at other times lapsing for many months, until the outbreak of war. Dozens of letters reveal a wonderful mixture of abstruse theory, keen interest in each other's work, and many warm personal expressions of concern and fellowship. The range of their subjects is extraordinary—from discussions of the laws of harmony and the nature of the spiritual to Schoenberg's request for the name of an inexpensive doctor (one who charged "artists' prices") who could treat his daughter's skin condition. It is worth noting that the friendship between Kandinsky and Schoenberg, while deeply felt and intellectually compelling, was essentially an epistolary relationship; as far as we know, the two spent very little time together in person. Kandinsky, at forty-four, eight years older than Schoenberg, was the more active and interested correspondent, frequently sending several missives between responses from Schoenberg. Despite their growing familiarity, throughout their correspondence the two friends used the formal means of address ("Sie"), which was not

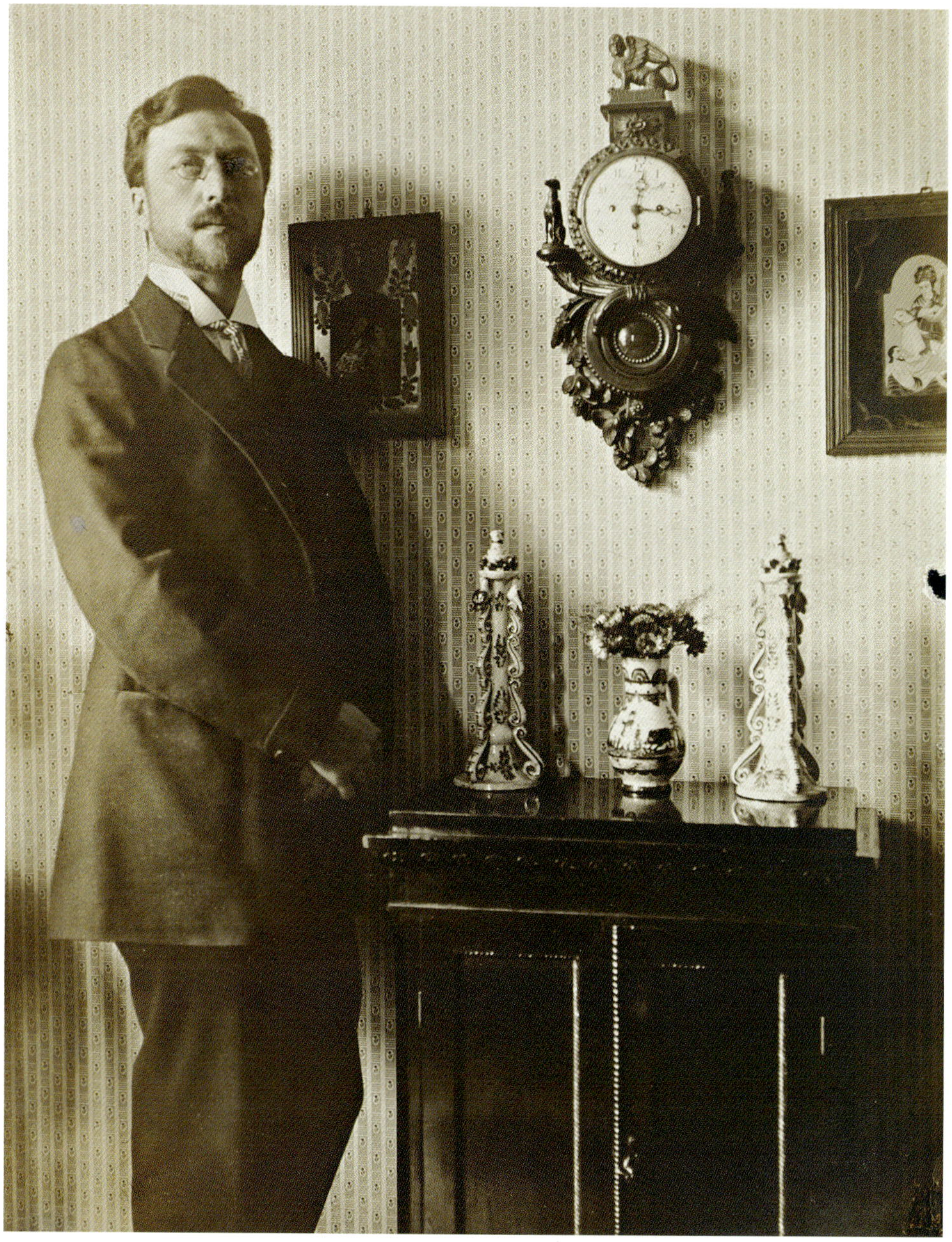

Fig. 17. Kandinsky sent this photograph of himself to the composer with the following inscription on the back: "To Arnold Schönberg, with feelings of profound affinity. Kandinsky, Munich, 9 April 1911."

unusual for the period, and generally addressed each other as "Mr. Schoenberg" and "Mr. Kandinsky."[42]

A number of photographs and books were exchanged. Personal photographs became a particular issue—after all, the two pen pals did not know what the other looked like. Kandinsky sent a photograph of himself on April 9, 1911 (fig. 17), and urged the composer to do likewise, but despite repeated requests Schoenberg waited until the following December to finally send one (fig. 18).[43] Along with the photograph, the composer sent an inscribed copy of his new book, *Theory of Harmony*, in which Schoenberg wrote that he and Kandinsky were on the same path and that they had indeed been brought together by this very same book (a reference, no doubt, to the artist's reaction to the excerpt printed on the poster and in the January 2, 1911, concert program).[44] Just a few days before, Kandinsky had sent Schoenberg an inscribed copy of his own just-published treatise, *On the Spiritual in Art* (figs. 19–20).

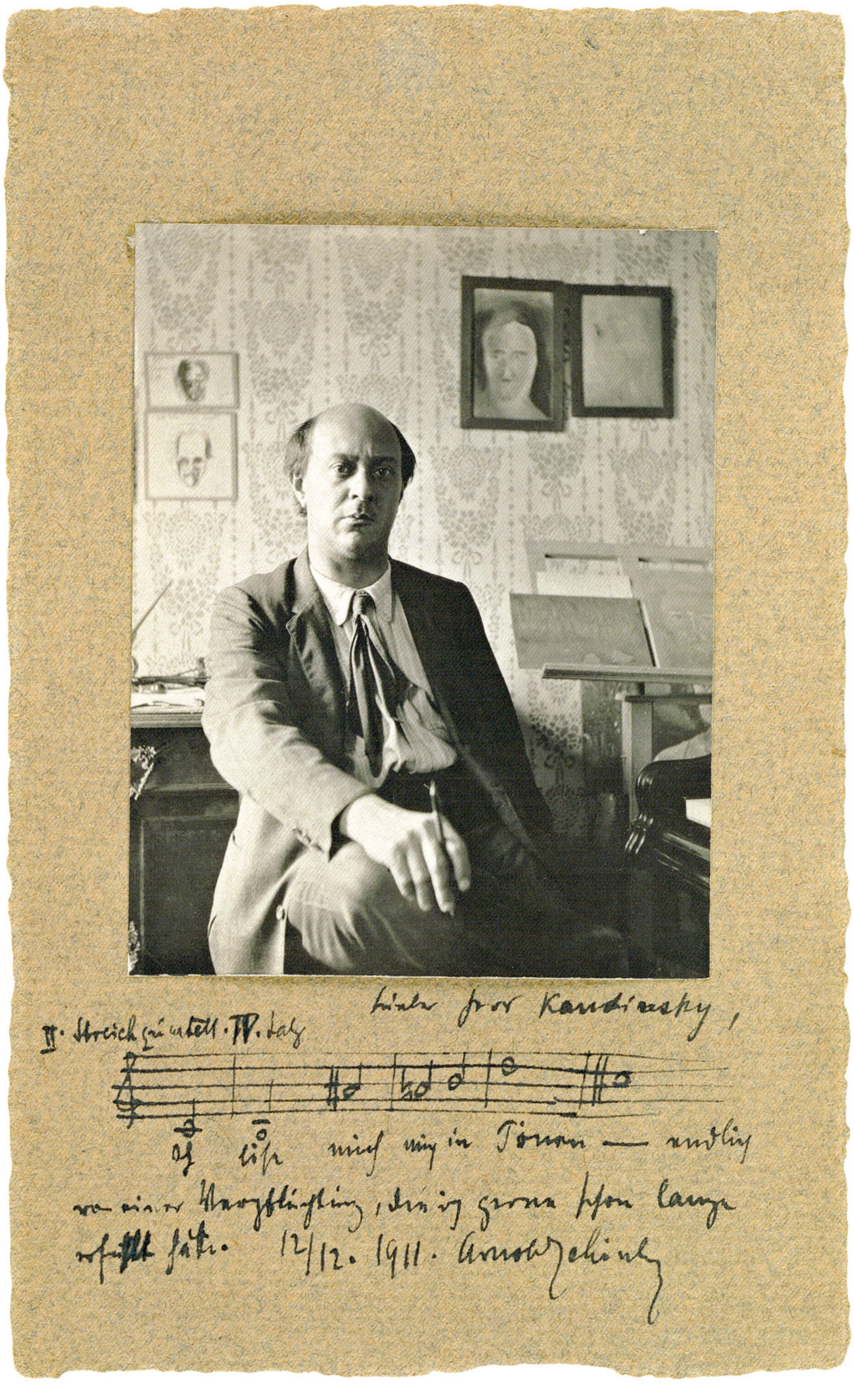

Fig. 18. Schoenberg sent this photograph of himself with the following dedication: "Dear Mr. Kandinsky, I am discharging in musical tones—an obligation I have long wished to fulfill. 12 December 1911. Arnold Schönberg."

Kandinsky was impressed with the photographs of Schoenberg's paintings that the composer sent in February 1911. "I am really enthusiastic about your pictures: their sources are a natural necessity and a fine sensitivity," he wrote, appreciating the composer's paintings as outstanding examples of the "purest realism," a painting option that he applauded, although he himself inclined toward "complete abstraction." Interestingly, Kandinsky preferred the composer's self-portraits and landscapes to his more abstract Gazes. The artist also mentioned that his partner, Gabriele Münter, was similarly delighted with his

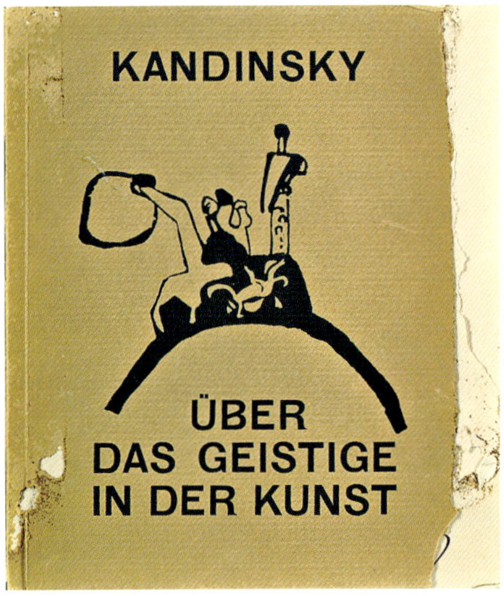

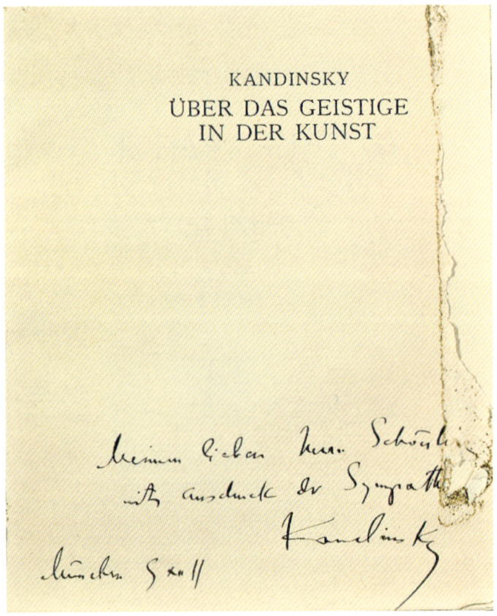

Figs. 19–20. Kandinsky sent this copy of his seminal treatise, *On the Spiritual in Art*, with the following inscription: "My dear Mr. Schönberg, in expression of sympathy, Kandinsky, Munich, 9 December 1911."

pictures.[45] When Kandinsky actually saw Schoenberg's paintings the following November, he rhapsodized about their "*inner* sonority" and observed that while they were the opposite of his own work, he felt that they grew "spiritually out of the same root."[46]

The two new friends met in person in mid-September 1911, while Schoenberg was staying in Berg, on the Starnberger See, in the foothills of the Bavarian Alps, not far from Murnau, where Kandinsky and Münter had a summer house. Franz Marc and Maria Franck were also at this first meeting. For some months, Kandinsky and Marc had been working on plans to publish an almanac that would present a synthesis of the arts by mixing the radical new work of an international group of modern artists and musicians with folk art, Asian art, and "primitive" art.[47] The volume, to be called the *Blue Rider Almanac*, would be published in May 1912.

During a brainstorming session in Murnau in October, the artists sent a postcard to Schoenberg wishing that the group could all be together again (figs. 21–22).[48] Schoenberg had already been asked to contribute to the volume, and Kandinsky was emphatic that he must participate. "Now the *Blaue Reiter*!" the artist wrote on November 16, 1911. "You have more than a month for your article. First number without Schoenberg! No, I won't have it. . . . Give us 10–15 pages! As I said, it *must* not be without Schoenberg."[49] The composer eventually submitted "The Relationship to the Text," a discussion of music and words, as well as the score for *Herzgewächse*, a setting of a Maeterlinck poem, which was included as a foldout facsimile. When Kandinsky and Marc left the Neue Künstlervereinigung München and decided to mount their own exhibition, they included four of Schoenberg's paintings in the first Blue Rider exhibition at the Moderne Galerie Thannhauser in Munich in December 1911 (pls. 39–42). Two of these paintings were subsequently reproduced in the *Blue Rider Almanac*.

Kandinsky also promoted Schoenberg in a number of other ways. He brought the composer's work to the attention of his colleagues in the Russian avant-garde; in early 1911, he translated "On Parallel Octaves and Fifths" into Russian for the catalogue of the touring version of the Second International Art Exhibition, which originated at the Salon Izdebsky in Odessa (fig. 23) and was instrumental in arranging for Schoenberg to conduct *Pelleas und Melisande* in Saint Petersburg in December 1912 (fig. 24). Kandinsky championed the composer's paintings, hoping to include them in other exhibitions (Schoenberg declined), and contributed a thoughtful piece about them ("The Pictures") for a Festschrift that was presented to Schoenberg in Prague on February 29, 1912 (fig. 25; see Hailey essay, fig. 1). Clearly influenced by the Munich concert and a new familiarity with the composer's ideas, Kandinsky added references to Schoenberg in his major theoretical opus, *On the Spiritual in Art*: "Schoenberg's music," he wrote, "leads us into a new realm, where musical experiences are no longer acoustic, but purely spiritual. Here begins the 'music of the future.'"[50]

Meanwhile, Kandinsky's paintings had also "made a great and lasting impression" on Schoenberg, who finally had the opportunity to see four of them in November 1911 at the *Neue Secession* exhibition in Berlin, where the composer

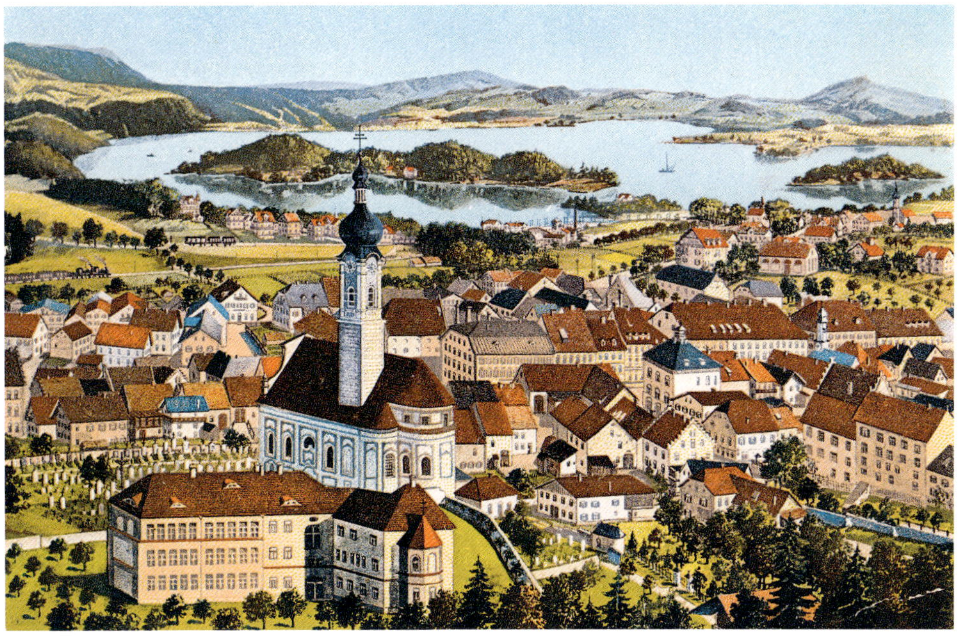

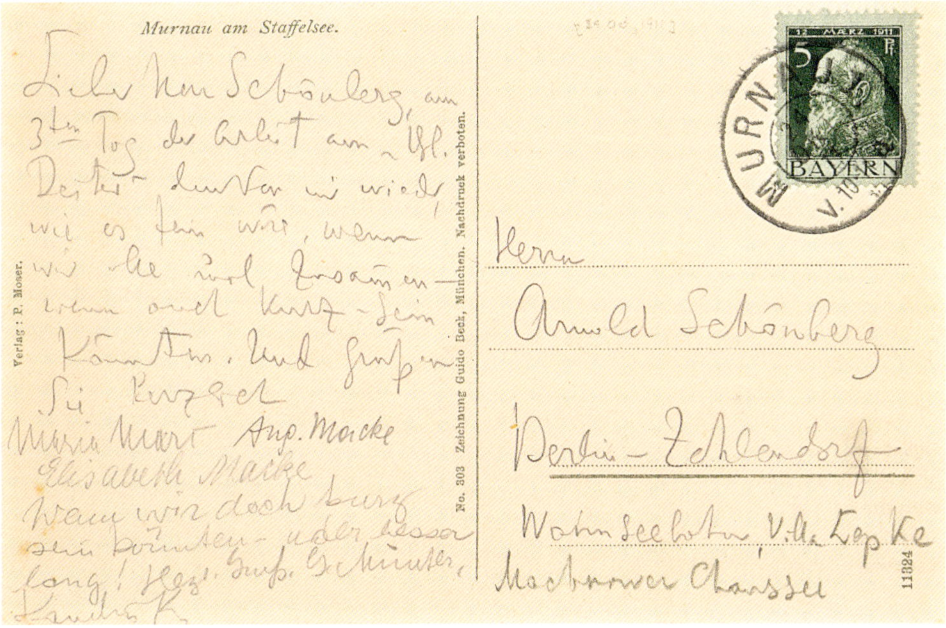

Figs. 21–22. This postcard, with an image of Murnau on the front, was sent to Schoenberg during an October 1911 planning session for the *Blue Rider Almanac*: "On the third day of the work on *Der blaue Reiter*, we think again how fine it would be if we could all be together once more—if only for a short time. And kindest regards from Maria Marc, Aug. Macke, Elisabeth Macke." Additionally, Gabriele Münter wrote, "If we just could be [together] for a short time—or better, for a long time! Kind regards, G. Münter, Kandinsky."

had moved a couple of months before. "Much is still before my eyes," he wrote the artist. "The dreamlike nature of the impressions, that which is wild and nevertheless clearly controlled, and in particular the incredibly strong effect of the colors. I would love to see them again."[51] The composer also mentioned how much he liked Münter's paintings ("The remarkable and yet womanly strength of her works touched me extraordinarily"),[52] as well as those of Franz Marc ("There is a curious gentleness in this 'giant'").[53]

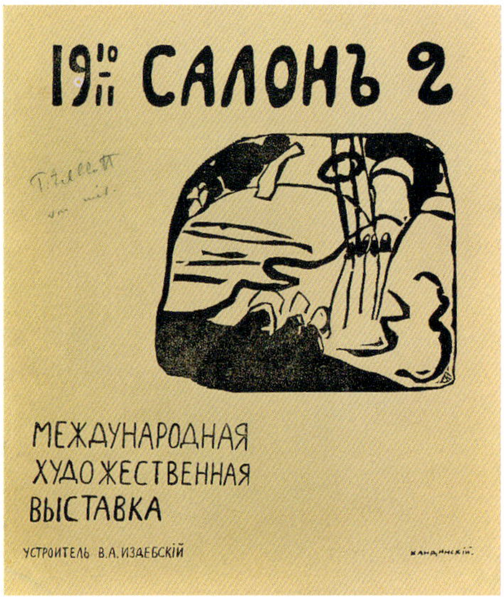

Fig. 23. Catalogue of the Second International Art Exhibition ("Salon 2") in Odessa, 1910/11. This exhibition subsequently toured Russia.

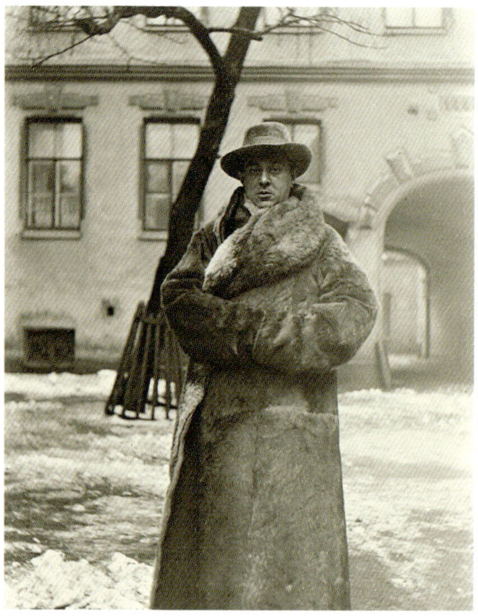

Fig. 24. Arnold Schoenberg in St. Petersburg, 1912.

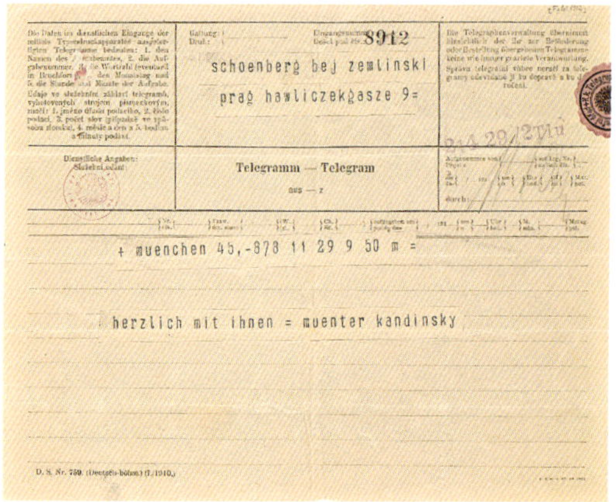
8912
schoenberg bej zemlinski
prag hawliczekgasze 9=
Telegramm — Telegram
+ muenchen 45,-878 11 29 9 50 m =
herzlich mit ihnen = muenter kandinsky

Fig. 25. Münter and Kandinsky sent this telegram to Schoenberg in Prague in February 1912 on the occasion of the performance of *Pelleas und Melisande* and the presentation of a Festschrift to the composer. It reads simply, "Thinking of you warmly—Muenter Kandinsky."

The correspondence between the two friends continued through 1912, with extended discussions about, among other things, their respective operas—Kandinsky's *Der gelbe Klang*, which had been published in the *Blue Rider Almanac*, and Schoenberg's current project, *Die glückliche Hand* (The lucky hand; pls. 59–61). In this instance, the composer praised the artist for his emphasis on conveying an "inner vision," and going further than Schoenberg himself in renouncing "any conscious thought, any conventional plot."[54] Münter sent Schoenberg a New Year's greeting (in the form of a woodcut) at the outset of 1913 (fig. 26), but otherwise the couple was out of touch with the composer for much of 1913, which prompted Schoenberg to apologize on September 28: "I am perpetually having to do unpleasant things and struggle with weariness afterwards. It is sad that one has no time to catch one's breath. When I am tired I have no desire to do anything: neither to work nor to write letters. Don't be angry with me!"[55] The following year, though, the two had the chance to be together when the Schoenbergs decided to spend the summer of 1914 in the Murnau area. Through May and June, Münter and Kandinsky spent a great deal of time finding a suitable house for them to rent. They sent numerous letters to the composer illustrated with Münter's detailed floor plans of the houses and Kandinsky's cartoonlike maps showing the locations of the properties in relation to the lake, the train station, and other facilities (fig. 27). Schoenberg and his family vacationed in Murnau in July, and no doubt visited with Kandinsky and Münter during that time. But their summer stay was cut short by the outbreak of war in August.

The Schoenbergs spent the war years in Austria, while Kandinsky went back to Russia, only returning to Germany in December 1921.[56] The two friends were completely out of touch for eight long years until Kandinsky renewed contact with Schoenberg in July 1922. "Everything has really changed since our time together in Bavaria," he wrote. "Much that was a daring dream at that time has now become the past. We have experienced centuries."[57] Schoenberg was thrilled to have finally heard from his old friend. "How often I've thought of you with anxiety during these eight years! And how many people I have asked about you, without ever getting any definite and reliable information." He echoed the artist in observing that perhaps the worst trial of all was "the overturning of everything one has believed in," and mentioned that he had found solace in religion ("belief in something higher, beyond") and the composition of his oratorio on such spiritual themes, *Die Jakobsleiter* (Jacob's ladder). The interest in religion—"though without any organizational fetters"—was new for Schoenberg, an assimilated Jew who had converted to Protestantism in 1898.[58]

Kandinsky had joined the faculty of the Bauhaus in Weimar in the spring of 1922, and in April 1923 he invited Schoenberg to come there to head up the music school. "How often I have said to myself: 'if only Schoenberg were here!' And imagine, now he could perhaps come," wrote the artist.[59] The composer immediately rejected the offer and, based on information from Alma Mahler, accused the artist of being anti-Semitic. Much as he would have liked to teach at the Bauhaus, Schoenberg responded to Kandinsky, "It cannot be. For I have at last learnt the lesson that has been forced upon me during this year, and I shall not ever forget it. It is that I am not a German, not a European, indeed perhaps scarcely even a human being (at least, the Europeans prefer the worst of their race to me), but I am a Jew." He continued that he had "heard that even a Kandinsky sees only evil in the actions of Jews and in their evil actions only the Jewishness, and at this point I give up hope of reaching any understanding. It was a dream. We are two kinds of people. Definitively!"[60]

Kandinsky was stunned. He quickly replied, "In earlier days I would never have been able to suppose that we—of all people—could write to each other in

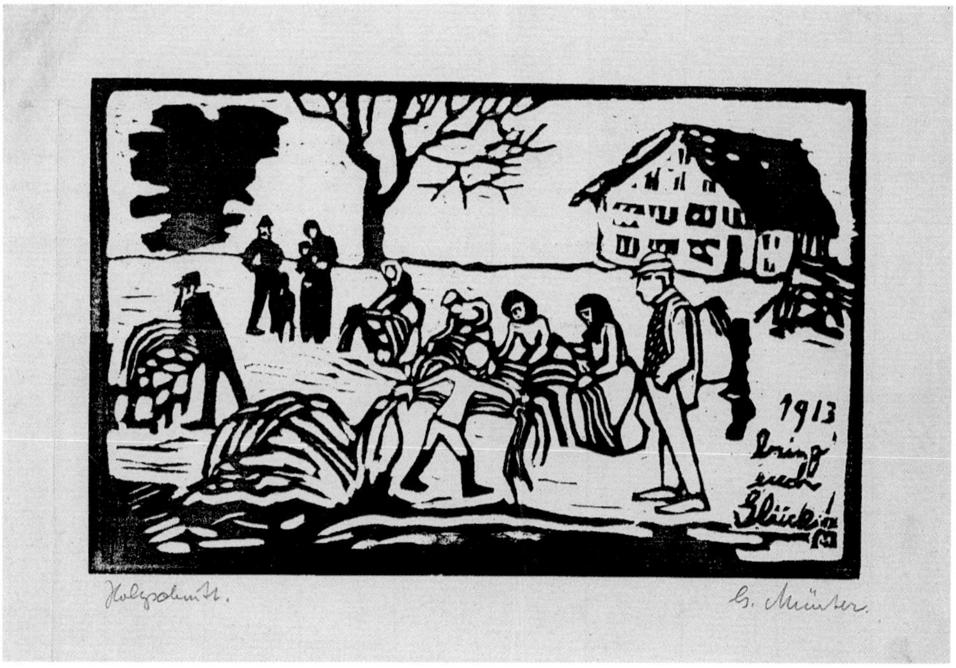

Fig. 26. Münter sent Schoenberg this New Year's woodcut, which reads, "1913 brings you luck!"

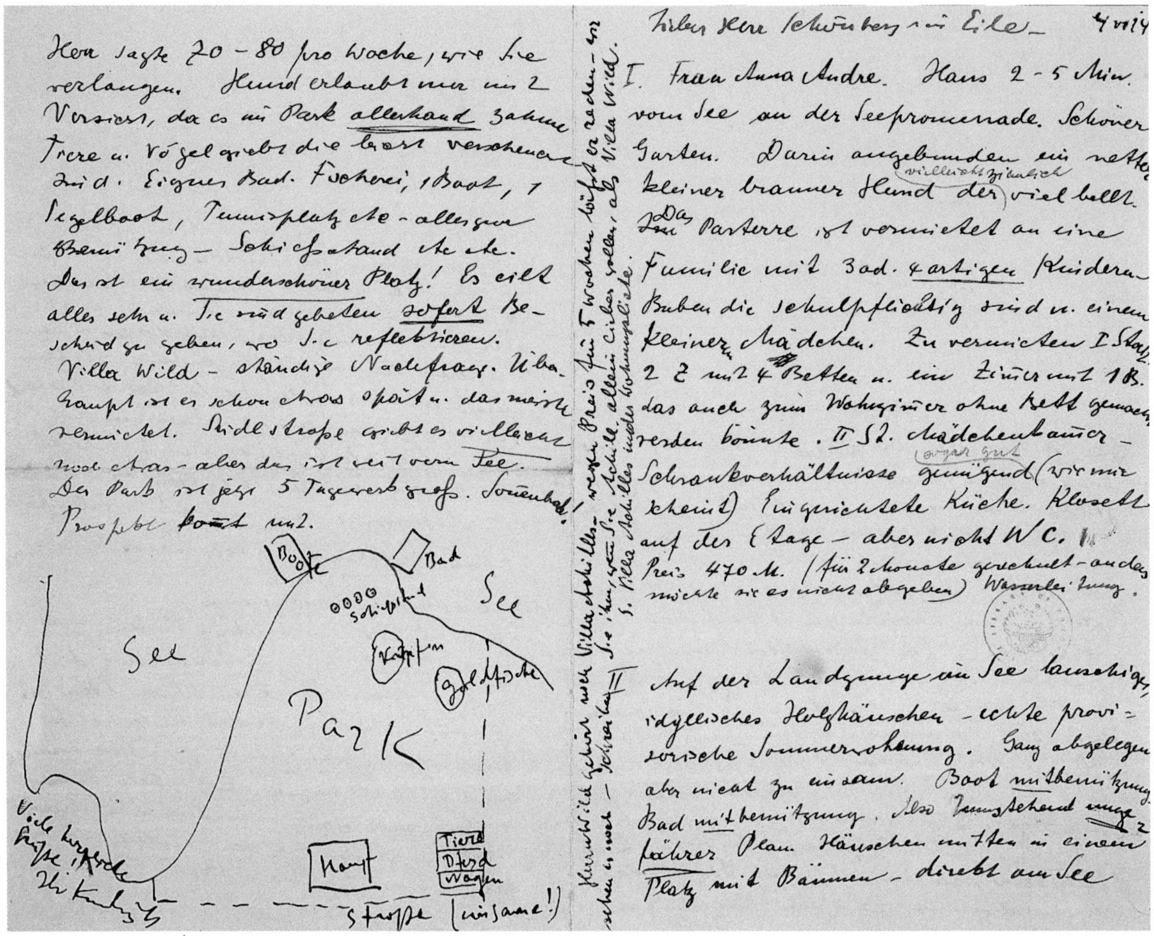

Fig. 27. Letter from Münter and Kandinsky to Schoenberg, June 4, 1914 (first page on right, final page on left). The letter, written by Münter, describes various houses for rent in the Murnau area; the drawing by Kandinsky shows one of the houses in a park by the lake.

such a way. . . . I love you as an artist and a human being, or perhaps as a human being and an artist. In such cases I think least of all about nationality—it is a matter of the greatest indifference to me."[61] Schoenberg was not swayed, and in a six-page diatribe, informed by recent firsthand experience, the composer attacked anti-Semitism. He stated: "When I walk along the street and each person looks at me to see whether I'm a Jew or a Christian, I can't very well tell each of them that I'm the one that Kandinsky and some others make an exception of, although of course that man Hitler is not of their opinion." And then, most presciently, he wrote, "But what is anti-Semitism to lead to if not to acts of violence? Is it so difficult to imagine that?" Schoenberg asked Kandinsky not to respond and observed that the two could simply no longer understand each other. This was extraordinarily painful for Schoenberg, who wrote that he still had respect for the Kandinsky he had once known and asked the artist "to convey greetings from me to my former friend Kandinsky." Finally, he expressed the hope that if they met up again they would not have "to be blind to each other."[62]

In 1927, the two old friends did indeed meet again when they ran into each other while they were both on vacation at Pörtschach on the Wörther See (fig. 28). It was the last time they saw each other. With the rise of the Nazis, Schoenberg left

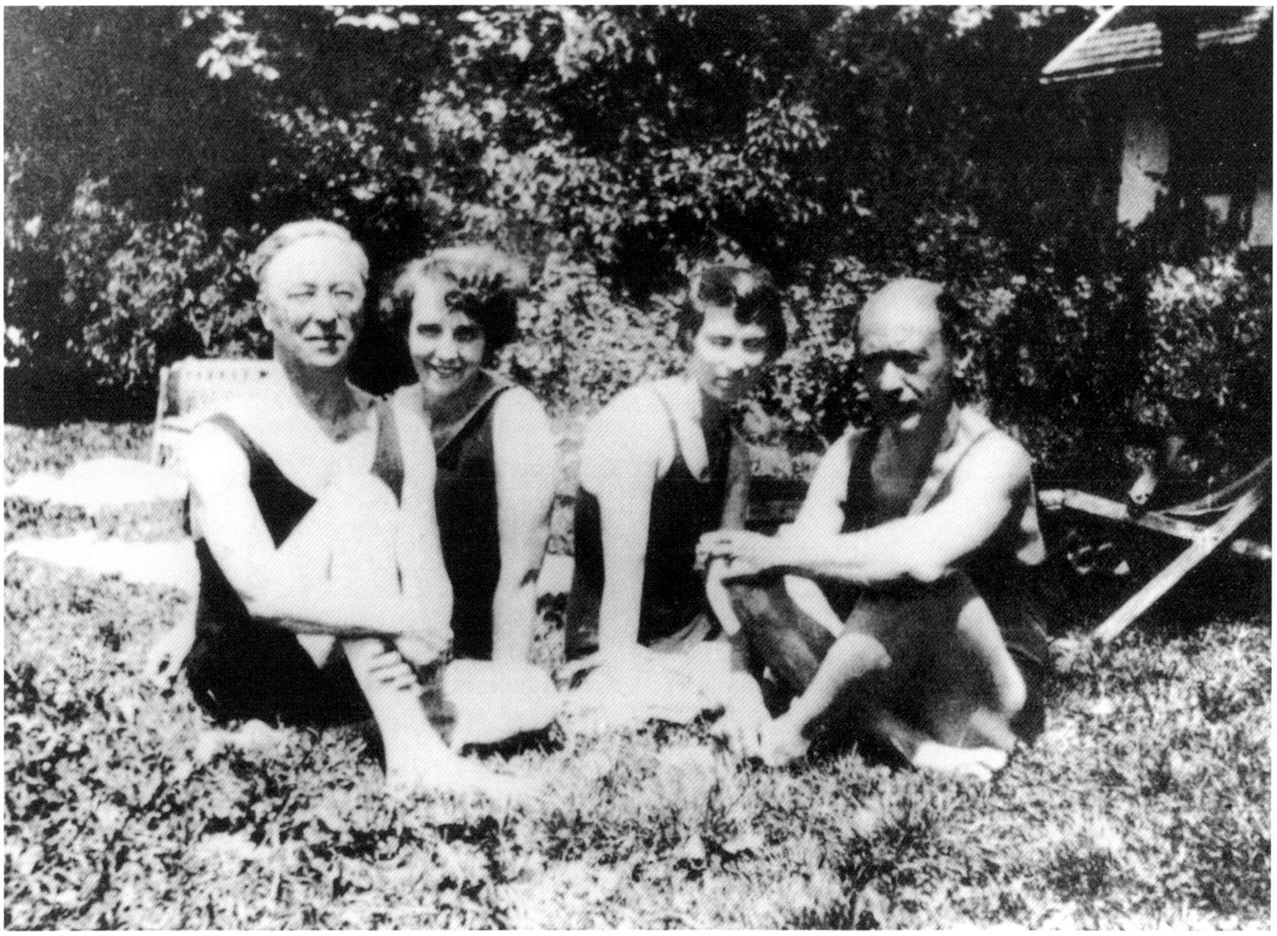

Fig. 28. Wassily and Nina Kandinsky with Gertrud and Arnold Schoenberg, Pörtschach on the Wörther See, 1927.

Berlin for Paris in 1933. Shortly thereafter, he and his family left for the United States, where he taught in Boston and New York before settling in Los Angeles in 1934. Kandinsky fled Germany in 1933 and settled in Neuilly-sur-Seine, near Paris. In one last letter between the two old friends, on July 1, 1936, Kandinsky fondly recalled their first meeting:

> Do you still remember, dear Schoenberg, how we met—I arrived on the steamer wearing short Lederhosen and saw a black-and-white graphic—you were dressed completely in white and only your face was deeply tanned. And later the summer in Murnau? All our contemporaries from that time sigh deeply when they remember that vanished epoch and say: "That was a beautiful time." . . . How wonderfully life pulsated then, what quick spiritual triumphs we expected.[63]

In a profound sense, however, their initial meeting was at the Munich concert on January 2, 1911, when Kandinsky heard Schoenberg's compositions for the first time. The composer's music spoke to the artist in a way that touched him very deeply. At that moment, he encountered another artist whose project paralleled his own artistic journey. Just as Kandinsky divined that Schoenberg, like himself, was striving to liberate the "individual voices" in his compositions, he also correctly sensed that he had just "met" one of the great individual voices of his time.

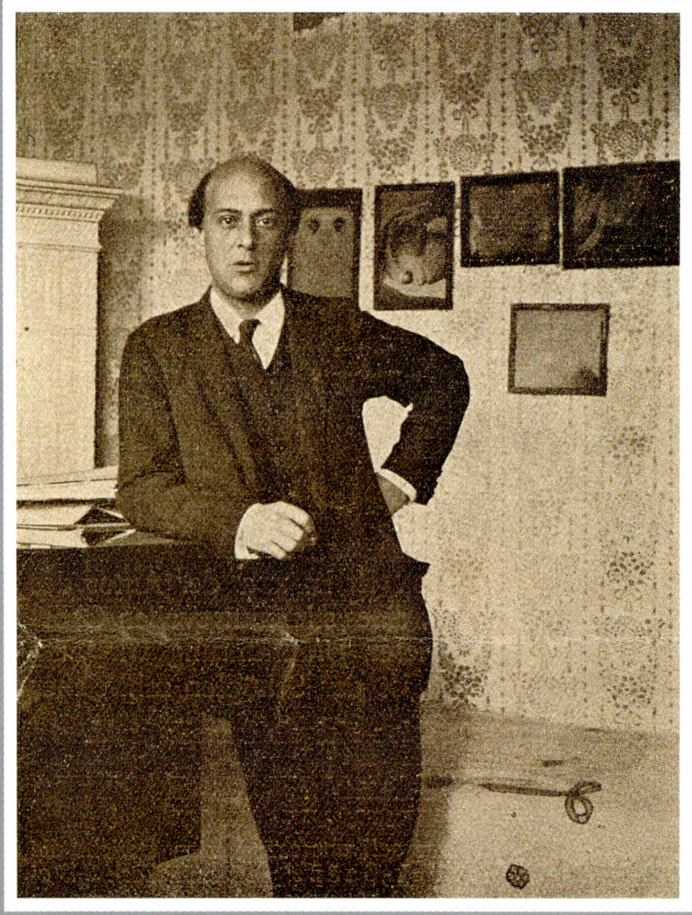

Schoenberg's Echo

The Composer as Painter

Esther da Costa Meyer

He arrived without much baggage, just when artists were avidly exploring the affinities between painting and the nonrepresentational art of music. Abstraction beckoned. Schoenberg's lightness must have seemed enviable to his new colleagues in the art world, or perhaps simply reckless. He was only passing through, rising in a year or so from amateur to member of the international avant-garde. A flash, and he was gone, reclaimed by music. But the products of this brief moment in time command attention: liquid faces dissolving into paint, a red-rimmed, incandescent pupil, fierce whisperings of the soul burst from its moorings.

Schoenberg probably learned the rudiments of painting from the gifted young artist Richard Gerstl, whom he met around 1905.[1] Rebellious and high-strung, Gerstl was attracted to the composer, already notorious for his principled and uncompromising struggle against Vienna's conservative musical establishment.[2] In 1907, Gerstl moved into the same building on Liechtensteinstrasse where both Schoenberg and his brother-in-law Alexander Zemlinsky lived, and was invited to spend the summer holidays with the Schoenbergs at Gmunden. Gerstl's remarkable portraits of Schoenberg, his family, and members of his circle attest to the growing intensity of their relationship. In the summer of 1908, Schoenberg's first wife, Mathilde, then thirty-one and a mother of two, left her family and went to live with the twenty-five-year-old artist. Only the intervention of Schoenberg's student Anton Webern, who begged her to think of the couple's two young children, convinced her to return. Gerstl did not survive the tension, and on the night of November 4–5 committed suicide, after destroying all the works in his studio. As the plots of Schoenberg's first two operas—*Erwartung* (Expectation; 1909) and *Die glückliche Hand* (The lucky hand; 1910–13)—reveal, this tragedy had repercussions not only in his life but in his work as well.

The motivations that drove Schoenberg to take up art are complex and overdetermined. Painting must have given him great pleasure: all his life, he revealed an affinity for handicraft, especially for bookbinding and making furniture. His urge to paint, however, was also deeply connected to his personal crisis: his earliest extant work, a self-portrait in pen and ink dated 1908, was produced

Fig. 1. Arnold Schoenberg standing in front of some of his paintings, as illustrated in the *Rheinische Musik und Theater Zeitung*, February 17, 1912.

six weeks after Gerstl's suicide (pl. 9). It is equally significant that he turned to art just after the gradual break with tonality. Given the unremitting hostility of critics and public to his music, painting permitted Schoenberg to expatriate himself to another field, where he was free to try out new ideas, and to question himself in an unfamiliar medium. Financial considerations also played a role: as the opposition to his music increased, he hoped, somewhat optimistically, to make a living from his portraits.

On March 7, 1910, he wrote to Emil Hertzka, his publisher in Vienna, asking him to find patrons willing to acquire his work, adding that "it is much more interesting to have one's portrait done by . . . a musician of my reputation than to be painted by some mere practitioner of painting whose name will be forgotten in 20 years, whereas even now my name belongs to the history of music."[3] In June, Schoenberg asked the artist Carl Moll, Alma Mahler's stepfather, to organize a show of his works at Vienna's prestigious Galerie Miethke. Moll refused, fearing that Schoenberg's hopes of selling his paintings were premature. Schoenberg then decided to exhibit his work at his own expense, at the bookshop of Hugo Heller, a well-known Viennese publisher. Since most of his dated paintings are from that year, they were probably completed for the occasion, prompted by financial need.

The exhibition, which opened on October 8, 1910, included forty-two works: eleven portraits and studies; two self-portraits; fourteen Impressions and Fantasies (*Eindrücke und Phantasien*); two caricatures; five portraits of Mahler; five Nightpieces (*Nachtstücke*); and five studies for his opera *Die glückliche Hand* (fig. 2).[4] Though the show was neither a financial nor a critical success, several important voices found the work striking, among them Arthur Schnitzler: "Talent unmistakable," he noted in his diary.[5] Only three of the paintings sold, and to an anonymous buyer—portraits of Mahler, all. Schoenberg only discovered the identity of his patron a year later. "Since yesterday evening I know who the buyer of your pictures was," wrote Webern in 1911. "He did not want you to know. Now he has gone to eternal rest. I do not think that he wants you not to know. . . . Your pictures were bought by GUSTAV MAHLER."[6] Mahler's generous gesture of support for his struggling young colleague was all the greater for being discreet.

Fig. 2. Catalogue of Schoenberg's first exhibition at the Kunstsalon Heller in Vienna, October 1910.

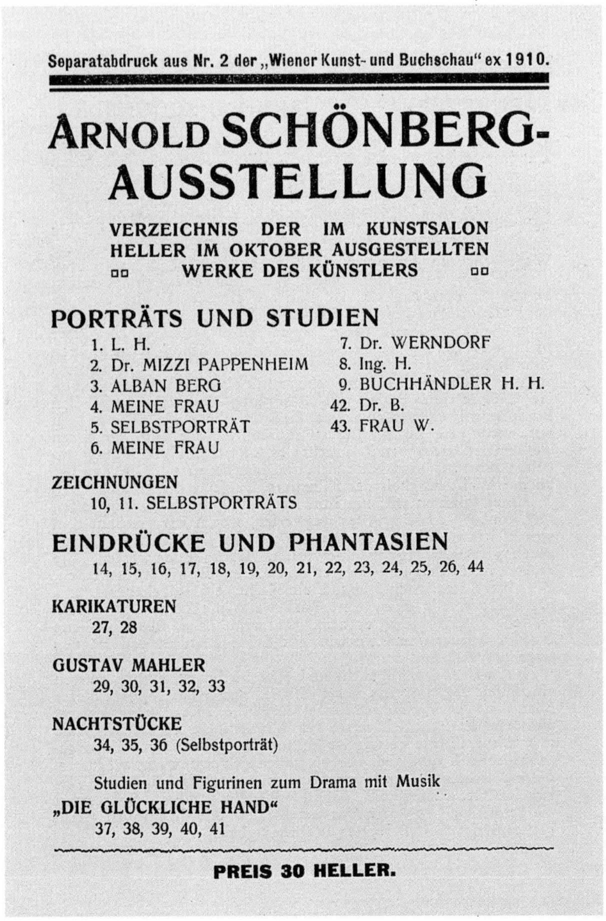

Separatabdruck aus Nr. 2 der „Wiener Kunst- und Buchschau" ex 1910.

ARNOLD SCHÖNBERG-AUSSTELLUNG

VERZEICHNIS DER IM KUNSTSALON HELLER IM OKTOBER AUSGESTELLTEN WERKE DES KÜNSTLERS

PORTRÄTS UND STUDIEN

1. L. H.
2. Dr. MIZZI PAPPENHEIM
3. ALBAN BERG
4. MEINE FRAU
5. SELBSTPORTRÄT
6. MEINE FRAU
7. Dr. WERNDORF
8. Ing. H.
9. BUCHHÄNDLER H. H.
42. Dr. B.
43. FRAU W.

ZEICHNUNGEN

10, 11. SELBSTPORTRÄTS

EINDRÜCKE UND PHANTASIEN

14, 15, 16, 17, 18, 19, 20, 21, 22, 23, 24, 25, 26, 44

KARIKATUREN

27, 28

GUSTAV MAHLER

29, 30, 31, 32, 33

NACHTSTÜCKE

34, 35, 36 (Selbstporträt)

Studien und Figurinen zum Drama mit Musik „DIE GLÜCKLICHE HAND"

37, 38, 39, 40, 41

PREIS 30 HELLER.

Critical response in Vienna seems to have been colored by the reaction to Schoenberg's music, though it is clear from the number of reviews that his art was taken seriously. Even the art world found positive things to say, along with serious reservations. "At first sight," wrote the reviewer of the *Illustriertes Wiener Extrablatt* of Schoenberg's work, "it is frightening. One is appalled and repulsed. It is a yawning chasm of the most ghastly dilettantism. Here is a manifesto of the first uncertain gropings. . . . Once the eye has recovered from all these surging, whorling, blurred, briny, snarling horrors, once it has learned 'to see,' a certain deeply rooted talent becomes apparent, a fantastic, bizarre, willful creative power that has misappropriated its medium and become mired in slime."[7] And the critic of the *Weltneuigkeits-Blatt* observed that "one cannot deny that his pictures and portrait studies have remarkable qualities. The self-portraits, the large portrait of a woman 'My Wife,' as well as the half-length Heller portrait show considerable promise."[8] Adalbert Franz Seligman, art critic of the prestigious *Neue Freie Presse*, was more dismissive: "Mr. Schoenberg, as Mr. Heller, my cicerone, assures me with an embarrassed smile, has been painting for only a year. One cannot tell from looking at these works. They look as if their author first took up the brush last week."[9]

Music critics were more accepting. Elsa Bienenfeld, who covered musical events for the *Neues Wiener Journal*, paid close attention to the works: "Schönberg paints these portraits and fantasies with brutal simplicity, in the style of Kokoschka. One large blot of color stands wild and mutinous next to another. . . . And yet one cannot deny, that as dreadful, as audacious, as childish as his manner of painting appears to be, there is always a flash of something elemental and peculiar to the person or mood portrayed." She concluded: "There is no doubt that this manner [of seeing] is very strong and original; it is also frightening."[10] Reviewing the opening night for the cultural magazine *Der Merker*, Paul Stefan observed, with somewhat less insight, that Schoenberg's art was born of his compositions: "Only musicians, only those who know Schönberg's music and its secrets, should look at these pictures, for only they will experience them elementally as sounds transposed across all the accidental boundaries of form. It was therefore virtually essential to have the music of Schönberg ringing in one's ears as one viewed this exhibition."[11]

The connection between Schoenberg's music and his art was underscored by a performance at the Heller Gallery, on October 12, of his first two string quartets, opp. 7 and 10, by the Rosé Quartet.[12] There is a beautiful symmetry in the fact that these same works would lead to his next exhibition. Less than two months later, on January 2, 1911, the Rosé Quartet performed the same program in Munich, along with five lieder and the newly published piano pieces, op. 11. The concert was attended by Wassily Kandinsky, his companion Gabriele Münter, Franz Marc, Alexei von Jawlensky, and Marianne von Werefkin—all members or supporters of the Neue Künstlervereinigung München (NKVM) who would soon break away to form the Blue Rider (*Blaue Reiter*). For Marc and Kandinsky, the concert was an epiphany. Both were extremely knowledgeable about music, and were struck by the String Quartet in F-sharp Minor (1907–8), where, in the final movement, Schoenberg first broke with tonality. A few days after the event Marc wrote to the painter August Macke: "Can you imagine a music in which tonality (that is, conformity to a given key) is entirely suspended? When listening to this music, I was constantly thinking of Kandinsky's large Composition, which disavows any trace of tonality . . . and also of Kandinsky's 'jumping spots'[*springende Flecke*], which permits each tone sounded to stand by itself (a sort of *white canvas* between the flecks of color!). Schönberg proceeds from the principle that the concepts of consonance and dissonance do not exist at all. A so-called disso-

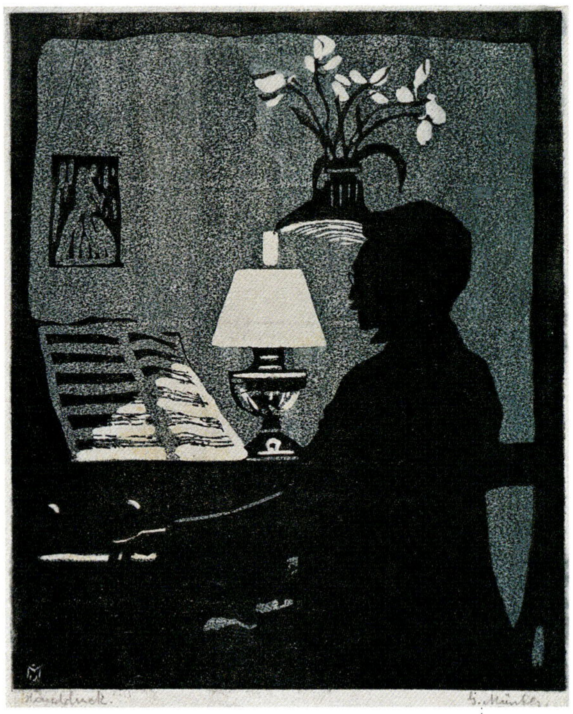

Fig. 3. Gabriele Münter (German, 1877–1962). *Kandinsky at the Harmonium*, 1907. Color linocut, 5⅞ x 4⅞ in. (14.8 x 12.4 cm). Städtische Galerie im Lenbachhaus, Munich, GMS 836.

nance is only a consonance that is situated further apart."[13]

Kandinsky was even more profoundly affected, not only by the music but also by the program notes, which he would soon translate into Russian and which were an excerpt of Schoenberg's forthcoming treatise, *Harmonielehre* (Theory of harmony). An accomplished pianist and cellist and occasional composer, Kandinsky had given much thought to the affinities between art and music (fig. 3). His two series, the Improvisations and Compositions, had explicitly musical titles. Like Marc, he sensed a relationship between Schoenberg's liberation of music from tonality and his own agonizing attempt to free art from the shackles of representation. Abstraction and atonality, Kandinsky thought, shared similar revolutionary goals. Two weeks later he wrote the composer to express his admiration: "In your works, you have realized what I, albeit in uncertain form, have so greatly longed for in music. The independent progress through their own destinies, the independent life of the individual voices in your compositions is exactly what I am trying to find in my paintings."[14] Kandinsky's letter initiated one of the great epistolary exchanges on the relation between art and music, with remarkable insights on both sides, and equally inspired misreadings.[15] Nevertheless, if this exchange was crucial for the development of Schoenberg's ideas, it had no impact on his art, since almost all his oil paintings were finished before the two men met. On the whole, the tendency to look at Schoenberg's art almost exclusively through the lens of his friendship with Kandinsky has prevented a thorough understanding of his oeuvre as an artist: his paintings, in fact, bear little resemblance to those of the Russian artist.

When the two men finally met for the first time on September 14, 1911, Kandinsky was involved with the NKVM, which was preparing an exhibition to be held at the Moderne Galerie Thannhauser in Munich later that year. Increasingly dissatisfied with the narrow outlook of the organization, Kandinsky, Münter, and Marc resigned in December and founded their own group, the Blue Rider. They immediately set about preparing a rival exhibition to be held at the same venue, and invited Schoenberg to participate. By then he had moved to Berlin, and it was left to his students Alban Berg and Webern to select eight paintings from his apartment in Vienna, which they sent to Munich.[16] Of these, Kandinsky chose four: *Self-Portrait, Walking* (1911), *Night Landscape* (1910), and two Visions of 1910 (pls. 39–42). Photographs of the exhibition taken by Gabriele Münter show that Schoenberg's small-scale works were not advantageously displayed (figs. 4–6). His *Self-Portrait, Walking*, for example, was placed rather high, next to Marc's *Yellow Cow* (1911), a large canvas saturated with glowing color (pl. 43). Schoenberg, whose palette tended toward dark tonalities, must have feared being upstaged, because when Kandinsky invited him to take part in the group's second show to be held in February 1912, Schoenberg declined. In the interim, he had been asked to exhibit in Budapest, under more favorable conditions. "I will have a room of my own (23 paintings) where I will not be overshadowed by the

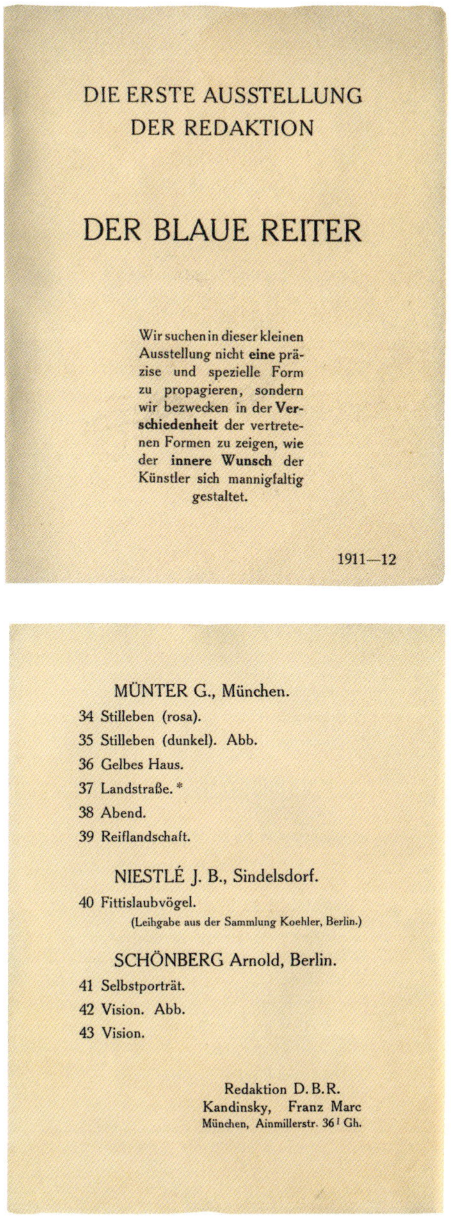
DIE ERSTE AUSSTELLUNG
DER REDAKTION

DER BLAUE REITER

Wir suchen in dieser kleinen Ausstellung nicht **eine** präzise und spezielle Form zu propagieren, sondern wir bezwecken in der **Verschiedenheit** der vertretenen Formen zu zeigen, wie der **innere Wunsch** der Künstler sich mannigfaltig gestaltet.

1911—12

MÜNTER G., München.
34 Stilleben (rosa).
35 Stilleben (dunkel). Abb.
36 Gelbes Haus.
37 Landstraße. *
38 Abend.
39 Reiflandschaft.

NIESTLÉ J. B., Sindelsdorf.
40 Fittislaubvögel.
(Leihgabe aus der Sammlung Koehler, Berlin.)

SCHÖNBERG Arnold, Berlin.
41 Selbstporträt.
42 Vision. Abb.
43 Vision.

Redaktion D.B.R.
Kandinsky, Franz Marc
München, Ainmillerstr. 36 I Gh.

Fig. 4. Two pages from the catalogue of the first Blue Rider exhibition at the Moderne Galerie Thannhauser in Munich, December 1911. Contrary to what was published in this catalogue, Schoenberg displayed four paintings in the exhibition.

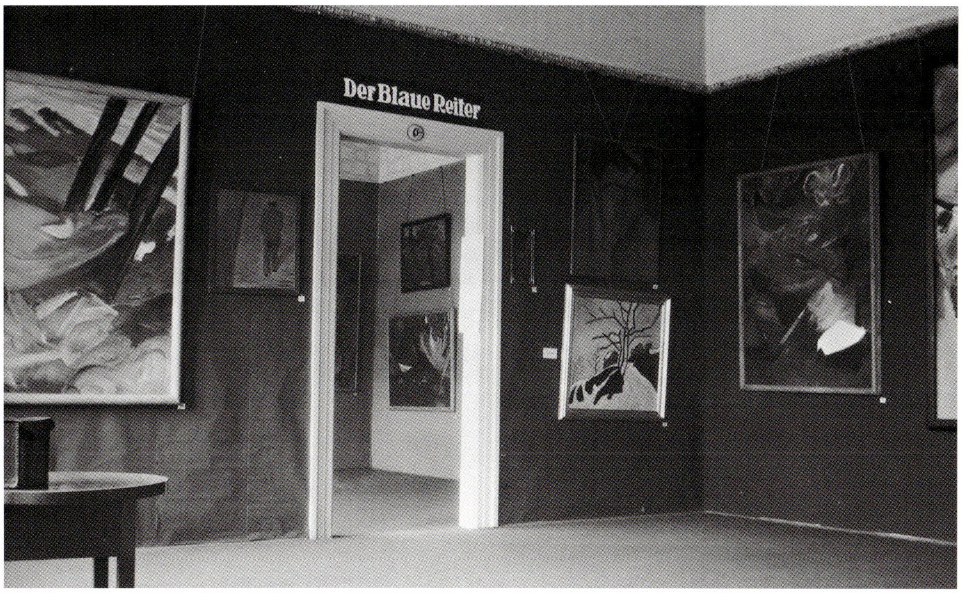

Fig. 5. First Blue Rider exhibition, Moderne Galerie Thannhauser, Munich, December 1911. On the left are Franz Marc's *Yellow Cow* (partially obscured) and Schoenberg's *Self-Portrait, Walking* (see pls. 42–43). Photograph by Münter.

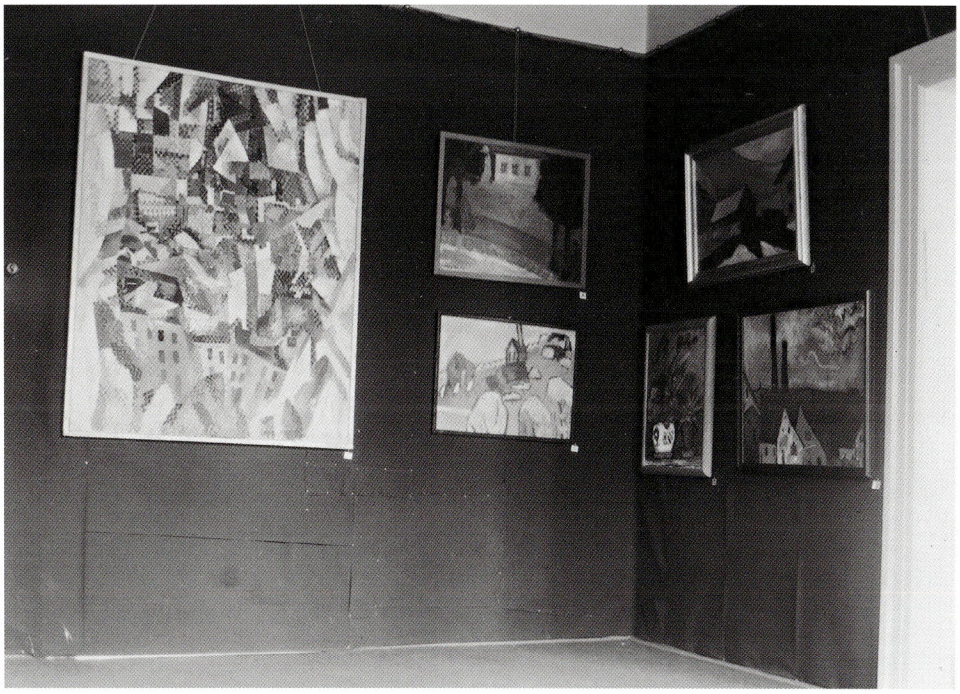

Fig. 6. First Blue Rider exhibition, Moderne Galerie Thannhauser, Munich, December 1911. Schoenberg's *Night Landscape* (pl. 41) hangs above Münter's *Frosty Landscape* and to the right of Robert Delaunay's *La Ville No. 2*. Photograph by Münter.

strong colors of the other painters," he explained to Kandinsky.[17]

Nonetheless, Schoenberg was well represented in the accompanying publication, the *Blue Rider Almanac*, which appeared in 1912. This collection of essays on art and music edited by Marc and Kandinsky contained lavish illustrations of art and ethnography from East and West, past and present. Both Schoenberg's *Self-Portrait, Walking* and one of the Visions were reproduced, as well as a facsimile of the autograph score of his *Herzgewächse* (Heart's foliage), op. 20, a setting of a poem by the Belgian Symbolist Maurice Maeterlinck. Lieder by Berg and Webern were also included. Most important, perhaps, was Schoenberg's remarkable essay "The Relationship to the Text" (*Das Verhältnis zum Text*), one of the great manifestos of modernity.[18] In this piece, written after meeting Kandinsky, Schoenberg proposed a new working model for the composer in which the music is not mortgaged to the text, but retains its autonomy, refusing to illustrate the poem or the libretto. Unlike Kandinsky, Schoenberg did not equate abstraction with atonality, but saw a parallel between the artist's renunciation of the object, and the composer's refusal to subordinate his music to literary texts (program music): "Kandinsky and Kokoschka paint pictures in which the external object is hardly more to them than a stimulus to improvise in color and form and to express themselves as only the composer expressed himself previously."[19]

Schoenberg's participation in the Blue Rider attracted a certain amount of international attention, and in January 1912, he was invited to take part in the *Neukunst Wien* exhibition in Budapest, along with his fellow Viennese Egon Schiele, Oskar Kokoschka, and Paris von Gütersloh, who helped organize the event.[20] Although he was allowed a greater number of paintings, these were hung unfavorably next to those of Kokoschka, contrary to what he had been led to expect. The reviews were largely negative. Ervin Ybl, later to become a prominent art historian, made some penetrating remarks, probably influenced by Wilhelm Worringer's *Abstraction and Empathy* (*Abstraktion und Einfühlung*; 1908), which linked abstraction to ornament: "Music provides expression, emotions and visions in an absolutely autonomous manner, as it is not restricted by imitation, and so Schoenberg in his painting too neglects to imitate nature. . . . Schoenberg neglects nature, but there is another course open to him on which he could bring pictorial values, namely ornamentation. In ornamentation the pictorial values are joined to expression even without imitation, but he spurns this course. He breaks with the imitation of nature and with ornamentation, yet he wants to be a painter."[21]

Despite all the international attention, Schoenberg did not fare too well with members of the Blue Rider. Macke did not think much of his paintings: "And now Schönberg! I am really enraged by these green-eyed watery rolls [*Wasserbrötchen*] with their astral stares. Against the self-portrait from behind I will say nothing, but are these morsels sufficient to justify cracking up Schönberg as an important painter?"[22] Even Marc, who had taken such interest in Schoenberg's music the previous year, and had visited him in Berlin, had cooled considerably.[23] In 1913, he and his wife, Maria, attended a performance of Schoenberg's *Pierrot lunaire* together with Paul Klee. "We were rather disappointed," his wife wrote to Macke; "the whole affair is too strongly Viennese—Egon Schiele, Klimt—also like Schönberg's heads with green eyes."[24] Klee, who had taken part in the second Blue Rider exhibition in February 1912, was devastating: "And the measure is not yet full!!" he wrote irritably in his diary. "Even Schönberg's insane melodrama *Pierrot lunaire* is being performed! Perish, Philistine, your last hour has struck!"[25] Kandinsky, too, had reservations about Schoenberg's visionary paintings, and preferred the portraits and landscapes. "And who told you that I do not like your pictures?" he wrote to Schoenberg in January 1912 with evident discomfort. "It is only that the origin of the 'Visions' is not clear to me."[26]

Though Schoenberg could not have known about all these comments, he must have felt his isolation as an artist. When Kandinsky invited him to participate in an exhibition organized by *Der Sturm* in 1912, he refused adamantly: "I do not believe it is advantageous for me to exhibit in the company of professional painters. I am surely an 'outsider,' an amateur, a dilettante. Whether I should exhibit *at all* is already a question. Whether I should exhibit with a group of painters is almost *no longer a question*."[27] There were other reasons for Schoenberg's refusal. Herwarth Walden (the pseudonym of Georg Lewin), director of the art gallery Der Sturm, editor of the periodical of the same name, and a composer by training, had written a withering review of Schoenberg's *Pelleas und Melisande*.[28] Far more important, Schoenberg's compositions were at last attracting attention abroad, and he had been invited to conduct concerts of his music in Amsterdam, London, and—thanks to Kandinsky—Saint Petersburg. Overwhelmed with commitments, he had no time for art. His career as a painter had come to an end, though he continued to draw until the end of his life.

Since most of Schoenberg's oils were painted in the space of a few years, the work is uneven, and there is no overarching stylistic development. Part of his oeuvre—some 65 oils and 200-odd drawings—is undated and undatable. While his first known work is from 1908, Schoenberg had already completed a number of paintings by then, as we may infer from an article by Paul Wilhelm, published in the *Neues Wiener Journal* in January 1909: "I visited Schönberg at his home on Liechtensteinstrasse. Pleasant rooms of uncluttered simplicity, enhanced by good taste. A few pictures on the walls told me the composer was also a painter. And one of remarkable talent at that, working in a broadly Impressionist manner, with a strong emphasis on planarity. A small head, an interesting self-portrait, struck me for the skill with which Schönberg captured the strangely mild yet sometimes flickering gaze of his eye."[29] It is highly unlikely that Schoenberg continued to paint immediately after Gerstl's suicide, even though he produced a self-portrait in 1908. The absence of any known works from 1909 seems to suggest a one-year hiatus between this early work and the majority of the oils, which were produced in 1910. On the other hand, Wilhelm's article raises the possibility that we are misdating the early paintings.

Despite the early lessons with Gerstl, Schoenberg was virtually self-taught, and fiercely denied being influenced by either Gerstl or Kandinsky.[30] Nevertheless, he was aware of his limitations as a painter, and acknowledged that he never gained in art the extraordinary literacy he acquired in music: "As a painter I was absolutely an amateur; I had no theoretical training and only a little esthetic training, and this only from general education, but not from an education which pertained to painting. In music it was different. . . . I had always had the opportunity to study the works of the masters and to study them in quite a professional manner, so that my technical ability grew in the normal manner. That is the difference

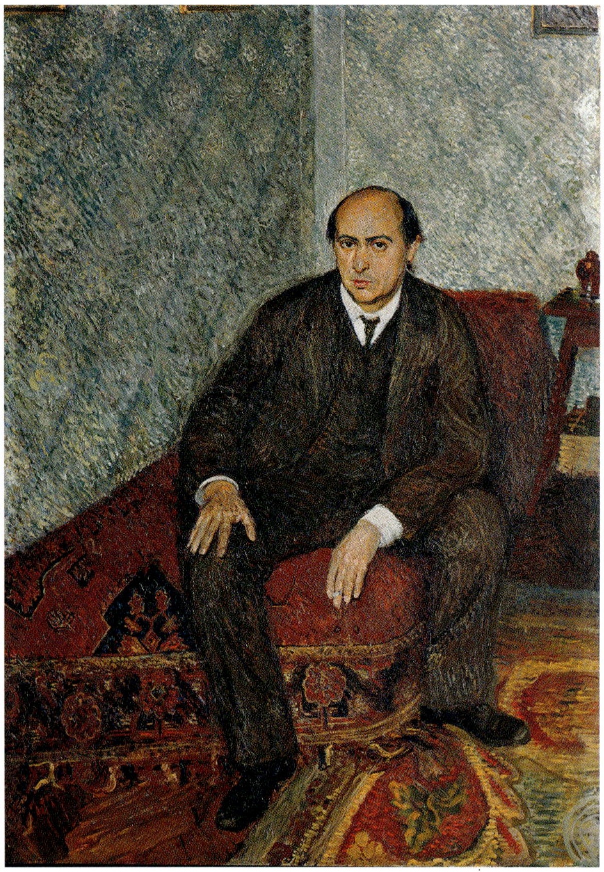

Fig. 7. Richard Gerstl (Austrian, 1883–1908). *Portrait of Arnold Schoenberg*, 1906. Oil on canvas, 71⅝ x 51⅛ in. (182 x 130 cm). Museen der Stadt Wien.

between my painting and my music."[31] Unlike Schoenberg the musician, Schoenberg the painter inhabited a universe that was considerably narrower. If the composer learned from Bach, Mozart, Liszt, Brahms, and Wagner; engaged with contemporaries like Strauss, Mahler, and Debussy; and explored theoretical and aesthetic questions of extraordinary breadth, the painter seems to have had a more restricted frame of reference. Yet his art interacts in a number of ways with that of other artists. Critics detected the influence of Kokoschka and Max Oppenheimer, though they, too, were still maturing.[32] So was Schiele, another personal friend. Gerstl's impact is harder to gauge. His pointillist portrait of Schoenberg, for example, differs radically from the bold impasto used in his portrayal of the entire family a year later (figs. 7–8). On the whole, even after Schoenberg's exposure to the Blue Rider, his allegiances remained close to home: as late as 1921, he confided to Webern that he considered Gustav Klimt "one of the greatest painters of all time."[33]

As a rule, Schoenberg did not work from preparatory sketches: revisions interfered with the intuitive spontaneity that he sought to express.[34] Paint was usually laid on thickly and palpably. Texture of this sort was self-referential, the trail left by the brush recording the gestural choreography of the hand, and calling attention away from the object of representation. Such heavy impasto became the trademark of the new generation. Turning their backs on the enameled surfaces of the Secessionists, the Expressionists dramatized the picture plane, stressing its flatness with tactility. Schoenberg may also have encountered brushwork of this kind in the paintings of Max Liebermann, Lovis Corinth, or Vincent van Gogh, all of whom had exhibited in Vienna, either at the Secession or at the Galerie Miethke.[35] The composer was perfectly conscious of his approach. "Smoothness," he wrote in 1912, "a quality formerly sought after, is today an error, for it is Kitsch-like [*kitschig*]. Yes, one paints with broad strokes today! Everyone paints with broad strokes, and he who does not paint with broad strokes produces Kitsch."[36]

It is in his portraiture that Schoenberg comes closest to the work of his fellow artists. With a few notable exceptions, portraits constitute the most traditional aspect of his work, as they were meant to be sold. Most depict family members, friends, or colleagues; a few are commissions that no doubt reflect the client's preferences; others were probably made as samples of his work as a portraitist. The genre, strongly circumscribed by patronage, did not encourage revolutionary departures. We find the same conformist stance in Schoenberg's paintings of his family: the radical modernity of his music coexisted with the placid, *bürgerlich* comforts of home, as we can see from the portrait of his first wife, *Mathilde* (pl. 53). In contrast to the self-portraits, Schoenberg faithfully reproduced the room's chairs, bookshelves, and wallpaper, which form a taut, space-defining grid of verticals and horizontals. The sitters are brought up close to the picture plane, and contained within the shallow, friezelike space favored by the

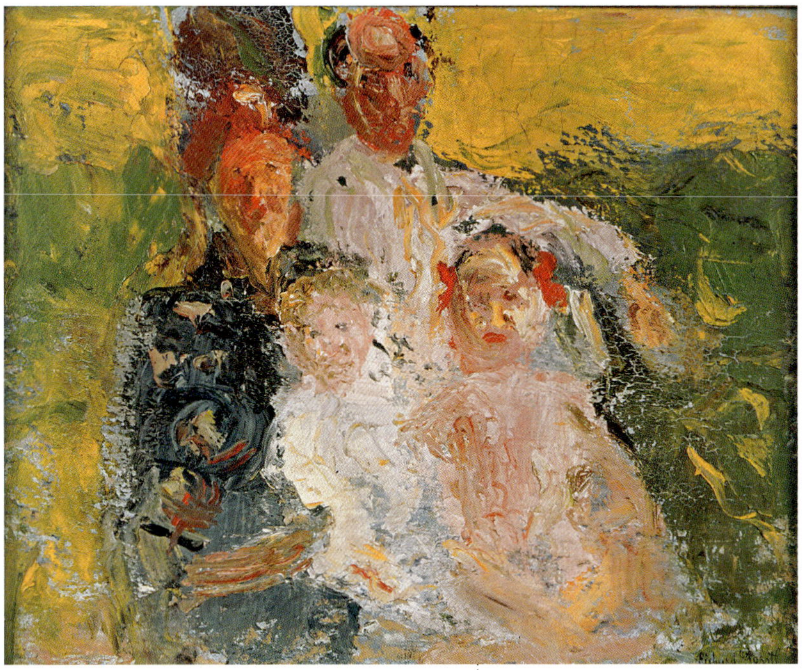

Fig. 8. Richard Gerstl. *The Schoenberg Family*, 1907. Oil on canvas, 35 x 43⅛ in. (88.8 x 109.7 cm). Museum Moderner Kunst Stiftung Ludwig Wien.

artists of the time, wary of illusionistic depth. Figure and ground are strongly interconnected. Schoenberg's grasp of anatomy was tenuous, but with typical aplomb he dismissed its mastery as unimportant. Mimesis was to painting what literary content was to program music: "With compositions based on poetry," he argued in his essay in the *Blue Rider Almanac*, "the exactness of rendering the action is as irrelevant to its artistic value as the resemblance to the model is for a portrait."[37]

Schoenberg's portraits of musicians or figures from the music world—Zemlinsky, Berg, Hertzka—constitute a category of their own, easily dominated by the five portraits of Mahler, all completed by 1910. Only *Gustav Mahler* survives today, an inscrutable, masklike effigy, in which a band of black hair awkwardly surmounts a huge forehead, meant to evoke Mahler's superior intelligence (pl. 54).[38] Schoenberg's feelings for Mahler were complex, "love that pursues with hate" (*Liebe, die mit Hass verfolgt*), as he wrote with characteristic bluntness in an extraordinary letter to the older composer that year.[39] Mahler had given him moral and financial assistance, and even on his deathbed is reported to have asked, "Who will take care of Schoenberg now?"[40] Admiration and gratitude vied with insecurity, and perhaps with resentment in the younger man. A photograph of Schoenberg at home taken in 1910 shows one of his portraits of Mahler beside a well-known photograph of the older composer: another glimpse of the anxiety of influence (fig. 9). Mahler's death in 1911 seems to have delivered Schoenberg from the all-too-human ambiguities of his deep and abiding affection for the great composer. Sorrow and guilt came to replace Oedipal rivalry. Mahler's relentless persecution in Vienna, self-imposed exile, and untimely death were read by Viennese modernists in terms of hagiography, if not martyrdom. The funeral wreath that Schoenberg and his pupils sent referred to the older composer as "saintly" (*heilig*); and just after Mahler's death, Schoenberg began an article with the words: "Gustav Mahler was a saint."[41]

Perhaps the most moving of all of Schoenberg's works is his painting of Mahler's funeral, which took place in Grinzing on May 21, 1911, and was attended by the entire Schoenberg circle, as well as by Klimt, Adolf Loos, Karl Kraus, and Peter Altenberg (pl. 55). A group of mourners is gathered around an open grave, their psychological turmoil evoked by two windswept trees. Executed in cursory strokes and tiny dabs of color, the painting seems to be guided less by artistic intention than by emotion: its very naïveté marks it out as an act of mourning, a lamentation. It was probably done soon after the funeral, when Schoenberg was feeling acutely bereft of his greatest support. Another grief-stricken response to Mahler's death is the poignant last movement of Schoenberg's Six Little Piano Pieces, op. 19, of the same year, a miniature requiem that includes one last trib-

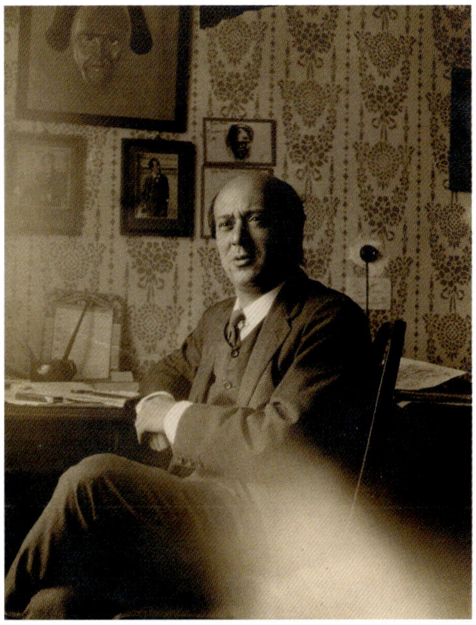

Fig. 9. Schoenberg with his portrait of Gustav Mahler and two photographs of the composer, 1911.

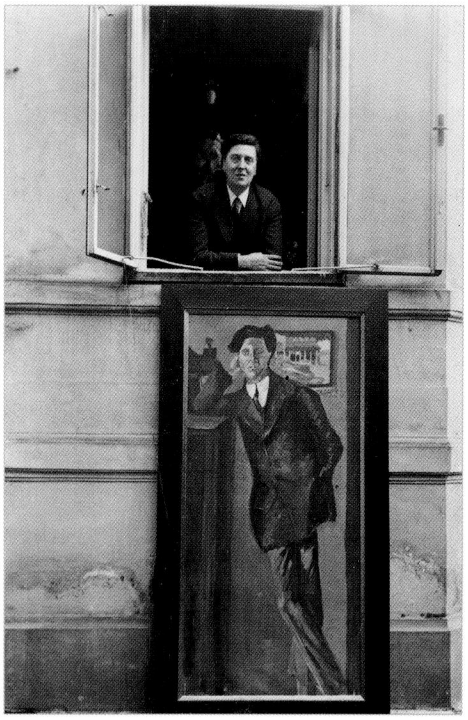

Fig. 10. Alban Berg with his portrait painted by Schoenberg, c. 1910.

ute to Mahler: a cascade of fluttering sounds softly falling earthward.[42]

As with most artists, the portraits of Berg and Mahler tell us much more about Schoenberg than they do about the sitters. "Everything I have written," Schoenberg once told Berg, "has a certain inner likeness to myself."[43] The same can be said of everything he painted. A case in point is precisely Schoenberg's portrait of Berg (pl. 50), probably finished in 1910, and in stark contrast to the ambivalence evident in his *Gustav Mahler*. We do not know the circumstances under which these works were executed. It is unlikely that Mahler, who had left for New York in 1908, would have posed for his image, as Berg undoubtedly did for his. Nonetheless, a comparison between the two portraits reveals the immense difference between painting a student and painting a revered master. In the case of Berg, we immediately sense that it was not just the younger musician who was more relaxed, but Schoenberg himself: there seems to be no affect. Mahler, who was very much alive at the time of his portrait, appears as a vision, whose disembodied head seems to float in the air, elevated above a mere mortal like the casually cross-legged Berg.

Berg's portrait is unusual for its large size and elongated shape, aptly chosen for the long, lanky musician (fig. 10). Schoenberg's preference for small paintings reflected his financial situation; canvas was expensive, and most of his works are on cardboard. But he also apparently disliked large formats because of their tendency to escape from the visual field. In a letter to Kandinsky of December 14, 1911, he criticized the scale of the latter's *Romantische Landschaft* (Romantic landscape; 1911), which Schoenberg had seen at the *Neue Secession* exhibition in Berlin. The large size of the canvas, he thought, inevitably miniaturized the painting by forcing the viewer to draw away from the painted surface to see it in its entirety.[44] As can be seen in his portraits of Berg and Helene Nahowski, Berg's future wife, Schoenberg clearly gave a great deal of thought to his compositions, making use of several strategies that question the nature of pictorial space (pls. 50–51). The relief given to the sitter collides with the emphatic flatness of the wall, and Schoenberg plays off the centrifugal, collagelike effect of the background against the near-symmetrical image in the center. In the portrait of Nahowski, he quoted from his own work, reproducing one of his self-portraits behind her. This was standard practice among the Impressionists, although they usually relished reproducing their work in miniature. In Schoenberg's portrait, the painting within the painting appears as a highly abstracted representation, greatly reduced in size and cut off by the frame.

Another work of historic significance is the portrait of Marie Pappenheim (fig. 11), the librettist of Schoenberg's first opera, *Erwartung*. It was probably executed at Steinakirchen, where he met Pappenheim while on vacation in 1909. Schoenberg had first read her poetry in Karl Kraus's magazine *Die Fackel*, and had asked her about writing a libretto for him.[45] Pappenheim, who had just finished medical school, agreed, and sent him the manuscript toward the end of August. Schoenberg set to work immediately, and completed the opera in seventeen days. Unlike most of his female sitters, Pappenheim is not shown in a

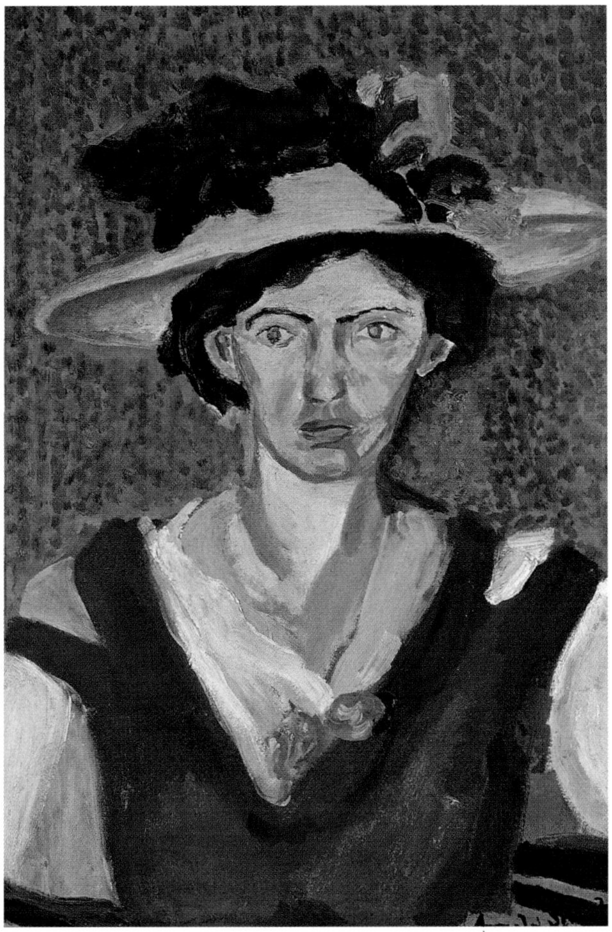

Fig. 11. Arnold Schoenberg (Austrian, 1874–1951). *Marie Pappenheim*, 1909. Oil on cardboard, 26¾ x 19¼ in. (68 x 49 cm). Collection of Prof. Dr. Franz Eckert.

domestic setting. Broad, disjointed swaths of color underscore the studied asymmetry of dress and hat. They were probably meant as allusions to the writer's Expressionist leanings, as were the drawn features and agitated eyes. In fact, Schoenberg seems to have deliberately transferred to his sitter qualities that she had imparted to the protagonist of *Erwartung*, a disturbed woman who has probably murdered her lover.

This portrait raises the issue of Schoenberg's tantalizing and tangential relationship with the world of Sigmund Freud. Pappenheim was not, as is often claimed, related to Bertha Pappenheim, who had been analyzed by Josef Breuer, but she was probably familiar with the famous volume that he coauthored with Freud, *Studies on Hysteria* (1895), where Bertha Pappenheim's case history appears under the pseudonym "Anna O."[46] The disconnected lines sung by the sole protagonist of *Erwartung*, as the conductor Robert Craft pointed out, resemble the truncated speech brought up by patients during the psychoanalytic process: syntax has broken down under the weight of traumatic memories (anamnesis), and the association of ideas overrides the flow of narrative. Freud's impact among Vienna's literary and artistic circles can hardly be overestimated. The descent into self enabled the dramatization of the quotidian, just when artists were discarding history and mythology as subject matter. There is, however, no record that Schoenberg ever read anything by Freud.[47] Nor did the two ever meet, although Schoenberg's apartment on Liechtensteinstrasse was around the corner from Freud's on Berggasse. Nonetheless, Schoenberg may have absorbed some of Freud's ideas from his entourage, though he would only refer to psychoanalysis explicitly much later.[48] Hugo Heller, in whose bookshop Schoenberg held his exhibition, was a major publisher of psychoanalytic literature (fig.12), including the influential journal *Imago* (1912–37), as well as Freud's series of applied psychology, *Schriften zur angewandten Seelenkunde* (Papers on applied psychology; 1907–11).[49] Max Graf, a well-known music critic friendly to Schoenberg, wrote the first psychoanalytical study of music, an analysis of Richard Wagner's opera *Der Fliegenden Holländer* (The flying Dutchman), in 1910. A year earlier, Freud had published the case history of Graf's son, Herbert, under the name "Little Hans."[50] "Little Hans," later a well-known opera director, would stage a successful production of *Die glückliche Hand* in Breslau in 1928. Though undoubtedly attracted to psychoanalysis, particularly between 1909 and 1911, Schoenberg chose to remain at a certain distance.

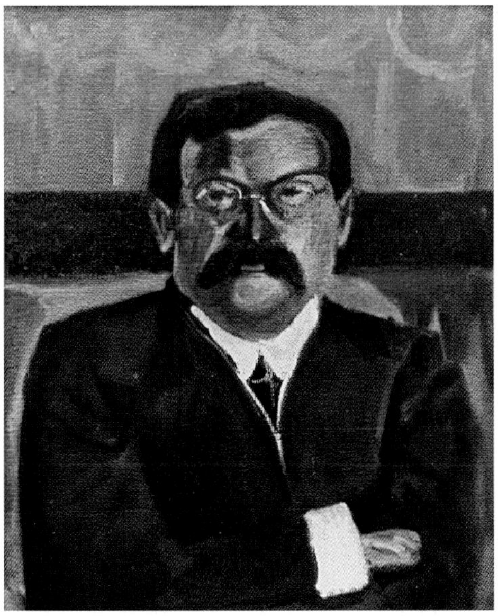

Fig. 12. Schoenberg's portrait of the publisher Hugo Heller, c. 1910, now lost.

It is again the world of Freud that resonates in the background of Schoenberg's self-portraits, which account for more than one-third of his output (pls. 9–15). Self-portraits are not unusual among autodidacts, who rarely have models or clients at their disposal. Nor can they be put down solely to narcissism, a component of all images of the self. In these works, Schoenberg shows himself in total isolation against a neutral background, formal, circumspect, and in the

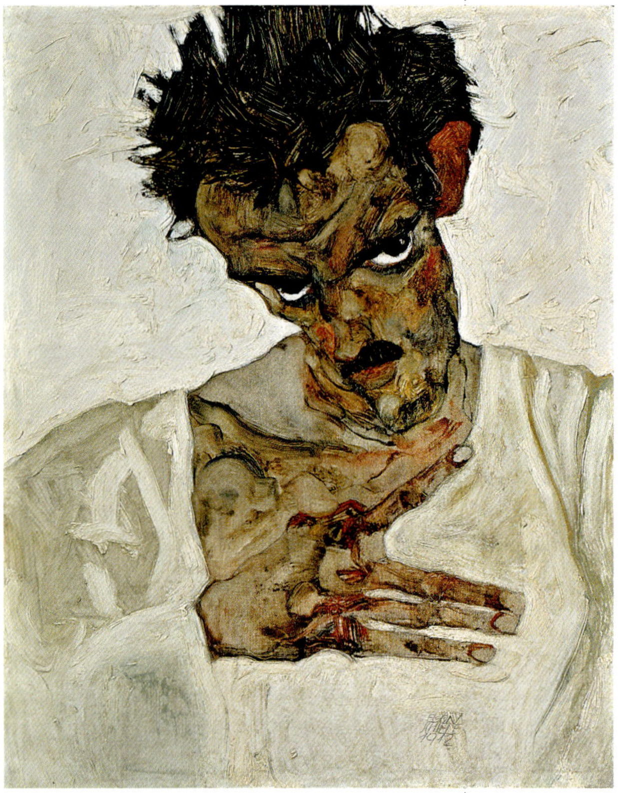

Fig. 13. Egon Schiele (Austrian, 1890–1918). *Self-Portrait with Head Lowered*, 1912. Oil on panel, 16⅝ x 13¼ in. (42.2 x 33.7 cm). Leopold Museum–Privatstiftung, Vienna.

unflattering stance of frontality. He rarely adopted the three-quarter view favored by most artists, an approach that in turn affected his portraits.[51] By leaving out all but the face's most distinguishing features, these closely cropped images are reminiscent of passport photos, with their overriding concern for identification rather than representation. This ego-driven penchant was one of the many traits that Schoenberg shared with Gerstl, Kokoschka, and Schiele (fig. 13). In contrast to the Secessionists, who dismissed the self as an ephemeral association of passing sensations, they reaffirm the messianic calling of the hero-artist, and in so doing appear to turn their backs on the sublimated anxieties of their predecessors. Together with diaries and journals, which figure prominently in Viennese literature at the time, self-portraits can be considered forms of expression that explore the construction of identity—a work of self-analysis not unlike that of Freud's *Interpretation of Dreams* (1900). The mood is introspective, even solipsistic; the outside world does not exist.

Self-portraiture is both a confessional mode and a form of fiction.[52] Schoenberg himself may have believed in the direct, unmediated expression of self, but artists always work within given genres and traditions. As Fritz Saxl once pointed out, "It is not the free, unmediated expression of inner life which determines artistic formulations of gesture and the face, but rather the generative dialogue with already established pictorial forms and conventions."[53] With their intense stare and iconic centering of the face within the frame, Schoenberg's self-portraits bring to mind the tradition of northern Romanticism taken up by his contemporaries, particularly in the disquieting look and low viewpoint found in some of the later drawings.[54] Yet, while we should be wary of trying to deduce inner thoughts from portraits, the sheer number of Schoenberg's self-portraits attests to their importance during a period of terrible loneliness, when the composer was battling self-doubt, marital problems, public incomprehension and financial hardship. Taken as a whole, they resemble an interminable soliloquy, a search for an endlessly deferred identity sustained week after week, in view of the stubborn opacity of the face—a form of relentless self-questioning all the more significant because there is no equivalent in his music, though it is not lacking in autobiographical elements.[55]

Schoenberg's self-portraits also evoke his sense of play and the ludic fascination with mirrors that occur in his music as well.[56] A clear example of the relation between his use of specular images in art and in music can be seen in *Self-Portrait, Walking* (1911; pl. 42), one of his best-known works and, ironically, the one self-portrait that could not have been based on a mirror (though this does not invalidate the principle). This work, as Hans Heinz Stuckenschmidt suggests, should be seen in connection with the contemporaneous "Mondfleck," the eighteenth episode of *Pierrot lunaire* (1912), in which Pierrot turns around and sees a bright spot of moonlight reflected on his back.[57] Four instruments, divided into two pairs, develop thematically, then reverse themselves, as if they were going through the mirror.

Self-Portrait, Walking is striking for its relationship to still other traditions. Schoenberg was no doubt familiar with similar portraits of Beethoven and Brahms. As a genre, the *Rückenfigur* (figure seen from behind) is prominent in the work of the German Romantics, especially that of Caspar David Friedrich.[58] But Schoenberg's self-portrait is also related to the art of his contemporaries: a sketch for this painting, one of the rare works of Schoenberg to include an urban context, bears an uncanny resemblance to Adolf Erbslöh's *Street* (1910), exhibited at the NKVM from which the Blue Rider artists broke away (figs. 14–15). It is telling that Schoenberg pared the city down to a minimum in the final painting, where it reads almost like wallpaper: unlike the painters of Die Brücke who often dealt with the metropolis, the Blue Rider and the Viennese Expressionists usually avoided ostensibly urban themes. They had an equal aversion to the machine aesthetic then being propounded by the Italian Futurists. Both their iconography and their strong sense of craftsmanship, with its exaltation of the human hand, betrays a certain nostalgia for the preindustrial age—in itself an expression of the layered temporalities of modernity.

If Schoenberg generally aligned himself with that younger generation of Viennese Expressionists, a smaller group of works reveals his ties with the cultural underpinnings of the Secession. In *Self-Portrait* (1910), for example, his features are beginning to dissolve (pl. 40), and in *Gaze* and *Thinking*, works teetering on the edge of abstraction, only the top of the head, with its unmistakably receding hairline, is visible (pls. 16–17). Here Schoenberg represented himself by synecdoche, the brow and sometimes the eyes standing for the whole. These are no longer anxious attempts at self-assertion, but "paintings of threatened identity in a kind of visionary self-dissolution."[59] It was Freud, of course, who said that the ego is not master in his own house, and for the older generation of Secessionists, the disintegration of the classical subject was one of the central tenets of Viennese modernity, whose ramifications were explored by Ernst Mach in *The Analysis of Sensations* (1885), Hugo von Hofmannsthal in *Letter of Lord Chandos* (1902), and in Hermann Bahr's "unsavable ego" (1904).[60] The huge distinction made by critics between the Secessionists and the younger Expressionists meant little to Schoenberg and his peers.[61]

The metaphysical intensity of Schoenberg's deliquescent images of self leads us directly to a consideration of his best-known works, the Visions. Initially called *Eindrücke und Phantasien* (Impressions and fantasies), and later *Blicke* (Gazes), they were named Visions by Kandinsky.[62] These were the paintings that

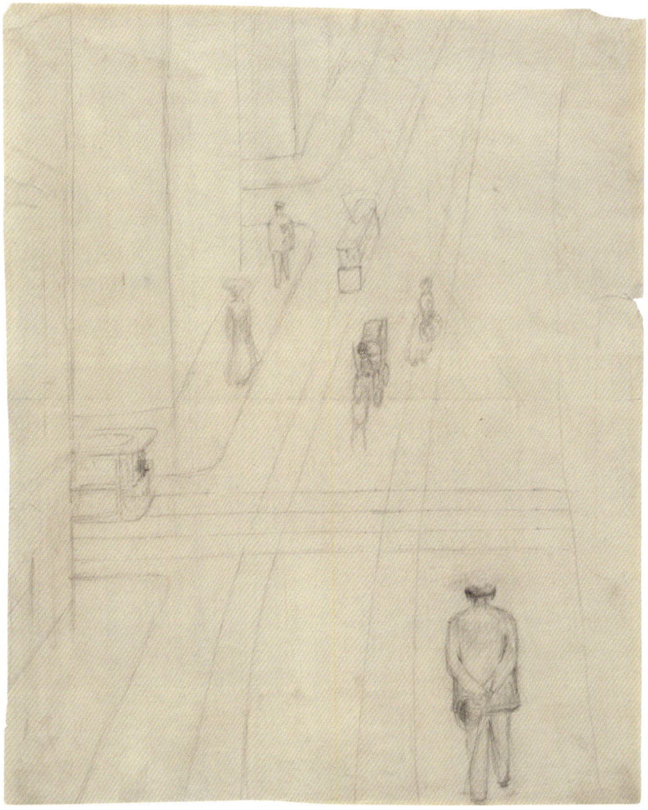

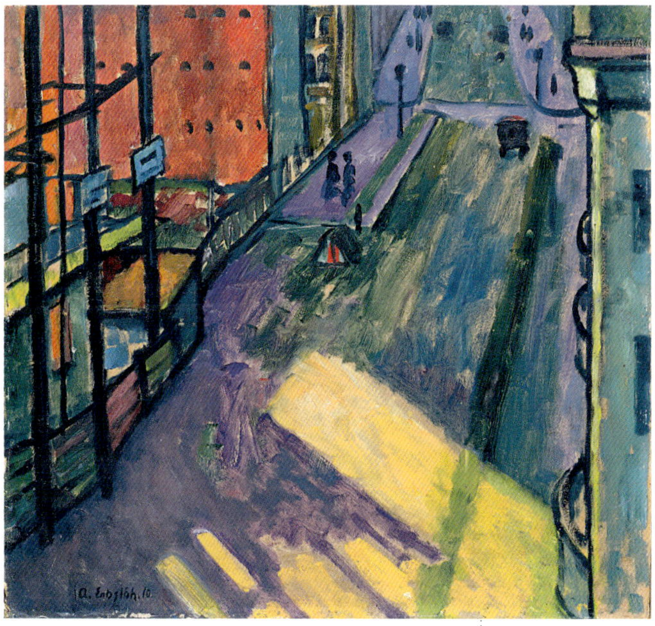

Fig. 14. Arnold Schoenberg. *Sketch for Self-Portrait, Walking*. Pencil on paper, 15⅜ x 12⅝ in. (39 x 32 cm). Arnold Schoenberg Center, Vienna.

Fig. 15. Adolf Erbslöh (German, b. United States, 1881–1947). *Street*, 1910. Oil on pasteboard, 20¼ x 21½ in. (51.5 x 54.5 cm). Museum Ludwig, Cologne.

Schoenberg rightly considered his most original: disembodied heads with enigmatic gazes, mouths giving utterance to voiceless screams, and faces racked by self-doubt and palsied by pain (pls. 18–20 and 39). They seem to rise from viscous depths, like *unheimlich* variations of his questioning views of himself. Significantly, in these works that were so close to his heart Schoenberg rejected the phenomenal world of the portraits and landscapes (fig. 1). Art here becomes a challenge to the visible, an affirmation of the elusive self that has shed the raiment of carnality. Hence the devaluation of the body, which is elided or drastically curtailed, in favor of the face. Hence, too, his impatience with the constricting nature of the frame: some of the Visions seem to extend beyond the confines of the cardboard support, suggesting the limitless world of the imagination.

At the time, artists as different as Edvard Munch, Kandinsky, and Kokoschka were developing a keen interest in the psychological and the instinctual. "Consciousness is a sea ringed about with visions," observed Kokoschka in a lecture titled "On the Nature of Visions" (1912). Schoenberg must have seen a connection between his paintings and the ideas of his younger colleague, for one of these works, *Vision (Eyes)*, is inscribed "Reminiscence of Oskar Kokoschka" (pl. 19). But if Kokoschka claimed that in his work it "is the psyche which speaks,"[63] Schoenberg specifically stressed the role of the unconscious in the process of artistic creation. As he wrote to the composer Ferruccio Busoni on August 24, 1909, "My only intention is to have *no* intentions! No formal, architectural or other artistic intentions (except perhaps of capturing the mood of a poem), no aesthetic intentions—none of any kind; at the most this: to place nothing inhibiting in the stream of my unconscious sensations. But to allow anything to infiltrate which may be invoked either by intelligence or consciousness."[64] A year and a half later, on January 24, 1911, Schoenberg wrote along similar lines to Kandinsky: "Art belongs to the *unconscious* [*Unbewusst*]! One must express *oneself*! Express oneself *directly*! Not one's taste, or one's upbringing, or one's intelligence, knowledge or skill. Not all these *acquired* characteristics, but that which is *inborn, instinctive* [*angeboren, triebhaft*]."[65] During the years when Schoenberg was painting (1908–11), he was also struggling to develop a musical language that could convey the unruly richness and complexity of the unconscious, music that was "unwilling to go on being the serving-maid to poetry," music that "cut out the detour of first expressing unconscious sensations in the language of consciousness, and then retranslating this translation into the language of the unconscious."[66] This once again brings Schoenberg close to Freud, for whom psychoanalysis was predicated upon recognition of the existence of the unconscious. But the very fact that Schoenberg believed that the unconscious could be summoned by fiat, or at least directly, shows how far he was from Freud, for whom the unconscious could rise to consciousness only indirectly, mediated and displaced by dreams, parapraxes, symptoms—or art.

The angst-ridden nature of the Visions also reveals Schoenberg's knowledge of Symbolist art. *Red Gaze* (pl. 39), for example, bears the unmistakable impact of Munch's *Scream* (1893; fig. 16), especially in the large, incandescent

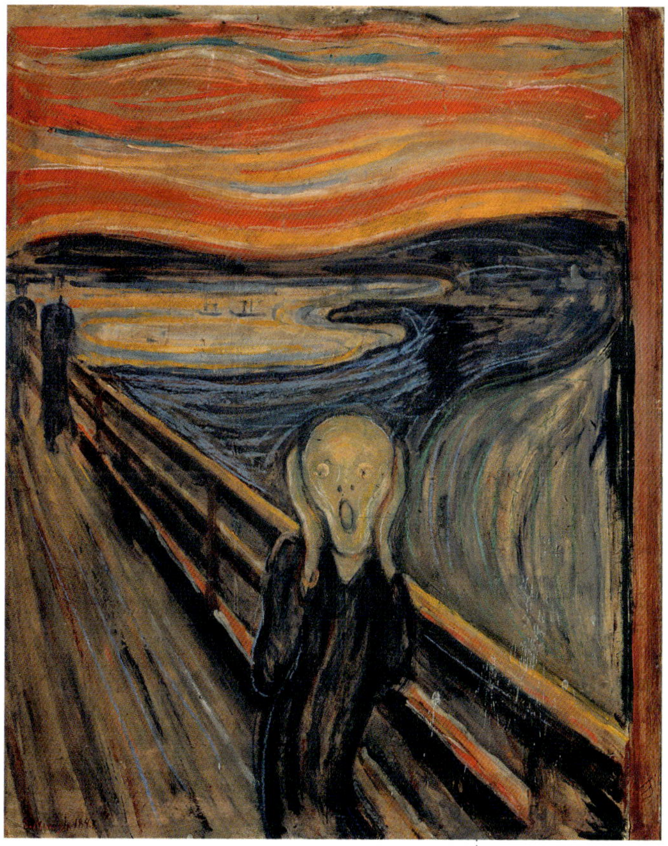

Fig 16. Edvard Munch (Norwegian, 1863–1944). *The Scream*, 1893. Tempera and pastel on cardboard, 35⅞ x 28⅞ in. (91 x 73.5 cm). Nasjonalgalleriet, Oslo, Norway.

eyes, and in the way the face seems to be held by two hands. (Munch's paintings had been exhibited in Vienna by the Secession in 1901, and at the Miethke Gallery in 1904.) But Schoenberg thrusts the image up close to the viewer, filling the entire frame. Close-ups of this kind, long since secularized, had emerged in the fifteenth century as a means of triggering the viewer's empathy.[67] *Red Gaze* produces the same dramatic effect. All anecdotal aspects have been stripped away, leaving only exaggerated features of frightening intensity and psychological pain, like a modern-day *écorché*, or vivisection, carried out without anaesthetic. Schoenberg was also familiar with the works of Max Klinger, Franz von Stuck, and Ferdinand Hodler, though their heavy-handed allegories were a far cry from his approach, as were those of Alfred Kubin.[68] Klinger had shown at the Secession in 1898 and 1899, and at the group's Beethoven exhibition in 1902. Given Schoenberg's great interest in Brahms, he was undoubtedly acquainted with the latter's Four Lieder, opp. 96 and 97, which had been published with lithographs by Klinger.[69] A more likely source for the Visions was French Symbolism. The severed head of John the Baptist in Gustave Moreau's *Apparition* (1874–76) circulated widely in different versions and copies; yet the illustrative nature of Moreau's work, which often implies a text external and anterior to the work itself, is absent in Schoenberg's oeuvre. He seems closer to Odilon Redon, as Pierre Boulez first pointed out, another artist who depicted floating faces brooding darkly and strange, haunting eyes, but without the macabre connotations.[70]

A few of Schoenberg's Visions, which have never been properly deciphered, show little more than hands or arms. In *Flesh*, two ghostly, elongated arms reach out eerily from unseen shoulders: the blood-red body has become a landscape, or perhaps the landscape is the objectification of the psyche (pl. 21). In another work, a pale, spectral hand seems to clasp a darker one that blurs into the cosmic background (pl. 23). Peeling the surface away, Schoenberg discloses the nervous energy beneath. And in the most hermetic of these, a dark, powerful hand bears down upon a bald head, while a single red-rimmed eye exudes a pale blue light from its pupil (pl. 22). These works may have been preliminary studies for Schoenberg's short one-act opera, *Die glückliche Hand*. Although it was only completed toward the end of 1913, four preparatory sketches for the sets were included in the Vienna exhibition of 1910. The fact that one hand is white and another is dark should probably be read in terms of gender distinction. Expressionists and Symbolists often used color contrast to express the war between the sexes—one of the themes of *Glückliche Hand*—as we can see, for example, in the work of Schiele, Kokoschka, or even Munch. This would explain the more aggressive impetus given to the dark hand as opposed to the passive white one.[71]

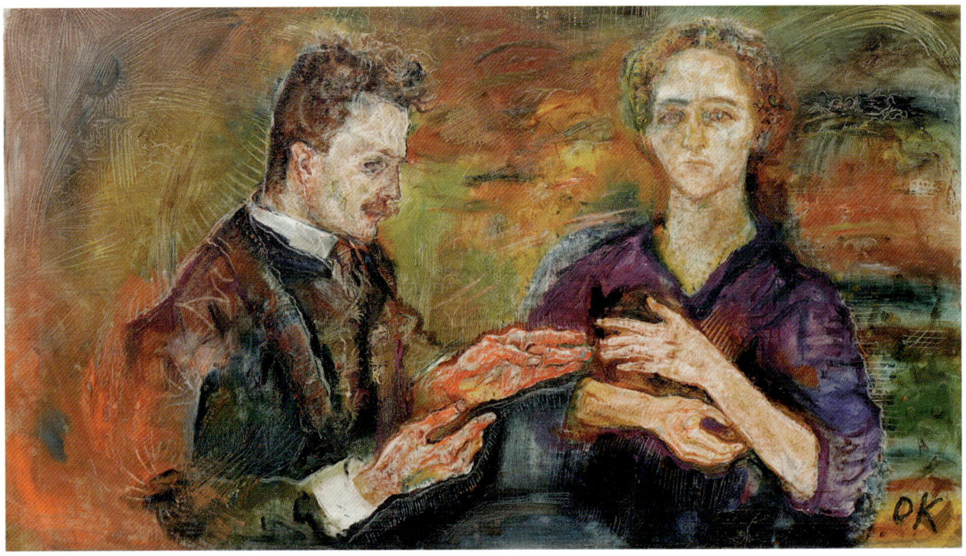

Fig. 17. Oskar Kokoschka (Austrian, 1886–1980). *Hans and Erika Tietze*, 1909. Oil on canvas, 30⅛ x 53⅝ in. (76.5 x 136.2 cm). The Museum of Modern Art, New York, Abby Aldrich Rockefeller Fund.

Schoenberg's Hands (pls. 22–23) were to have a fascinating afterlife in the world of music. In 1911, Franz Schreker wrote a libretto for Zemlinsky, but then decided to compose the music himself. In that opera, *Die Gezeichneten* (The marked ones) of 1918, Carlotta Nardi, the female protagonist, describes her own paintings of hands in terms that bear a close resemblance to those of Schoenberg: "But the strangest of these was the picture of a hand pale and waxen, like that of a corpse, with uncannily long withered fingers, clenched round something that could not be seen. Only a faint purple glow leaked out through the ghostly fingers, but this gleam was like a silent lament, like a suppressed whimpering sob and like a scream, restrained and in deathly fear, like a stifled cry for deliverance."[72] Schoenberg was well aware of Schreker's reference, and after hearing a new production of the opera at the Städtische Oper in Berlin in December 1929, he gave Schreker a watercolor of one of his hand paintings (pl. 22).

Hands play a cardinal role as a vehicle for expression in the iconography of Schoenberg's fellow painters like Kokoschka (fig. 17), Schiele (fig. 13), Oppenheimer, or even Munch. None, however, had shown them separate from the body, though one could argue that studies of hands had a tradition in German art stretching back to Albrecht Dürer. Schoenberg's use of close-ups has often been associated with his interest in film, but in 1910 they were not yet clearly established as part of cinematic narrative. Nonetheless, Schoenberg's Hands, wrested from their narrative matrix and from the flow of musical time in *Die glückliche Hand* (if that is what they are), seem to anticipate film music. By refusing to defer to the big picture, these mute, enlarged details suggest "a fragment whose existence never exceeds the fragment," as Roland Barthes pointed out in his analysis of the film still in the work of Sergei Eisenstein.[73] Works like these may also be likened to Schoenberg's short, miniature-like compositions, which, in the words of Charles Rosen, do not "diminish the emotions they express but enlarge them, as if fragments of feeling were blown up by a powerful microscope."[74]

Eyes figure prominently in Schoenberg's Visions, as they do in his two operas of those years, especially *Die glückliche Hand* (pls. 59–61). In 1922, the composers Darius Milhaud and Francis Poulenc visited Schoenberg at his home in Mödling, outside Vienna: "We had coffee in the dining-room, the walls of which were hung about with Schoenberg's paintings," wrote Milhaud. "Faces and eyes, eyes, eyes everywhere!"[75] Elsa Bienenfeld had a similar experience when she visited Schoenberg's solo exhibition in 1910: "On entering the gallery, one has the impression of being stared at from all sides by eyes, glowing, burning, wide-gaping, dreadful, yearning, insane eyes."[76]

Like hands, eyes have a long history in art and literature, and are central to the work of Gerstl, Schiele, and Kokoschka. However, in Schoenberg's paintings, the eyes have severed their links with anatomy and float adrift in the uncontoured features of the face. The very way in which he presented a single eye—or two unconnected ones—calls attention to its incorporeal, nonmimetic nature (pls. 18–19). With regard to the primacy accorded the eye, Schoenberg stood firmly in a tradition stretching back to Romanticism. One need only think of Caspar David Friedrich's famous statement that the artist should close his outer eye in order to see his painting with his inner, spiritual eye.[77] This iconographic theme was very much alive in Schoenberg's day, when the eye had become a key image of Theosophy, a movement in which both Mahler and Kandinsky took great interest. Although the degree of Schoenberg's involvement with Theosophy is unclear, his beautiful panegyric to Mahler, written in 1912, is redolent of Theosophical terminology: "We are to remain blind until we have acquired eyes. Eyes that see the future. Eyes that penetrate more than the sensual, which is only a likeness; that penetrate the super-sensual. Our soul shall be the eye."[78] The equation of the soul with the eye was part of the stock-in-trade of the fin de siècle, a remnant of Romanticism that had survived into the modern age.

Schoenberg did not entirely have faith in the *Aufklärung*—the German Enlightenment—that rock of assimilation that sustained the secular beliefs of a Freud or a Schnitzler. He traded in the indeterminate currencies of Symbolism and perhaps of Theosophy, which were part of the revolt against materialism. High modernism, of course, filtered out the metaphysical paraphernalia of the fin de siècle, which did not fit the lean intellectual profile to which its proponents aspired. Yet it is not by chance that the pioneers who first made the leap to nonobjective art, like Piet Mondrian and Kandinsky, or radical innovators like Mahler and Schoenberg, so often invoke the language of the soul, concepts of spirituality, and even Theosophy. Abstraction was the best vehicle for the absolute, an ideal signifier of transcendence. These artists and musicians drained their art of the figurative—cleansed it of the immanent and the secular, which imperiled the higher truths they wished to convey. The metaphysics, if not the theology, of abstraction required the departure of figuration or tonality. Robert Rosenblum has called attention to the redemptive lining of abstraction, suggesting that in some cases this revolutionary step must also be understood in relation to the Mosaic law against graven images: "The sense of divinity in boundless voids, where figures, objects, and finally matter itself are excluded, belongs to a Romantic tradition primarily sustained by non-Catholic artists—Protestants, Jews, or members of such modern spiritualist sects as Theosophy—for the iconoclastic attitudes of these religions were conducive to the presentation of transcendental experience through immaterial images."[79]

As a composer, Schoenberg was less bound to the visual than Kandinsky. Having already made the leap into atonality independently, he did not agonize over abstraction.[80] "I myself don't believe that painting must necessarily be figurative [*gegenständlich*]," he wrote to Kandinsky in 1911. "Indeed, I firmly believe the contrary. Nevertheless, when the imagination suggests figurative things to us, then, well and good—perhaps that is because our eyes perceive only figurative things. The ear has an advantage in this regard! But when the artist reaches the point at which he desires only the expression of inner events and inner scenes in his rhythms and tones, then the 'object in painting' has ceased to exist for the reproducing eye [*dem reproduzierenden Auge*]."[81]

Strictly speaking, none of Schoenberg's paintings is abstract: all have a referent, clearly invoked by the title, even if irreducible to mimesis and lacking corporeality. The viewer's eye, unfettered by subject matter, focuses on the thick impasto and self-referential brushstrokes that call attention to the materiality of paint and canvas, almost contradicting the ideality they are meant to convey. The emphatic gestural quality of the works almost foreshadows Abstract Expressionism. Schoenberg's thought was still essentially dualistic, premised on the existence of both form and content, and hence freighted with metaphysics. The musician in him never entirely abdicated control. In *Blue Gaze*, one of the rare Visions to show a mouth, the brushwork suggests sound issuing forth silently (pl. 20). In this work, Schoenberg also juggled the modalities of time and space inherent in music and painting. Accustomed, as a composer, to making time audible, he tried here to make it visible. One is reminded of Paul Claudel's beautiful aphorism "The eye listens," though the subject is here given a more pessimistic twist: the silent scream also evokes the isolation of the modern artist, the seer reduced to aphasia, a topic that reverberates in other Visions.[82]

Among these, Schoenberg's painting of a head of Christ takes on particular significance (pl. 24). Only the upper portion of the face, with its sad, piercing eyes, emerges from the gloom, after the manner of the French Symbolists, a defeatist vision, bereft of hope, that hardly suggests a redeemer. In a curious watercolor of 1919, Schoenberg took up the same theme, but the crossed legs and outstretched arms denoting the Crucifixion seem to be contradicted by the disconcertingly stylized figure with extravagant hair (pl. 26).[83] Images of Jesus were hardly unusual among Jewish artists: there are several representations of the Jewish Jesus, who does not represent the Messiah, but "a Jewish martyr who holds out no suggestion of salvation."[84]

Christ, of course, was another matter. It was neither the religious nor the historical aspect that appealed to Schoenberg, but the availability of the metaphor. Since the days of Romanticism, Christ had been a well-established trope for the lonely artist, persecuted and forsaken by all. Albert Bloch, the only American artist to take part in the first Blue Rider exhibition, had shown a painting of Christ with

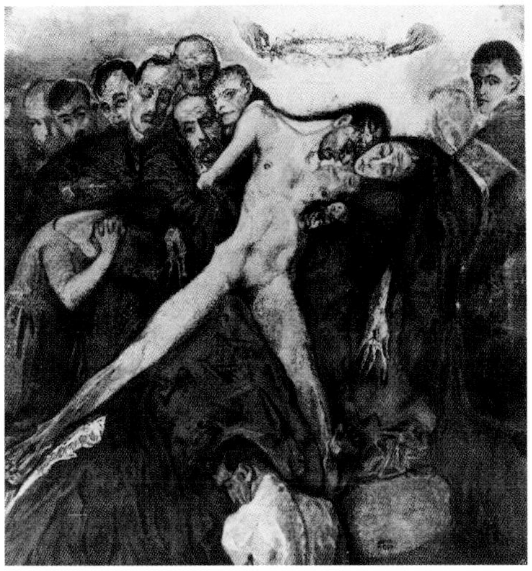

Fig. 18. Max Oppenheimer (Austrian, 1885–1954). *Descent from the Cross*, 1910–11. Oil on canvas. Location unknown. Karl Kraus, Peter Altenberg, and Heinrich Mann are portrayed to the right of Christ.

the stigmata (pl. 49).[85] In Max Oppenheimer's *Descent from the Cross (Kreuzabnahme*; 1910–11), the artist depicts himself as Christ, surrounded by sympathetic onlookers including Karl Kraus, Peter Altenberg, and Heinrich Mann (fig. 18).[86] Schoenberg himself had already turned to the subject in "Gethsemane," a poem by Richard Dehmel that he set to music in 1899.[87] Christ-as-artist would reappear even more forcefully in *Pierrot lunaire* (1912): in "Red Mass," the eleventh song of the cycle, Pierrot "shows the frightened souls the dripping red host; his heart—in bloody fingers—at the gruesome communion."[88] Significantly, Pierrot was also identified with Christ—and with the artist—in Bloch's paintings, especially in *Death of Pierrot* (1912–13).[89] Schoenberg's appropriation of the image of Christ, like his later identification with Moses, also served autobiographical ends, as one of his self-portraits suggests (pl. 25). "The artist who identifies himself with Moses and Christ," notes Karin von Maur, "clearly sees himself as prophet, redeemer, and victim in one."[90]

If in the Visions Schoenberg explored the role of suffering martyr, in his caricatures he took on the mantle of avenging judge. The composer, whose animosity toward music critics was proverbial, channeled his anger into several caricatures, executed with burlesque, hyperbolic traits; among these are *Critic I*, with its exaggerated ears, and *Art Patron*, with its eyes conspicuously closed (pls. 27–28). As we might expect, these works show violence not only in the overdrawn features, but in the very mode of production—the abrupt brushwork and dissonant colors. Another characteristic of both the caricatures and the Visions was condensation, a quality that Ernst Gombrich saw as crucial to wit.[91] In *Jokes and Their Relation to the Unconscious* (1905), Freud claimed that caricatures are attempts to relieve the ego of a burden, to help it obtain mastery over aggressive impulses by displacing them onto a surrogate.[92] The ego is thus able to ward off hostility by assigning it an outlet in the comic. Caricature empowers.

Schoenberg's need for safety valves for his anger extended beyond his painting. Pieces like Three Satires for Mixed Chorus, op. 28 (1925), were composed in response to colleagues like Igor Stravinsky and Ernst Krenek. "I wrote them when I was very much angered by attacks of some of my younger contemporaries at this time and I wanted to give them a warning that it is not good to attack me," he wrote years later.[93] In cooler moments, Schoenberg recognized the often self-defeating nature of invective. "I don't think it is a good idea for you to skirmish with journalists," he once wrote Berg. "It intensifies hate, but lessens contempt, thereby serving the journalists and injuring you! . . . And you can see where that leads by looking at [Karl] Kraus, of whom it has made a prisoner who cannot escape."[94]

Schoenberg's landscapes, one of which was exhibited at the Blue Rider, are of an altogether different character (pl. 41). Apart from two outdoor scenes with dappled sunlight, all his works in this field are nocturnes: mood prevails over description. Spare, simplified forms, melancholy hues, and the absence of light convey a particular *Stimmung*, a sense of emptiness and lingering sadness reminiscent of Munch. Some recall Gerstl: disheveled trees or tufts emerging from the gray-green background. For Schoenberg, color was an expressive adjunct and bore little relation to the colorism of Kandinsky and his circle, which often became an end in itself. Kandinsky admired Schoenberg's indistinct, monochromatic hues, which struck him as a liberation from conventional aesthetic constraints. Marc wrote to his future wife, Maria Franck, in 1911 that Kandinsky "sees in this murky mixture of Schönberg his immense greatness; he says: Look here, I still cannot do without the beautiful clear colors; I still paint, in spite of myself, in old color harmonies, which I don't really want to. Schönberg has made this great step over and beyond me. I would like to paint in really dirty colors, as only then can my thoughts express all that they should."[95]

The death-haunted sensibility and ominous sense of foreboding we find in some of Schoenberg's landscapes are very close to the atmosphere of his first opera, *Erwartung*, and his sketches for this work are among the most successful of his watercolors (pls. 56–58). The dark tones and liquid paint aptly capture the somber mood of the opera, in which a woman in a highly unstable state of mind stumbles through the woods at night in search of her lover. At the end, when she finally comes across his corpse, the music refuses to spell out whether she murdered him or not. Like the Visions, these watercolors partake of the twilit universe of Symbolism. The labyrinthine woods do not reflect the empirical world but the protagonist's state of psychological disarray (pls. 56–57). As such, the set designs support the gendered Manichaeism at the heart of *Erwartung* and *Die glückliche Hand*. Darkness is associated with women in the tradition of Strindberg, who had a profound impact on Schoenberg, an impact that the Gerstl affair did nothing to lessen. The watercolors also point up a discrepancy between Schoenberg's music and his art. His music had already emancipated itself from the nebulous indeterminacy of Symbolism, which had been briefly explored in *Pelleas und Melisande*. His thoughts on painting were of more recent date and inevitably lacked the firm technical grounding and historical perspective of his compositions. The sketches for *Erwartung*—a modern Gothic—are thus wholly indebted to the tested, crepuscular world he had largely left behind in his compositions. In a way, the music that Schoenberg was composing in 1909 and 1910 did not have a counterpart in his painting.

With *Die glückliche Hand*, Schoenberg struck out in a new direction. In its final form, the opera must be seen as a reformulation of his article "The Relationship to the Text," in which he had problematized the connection between text and music. But the opera had a long period of gestation. By the time the opera was completed in 1913, Kandinsky's revolutionary abstract drama, *Der gelbe Klang* (The yellow sound), which broke with the anthropocentric tradition of Expressionist theater, had been published in the *Blue Rider Almanac* (1912).[96] Yet if Kandinsky's object-oriented dramaturgy was pivotal to the final version of *Die glückliche Hand*, Schoenberg's sketches for the sets represent an earlier stage in his development, since they were shown at the Heller exhibition in 1910 (pls. 59–61). Another modern-day *Gesamtkunstwerk* known to Schoenberg was Kokoschka's *Mörder, Hoffnung der Frauen* (Murderer, hope of women) of 1907,

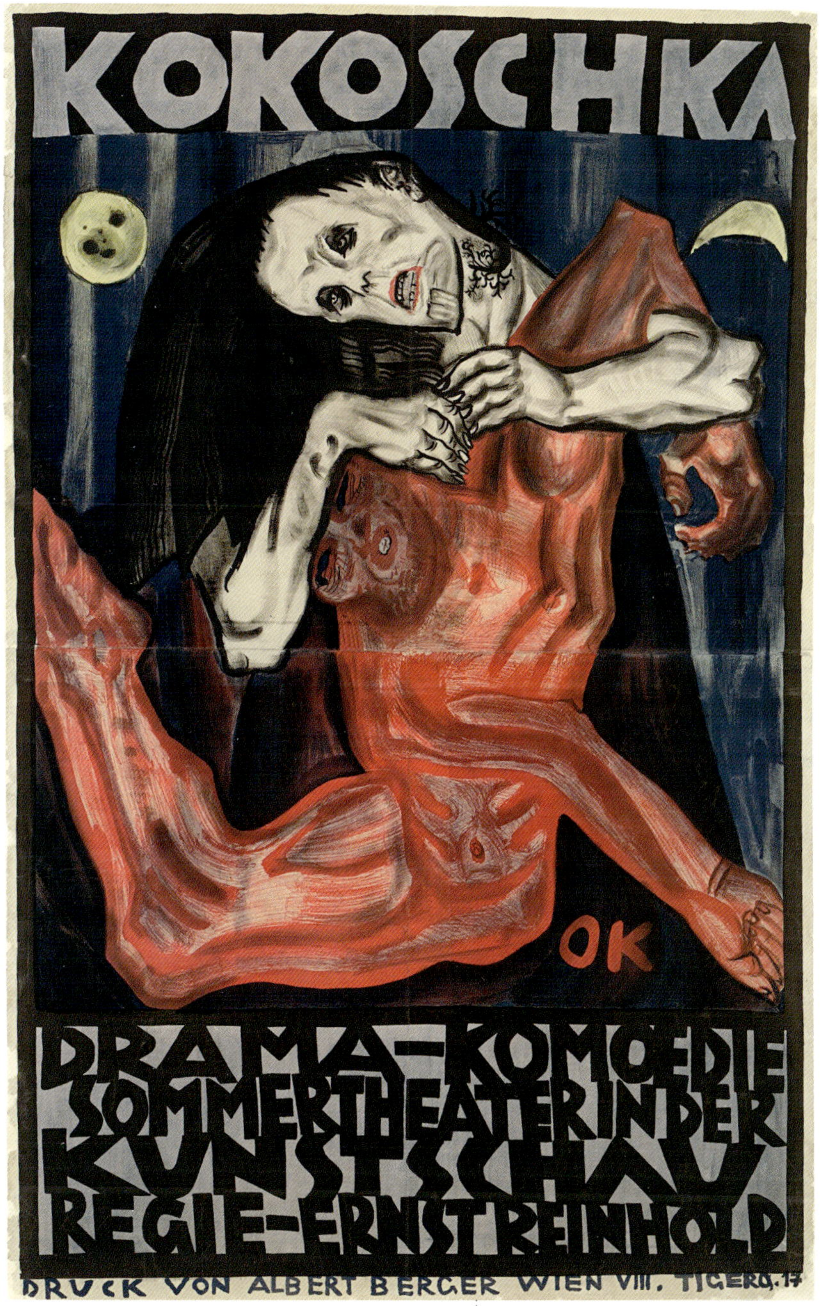

Fig. 19. Oskar Kokoschka. Poster for his play *Murderer, Hope of Women*, 1909. Color lithograph on paper, 49⅛ x 31⅞ in. (125 x 81 cm). MAK–Austrian Museum of Applied Arts/Contemporary Art, Vienna. Kokoschka made this poster for the summer theater of the 1909 Kunstschau in Vienna, where *Murderer, Hope of Women* (1907) received its premiere.

which, like *Die glückliche Hand*, deals with the war between the sexes (fig. 19). *Die glückliche Hand* has no plot in the conventional sense of the word: a triangle resolves itself unfavorably when the artist loses the woman he loves to a lesser man. The sketches follow the stage directions closely. In the first scene, the fantastic animal sinking his teeth into the protagonist reveals the composer's continuing interest in Symbolism. An ink drawing showing the gaze of the twelve chorus members is reminiscent of Redon, who drew much of his inspiration from Wagner's operas (pl. 59). Since Redon's work was exhibited at the Berlin Secession, which Schoenberg visited in December 1911 while working on *Die glückliche Hand*, it is fair to assume that this sketch was done after seeing the show.[97]

Schoenberg's paintings cannot be instrumentalized and reduced to illustrations of his life or his music. Defying easy interpretation, his art raises challenging questions concerning the dilemmas of a major intellectual figure of the twentieth century. Works like *Red Gaze* show how powerful his contribution to expressionist art really was. Few people have achieved recognition in two different fields in the liberal arts. Strindberg, a man much admired by Schoenberg and his circle, came close, as did the Lithuanian artist-composer Mikalojus Čiurlionis. The fact that most of Schoenberg's oils were done in a single year is part of what makes them unique. But what a year! Under the pressure of events, Schoenberg grew. The isolation resulting from his dissolution of tonality threw him into a state of intellectual speculation that sharpened his analytical skills; work on *Erwartung* and *Die glückliche Hand* encouraged his radical rethinking of the connection of color and light to music and sound; his interest in the unconscious led to a visionary form of art that hovered effortlessly on the verge of abstraction—that crucible where the mystical and the modern coincided. Even the searing pain brought about by his marital crisis made his painting an impassioned vehicle for his times. "Art," he wrote in 1910,

> is the cry of distress uttered by those who experience at first hand the fate of mankind. Who are not reconciled to it, but come to grips with it. Who do not apathetically wait upon the motor called "hidden forces," but hurl themselves in among the moving wheels to understand how it all works. Who do not turn their eyes away to shield themselves from emotions, but open them wide, so as to tackle what must be tackled. Who do, however,

often close their eyes, in order to perceive things incommunicable by the senses, to envision within themselves the process that only seems to be in the world outside. The world revolves within—inside them: what bursts out is merely the echo—the work of art![98]

Schoenberg's paintings raise the issue of his changing relation to Judaism and of assimilation—once described by George Steiner as "the diaspora within the diaspora."[99] In 1898, when he was twenty-four, Schoenberg converted to Protestantism, most likely due to his profound identification with German culture, and especially with the music of Bach and Brahms, which he so deeply admired.[100] Converted or not, it was hard for Jewish intellectuals to avoid a culture of syncretism: the difficulty of staying on one side of the divide must have presented itself to them continuously. Much of Schoenberg's work, after all, is about straddling fault lines: Moses/Aaron; Saul/Paul; and, at a different level, music/painting; Germany/Austria; Europe/America; heart/brain.[101] In his famous lecture on Mahler, for example, Schoenberg acknowledged that he had initially misunderstood Mahler's music: "I was Saul before I became Paul," he wrote, once more identifying Mahler as Christ, that is, as the persecuted artist.[102] Thrust into a position of compulsory brinkmanship, he would not be drawn into a passive role of victimization and refused to relinquish the dominant culture to which he had contributed so richly, negotiating the borderlines critically, and transmuting the inevitable tensions into art. The palimpsests show. Schoenberg never finished high school and lacked the remarkable *Bildung* that characterized a Freud, a Schnitzler, or a Hofmannsthal (a fact that no doubt played an emancipatory role in his work). His classics were limited to the Bible.[103] And the Bible, in Martin Luther's translation, remained his steady companion "in the course of a lifetime that embraced two world wars, various revolutions, and long years of exile in Europe and the United States," to quote Alexander Ringer.[104]

Political events were to shatter the fragile status conferred on Schoenberg by assimilation. In 1921, when he was vacationing in Mattsee, the town council demanded proof that he was not Jewish. Schoenberg refused to show his certificate of baptism and left town.[105] This was his most serious encounter with anti-Semitism up to that point in his life. Because of the central role represented by music in acculturation, many of the music critics who attacked him in Austria and Germany were themselves Jewish. Their disagreements, noted Leon Botstein, reflected "an intra-ethnic debate regarding political security, cultural identity and assimilation."[106] It was in the United States, in fact, that one of the earliest attempts to link Schoenberg's music with his Jewishness appeared, in a review published in 1913 by James Huneker, foreign correspondent of the *New York Times* (fig. 20): "Perhaps the Hebraic strain in the composer's blood has endowed him with the gift of expressing sorrow and desolation and the abomination of living." That Huneker's judeophobia was racialist becomes clear in his conclusions: "The aura of Arnold Schoenberg is, for me, the aura of original depravity, of subtle ugliness, of basest egotism, of hatred and contempt, of cruelty, and of the mystic grandiose." Huneker—who was also the first to publish Schoenberg's paint-

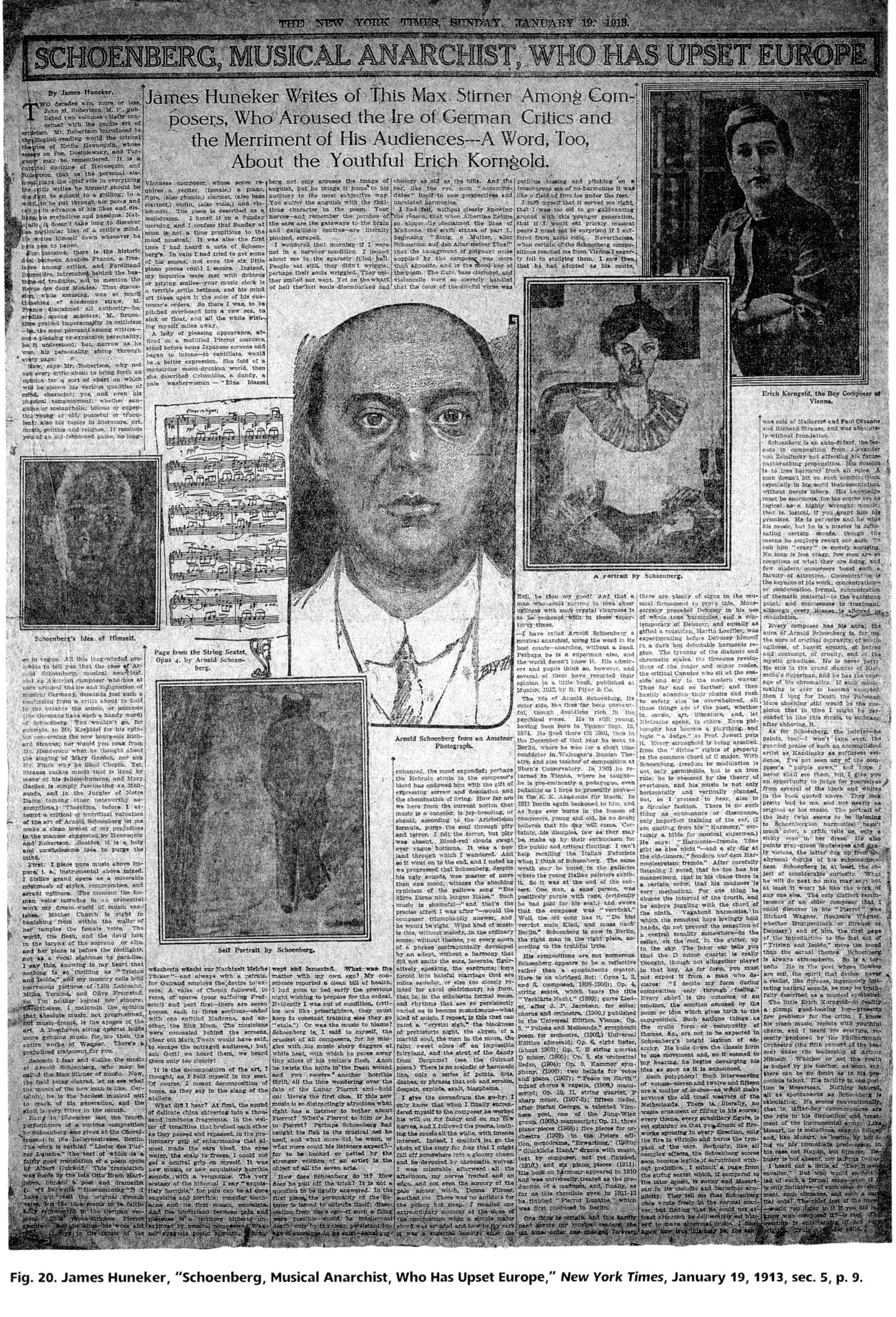

Fig. 20. James Huneker, "Schoenberg, Musical Anarchist, Who Has Upset Europe," *New York Times*, January 19, 1913, sec. 5, p. 9.

ings in this country—added that the composer "also paints gray-green landscapes and sickly visions, the latter dug up from the abysmal depths of his subconsciousness."[107]

Mattsee was a clarion call. Yet the painful episode did not dislodge Schoenberg's profound allegiance to a German culture he had helped shape. In an unpublished letter to Alma Mahler, he wrote that he had finally begun to work again, and on something new, "something that those Aryan Germans who persecuted me in Mattsee will have to thank me for when, even a hundred years from now, they enjoy international esteem because they belong to a state that has recently assured its hegemony in the field of music!"[108] The full extent of the incident at Mattsee seems to have hit home only in 1923, in the course of an exchange with Kandinsky. Their correspondence had been interrupted during World War I, when the two men lost sight of each other for a few years. It resumed when Kandinsky returned to Germany to teach at the Weimar Bauhaus, at the behest of Walter Gropius (who had married, then divorced, Schoenberg's old friend Alma Mahler). In 1923, Kandinsky wrote to Schoenberg, inviting him to join the Bauhaus faculty as head of the Weimar Musikhochschule. In the meantime, Schoenberg had heard from Alma Mahler that the Russian artist had made anti-Semitic remarks. The composer was deeply affected, and on April 19 he sent the artist a furious letter: "For I have at last learnt the lesson that has been forced upon me during this year, and I shall never forget it. It is that I am not a German, not a European, indeed perhaps scarcely even a human being (at least, the Europeans prefer the worst of their race to me), but I am a Jew."[109] A few days later he wrote even more forcefully: "You are perhaps satisfied with depriving Jews of their civil rights. Then certainly Einstein, Mahler, I and many others, will have been got rid of. But one thing is certain: they will not be able to exterminate those much tougher elements thanks to whose endurance Jewry has maintained itself unaided against the whole of mankind for 20 centuries. For these are evidently so constituted that they can accomplish the task that their God has imposed upon them: To survive in exile, uncorrupted and unbroken, until the hour of salvation comes!"[110] After this traumatic experience, Schoenberg's commitment to Judaism would occupy an increasingly prominent place in his music and in his writing.

Though opposition to his work did not let up, Schoenberg was appointed to the Prussian Academy of the Arts in Berlin in 1925. But at the very moment when he appeared to have succeeded, his career seemed headed toward a collision between conflicting identities. While Schoenberg hoped that his culminating achievement would lead to the acknowledgment of his contribution to the German musical tradition, his personal development was moving toward self-definition as a Jew. When, in 1933, he was dismissed from his post by the Nazis, he escaped to Paris, where he publicly reaffirmed his return to Judaism (fig. 21). As he had written to Alban Berg the previous year: "More and more I am forced to concern myself here with the question whether and to what extent it is wise to count myself in this camp or that, whether it depends upon my volition, determination, inclination, or whether it is coercion. Naturally, even without the

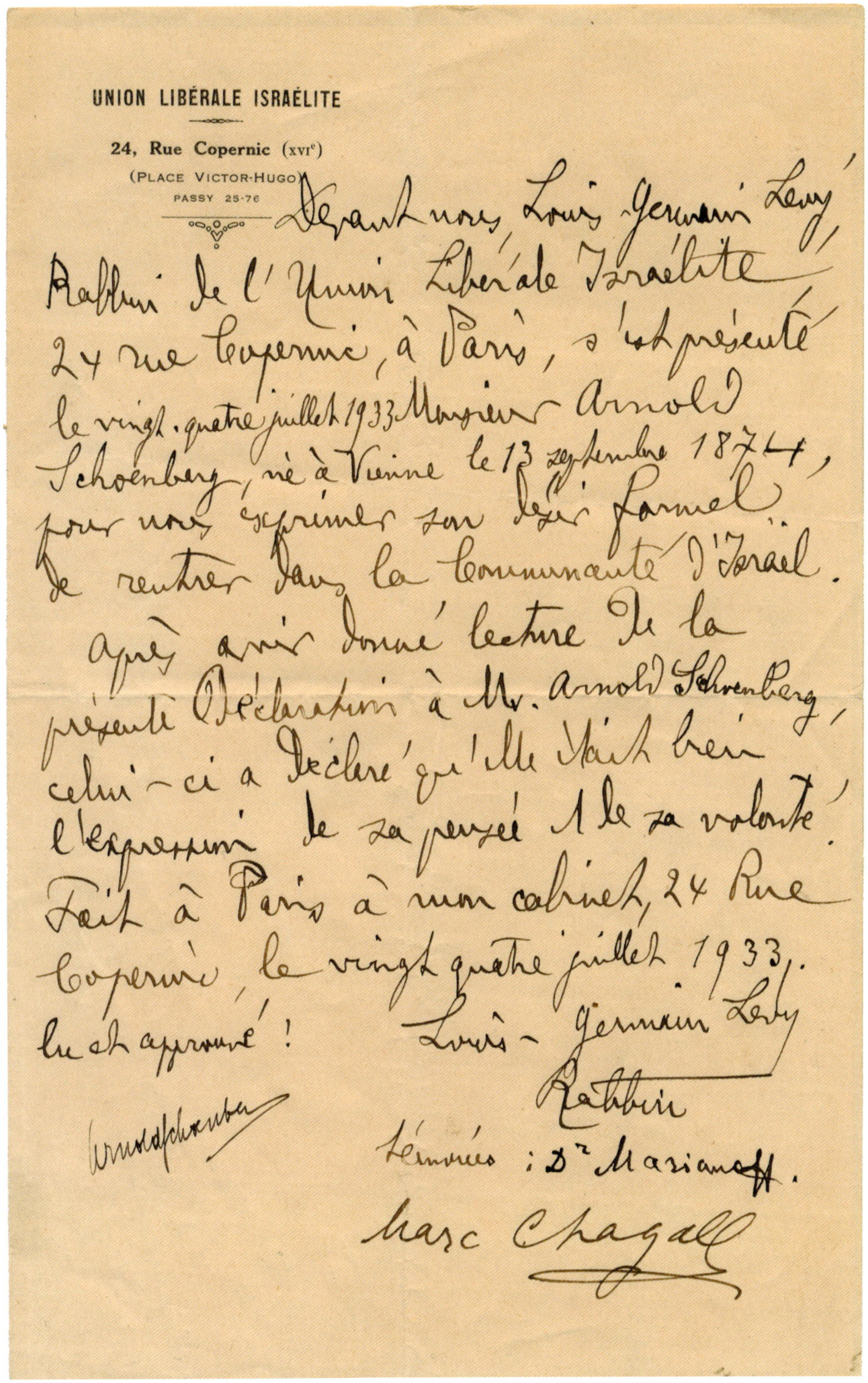
UNION LIBÉRALE ISRAÉLITE

24, Rue Copernic (XVIe)

(PLACE VICTOR-HUGO)

PASSY 25·76

Devant nous, Louis Germain Lévy
Rabbin de l'Union Libérale Israélite
24 rue Copernic, à Paris, s'est présenté
le vingt-quatre juillet 1933 Monsieur Arnold
Schoenberg, né à Vienne le 13 septembre 1874,
pour nous exprimer son désir formel
de rentrer dans la Communauté d'Israël.
Après avoir donné lecture de la
présente Déclaration à Mr. Arnold Schoenberg,
celui-ci a déclaré qu'elle était bien
l'expression de sa pensée et de sa volonté.
Fait à Paris à mon cabinet, 24 Rue
Copernic, le vingt quatre juillet 1933.

Lu et approuvé! Louis-Germain Lévy
Rabbin

Arnold Schoenberg

Témoins : Dr Marianoff.

Marc Chagall

Fig. 21. Arnold Schoenberg's reaffirmation of his Jewish faith, signed by the rabbi, Louis-Germain Lévy, and two witnesses, Dimitri Marianoff (Albert Einstein's son-in-law) and Marc Chagall. Paris, July 24, 1933.

nationalist hints of the last few years, I know exactly where I belong. It's just that it's not as easy to switch places as one would imagine." And he added: "Today it is with pride that I call myself a Jew; however, I am aware of the difficulties of really being one."[111] Like the self-portraits, his words underscore the painful and ever-perilous quest for self-discovery of a thinker who refused to paper over the fault lines, but gave eloquent expression to the irreducible duality of German-Jewish identity.

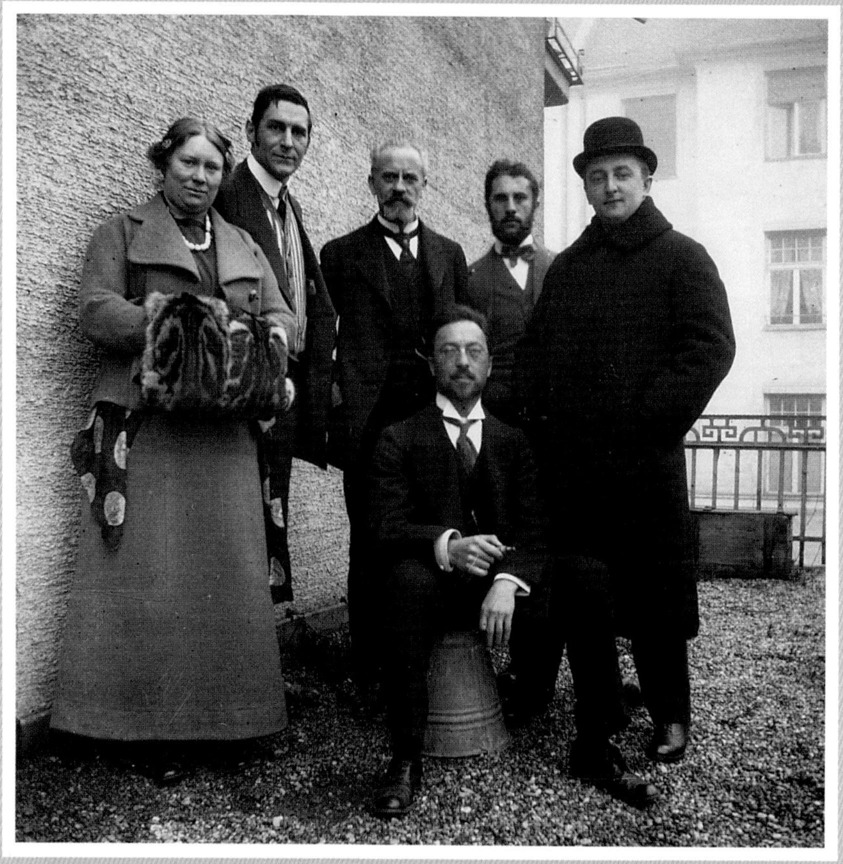

The Blue Rider

Reinhold Heller

Munich was radiant. . . . Art blossomed, art reigned, art stretched its rose-entwined scepter over the city and smiled. A universal, respectful participation in its flourishing, a universal, diligent and generous practice and propagation in its service . . . reigned. . . . Munich was radiant.

—Thomas Mann, "Gladius Dei"

Many discussions of Munich's visual arts avant-garde in the early twentieth century begin with such a quotation from Thomas Mann's 1902 short story "Gladius Dei."[1] Although Mann ignored the continuing dominance of a puritanical, conservatively Catholic government and social hierarchy, which were not infrequently reactionary in their attitudes toward both style and content in art, his optimistic presentation of the Bavarian capital city's artistic life reflected a widely perceived reality. For example, in 1930, Wassily Kandinsky, in one of his few reminiscences about his years in Munich, similarly recalled a city where art was a major presence and a preeminent focus of identity, especially in Schwabing, the bohemian and student section of the city: "[In] funny, somewhat eccentric and self-confident Schwabing, . . . a person—whether man or woman . . .—not carrying a palette, a canvas, or at the very least a portfolio was immediately conspicuous. Like an 'intruder' in a 'nest.' Everybody painted . . . or wrote poetry, or played music, or learned to dance. . . . Schwabing was a spiritual island amid the wide world, in Germany, for the most part even in Munich."[2]

Just as Mann's characterization is overly roseate, nostalgia surely colors Kandinsky's recollections. Nonetheless, there is ample justification for citing Mann's and Kandinsky's glowing testimonials to Munich and its art community—the city was in the ranks of international art centers such as Paris or Berlin with its newly active German art community. And although around 1900 Munich's glory was slowly diminishing, its numerous art schools, museums, and galleries remained a major magnet for artists from Germany and other European countries and the Americas.

Despite the wealth of artistic activity, however, modernist explorations and

Fig. 1. Artists on the balcony of Wassily Kandinsky and Gabriele Münter's apartment in Munich, 1911. Left to right, standing: Maria Franck, Franz Marc, art collector Bernhard Koehler, Heinrich Campendonk, and Thomas von Hartmann; sitting: Wassily Kandinsky. Photograph by Münter.

experimentation found relatively little support and were rarely presented publicly. Neither the tradition-bound Association of Pictorial Artists of Munich nor the nominally more progressive Munich Secession opened their exhibitions to radical artistic innovation. To overcome this impasse, younger artists formed groups to sponsor their exhibitions and raise funds by various means, including by opening small art schools. Thus, Kandinsky and others founded the Phalanx Society in May 1901 for the purpose of "providing these artists with exhibition opportunities, since the Munich Secession shut out all the young, and in order to bring modern (i.e., at the time, predominantly Impressionist) foreign artists to Munich" (figs. 2–3).[3] Chronically short of funds, limited in their exhibition possibilities, often collected around one or two individuals, most of these splinter groups were short-lived. Phalanx's life span, from June 1901 to December 1904, was comparatively long, but its exhibition activity, which focused especially on non-German artists, ceased after Kandinsky—the group's guiding light—left Munich to travel with Gabriele Münter in Tunisia, Italy, and France for several years.

The impact of these small, progressive artists' groups on Munich's larger artistic milieu was necessarily minimal, so the artistic face of the city remained largely conventional, as Gauguin's Polish disciple Władisław Ślewiński observed derisively during a visit in early 1908. "We are in Munich now," Ślewiński wrote, "and will remain for some time. The atmosphere is little encouraging; here there are only paint smearers and beer. The paint smearers are horrible, but the beer is excellent. The artistic niveau [level] is so horribly low that one has absolutely no desire to have an exhibition."[4]

Despite his denigration of Munich from the artist's point of view, Ślewiński met with Jan Verkade and Paul Sérusier, two other followers of Gauguin from

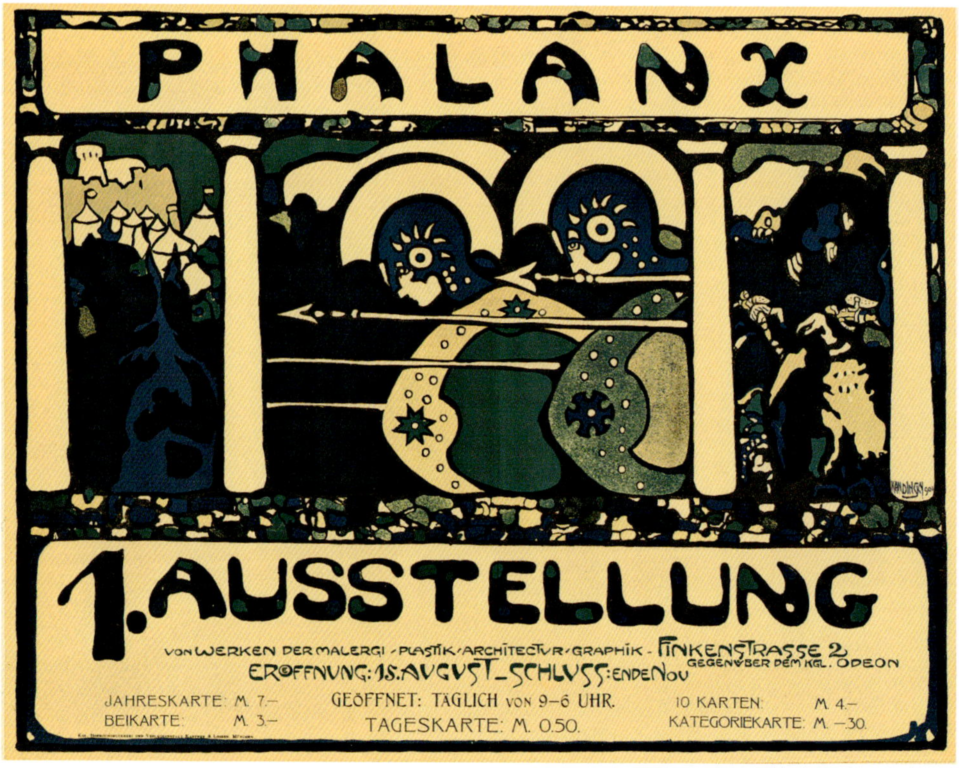

Fig. 2. Wassily Kandinsky (Russian, 1866–1944). *Poster for First Phalanx Exhibition*, 1901. Color lithograph on paper, 18⅝ x 23¾ in. (47.3 x 60.3 cm). The Solomon R. Guggenheim Museum, New York, Gift of Kenneth C. Lindsay, Binghamton, New York.

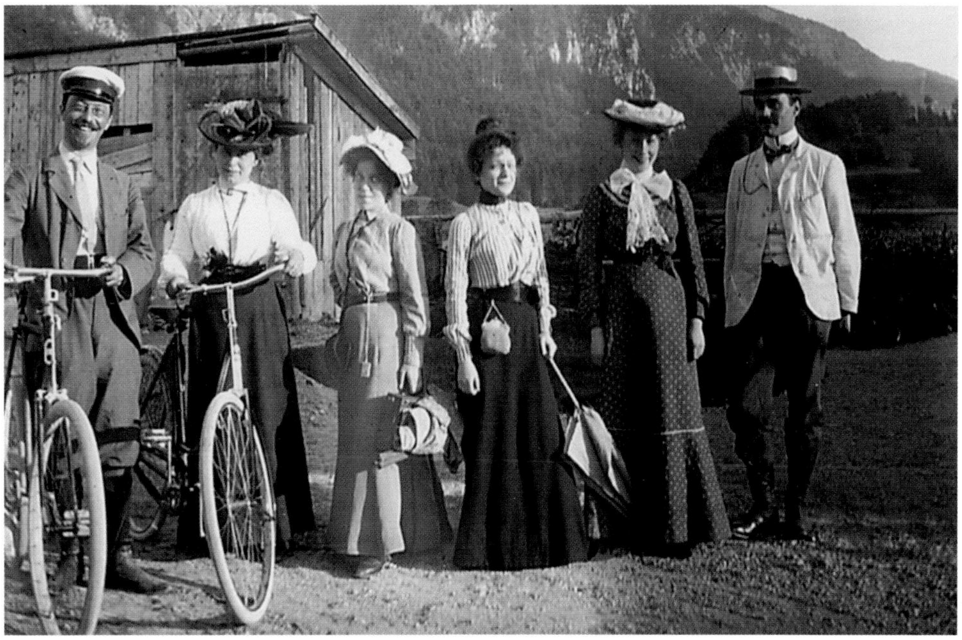

Fig. 3. Kandinsky (left) with his Phalanx painting class in Kochel, in the foothills of the Bavarian Alps, 1902.

Pont-Aven who were already studying and working there, and through them met the Russian expatriate artists Marianne von Werefkin and Alexei von Jawlensky.[5] The two most stylistically progressive artists resident in Munich after Kandinsky and Münter left at the end of 1904, Werefkin and Jawlensky applied Gauguin's Synthetist or Cloisonniste marked lines around flattened areas of subjective color in their own work, boldly integrating them into the expansive colorism and vigorous brushstrokes they learned from Henri Matisse and the other Fauves during visits to Paris.

By the time Münter and Kandinsky returned to Munich in the early summer of 1908, the trio of Gauguin's disciples had moved on. A meeting of all five, along with Jawlensky and Werefkin, might well have been of momentous significance for the development of modern art, but instead the three Frenchmen and their Gauguin-derived aesthetic proved more indirectly meaningful for Kandinsky and Münter, as their thoughts on art were transmitted through Jawlensky and Werefkin. Although their most recent paintings, of early summer 1908, emphasized a modified Impressionist technique, Kandinsky and Münter brought with them from France the same fascination with a Gauguinesque flattening of forms, fused with Matisse's vibrant coloration and formal experimentation. During August and September, painting together in the nearby picturesque Bavarian Alpine village of Murnau, Jawlensky, Kandinsky, Münter, and Werefkin—the last less than the first three—put into practice and defined a collective new style that was identifiably Expressionist (see fig. 4; pl. 8; and Dabrowski essay, fig. 3).[6]

Münter recalled the weeks in Murnau as a key moment in the rapid transformation of all their work as they sought new directions: "It was a wonderful, interesting, happy period of work with many discussions about art with the enchanting 'Giselists' [Werefkin and Jawlensky, who lived in Munich on the Gisela Strasse]. . . . We all tried hard and each one of us matured [in our art]. I made a mass of studies. . . . We all worked hard."[7] In a diary-like entry of 1911, Münter

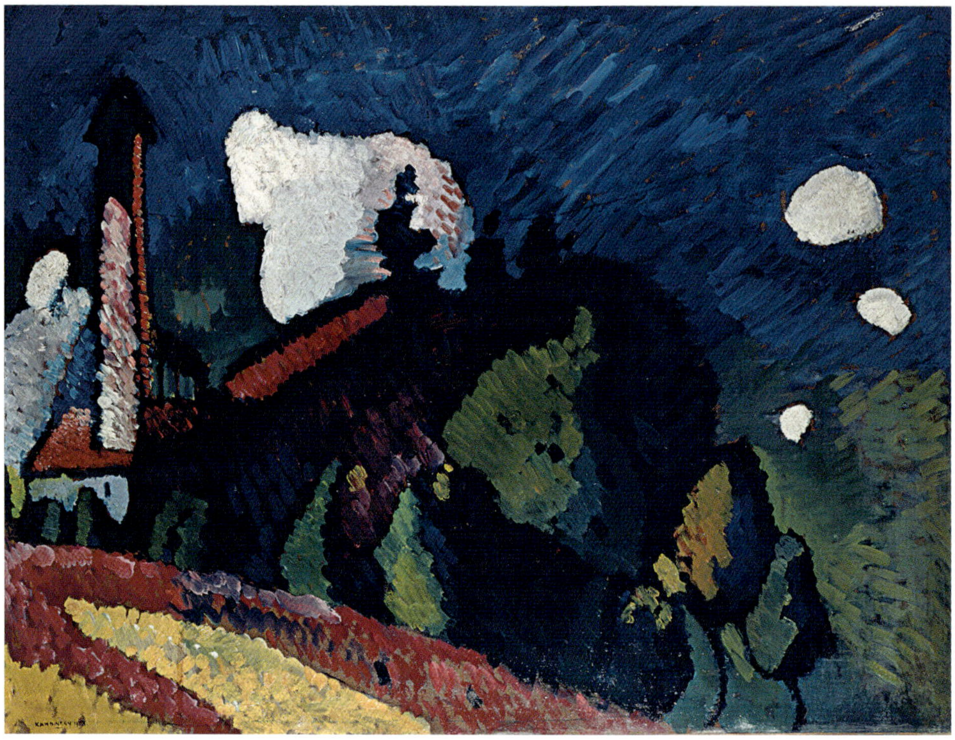

Fig. 4. Wassily Kandinsky. *Landscape with Tower*, 1908. Oil on board, 29⅛ x 38¾ in. (75 x 98.5 cm). Musée National d'Art Moderne, Centre Georges Pompidou, Paris.

recalled painting alongside Jawlensky, showing him her works, comparing them to his, and absorbing his understanding of the concept of "synthesis." Even later, in a letter of 1934, Kandinsky likewise still recognized his indebtedness to his Russian compatriot, acknowledging that "I learned much from you then, and will be eternally grateful for it."[8]

Münter's painting of Werefkin and Jawlensky reclining in a springtime mountain meadow, probably dating from 1909 (pl. 6), exemplifies the common vocabulary their works achieved. Although figures and landscape are reduced to flattened hieroglyphic renderings, lacking even the details of facial features, this reductiveness does not prevent the viewer from readily identifying female and male figures, as well as elements of the landscape, which retain a perspectival reference in their relative sizes. The colors remain largely true to their model, but are simplified, intensified, and limited in range, and are applied—mixed but avoiding all illusion of modeling—with active but not gesturally emphatic brushstrokes. Finally, the effect of flatness is accented further by the notably Cloisonniste outlining of shapes and by expanses of unpainted cardboard. While the painters' individual vocabularies are usually easily discernible in the works of the summer and fall of 1908 and early 1909, they share a basic approach and common stylistic principles.

If Jawlensky provided the impetus for the quartet's stylistic transformation in Murnau during the summer of 1908, it was Kandinsky who soon became the group's guiding force. Significantly contributing to Kandinsky's rise to prominence in the group was their inability to exhibit their newly radicalized work at the existing exhibition venues. On January 22, 1909, the painting quartet from Murnau, joined by a number of artists who were studying with Jawlensky or who visited his and Werefkin's Gisela Strasse apartment regularly as well as by several art collectors, decided to organize formally into a new artists' association, modeled on the earlier Phalanx group. Within a month the artists decided to name it quite simply Neue Künstlervereinigung München (New Association of Artists Munich), frequently identified solely by its initials as NKVM.[9] In large part because of his prior experience with Phalanx, Kandinsky was selected to head the new exhibition society, or, as Münter recalled admiringly a few years later, "Kandinsky resolved to become its head since no one else could do it."[10] Jawlensky became the second executive officer. Initially the Association numbered twenty-one members, between artists and a few patrons, but the number fluctuated, with members resigning and new ones joining for personal reasons or—more frequently—in response to the core group's stylistic radicalism.[11]

In the spring of 1909, Kandinsky designed a membership card (fig. 5) and an identifying symbol for the group, and wrote the programmatic circular sent out to gather additional support and membership:

> We permit ourselves to call your attention to a new association of artists, which came to life in January 1909 and which cherishes the hope of aiding with all its might in the propagation of artistic culture with exhibitions of serious artworks. Our point of departure is the thought that the artist, in addition to the impressions he receives from the external world, from nature, continuously collects experiences in an inner world. And [our point of departure] is the search for artistic forms that should give expression to the reciprocal permeation of all these experiences—for artistic forms that must be freed of everything incidental, in order to give what is essential a strong expression—in short, the striving for artistic synthesis. This seems to us to be the phrase that currently is uniting ever more artists in spirit. By founding this organization, we hope to grant these spiritual relationships among artists a material form that will create the opportunity to speak to the public with a united strength.[12]

The succinct circular offered a condensed formulation of the aesthetic principles guiding Kandinsky's, Münter's, and Jawlensky's new works at the time. Grounded in an opposition to, but—significantly—not a total rejection of, the post-Renaissance artist's dependence on an illusionistic imitation of visible nature, which remained a basic principle of Impressionism as they saw it, the NKVM called for a new recognition of subjective responses and experiences that would produce images representing a fusion of "external objectivity" and "internal subjectivity." This fusion of interacting, complementary, and antithetical principles they then identified—adopting Jawlensky's predilection for Gauguin's term but shifting its meaning—as an expansive "synthesis," an innovative and independent realm of artistic production.[13]

If Jawlensky offered the NKVM Gauguin's Symbolist terminology as the cornerstone of the group's modernist artistic developments, it was Kandinsky who most systematically developed its implications and justifications.[14] At the time the NKVM was founded, he had completed the first draft of his book, *On the Spiritual in Art*, which established theoretical principles for the Expressionist art he, his friends, and other artists were producing.[15] The term "synthesis" no longer played a meaningful role; shortly before 1900, Kandinsky had substituted for it

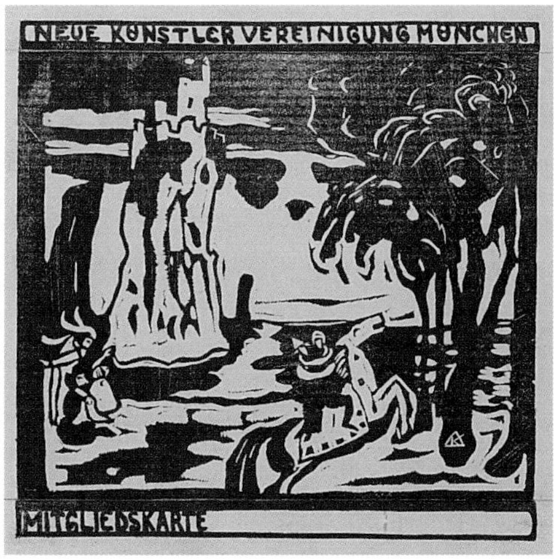

Fig. 5. Membership card for the Neue Künstlervereinigung München (1909), illustrated by Kandinsky.

the Hegelian term "inner necessity" (*innere Notwendigkeit*), which had once again become current in German art theory. For this "inner necessity" Kandinsky posited three "mystical sources":

1. every artist, as creator, must give expression to what is characteristic of him (the element of personality),
2. every artist, as child of his epoch, must give expression to what is characteristic of his epoch (the element of style contained in its innermost value, composed of the language of the epoch and the language of the nation, as long as the nation as such exists),
3. every artist, as a servant of art, must present what is unique to art generally (the element of the purely and eternally artistic, which resides in all persons, peoples, and times, which is visible in every artwork of every artist, of every nation, of every time, and which, as the principal element of art, knows neither place nor time).[16]

Grounding his position in Hegel's view of a necessary perpetual spiritual progression away from dependence on the external material world, Kandinsky then argued that "the path on which we find ourselves today, and which is the greatest good fortune of our time, is the path through which we shall rid ourselves of the external in order to counteract this main principle with its antithesis: the fundamental principle of inner necessity."[17] "Inner necessity" would subordinate dialectically the subjective elements of personality, time, and place in an artwork's creation and counteract them with a conscious adherence to art's eternal "objective" principles, which make it possible, for example, to recognize "that a 'crudely' carved column from a Hindu temple is absolutely animated by the very same soul as any living work, no matter how 'modern.'"[18] Aligning himself and the other artists of the NKVM with the progressive, historically forward-moving principle of "inner necessity," Kandinsky sought to assure the readers of his tract that the "modern" art of the NKVM represented both an ineluctable future and the universal, unchanging values of true art.

Had it come out in the fall of 1909 (and not been rejected by a series of publishers), the book would have functioned as a panegyric defense and reasoned justification addressed to an antagonistic or uncomprehending audience for the works the NKVM included in its first exhibition (fig. 6). In a venue made available through the intercession of the recently appointed general director of the Bavarian museums, Hugo von Tschudi—who had been dismissed from his prior position as director of Berlin's National Gallery for favoring modernist French painting over traditional German art[19]—the exhibition was held at Heinrich Thannhauser's Moderne Galerie in Munich from December 1 to December 15, 1909, then traveled to eight other German cities.[20] Because of their provocative, radically intense colorism and drastically reductive simplifications within which the recognizable forms of objects threatened to dissolve, the paintings of Jawlensky, Kandinsky, and Münter dominated the exhibition (fig. 7). For them, "synthesis" and

Fig. 6. Wassily Kandinsky. *Poster for the First Exhibition of the Neue Künstlervereinigung München*, 1909. Color lithograph on paper, 37 x 25¼ in. (94 x 64 cm). Städtische Galerie im Lenbachhaus, Munich.

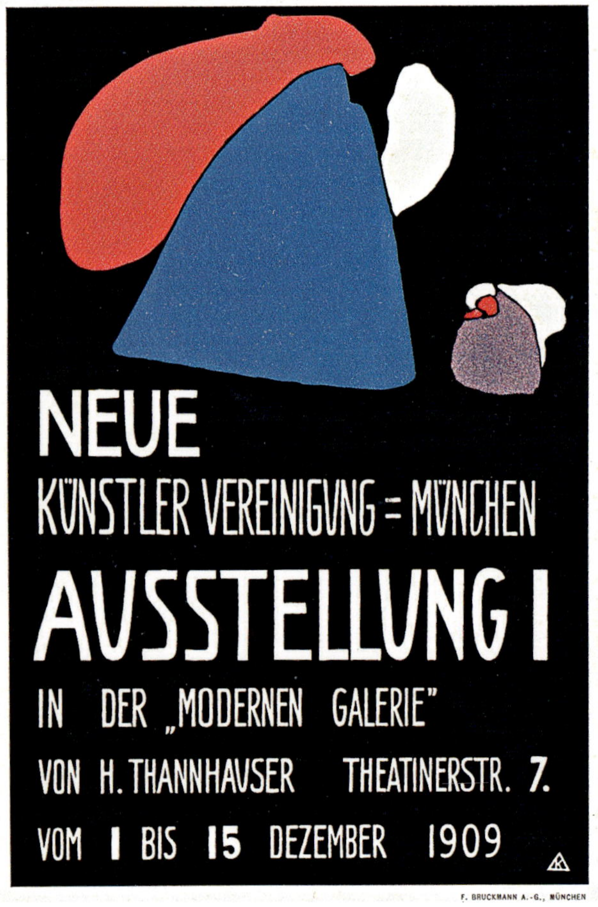

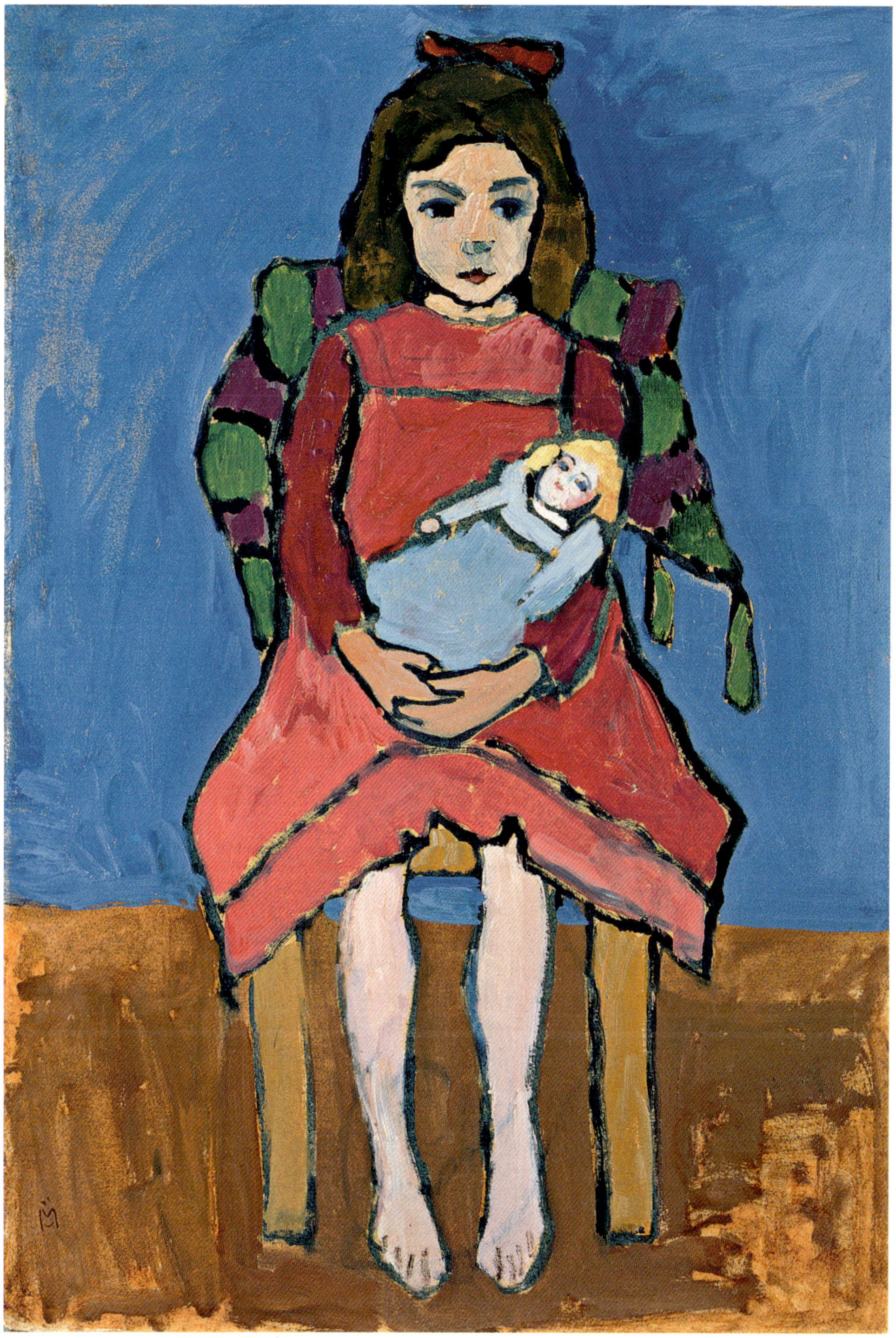

Fig. 7. Gabriele Münter (German, 1877–1962). *Girl with Doll*, 1908/9. Oil on canvas, 27½ x 19 in. (70 x 48.8 cm). Milwaukee Art Museum, Gift of Mrs. Harry Lynde Bradley, M1966.165. This painting was shown in the first NKVM exhibition in December 1909.

"inner necessity" provided the justification for a dramatically liberated formal vocabulary that no longer required ready referentiality.

The critical reception in Munich was vehemently negative. The exhibition did make one major convert, however: the painter Franz Marc visited the Moderne Galerie Thannhauser repeatedly, and under the exhibition's influence transformed his own work, which gradually moved away from the modified Impressionism he had practiced to that point. When the second NKVM exhibition took place, again at Thannhauser's, in September 1910, Marc wrote a lengthy refutation of the negative criticism that met it once more. Like Kandinsky, he pointed to the rejection of Impressionism, which remained "solidly stuck in the 'material realm,'" as the premise for the new art with its "fully spiritualized and de-materialized interiority of perception" and its goal of an absolute "spiritualization of the 'material realm.'" Marc simplified Kandinsky's arguments but strongly iterated his belief in an art that would no longer depend on the "material" visual world for its imagery and proclaim instead its reliance on painting's "consequentially accomplished *division of the surface*, the mysterious lines of the one, the coloristic harmonies of the other [that] seek to generate spiritual moods [*geistige Stimmungen*] that have little to do with the material makeup of what is depicted but instead prepare the soil of a new, very much spiritualized aesthetic."[21] The Neue Künstlervereinigung München, in short, represented the initial adventurous efforts of an art wholeheartedly of the future.

In addition to works by its members, the second NKVM exhibition included paintings by French artists.[22] Georges Braque, Pablo Picasso, Henri Le Fauconnier, and André Derain presented early Cubist works, while Kees van Dongen and Georges Rouault represented variants of Fauvism. (Henri Matisse was invited but declined to exhibit.) The international manifestations of the new non-naturalistic "spiritual art" were therefore accented as never before in a Munich exhibition; the Munich artists were also manifestly positioned within a context of artistic activity that reached well beyond local Bavarian considerations.[23] The most controversial works in the exhibition, however, were not the avant-garde Parisian paintings but Kandinsky's, especially his large *Composition II*, which clearly distinguished itself from every other work in the exhibition by the degree of its departure from coherently recognizable imagery. Although destroyed, its penultimate study is extant (pl. 2), and we can see that it is a work in which he retained his outlined forms, flattened areas of color, and collapsed spatial renderings, but the degree of stylization and non-naturalistic coloration renders the scene all but indecipherable in terms of referentiality to the visual world outside the painting's own limits. This determined antireferentiality is also announced by the title—*Composition II*—which has potentially musical and overtly serial connotations, but otherwise offers the viewer no verbal clues to decipher the medley of shapes, colors, and lines. Recent scholarship has assiduously attempted to decipher the symbolism of Kandinsky's "hidden imagery" and recognizes in the study two levels of reference: on the one hand, a landscape scene with figures that translates into contrasting representations of apocalyptic conflagration, and, on the other, the paradisiacal sacred grove or Garden of Love.[24] The public of 1910, however, lacked both the tools of archival documentation and the viewing habits of today's art lovers instilled by nearly one hundred years of abstract painting. The first audiences saw in *Composition II*—if their response was positive—a revolutionary shift toward a nonrepresentational independence on the part of the essential components that constitute painting itself. Alternatively—if their response was negative—the work was an anarchic, incomprehensible, and inarticulate jumble testifying only to the maker's madness, lack of talent, or desire for sensationalism.[25] Just as today it may be difficult to imagine the urgent sense of unprecedented innovation and liberation that Kandinsky's painting generated in 1910—and that seemed either to threaten the very tradition of painting itself or to promise a new future, filled with excitement and adventure—so in 1910 it was impossible not to recognize the work's pivotal significance.[26] With *Composition II* as its focal piece, the second NKVM exhibition was a site of extreme antagonism and vituperative confrontation such as had rarely, if ever, been seen in Munich before.[27]

The controversy, with its heated arguments pro and con, extended into the NKVM itself. By December, Kandinsky was openly questioning his determination to keep the group together: "Yes, I really have to admit that I think of our group with little pleasure and would like nothing better than to resign from it. But I do not know if my conscience will permit it."[28] On January 10, 1911, he resigned his position as president of the NKVM because his vision of the group and its activities differed dramatically from that of the majority of members.[29] Despite Kandinsky's continuing dissatisfaction and impatience with the other artists, he retained his membership, however. Moreover, he gained a new ally, open to his ideas, in Franz Marc.

The two met shortly before they attended the Arnold Schoenberg concert together on January 2, 1911, after which Kandinsky also developed a friendship with the Viennese composer. As his relationship with other NKVM members deteriorated, and they rejected his drive toward abstraction, Kandinsky rapidly cultivated an alternative group of artists who, like him, were intent on laying the groundwork for a radically new art of the future (fig. 1). Marc characterized their shared utopian convictions in a letter to his future wife, Maria Franck: "Today we live in one of the most significant moments in the history of culture. Everything that we still carry with us of the 'old culture' (religion, monarchism, aristocracy, privileges [including purely spiritual ones], humanism, etc.) is a 'present time already belonging to the past.' . . . What kind of new culture we are approaching, no one is able to say today, simply because we stand in the midst of the transformations themselves."[30]

Firmly convinced that their reformist, avant-garde art was the harbinger of inevitable future developments in art, culture, and society, Kandinsky and his cohorts found themselves consistently at odds with the NKVM majority, especially over exhibition policies and practices.

The differences festered throughout the year 1911. The final confrontation between Kandinsky and his supporters and the remainder of the NKVM membership occurred at the beginning of December, when the selection jury for the third NKVM exhibition rejected Kandinsky's *Composition V* (see Dabrowski essay, fig. 5), ostensibly for exceeding the size limits Kandinsky himself had written into the organization's statutes, but really because Kandinsky's near-abstraction broke with the other artists' continuing commitment to a greater degree of figuration. Personal animosities played a role as well, as a letter from one of the artists voting against Kandinsky makes apparent: "Within the Association major changes have taken place . . . : Kandinsky, [Alfred] Kubin, Marc, Miss Münter are

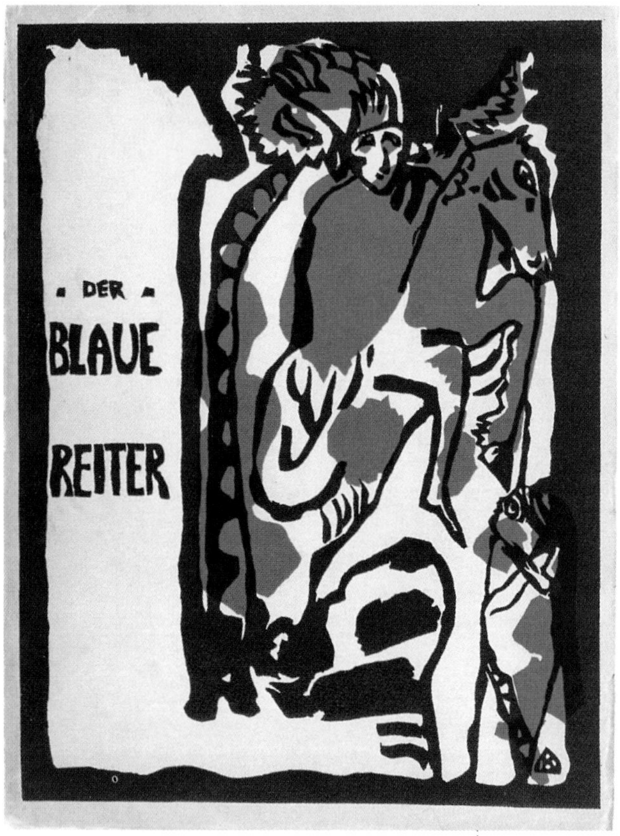

Fig. 8. Cover of the first edition of the *Blue Rider Almanac* (1912), illustrated by Kandinsky.

no longer members. . . . We do not believe there is a reason for great regret, since these individuals did nothing but perpetually create difficulties for us."[31] After resigning from the NKVM, Kandinsky, Marc, and Münter immediately began to put into effect a tentative plan for an exhibition to counter that of the NKVM, and to be positioned alongside it in three small rooms at the Moderne Galerie Thannhauser.

Marc and Kandinsky had already been very active outside the NKVM with a series of publications that fostered their ideas. When the conservative painter Carl Vinnen compiled his controversial pamphlet *Protest deutscher Künstler* (Protest of German artists), which in effect accused German museums and critics—an "interest group" supported by "aesthetes and snobs"—of supporting modern French art at the expense of German artists, deemed to be suffering severe financial losses as a result,[32] it was Kandinsky and Marc who were instrumental in organizing an anthology of writings by artists, critics, and museum people countering Vinnen's "Protest." In his contribution to their own pamphlet, *Im Kampf um die Kunst: Die Antwort auf den "Protest deutscher Künstler* (In the struggle for art: response to the protest of German artists), Marc sarcastically retorted that German art needed the infusion of foreign influences to regain the universal quality undermined by the provincialism of Vinnen and others. "A strong wind," Marc wrote, "blows the seeds of a new art over all of Europe today. . . . The anger of a few artists on German soil at a wind that happens to be from the west is nothing but comical. They prefer dead calm."[33]

Although the "Protest" identified the NKVM as a manifestation of anti-German internationalism, the refusal of the group in 1911 to expand the selection of artists invited to exhibit was one of the sources of Marc, Münter, and Kandinsky's dissatisfaction with their fellows. The willingness to look beyond national and local boundaries, to "extend our hand" to French and other artists, meant, according to Marc, participating, even if haltingly, in the active formation of a new cultural era.

It was to further this project and to examine the international status of contemporary art's progress toward its utopian goal that Kandinsky conceived of another project for him and Marc to carry out in June. "Now! I have a new plan," he wrote enthusiastically, "We two must be the editors. A sort of almanac (annual) with reproductions and articles only by artists. The entire year must be mirrored in the book, and a link to the past as well as a beam of light into the future must grant full life to this mirror."[34] He added in a postscript: "and a *chronicle*!! i.e., reports about exhibitions = criticism also written by *artists*." The "almanac" would compare works by contemporary artists with examples from ancient Egypt, by children, or by naïve or folk artists, in order to demonstrate visually an "inner," or "spiritual," kinship between them. Finally, he wished to extend the "chronicle" to include literature and music, producing conceptually a new union of the arts in which the juxtaposition of the various genres—like the pictorial comparisons—would make their common concerns, means, and goals apparent to the publication's readers without any need for discrete theoretical arguments. Briefly here, almost as an aside, Kandinsky had outlined the program of one of modern art's key documents, the *Blue Rider Almanac* (fig. 8).[35]

Throughout the summer and early fall, Kandinsky and Marc worked on the *Almanac*, writing essays, corresponding with other artists, collecting articles and photographs of artworks, planning the layout, and signing with Reinhardt Piper as publisher. They also sought out or renewed their friendships with the Rhineland painters August Macke (fig. 9) and Heinrich Campendonk, as well as with Paul Klee and Arnold Schoenberg, so that at the same time as the *Almanac* was being planned a new association of artists began to take shape outside the NKVM. On September 10, Marc sent Reinhardt Piper an ambitious provisional table of contents with separate sections devoted to painting, music, books, a chronicle, and reproductions.[36] Also early in September, they named the almanac *Der Blaue Reiter* (The blue rider), because, as Kandinsky laconically recalled nearly two decades later, "we both loved blue, Marc—horses, I—riders."[37]

Fig. 9. August Macke (German, 1887–1914). *The Storm*, 1911. Oil on canvas, 33¹⁄₁₆ x 44¹⁄₁₆ in. (84 x 112 cm). Saarland Museum, Saarbrücken. This work was shown in the first Blue Rider exhibition and also reproduced in the *Blue Rider Almanac*.

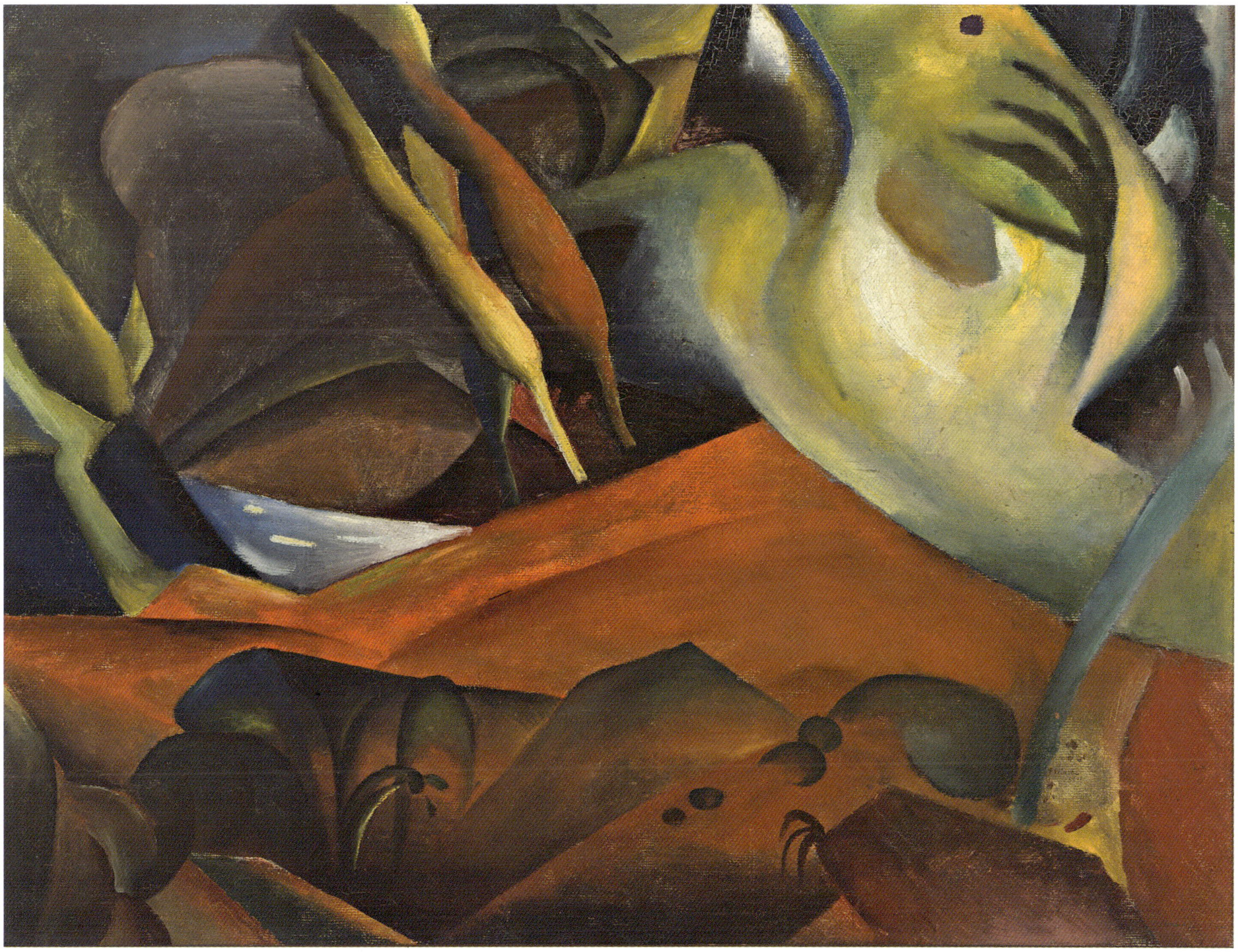

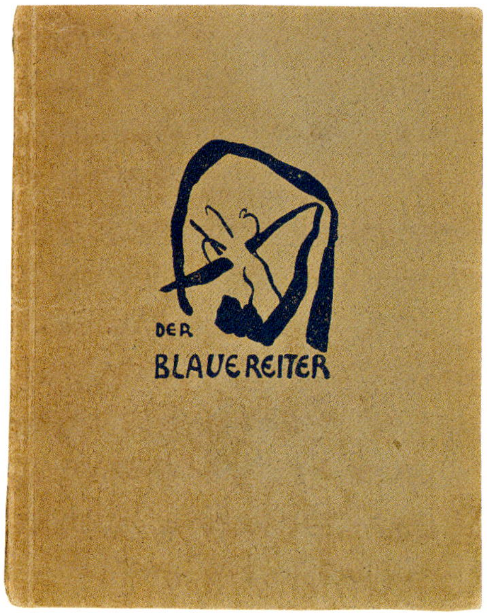

Fig. 10. Cover of the catalogue for the first Blue Rider exhibition (1911), illustrated by Kandinsky.

In a typed preliminary preface to the volume, the co-editors enthusiastically proclaimed, "We are standing at the threshold of one of the greatest epochs that mankind has ever experienced, the epoch of great spirituality."[38] The *Almanac* was to serve as the first collective voice of this new era, a kind of artistic holy scripture, at once a historical record and a prophecy.

Work on the *Almanac* was interrupted by the dispute within the NKVM that resulted in Münter, Marc, and Kandinsky's resignations early in December and the subsequent rush to plan the alternative exhibition. The *Almanac*'s emphasis on the internationalism of contemporary art and on the "inner relationship" between works that "may appear unrelated on the surface" also served as the dual basis of the new exhibition. Similarly, the artists whose artworks and essays were reproduced in the *Almanac* became the core group fielding paintings to the exhibition. Through urgent correspondence, the show was orchestrated amazingly quickly.

The fateful meeting of the NKVM jury had taken place on December 2; on December 18—or perhaps even a day earlier—"The 1st Exhibition by the Editorship of the Blue Rider" opened with some forty-eight paintings by Albert Bloch, David Burliuk, Vladimir Burljuk, Heinrich Campendonk, Robert Delaunay, Elisabeth Epstein, Eugen von Kahler, Kandinsky, Macke, Marc, Münter, Jean Bloé Niestlé, Henri Rousseau, and Schoenberg (figs. 10–14; see da Costa Meyer essay, figs. 5–6).[39] It was a heterogeneous collection, with works ranging stylistically from Delaunay's Cubist-influenced architectural paintings to Kandinsky's radically abstracted *Composition V* (see Dabrowski essay, fig. 9) to Rousseau's "naïve" imagery, held together by Marc and Kandinsky's perception of the unifying "inner relationship" and, visually, by the strategically rhythmic placement of large paintings by Kandinsky, Marc, and Münter. A single sentence in the exhibition brochure condensed the grand utopian program of the Blue Rider: "Through this small exhibition we do not wish to propagate a *single* precise and special form; rather we intend to demonstrate through the *diversity* of the represented forms how the *inner desire* of the artists manifests itself multifariously."

Another brochure also advertised the forthcoming publication of the *Almanac*, even as it iterated Marc and Kandinsky's editorial intentions and their prophetic faith:

The great upheaval,
The shifting emphasis in art, literature, and music,
The multifariousness of form: the constructive principle, the composition of these forms,
The intensive turn to the inner realm of nature and, associated with it, the rejection of the beautification of nature's exterior—
—Such are, generally sketched out, the signs of the new inner renaissance.
To show the characteristics and manifestations of this turn,
To emphasize their inner cohesion with epochs of the past,
To make known the expression of inner intentions in every form that has an inner resonance—
Such is the goal that "The Blue Rider" shall strive to reach.[40]

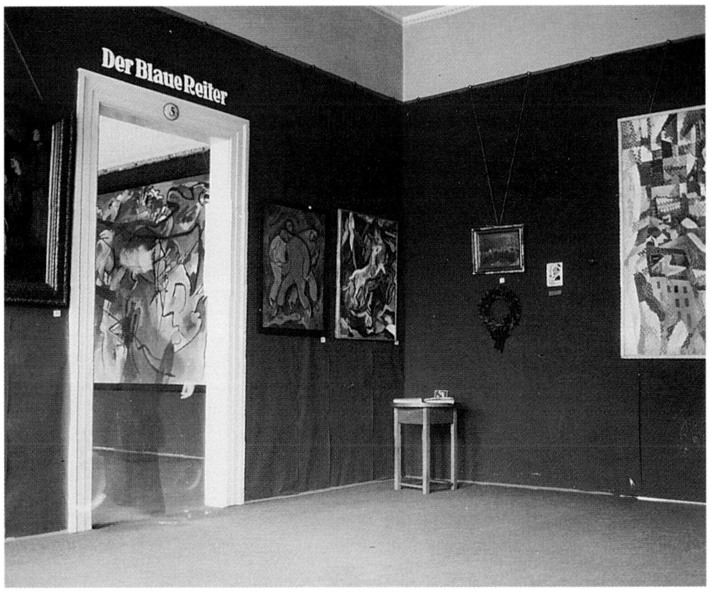

Fig. 11. First Blue Rider exhibition, Moderne Galerie Thannhauser, Munich, December 1911. Room 1, with paintings by (left to right): Münter, Albert Bloch, Campendonk, Henri Rousseau, Marc, and Robert Delaunay. Kandinsky's *Composition V* (1911) can be seen through the doorway. Photograph by Münter.

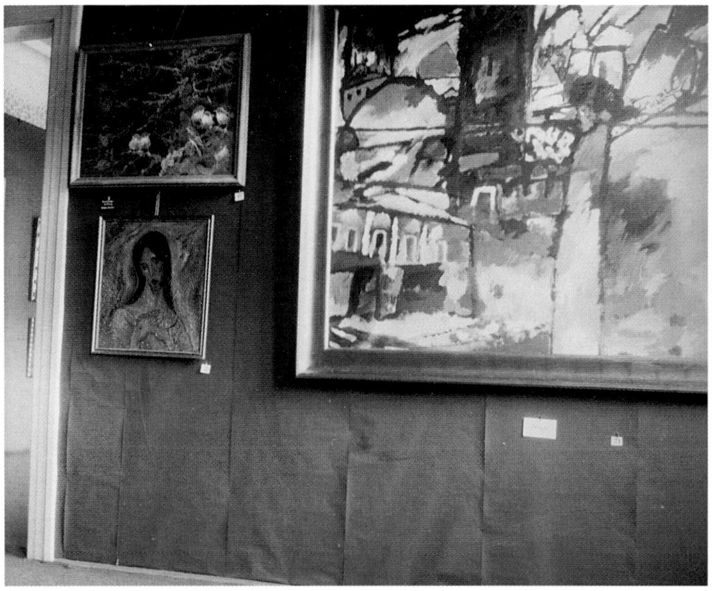

Fig. 12. First Blue Rider exhibition, Moderne Galerie Thannhauser, Munich, December 1911. Room 1, with paintings by (left to right): Jean Bloé Niestlé, Bloch (see pl. 49 in this volume), and Kandinsky. Photograph by Münter.

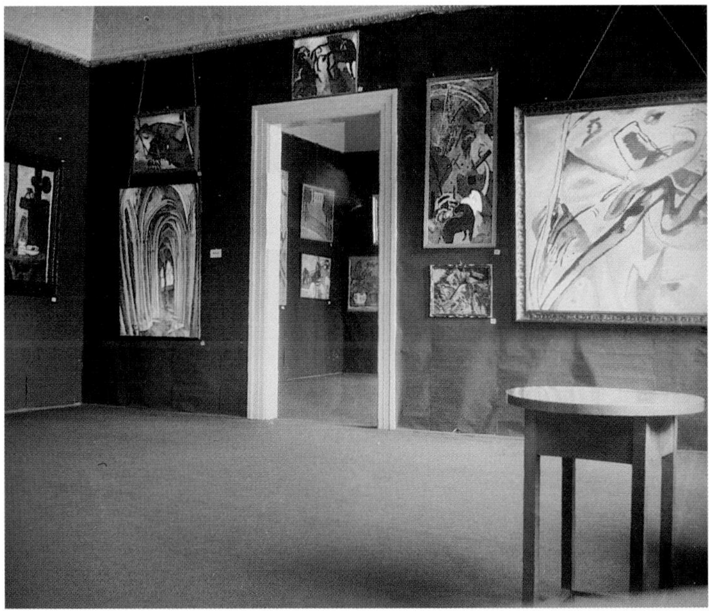

Fig. 13. First Blue Rider exhibition, Moderne Galerie Thannhauser, Munich, December 1911. Room 2, with paintings by (left to right): Münter, August Macke, Delaunay, David Burliuk, Marc, and Kandinsky. Arnold Schoenberg's *Night Landscape* (1910) can be seen through the doorway. Photograph by Münter.

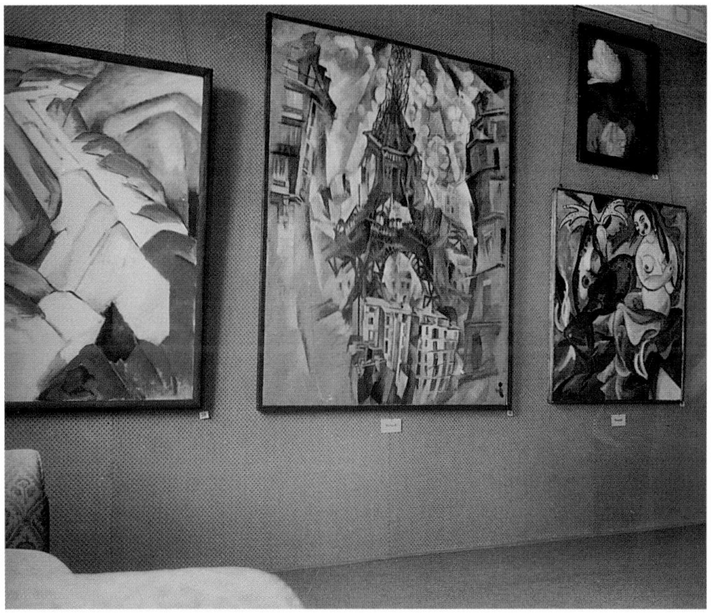

Fig. 14. First Blue Rider exhibition, Moderne Galerie Thannhauser, Munich, December 1911. Room 3, with paintings by (left to right): Marc, Delaunay, Elisabeth Epstein, and Campendonk. Photograph by Münter.

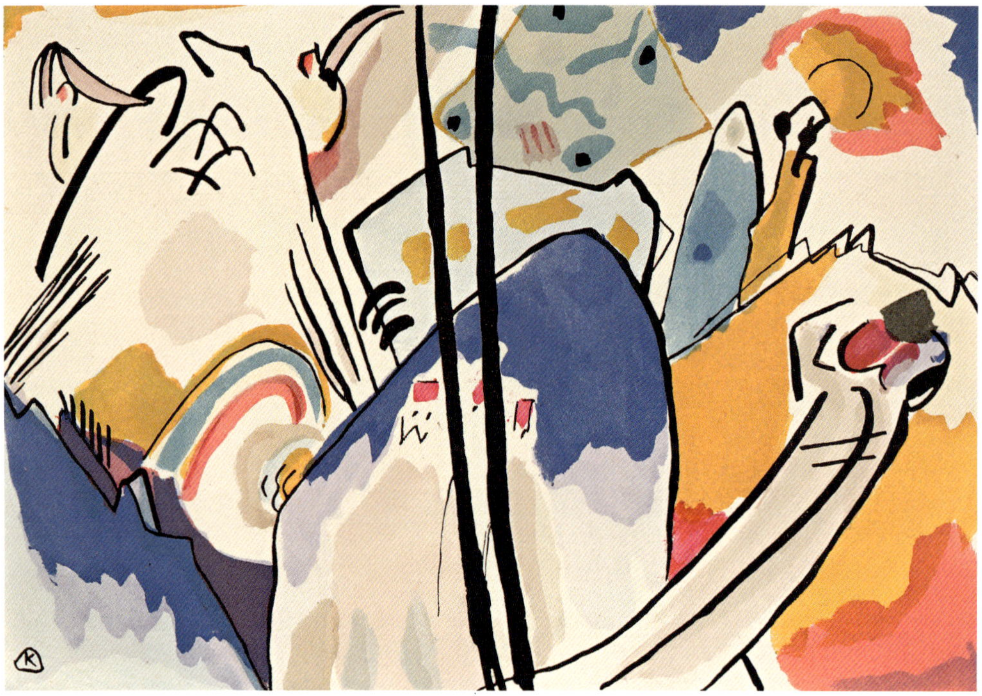

Fig. 15. Kandinsky's *Study for Composition IV* as reproduced in the first edition of the *Blue Rider Almanac*.

As if it were an expansion of these brief statements, Kandinsky's book, *On the Spiritual in Art*, was finally published by Piper while the exhibition was on display and was available for purchase there. However, the *Almanac* remained projected as the fundamental collective identity through which other projects were filtered and through which a collective identity was achieved. This enterprise was as short-lived as it was productive: the second and last Blue Rider exhibition, devoted to more than 315 prints, drawings, and watercolors by numerous artists, opened on February 12, 1912.

The first Blue Rider exhibition traveled to Cologne, Bremen, Zurich, Hagen, and Frankfurt during 1912. Herwarth Walden's unexpected but very welcome request that the exhibition open his gallery Der Sturm in Berlin in early spring—while the works were still on tour—was fulfilled with other paintings by the Blue Rider artists and by Jawlensky and Werefkin. Work on the *Almanac* continued throughout this time. The number of contributions was reduced because some of the artists could not meet the deadlines; Kandinsky's design for the woodcut for the cover revealed "The Blue Rider" to be less a haphazard title than an expression of his and Marc's vision of avant-garde artists as modern embodiments of Saint George, engaged in a struggle against the dragon of materialism; and final selections were made for more than 140 illustrations. In May 1912, the *Almanac* was published, its contents dominated by the contributions of Kandinsky and Marc (figs. 15–16). Marc's three initial essays tracked the history of modern art in Germany and introduced comparative principles to guide readers in viewing the illustrations. Kandinsky's offerings were the three important closing contributions: the essay "On the Question of Form," which expanded upon aspects of *On the Spiritual in Art*; his discussion of stage design, or—in his transgenre terminology—"composition"; and the text of his dramatic "stage composition" *Der gelbe Klang* (The yellow sound). Framed by Kandinsky's and Marc's writings were Macke's essay "Masks"; Schoenberg's discussion of the interactions between music and text; David Burliuk's review of contemporary Russian art; the French critic Roger Allard's review of current French artistic developments; the Russian composer Thomas von Hartmann's essay "Anarchy in Music"; a consideration of Delaunay's works; and studies of Alexander Scriabin's music and of "free music"—all accompanied by a network of illustrations of contemporary, non-European, and medieval works and a selection of scores by Schoenberg, Alban Berg, and Anton Webern. Kandinsky's great plan was for a synthesis of the

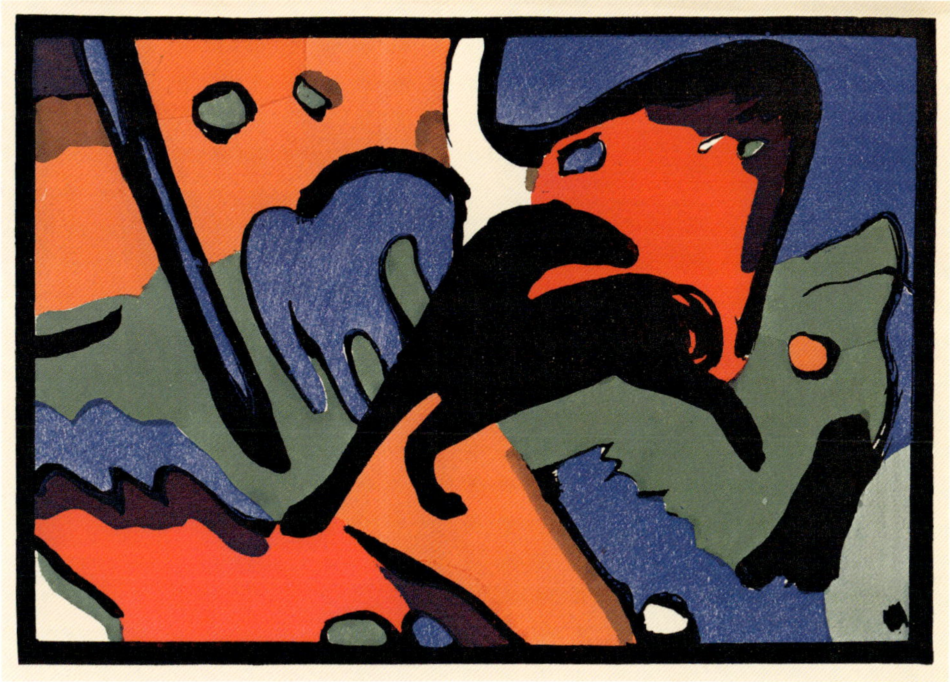

Fig. 16. Franz Marc's *Horses* as reproduced in the first edition of the *Blue Rider Almanac*.

arts, in which magical intersections and interpolations of works and media would provide a subjective sense of the "inner necessity" that was shaping the art of the time and the anticipated, imminent age of the "spiritual," the time when "budding blossoms," the "spiritual violets" of an artistic springtime, would finally bloom into maturity.[41] To a great extent, his vision was realized between the covers of the *Blue Rider Almanac*.

In 1935, Kandinsky wrote, "There never really was a 'Blue Rider' organization, not even a 'group,' as is so often erroneously written. Marc and I took what seemed right to us, what we freely selected. . . ."[42] That assessment is largely true. Around Marc's and Kandinsky's personalities, supportive artists collected their energies, producing artworks, exhibitions, and the ideas, gathered in the *Almanac*, that gave shape or direction to major aspects of the twentieth century's most forward-looking art. A planned second *Almanac* and an incremental growth, even perhaps a more formal organization of the Blue Rider, never came to be, nor did the Blue Rider's utopian vision of a spiritual future. When World War I broke out in the summer of 1914, the fused figure of the Blue Rider, composed of Marc and Kandinsky, broke apart. Marc was activated into the German imperial army and shot dead in 1916. Kandinsky went back to Russia; when he returned to Germany in 1921, Munich without Marc was no longer "radiant." The Blue Rider could not be resurrected.

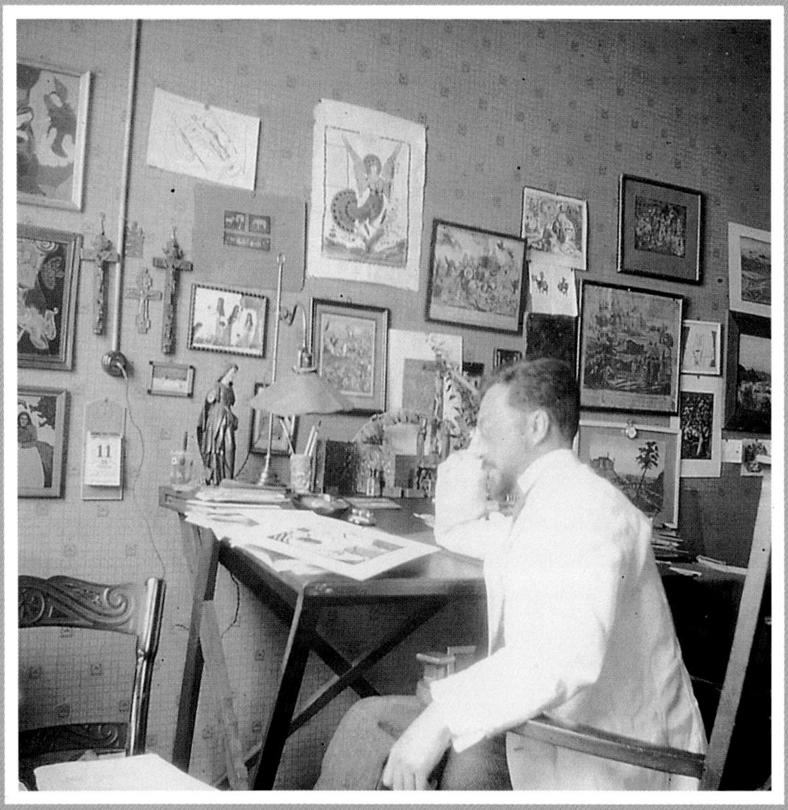

Kandinsky & Schoenberg

Abstraction as a Visual Metaphor of Emancipated Dissonance

Magdalena Dabrowski

> *I have just heard your concert here and it has given me real pleasure. You do not know me, of course—that is, my works—since I do not exhibit much in general and have exhibited in Vienna only briefly. . . . However, what we are striving for and our whole manner of thought and feeling have so much in common that I feel completely justified in expressing my empathy. In your works, you have realized, what I . . . have so greatly longed for in music. The independent progress through their own destinies, the independent life of the individual voices in your compositions, is exactly what I am trying to find in my paintings.*
>
> **—Wassily Kandinsky**

Thus wrote Wassily Kandinsky from Munich on January 18, 1911, to the Viennese composer Arnold Schoenberg, whose music, heard at a concert on January 2, 1911, made a great impression on Kandinsky.[1] At the time Kandinsky wrote this letter, he had already formulated his ideas about the goals and role of visual art in his first theoretical treatise, *On the Spiritual in Art*.[2] There he had articulated the concepts that he subsequently felt correlated explicitly with Schoenberg's music.

In his search for a new pictorial idiom that could adequately reflect the philosophical and aesthetic concerns of the contemporary world, Kandinsky looked for expressive means to free the human soul from the materialistic notions fostered by nineteenth-century positivist philosophy. Disillusioned by the effects of positivism on society, he felt that it was the role of art and artists to imbue the world with new spiritual values. The artistic innovations of Fauvism and Cubism influenced Kandinsky's belief that the world was indeed on the threshold of a "new epoch of the great spiritual."[3] He felt that to imbue art with new and spiritual meaning, any innovative aesthetic language should reflect both the internal and external elements—emotions or "vibrations" of the soul, as well as an unprecedented visual form. The visual form of the work of art was to strike the proper chord in the viewer, who would be transported into a spiritual realm by means of the work's expressive qualities. In Kandinsky's opinion, this process could only be achieved through a visual language independent of the forms of

Fig. 1. Wassily Kandinsky at his desk in his Munich apartment, 1911. Photograph by Gabriele Münter.

reality. The art that he believed spoke to the soul most directly—without references to the surrounding world—was music.

In 1908–9, Kandinsky had already introduced musical terms such as "impression," "improvisation," and "composition" into the titles of his pictorial works. These titles manifested his belief that his path toward an art form devoid of both representation and subject matter should follow the example of music, the most abstract of the arts. Schoenberg's music only confirmed and strengthened Kandinsky's conviction. The famous concert, whose program included Schoenberg's First and Second String Quartets, opp. 7 and 10; the Three Piano Pieces, op. 11; and five lieder,[4] not only prompted Kandinsky's immediate visual response—the painting *Impression III (Concert)* (January 3, 1911; pl. 1)—but also initiated a fruitful exchange of aesthetic ideas between the painter and the composer that lasted until 1914, when, at the outbreak of World War I, Kandinsky felt obligated to return to his native Russia. After an interval of several years, prompted by an unfortunate falling-out, Kandinsky and Schoenberg corresponded sporadically through the 1920s and into the mid-1930s.[5]

From the initial exchange of letters, Kandinsky learned that Schoenberg was not only a composer but also a painter whose pictorial works were almost as untraditional as his music, and in whose view a painting did not have to be representational. Schoenberg was, in fact, convinced that "when the artist reaches the point at which he desires only the expression of inner events and inner scenes in his rhythms and tones, then the 'object in painting' has ceased to belong to the reproducing eye."[6]

Such an approach to painting was manifestly akin to that of Kandinsky. When Kandinsky later received photographs of Schoenberg's canvases, however, he thought more highly of the landscapes and the more realistic works than of the self-portraits that Schoenberg initially called Gazes (and that Kandinsky referred to as Visions). These were painted in a more abstract way and feature wide-open eyes that stare at the viewer from a broadly brushed, empty background. Nevertheless, Kandinsky was sufficiently impressed to ask Schoenberg to contribute an essay, and to allow reproductions of his paintings, as well as a music score, in the *Blue Rider Almanac*, a compendium of articles and works on music, painting, "primitive" arts, and other art-related subjects. Kandinsky was preparing this publication with his close friend the painter Franz Marc.[7] Marc, too, had attended the January 1911 concert, along with Kandinsky and their other good friends, all of whom became members of the Blue Rider group: Gabriele Münter, Alexei von Jawlensky, and Marianne von Werefkin. All of them found Schoenberg's music fascinating and unequivocally avant-garde, but for Kandinsky the music offered a true revelation.

As his writings indicate, Kandinsky had always considered music the most advanced of the arts, since it spoke to the audience through an abstract expressive language composed of sound and time. This is not to say that he sought to paint "musical" works; rather, that it was his ambition to develop a visual language consisting of equally abstract means of expression. These would be based

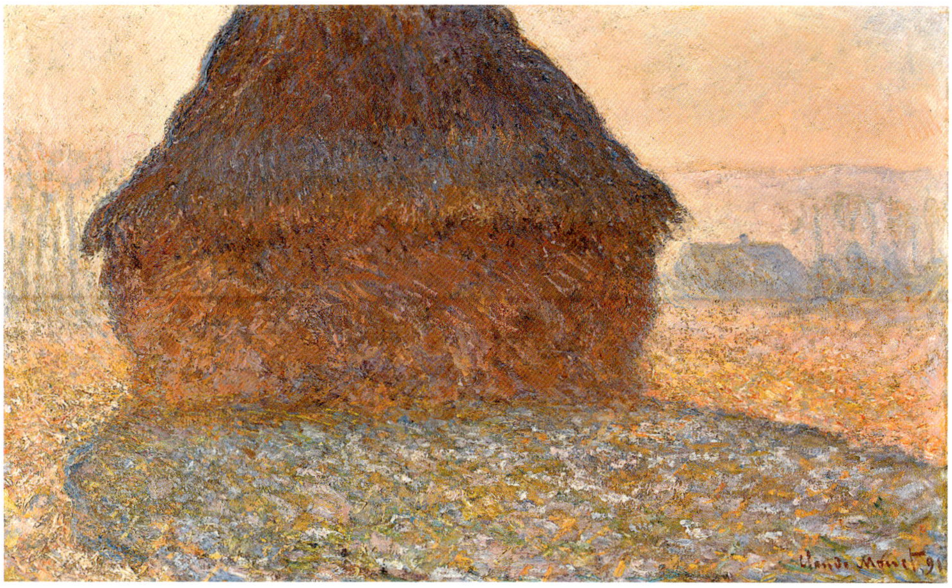

Fig. 2. Claude Monet (French, 1840–1926). *Wheatstack in the Sun*, 1891. Oil on canvas, 23⅝ x 39⅜ in. (60 x 100 cm). Kunsthaus Zürich.

on painting's formal vocabulary and syntax, which could free the viewer's imagination and elicit emotional and spiritual responses. This language, he imagined, would appeal to the viewers' "soul" by generating in them "inner vibrations," or the most profound and satisfying understanding of art, resulting solely from the combinations of color, form, and the ensuing compositional organization, rather than from the mimetic qualities of traditional compositions, which were predicated on perspectival space and narrative content. This desire to eliminate the object was awakened in Kandinsky when he first saw one of Claude Monet's Wheatstacks at the French Industrial Exhibition in Moscow in the summer of 1896 (fig. 2) and admired it before recognizing the subject. He realized that the viewer need not recognize the object portrayed in order to appreciate a painting, but can simply enjoy the particular combination of colors and forms that build up the specific composition.

Schoenberg's inventions, which revolutionized traditional musical conventions by introducing a free use of chromatic scale and atonality, were an entirely new expressive form of composition, exactly the elements that Kandinsky had been striving for in his painting. Schoenberg's most remarkable and controversial innovation was the "emancipation of the dissonance"—the principle that there is no real difference between consonance (musical chords that sound soothing) and dissonance (chords that sound tense), but that dissonance simply represents differently spaced, and frequently further removed, consonances.[8]

As a result of this revolutionary compositional discovery, Schoenberg's musical works acquired greater complexity, with each element of the composition—rhythm, form, and texture—pushed to its furthest possible limit. Traditional works use consonance and dissonance sequentially, in conjunction with each other; when dissonance is followed by consonance, the result is a sense of satisfaction or resolution of tension. By the emancipation of dissonance, Schoenberg subverted that effect, allowing every inner voice to participate in the thematic content of the work to the fullest and thus "bombarding" the listener with an unlimited amount of expressive information that is often difficult to absorb. This dissonant harmony places great intellectual demands on the listener as well.

Compared with conventional musical compositions, and especially those of the then dominant late-Romantic school, Schoenberg's works display a radically increased chromaticism (the use of all or most of the twelve notes of the chromatic scale) and atonality (lack of the sense of focus around a single pitch or key). At that landmark Schoenberg concert, Kandinsky understood these principles remarkably well, and realized that he had essentially been attempting to do the same in his paintings, by rejecting the traditional systems of pictorial composition and emphasizing instead harmonies of color and form, devoid of obvious representational associations. He distributed these elements equally throughout the pictorial field, without hierarchical structure, to achieve a maximum of visual and emotional resonance.

As a well-educated, intellectually sophisticated artist, Kandinsky was deeply conversant with all the newest European and Russian artistic theories and cultural developments. Not only was he a Munich correspondent for the Russian art monthly *Apollon*, reporting on various German and other European exhibitions, but he was extremely well read. He was particularly interested in philosophy, especially the work of Arthur Schopenhauer, and in Theosophy, including the writings of Madame Blavatsky, and Russian theories of mysticism. He also attended lectures and readings by the German Theosophist Rudolf Steiner. Kandinsky had lived in France—at Sèvres, near Paris—in the crucial years 1906–7, which saw the beginnings of Fauvism and Cubism, and had traveled widely throughout Europe and in North Africa. All these experiences had provided him with a broad spectrum of ideas on which to draw in order to attempt pictorial innovations.

Kandinsky's fascination with the affinities between painting and music was initially stimulated by theories of synaesthesia, that is, the spontaneous associations or exchanges between sensations (specifically, sounds and colors), popularized by the French Symbolists at the end of the nineteenth century. These, in turn, had drawn upon a theory of correspondences formulated some fifty years earlier by the poet, critic, and man of letters Charles Baudelaire.[9]

Kandinsky's interest in synaesthesia was further articulated through his belief in Richard Wagner's concept of *Gesamtkunstwerk*, or a total work of art, encompassing language, music, and the visual arts as crucial elements playing equally important roles in a musical drama and in the viewer's perception of the work. It was, in fact, according to Kandinsky's "Reminiscences" (1913), the performance of Wagner's *Lohengrin* that he saw in Moscow in 1896 that initially called his attention to both the expressive power of music—its emotive grip on the beholder—and its ability to conjure images. Describing his vivid memories of that experience, he recalled the musical evocation of a certain hour in Moscow that had always enchanted him: "The violins, the deep tones of the basses, and especially the wind instruments at that time embodied for me all the power of that pre-nocturnal hour. I saw all my colors in my mind; they stood before my eyes. Wild, almost crazy lines were sketched in front of me. I did not dare use the expression that Wagner had painted 'my hour' musically."[10]

During *Lohengrin*, Kandinsky realized that painting can affect viewers as powerfully as music does listeners. Fifteen years later, Schoenberg's music refreshed this early discovery, revitalizing Kandinsky's conviction regarding the need to evolve a new and modern language of pictorial expression that would help the viewer reach "the new epoch of the great spiritual."

Marc, who was especially well versed in music, commented on the parallels between Schoenberg's innovations in music and those in Kandinsky's painting in a letter, of January 14, 1911, to their mutual friend the artist August Macke. Describing his own impressions of the concert, Marc noted:

> Can you imagine a music in which tonality (that is, the adherence to any key) is completely suspended? I was constantly reminded of Kandinsky's large *Composition*, which also permits no trace of tonality . . . and also of Kandinsky's "jumping spots" in hearing this music, which allows each tone sounded to stand on its own (a kind of *white canvas* between the spots of color!). . . . Schoenberg seems, like the Association [Neue Künstlervereinigung München], to be convinced of the irresistible dissolution of the European laws of art and harmony and seizes upon the musical art-means of the Orient, which have remained primitive (until today).[11]

Marc's last reference is clearly to the work of the French Cubists—whose idiom was strongly influenced by what they referred to as "primitive art"—as Marc clarified in his letter to Macke of February 14, 1911.[12] His comment also confirms as a reference to Cubism an observation that Kandinsky shared with Schoenberg in his first letter to the composer:

> At the moment there is a great tendency in painting to discover the "new" harmony by constructive means, whereby the rhythmic is built on an almost geometric form. My own instinct and striving can support these tendencies only half-way. . . . I am certain that our own modern harmony is not to be found in the "geometric" way, but rather in the anti-geometric, antilogical [*antilogischen*] way. And this way is that of "dissonances in *art*," in painting, therefore, just as much as in music. And "today's" dissonance in painting and music is merely the consonance of "tomorrow."[13]

Kandinsky was in all likelihood describing the geometries of Analytical Cubism. In these works, the gridlike, rhythmical compositional scaffolding and the planar elements interact according to the laws of a Cézannesque "passage."[14] Such a method of constructing pictorial composition was incompatible with Kandinsky's own philosophy of painting and his explorations of its inherent spiritual complexity. Only later, in 1922, when Kandinsky began to teach at the Bauhaus in Weimar, Germany, did his views about geometry change. After seven years of exposure to the innovative forms of geometric abstraction pursued by such Russian avant-garde artists as Kazimir Malevich, the originator of Suprematism,[15] Kandinsky began to see geometric form and its interplay with color as expressive options.

In 1911, however, he was greatly reassured by Schoenberg's response to his first missive. In it, Schoenberg emphasized his conviction that their ideas and artistic solutions had a great deal in common, both in music and in painting. Yet, despite the many similarities in their artistic philosophies, theoretical discoveries, and innovative artistic solutions—as well as an interest in Theosophy—there were also very distinct differences between the painter and the composer, due to their individual understandings of the origins and goals of their art. When we compare their biographies, we are struck by the fact that their first theoretical treatises—Kandinsky's *On the Spiritual in Art* and Schoenberg's *Theory of Harmony*—which contain the fundamentals of their revolutionary concepts, had both evolved around the same time, before 1910, and were then published in the same year, 1911. Kandinsky's prose poems *Klänge* (Sounds; 1912); his opera, *Der gelbe Klang* (The yellow sound; 1911); his essay "On Stage Composition" (1911); and Schoenberg's *Die glückliche Hand* (The lucky hand; 1911) all represented examples of their respective concepts of the Wagnerian *Gesamtkunstwerk*.

Schoenberg, however, firmly believed that "art belongs to the *unconscious*! One must express *oneself*! Express oneself *directly*!" He saw art as "*inborn, instinctive*," totally independent of the external circumstances.[16] Kandinsky, on the other hand, conceived of painting as "a thundering collision of different worlds that are destined in and through conflict to create that new world called the work. Technically, every work of art comes into being in the same way as the cosmos—by means of catastrophes, which ultimately create out of the cacophony of the various instruments that symphony we call the music of the spheres. The creation of the work of art is the creation of the world."[17]

Kandinsky, then, saw a work of art from essentially the opposite viewpoint of his musical colleague: the artist was just a mediator, a conduit for what Schopenhauer defined as "abstract concepts" which were formed by reason and predicated on individual experience. As a percipient subject the artist released the emotional power of the work of art by manipulating the pictorial vocabulary and compositional structure. Schoenberg's musical innovations, such as his use of dissonance and atonality, seemed to Kandinsky to represent not only the exact counterparts of his pictorial research, but also a remarkable understanding of the demands placed on contemporary artists. For the artist, who himself was quite adept at playing the cello and the piano and who also tried his hand at composing, the discovery of these analogies provided distinct reassurance that his artistic path was appropriate for the new age. His paintings, where the figuration and narrative subject were obstructed or veiled through the use of colors and forms, devoid of clear contours and related to each other in a nonhierarchical manner, could be seen metaphorically as visual dissonances and absence of narrative key. Another aspect stressed by Kandinsky was the importance of "construction" as a vital element of pictorial work, an element that Schoenberg acknowledged was of no particular interest to him.

We can follow Kandinsky's evolution toward his first entirely abstract works beginning in 1908, with paintings such as *Murnau, Castle Courtyard I* (fig. 3). Kandinsky at this point became more attracted to the physical side of painting rather than to its subject matter. Although visibly figurative, this brilliant compo-

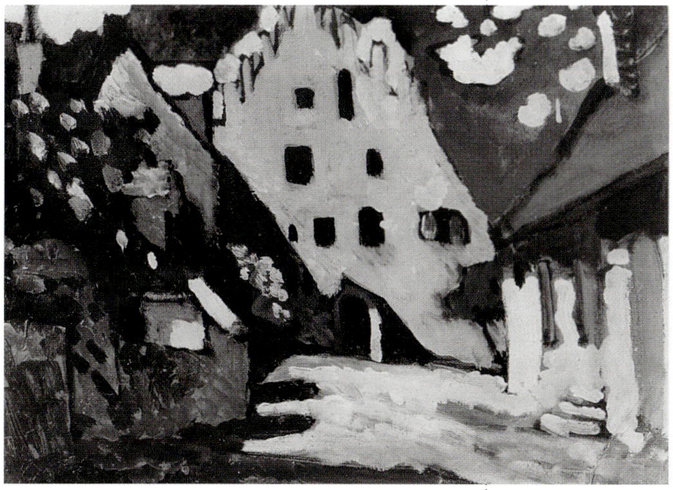

Fig. 3. Wassily Kandinsky (Russian, 1866–1944). *Murnau, Castle Courtyard I*, 1908. Oil on cardboard, 13 × 17 7/16 in. (33 × 44.3 cm). State Tretyakov Gallery, Moscow.

sition in jewel-like colors dispenses with clearly delineated forms, defining the masses of the buildings and the courtyard in front of them with large expanses of overlapping color, which creates a sense of solid form and space. Yet, the looming, bright yellow shape of the castle in the background of the composition simultaneously produces the illusion of enclosure. We contemplate the painting not so much as a landscape but as an arrangement of vivid colors and strong forms. The artist's use of dramatic foreshortening and the scale of the forms depicted draw the viewer's attention to the surface rather than into the space. The colors resound vibrantly against each other, creating a symphonic composition.

The artist further elaborated these effects in *Improvisation 3* (1909; fig. 4), which attempts to strike a proper balance between form and content. The seemingly "Oriental" scene—the exoticism is suggested by the North African architecture that occupies a large part of the right section of the painting—would appear to justify the artist's emphasis on the expressive values of color, form, and surface. The figure of a rider cloaked in bright orange, the green horse, and a large, looming, bright yellow building are all treated with flat areas of color, some in more strongly delineated forms and others in heavily brushed, almost abstract shapes. Structurally, all the compositional elements together stress the flatness of the pictorial surface rather than compositional depth. Although Kandinsky felt that the public was not yet ready for complete abstraction,[18] the identification of objects and figures does not play an essential part in our aesthetic appreciation

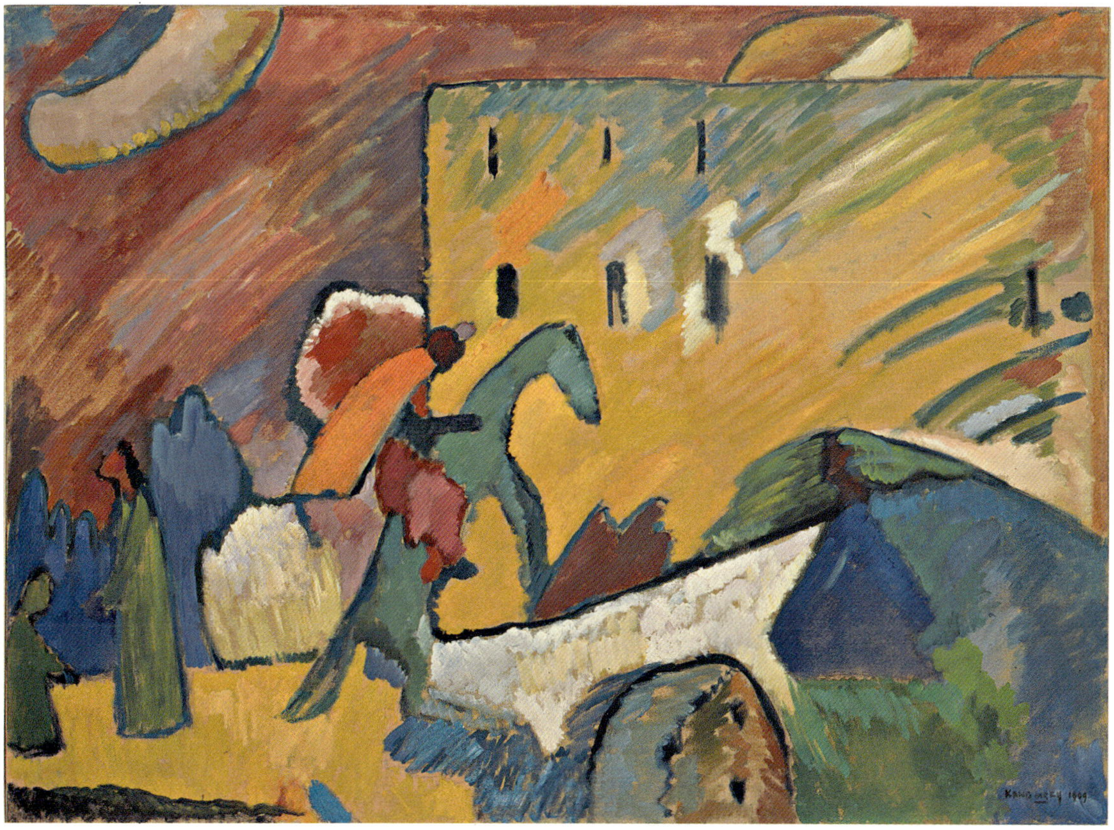

Fig. 4. Wassily Kandinsky. *Improvisation 3*, 1909. Oil on canvas, 37 × 51 1/8 in. (94 × 130 cm). Musée National d'Art Moderne, Centre Georges Pompidou, Paris.

of the work. In it, the artist stressed compositional freedom by dispensing with a hierarchical composition and assigning different voices to individual colors, thereby allowing the viewer a personal response.

The key to understanding Kandinsky's construction of his Improvisations can be found in the artist's conclusion to *On the Spiritual in Art.* There he included reproductions of three paintings representing "examples of the new symphonic type of [pictorial] construction, in which the melodic element is used only occasionally, as one of the subordinate parts—thus taking on a new form."[19] Kandinsky also identified the three categories of his works. The first, "Impressions," defines "the direct impressions of 'external nature' expressed in linear-painterly form." The second, "Improvisations," encompasses "chiefly unconscious, for the most part suddenly arising expressions of events of an inner character, hence impressions of 'internal nature.'"[20] Works in this second category, such as *Improvisation 3*, or the even more abstractly conceived *Improvisation 7* (*Storm*) (pl. 3), and *Improvisation 7* (fig. 5), convey the artist's response, or, in his words, "an expression of inner necessity," stimulated by his imagination.[21] (The third category, "Compositions," is discussed below.) Particularly in *Improvisation 7*, where the decipherable forms are much more obscure and we are attracted to a nonhierarchical, overall composition of dramatic forms and brilliant colors, the primary content of the picture becomes pure painting. It opens to the viewer unlimited opportunities of intellectual and emotional interpretation, arising from his or her inner feelings and individual imagination.

In a manner similar to music's free chromatic scale, *Improvisation 7* (*Storm*) conjures in the viewer's psyche unique images corresponding to personal (internal) experiences. As Kandinsky points out in the chapter "Effects of Color" in *On the Spiritual in Art*, different colors elicit different emotional and psychological responses in the viewer by inspiring in him or her "vibrations of the soul." Furthermore, these colors transcend the sense of sight: they can be heard and have their own scent. To demonstrate that interdependence of the senses, Kandinsky compared bright yellow to the higher notes of the piano and dark madder (vermilion) to a soprano voice.[22] *Improvisation 7* (*Storm*), in particular, shows parallels with a Schoenbergian musical piece based on free chromaticism, atonality, and dissonant harmony. The painting's antihierarchical composition is not really in any key; rather, it is full of "emancipated dissonances" that result in a turbulent harmony of vibrant, independent voices.

This open-ended freedom of organization in a painting appears forcefully in the third category of works, which Kandinsky described as a "new symphonic type of construction."[23] These are the Compositions, ten of his most monumental mural-size paintings, seven of which were executed by 1914, while the other three were created in 1923, 1936, and 1939, respectively.[24] Although the first three Compositions, painted primarily in 1910, are no longer extant, the *Sketch for Composition II* (pl. 2) gives us an excellent idea of Kandinsky's creative concept. As he again wrote in the "Conclusion" of *On the Spiritual in Art*, the Compositions were "the expressions of feelings that have been forming within me in a similar way [to the "Improvisations"] (but over a long period of time), which after the first preliminary sketches, I have slowly and almost pedantically examined and worked out. . . . Here, reason, the conscious, the deliberate, and the purposeful play a preponderant role. Except that I always decide in favour of feeling rather than calculation."[25]

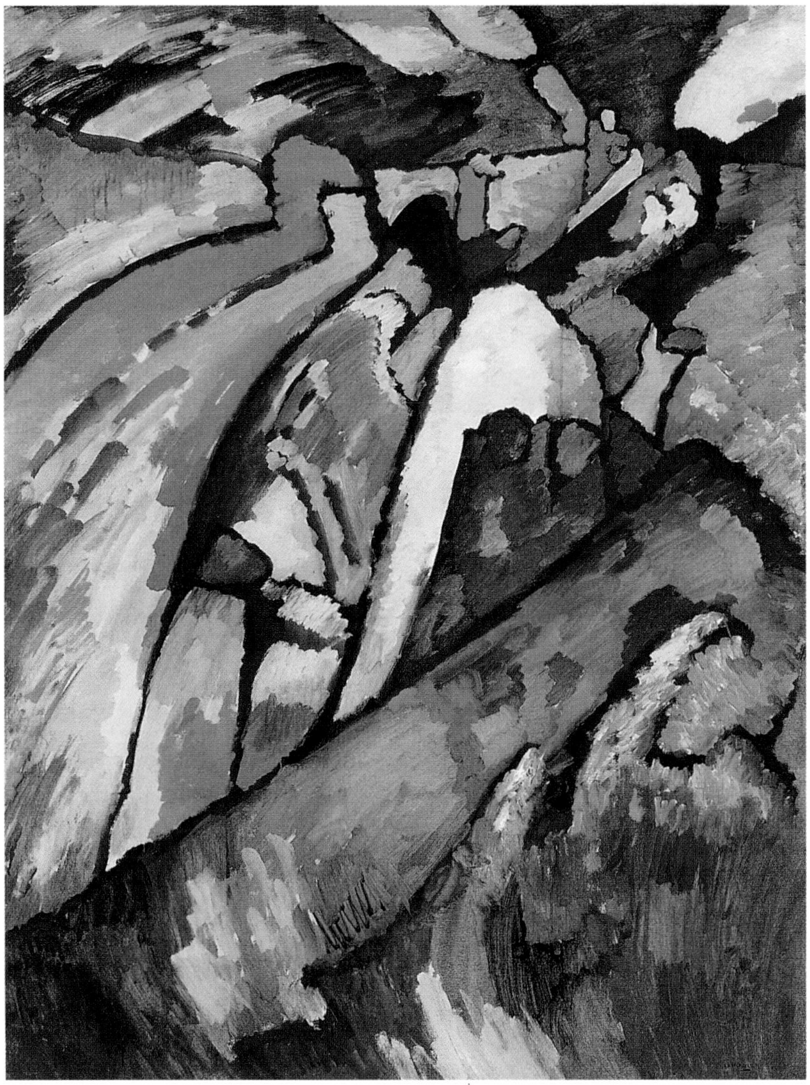

Fig. 5. Wassily Kandinsky. *Improvisation 7*, 1910. Oil on canvas, 51½ x 38³⁄₁₆ in. (130.8 x 97 cm). State Tretyakov Gallery, Moscow.

Analyzing *Sketch for Composition II* and the other extant sketches, we can clearly see many narrative elements in different areas of the canvas, yet each image provides only fragmentary explicative material.[26] These figurative fragments can help us interpret the iconography of the final work, yet we are still left with an ambiguous reading of the picture as a whole, due to the equal importance given to the various compositional parts. Such an open-ended freedom of response to very complex pictorial and iconographic motifs again recalls Schoenberg's concept of "developing variation." Kandinsky's forms continually evolve, unfolding rich visual and emotional interpretative possibilities. The viewer's response arises from perceptual clues offered throughout the painting rather than from any specific subject or figuration. Many forms are outlined in heavy black contours, creating a mosaic of unusual shapes, vibrant colors, and an exuberant profusion of planar forms. The central white element that runs diagonally through the middle of the painting should result in an illusion of depth, but it flips the overcrowded composition forward to the pictorial plane. Pure painting—the paint itself and the surface of the canvas—is the essence of the work and of the artist's preoccupation.

Other works of 1910, such as *Landscape with Factory Chimney* (pl. 4) and *Murnau with Church I* (pl. 5), represent different stages in Kandinsky's pictorial search; they increasingly show the dissolution of the contour and the emergence of flat, irregularly shaped planes of color. In *Landscape with Factory Chimney*, only the mountains are represented by outlined forms; the other elements are simply shaped by areas of broadly brushed color. Kandinsky's use of different chromatic values creates a striking analogy to Schoenberg's free chromaticism. Such effects are even more obvious in *Murnau with Church I*, where brilliant expanses of color, mostly without delineation (except for a clearly figurative church tower), define the masses of trees, bushes, fields of flowers, the winding road, and hills. The overlapping areas build a sense of form and suggest spatial contraction, bringing the composition forward to the surface. The composition is strikingly fluid, and the viewer does not need to recognize the narrative (implied by the figuration

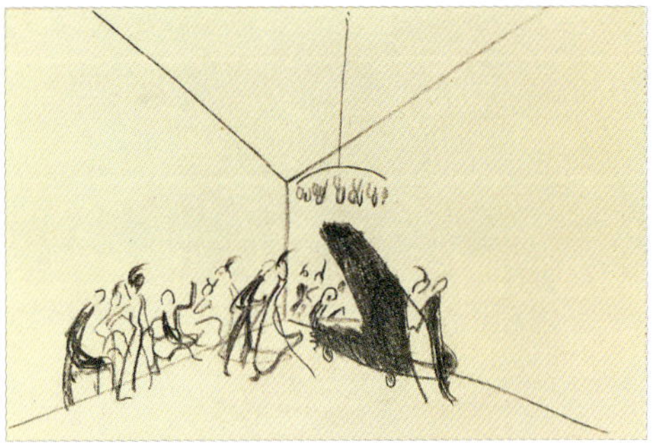

Fig. 6. Wassily Kandinsky. *Sketch for Impression III (Concert)*, 1911. Crayon on paper, $3\frac{15}{16} \times 5\frac{7}{8}$ in. (10 × 14.9 cm). Musée National d'Art Moderne, Centre Georges Pompidou, Paris.

Fig. 7. Wassily Kandinsky. *Sketch for Impression III (Concert)*, 1911. Crayon on paper, $3\frac{15}{16} \times 5\frac{7}{8}$ in. (10 × 14.8 cm). Musée National d'Art Moderne, Centre Georges Pompidou, Paris.

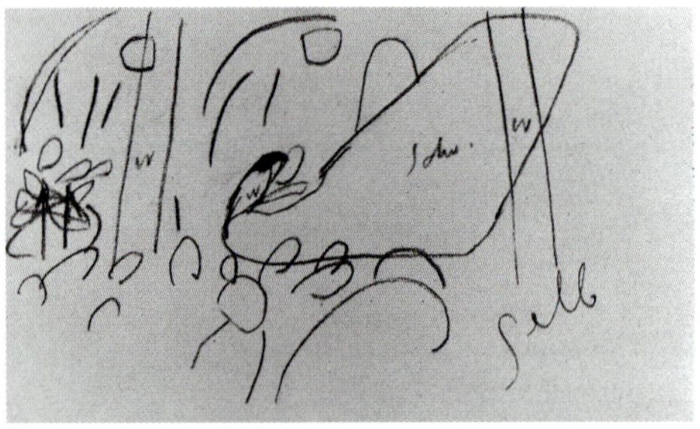

referred to in the title) in order to appreciate the painting as an arrangement of pure colors and forms.

Color is much more independent of descriptive form in Kandinsky's "response" to Schoenberg's concert—the striking canvas titled *Impression III (Concert)*, which Kandinsky executed the following day. It was preceded by two small pencil sketches (figs. 6–7) that record the artist's immediate reaction to the event and demonstrate his thinking processes. The first sketch represents a corner of the concert hall with a clearly identifiable black piano and the people in the audience, while the second is much more schematic, simply signaling the subject of the composition through a series of linear forms and color notations. This second sketch recalls Kandinsky's observation that when he heard Wagner's *Lohengrin*, crazy lines seemed to dance in front of his eyes, and the sounds of the orchestra brought certain colors to mind. The composition of the painting is dominated by a large expanse of bright yellow, which, as already noted, Kandinsky associated with the lower register of the piano. This brilliant yellow is strikingly juxtaposed with the looming black form of the piano: as viewers we can translate this visual combination into the aural tension experienced by the audience grouped on the left.

The composition's resounding overall effect is of dissonant harmony and turbulent, even violent movement, yet it invites the viewer to understand and respond to it emotionally. The loose and rapidly executed lines on the left of the composition, depicting the excitement of the audience on hearing the music, contrast strongly with the large, calmer planes of color on the right, resulting in a satisfyingly balanced painting. Although the subtitle *Concert* brings in narrative references, the painting is effectively read as a composition of nonobjective forms and brilliant colors. Like Schoenberg's different pitches, the black outlines, large black form, and bold yellow jolt the viewer's consciousness and soul, providing him or her with both a spiritual and a musical experience. The painting embodies Kandinsky's belief that "color is a means of exerting a direct influence upon the soul. Color is the keyboard. The eye is the hammer. The soul is the piano, with its many strings. The artist is the hand that purposefully sets the soul vibrating by means of this or that key."[27]

In addition, the intensity of the soul's "vibrations," Kandinsky believed, is directly related to specific combinations of color and form, and the visual "music" they produce. He experimented with a variety of solutions, some more painterly, others more graphic, and explored as well the effects of the suggestion of movement. The feeling of powerful motion—a rider rushing like lightning through space and landscape—reaches its climax in Kandinsky's colored woodcut *Lyrical*, (fig. 8; the painted version was reproduced in the first and only issue of the *Blue Rider Almanac*). The very title bespeaks Kandinsky's aspirations to embody the musical and spiritual aspects of art through language, form, and color. The emphasis here is on graphic means: the remarkable linearity of the composition, bursting with unrestrained energy, conveys the thundering speed of horse and rider. The extraordinary extension of the horse's body and head, which span the entire width of the pictorial field, and the half-suspended position of the rider, which implies tremendous speed, suggest the sound of the horse and rider flying through the landscape. The combination and intensity of the colors selected by the artist strengthen this impression.

The "inner sonority" of color has special impact in Kandinsky's unusual canvas of 1911, *Arabs II* (pl. 29). Here, the large expanse of white desert—silence—is punctured by a group of Arab riders on rearing horses, their white flowing robes merging with the pale blue of their horses and a ridge of blue mountain. This exotic subject, inspired perhaps by the artist's North African travels, brings to mind the earlier *Impression III* (*Concert*). The yellow, so dominant in *Impression III* (*Concert*), is limited in *Arabs II* to smaller but vibrant passages, which contrast with and accentuate the blues and whites. At first, *Arabs II* seems almost abstract, with the figurative elements becoming apparent only upon prolonged study. The large patches of black surge like unpredictable chords in an otherwise serene composition, a jarring effect akin to Schoenberg's "emancipated dissonances."

Even more dissonant notes ring in another 1911 work, *All Saints II* (pl. 33). Although the artist obviously returned here to figuration, showing the dead being resurrected on Judgment Day, the figurative motifs are not depicted in a naturalistic manner, but are evoked by the forms of heads and bodies. Tumultuous motion caught in a whirling arrangement of figures and forms results in a circular composition. Aural motifs, such as the angel blowing a trumpet in the upper left corner, make us hear the sound raising the saints. There is an overall riotous quality of cacophony and general upheaval within the brightly colored composition, whose title suggests order, peace, and quiet.

Kandinsky fulfilled his ambitious goal of a pictorial form that would unite in equal measure the spiritual and the musical in his Compositions. *All Saints II* laid the groundwork for a later work of that year, *Composition V* (fig. 9; see *Sketch for Composition V*, pl. 30), one of his largest and most controversial paintings.[28] Like *All Saints II*, it is devoted to the theme of the Resurrection, as Kandinsky explained in the second of his crucial early texts, written to be delivered as a lecture in conjunction with an exhibition of his works organized by the Kreis für Kunst society in Cologne in early 1914.[29] He described *Composition V* as an attempt at pure painting, but pointed out that a theme of such major significance posed a daunting problem for a contemporary painter, and therefore required a novel pictorial approach. The painting, which at first glance appears almost entirely abstract, is actually a compendium of veiled imagery representing different sequences constituting the moment of the Resurrection of the Dead: the trumpeting angels, the rising dead, all the saints, and other related motifs are reworked "quotations" from the artist's earlier works.[30] The composition's analogies to music seem to operate on two levels. One—the more literal—is the presence of musical instruments,

Fig. 8. Wassily Kandinsky. *Lyrical*, 1911. Plate 5 in *Klänge* (Sounds). Woodcut, $5^{11}/_{16} \times 8^{1}/_{2}$ in. (14.5 x 21.6 cm). Arnold Schoenberg Center, Vienna.

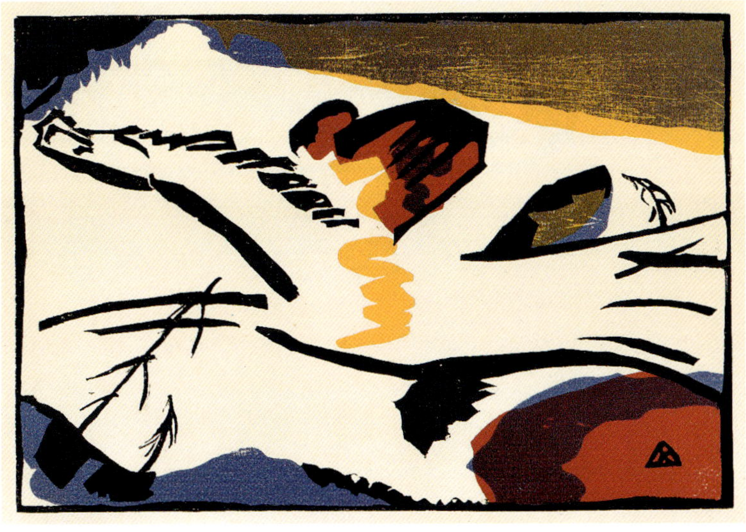

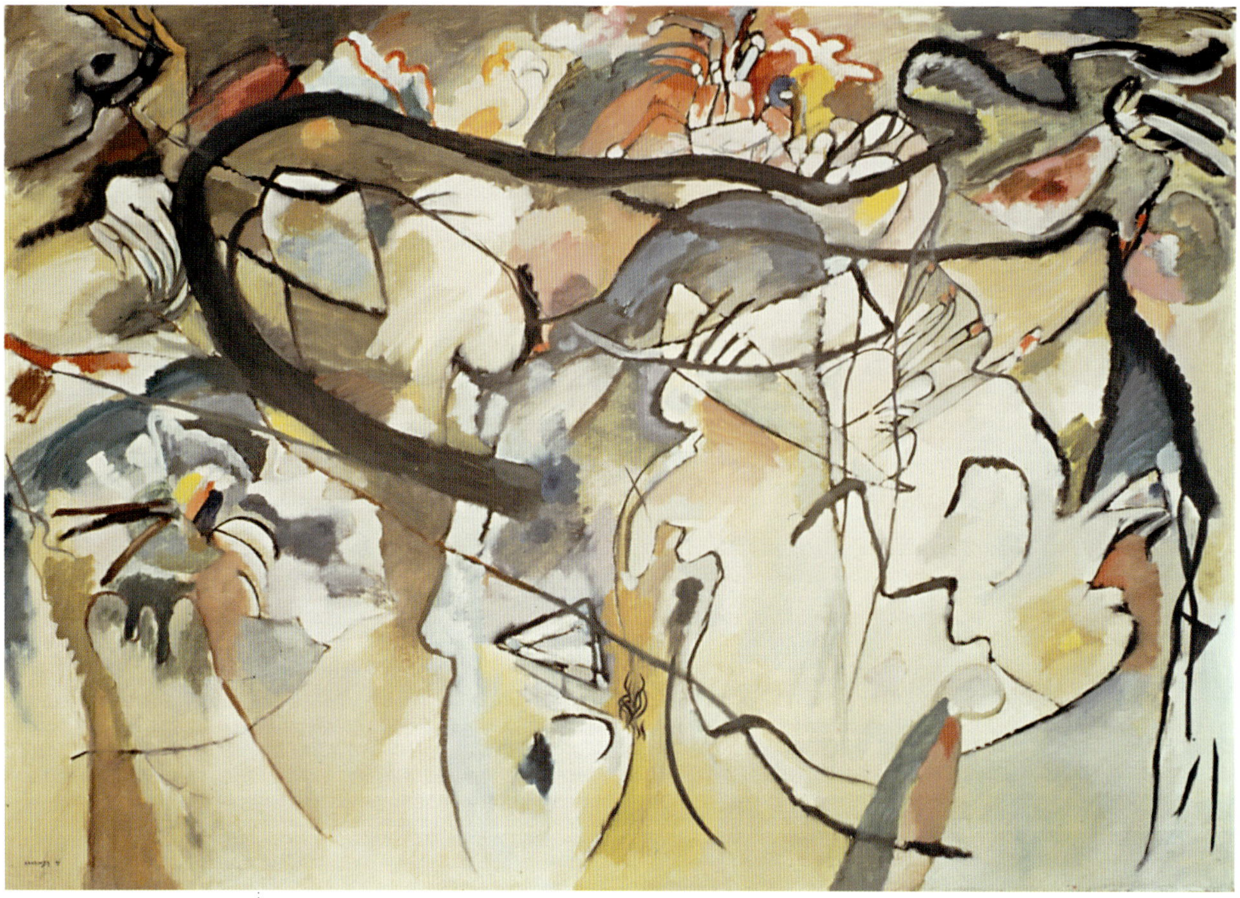

Fig. 9. Wassily Kandinsky. *Composition V*, 1911. Oil on canvas, 74¾ x 108¼ in. (190 x 275 cm). Private collection.

such as the trumpets, which are sounded to wake the dead. The large, sweeping black whiplash line dominating the composition, crossing almost the entire pictorial surface, may be seen as the loudest of these. The viewer's experience of the painting is the second, more subtle, level. The monumental canvas, executed in muted grays with only a few touches of brighter colors distributed unevenly throughout the composition, presents a crashing symphony of colliding forms—another instance of a visual equivalent of Schoenberg's "emancipated dissonances." By combining veiled imagery with the elimination of a single pictorial "key," Kandinsky made an enormous leap of imagination on the path from figuration to abstraction. He was evolving a new expressive formal language of color and emotion; significant in *Composition V* is the overall gray tonality, reflecting his belief that an apocalyptic event—any cosmic cataclysm—should always be conveyed by cool, grayish colors.

The culmination of Kandinsky's efforts to invent an abstract form suitable for the "new epoch of the great spiritual" (the threshold he believed humanity was about to cross), *Composition VII* (fig. 10) was the most monumental and complex of his pre-1914 canvases, executed within a remarkably short period of four days in November 1913.[31] A preparatory oil, *Fragment 2 for Composition VII* [*Center and Corners*] (pl. 32), presents a vibrant, seemingly abstract arrangement of forms depicted in circular motion. We can almost hear the ringing sonority of the colors.

Watercolor with Red Spot (Study for Composition VII) (pl.31), a sketch for the upper central section of the final work, presents a segment of a riotous arrangement of apparently abstract forms that clash with one another, creating a swirling composition. Like a musical grand finale where all instruments participate in achieving a highly expressive emotive effect, the profusion of circular forms and the multitude of irregular patches of vibrant colors build up to a striking dynamic whole.

According to Kandinsky, *Composition VII* was constructed to evoke the combined apocalyptic themes of the Flood, the Last Judgment, and the Resurrection, as well as the Garden of Eden, in one grand pictorial scheme. This painting was intended to express catastrophe and destruction as much as the hope of spiritual and aesthetic renewal, stunning the viewer with its inherent energy of expression.[32] Ascribing equal importance to all the compositional parts, Kandinsky places the viewer "within" the picture, creating a sensation of being enveloped by a riot of dynamic forms and colors.[33] The irregular forms swirling in an unstructured space and the interaction of colors might awake in the viewer a feeling similar to that evoked by an atonal musical piece with numerous pitches and free chromatic scale.

Although the outbreak of World War I and Kandinsky's return for a seven-year interlude in Russia interrupted the creative dialogue between the artist and Schoenberg, James Leggio has pointed out in his essay "Kandinsky, Schoenberg, and the Music of the Spheres" that Kandinsky's music/painting connection did

Fig. 10. Wassily Kandinsky. *Composition VII*, 1913. Oil on canvas, 78¾ in. x 119⅛ in. (200 x 300 cm). State Tretyakov Gallery, Moscow.

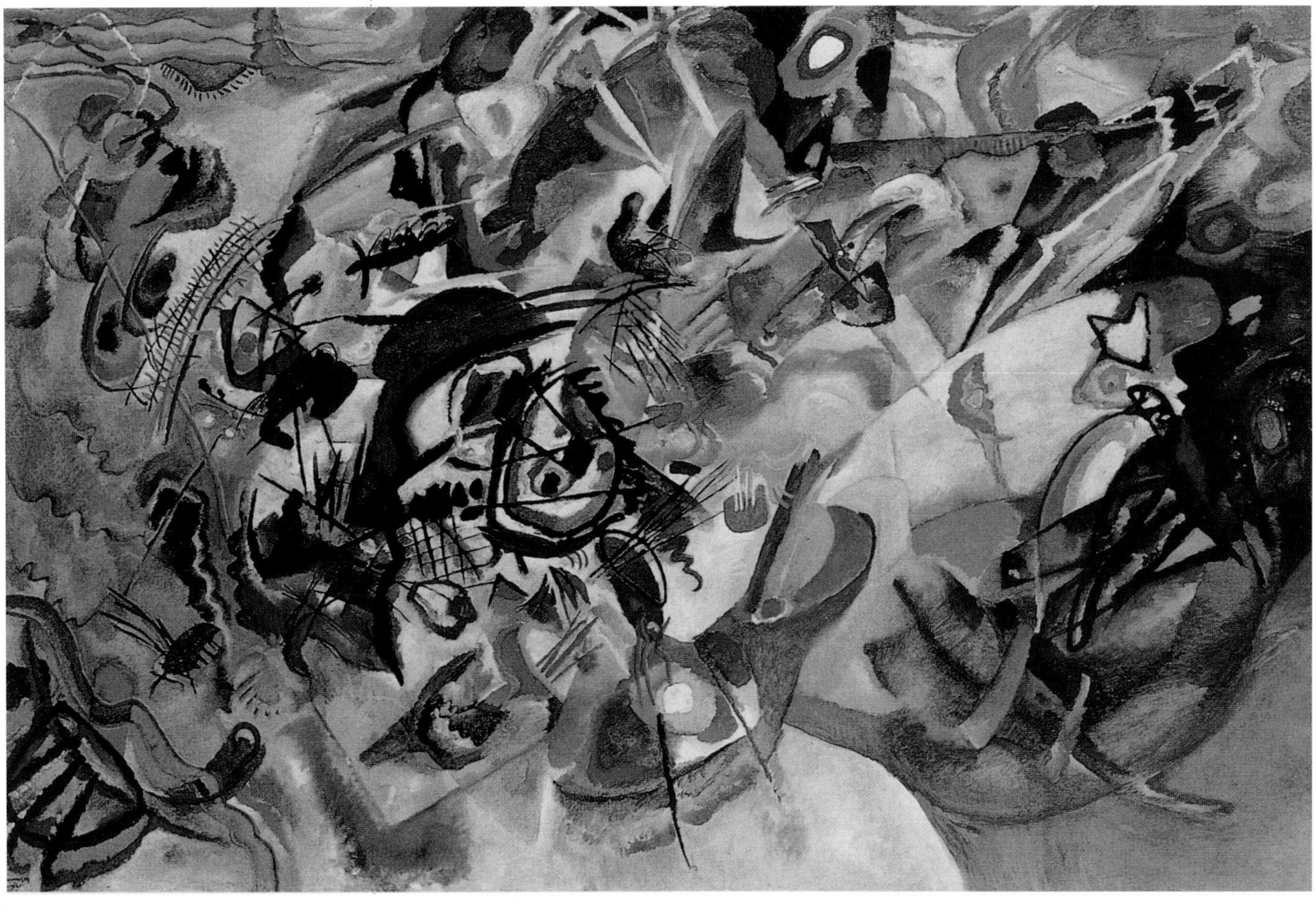

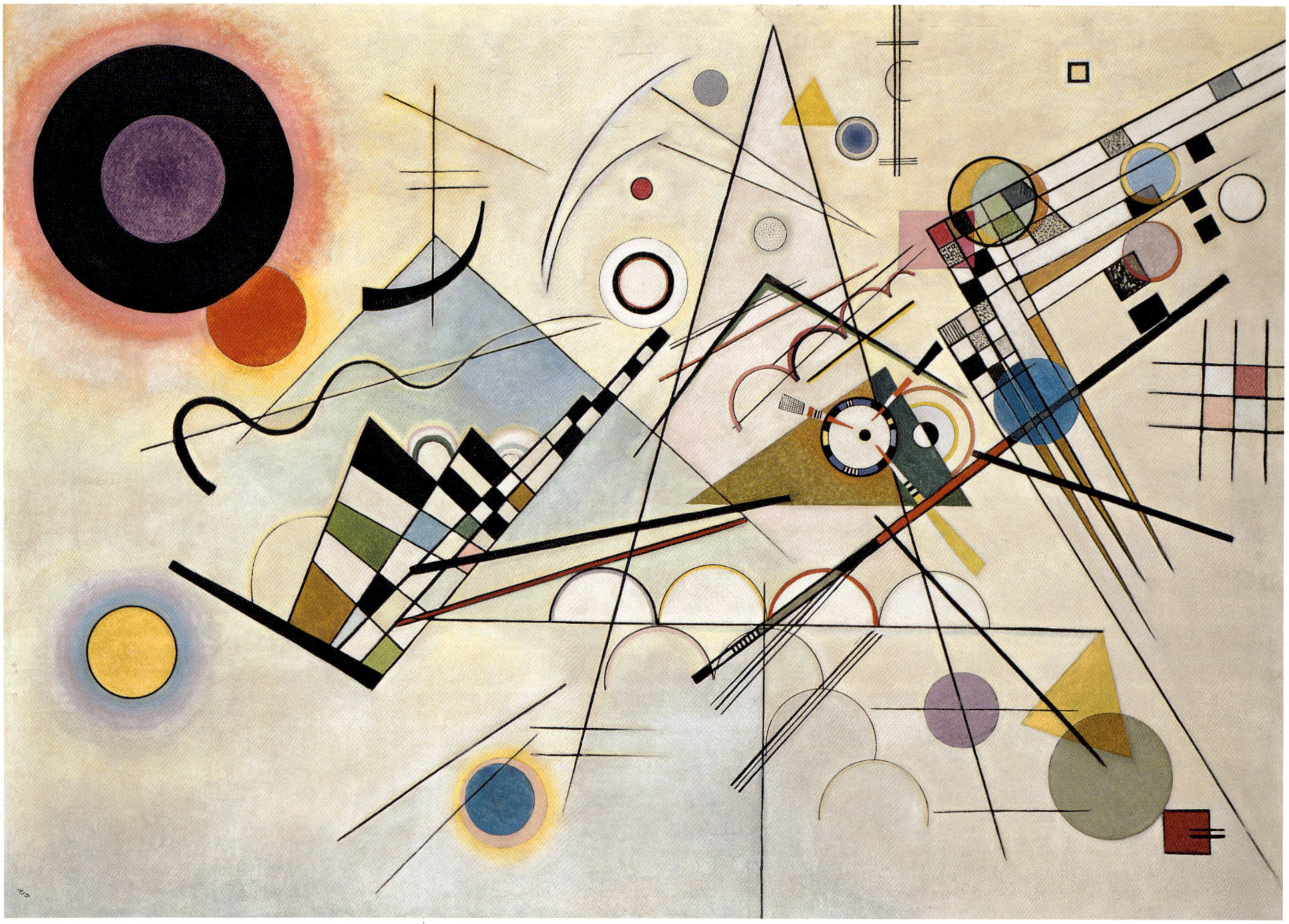

Fig. 11. Wassily Kandinsky. *Composition VIII*, 1923. Oil on canvas, 55⅛ x 79⅛ in. (140 x 201 cm). Solomon R. Guggenheim Museum, New York, Gift of Solomon R. Guggenheim, 1937.

not cease, but continued, during his Bauhaus years (1922–33).[34] *Composition VIII* (1923, fig. 11); his other paintings and graphic works of the Bauhaus period; and his second important treatise on art, *Point and Line to Plane* (begun in 1914 and finally published in 1926) present later aspects of Kandinsky's fascination with musical metaphors in painting. As he stated in *On the Spiritual in Art*, painting comes about in the same way as the cosmos, hence his ambition to paint the celestial harmony of the cosmos and to create art that would be equally universal.[35]

Composition VIII, like the painting *Circles Within a Circle* (fig. 12), both of 1923, embody this desire by means of a compositional structure of geometric elements floating within an infinite, all-enveloping cosmic space. They bring to mind Kandinsky's ideas of musical cosmology, already published in the *Blue Rider Almanac* and cited in *Point and Line to Plane*.[36] As Leggio convincingly argues, Kandinsky's pictorial correlations to music during the Bauhaus years are situated within the context of his desire to develop a cosmic and aesthetic model based not only on music, but on the analogy of geometric and harmonic principles that underlie the concept of celestial harmony; such principles—including those that guide the planetary system and determine the distances between planets—were prevalent from the times of Pythagoras and Plato to their nineteenth-century revival by Hermann Helmholtz.[37] To quote Kandinsky from *Point and Line to Plane*: "It is particularly interesting and significant that the graphic musical representation in common use today—musical notation—is nothing other than various combinations of point and line"; he felt that "painting and dance should be in search of their own notes."[38] Kandinsky considered the point to be the geometric origin of both line and plane through the interrelations of various tensions, and conceived of distinct tensions of the picture plane as the metaphorical equivalents of Schoenberg's dissonances.

Circular elements have long symbolized the perfection both of the world and of form—indeed, of creation itself. *Circles Within a Circle*, with its harmonious resolution of circles and straight lines, strikes us as an image of the closed circuit of creation, like a musical interaction between spheres.[39]

The continuous search for analogies to music permeated Kandinsky's creativity throughout his career. His great desire during the Bauhaus years was that Schoenberg would take over the directorship of the Weimar School of Music, thus bringing their pre–World War I collaboration and aesthetic dialogue full circle. In his own work, Kandinsky would always continue to overthrow the "eternal" laws of harmony, as Schoenberg did in his music, in his passion to create a pictorial universe that would manifest the music of the spheres.

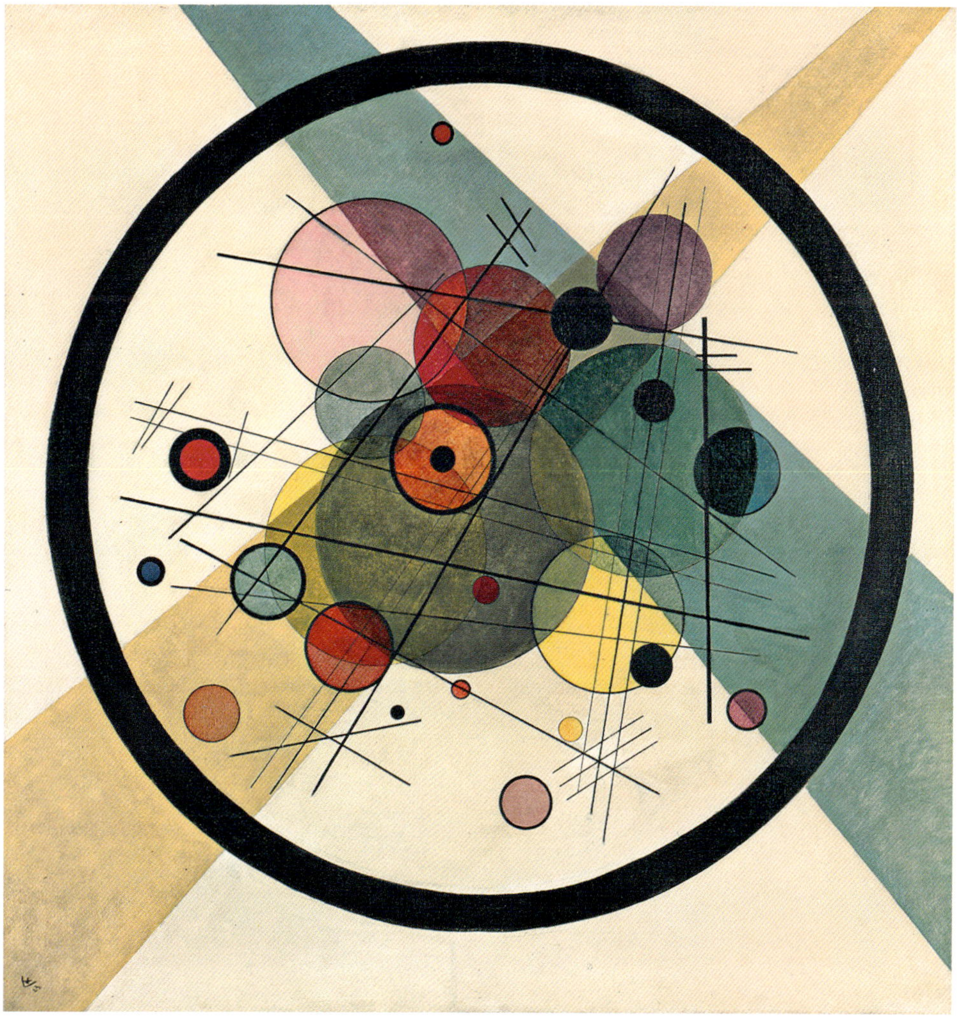

Fig. 12. Wassily Kandinsky. *Circles Within a Circle*, 1923. Oil on canvas, 38⅜ x 37⅝ in. (97 x 95 cm). Philadelphia Museum of Art, The Louise and Walter Arensberg Collection.

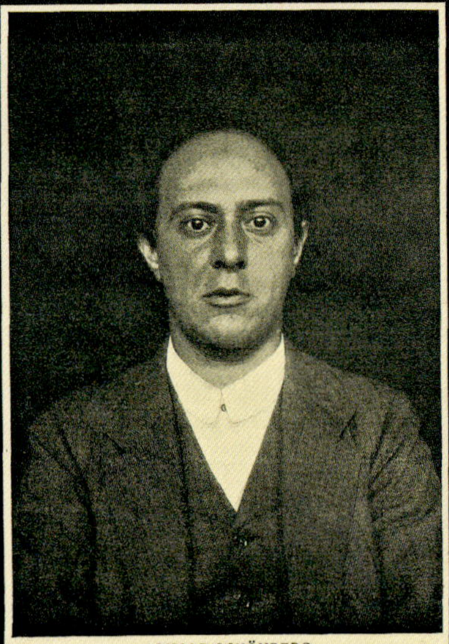

ARNOLD SCHÖNBERG
Nach einer Amateur-Aufnahme

ARNOLD SCHÖNBERG

MIT BEITRÄGEN VON ALBAN BERG
PARIS VON GÜTERSLOH · K. HORWITZ
HEINRICH JALOWETZ · W. KANDINSKY
PAUL KÖNIGER · KARL LINKE
ROBERT NEUMANN · ERWIN STEIN
ANT. V. WEBERN · EGON WELLESZ

R. PIPER & CO · MÜNCHEN 1912

First Loyalties

Schoenberg and Vienna's Classical Tradition

Christopher Hailey

By 1911, the year of his encounter with Wassily Kandinsky, Arnold Schoenberg had established credentials as a radical revolutionary. His plunge into atonality, like Kandinsky's venture into abstraction, unleashed a force of enormous moment for twentieth-century modernism, but Schoenberg was a modernist by impulse, not conviction. By 1911, he had already begun evolving a strategy for containing the consequences of his actions within a grid of aesthetic and technical coordinates largely defined by the cultural traditions of the city of his birth.

The Vienna of 1911 was the swollen capital of a disintegrating empire. By that year the city's population had topped two million, more than doubling its size from the 1880s. A significant portion of the city's recent immigrants were Jews, who by 1911 made up 10 percent of the population. Many came from German-speaking enclaves in Czech and Hungarian territories, including Schoenberg's father, Samuel, who had arrived from nearby Pressburg in Hungary (today the Slovakian capital of Bratislava), and his mother, Pauline Nachod, who had been born in Prague, descended from a distinguished line of cantors. All these recent immigrants sought new opportunities in Vienna, and within a generation most families had undergone various degrees of cultural and religious integration. This sudden influx of a highly motivated body of immigrants intent upon assimilation contributed to the particular quality of Vienna's turn-of-the-century culture, which was characterized by an articulate and productive tension between progressive and conservative tendencies, between loyal identification with and critical dissection of the city's cultural traditions. This experience of immigration and assimilation is thus the central backdrop for Schoenberg's distinctive brand of modernism.

For musicians, one vital facet of that process of acculturation was absorbing the precepts of Vienna's classical tradition, the heritage of Haydn, Mozart, Beethoven, and, more recently, Brahms. To better understand Schoenberg's creative response to this legacy, one might consider the examples of three Jewish composers to whom he was closely bound by ties of marriage, friendship, or moral allegiance. Gustav Mahler (1860–1911), Alexander Zemlinsky (1871–1942), and Franz Schreker (1878–1934) (fig. 2) were graduates of the Vienna Conservatory and

Fig. 1. The title page for the 1912 Festschrift for Arnold Schoenberg produced by his students and admirers. An image of the composer served as the frontispiece.

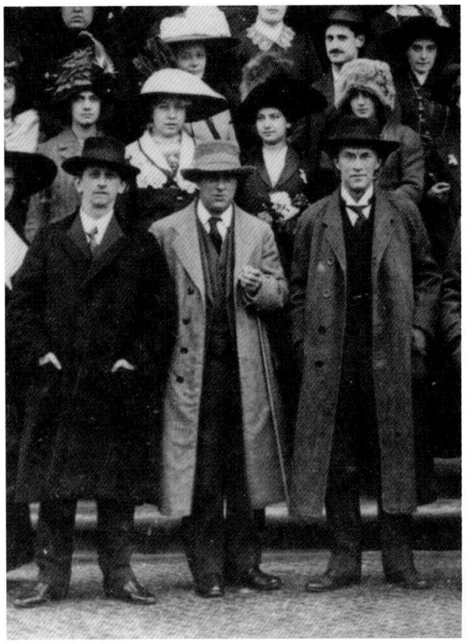

Fig. 2. Alexander Zemlinsky, Schoenberg, and Franz Schreker in Prague in 1912, on the occasion of the first performance there of Gustav Mahler's Symphony No. 8 under Zemlinsky with the participation of Schreker's Philharmonic Chorus from Vienna.

had studied with Robert Fuchs (1847–1927), a close friend of Brahms. In a sense, they had absorbed the classical tradition at the source, and its principles had readily become second nature in their craft. However, both Mahler and Schreker had spent their childhoods on the periphery of the empire (Mahler in Bohemia, Schreker in southern and western Europe) and arrived in Vienna quite literally as outsiders. It may be for this reason that these two composers were also less constrained by the weight of tradition and that their works embrace disjunction as a formal and stylistic principle. Interestingly, both Mahler and Schreker became powerful insiders—Mahler as director of the Vienna Court Opera, Schreker as director of the Berlin Hochschule für Musik (State Academy for Music)—but maintained their place on the periphery through works that insist upon an alternate musical universe whose links to Viennese classicism are decidedly attenuated. To a certain extent this was also the strategy of Zemlinsky, Schoenberg's brother-in-law. He, too, became a successful insider, at least during his years as music director of the German Opera in Prague (1911–27), but he thematized his physical and psychological insecurities in works that frequently undermine classical notions of organicism with ironic commentary and stylistic pluralism. The self-taught Schoenberg, on the other hand, had acquired his craft by dint of persistent questioning (his only acknowledged teacher was Zemlinsky), and he was alone among his contemporaries in his determination to force his way into the cultural mainstream by appropriating tradition and redefining its fundamental structures. Little wonder that it took Schoenberg considerably longer to join the musical establishment. Although each of these composers channeled an outsider's consciousness into his music, we must be cautious about reducing all their strategies to a single pattern of assimilation; for that their backgrounds were too dissimilar, their personalities too distinctly different.[1]

The contours of Schoenberg's personality are evident in the very succession of his works. Taking the long view of his compositional development from, say, 1899 to 1923, from *Verklärte Nacht* (Transfigured night) to the piano pieces opp. 23 and 25, one observes a series of works veering between excess and concentration, compression and expansion. *Verklärte Nacht* is a young man's piece, full to the bursting, an orchestral tone poem for six instruments. The composer's pungent harmonies shocked the pedants, but the real affront was his assault upon the sheltered confines of chamber music.

There is nothing sheltered or confined about the epic *Gurrelieder* (Songs of Gurre), begun in 1900, but Schoenberg abandoned that mammoth project in 1902 to compose *Pelleas und Melisande* (1903). If *Verklärte Nacht* aspires to orchestral mass, *Pelleas und Melisande* attempts to wed instrumental mass with the motivic mesh of chamber music. In its layered polyphony and wealth of instrumental effects, *Pelleas und Melisande* is a compendium of Schoenberg's self-acquired mastery, though here, too, he was pushing at limits; Zemlinsky warned his brother-in-law that the work's instrumental texture was impractically intricate: "It is humanly impossible to shade so many various themes simultaneously and each according to its significance. . . . All the more since each theme has its own timbral identity made up of the most varied combinations of instruments: chaos!"[2]

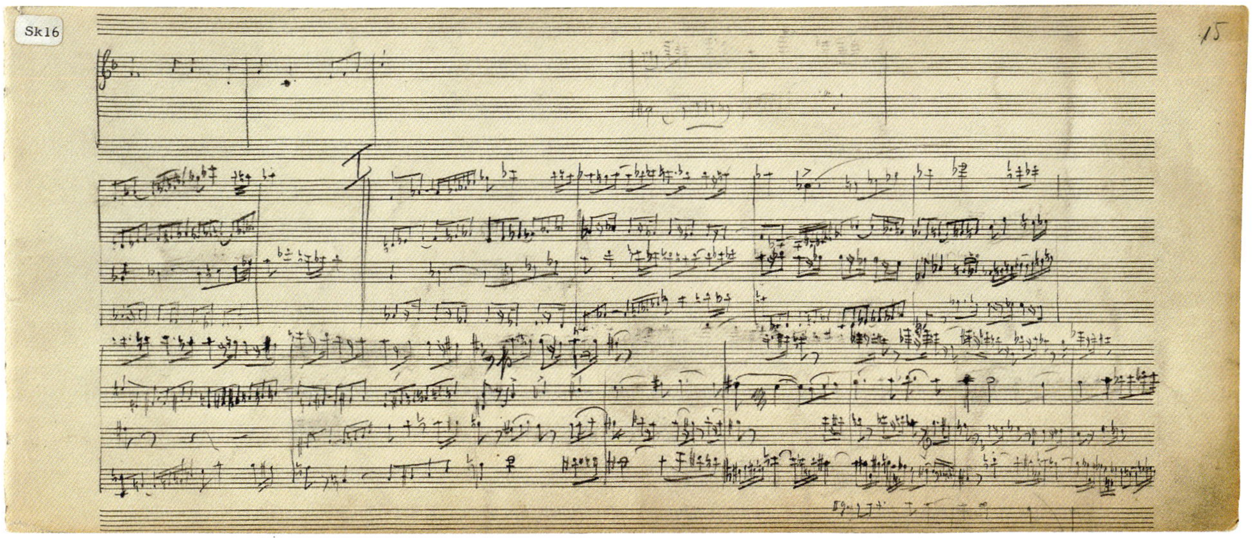

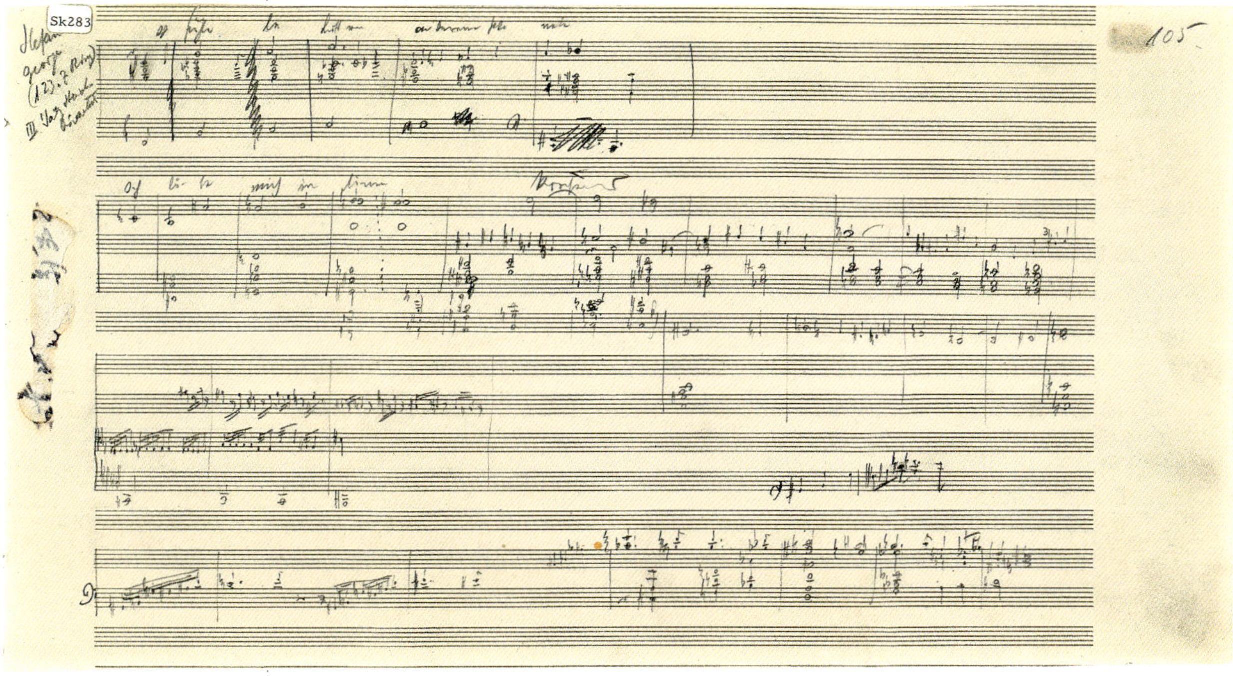

Figs. 3–4: Schoenberg's autograph sketches of his First String Quartet in D Minor, op. 7 (1905) and Second String Quartet in F-sharp Minor, op. 10 (1907–8).

Zemlinsky articulated what was in fact a common critique of Viennese music of the time, often leveled at Mahler, Schreker, and even Zemlinsky himself: that this music was saturated with information too complex or too disparate for the normal listener to grasp.[3] In these early years of the century, Schoenberg and his Viennese contemporaries mined the riches of a culture agitated by the centrifugal energies of a slackening empire. Hypertrophic density and expanse—think, too of Mahler's Eighth Symphony (1908), Zemlinsky's Second String Quartet (1915), or Schreker's opera *Die Gezeichneten* (The marked ones; 1915)—were aspects of fullness, but after *Pelleas und Melisande* Schoenberg abruptly switched course to begin a process of radical concentration that led him, via the dense but still sprawling First String Quartet of 1905 (fig. 3), to the coiled intensity of the Chamber Symphony of 1906. What followed was a kind of implosion, a distillation and further reduction of means, each work a seeming retrenchment from its predecessor, a paring down to essences, from the First to the Second String Quartet (1907–8; fig. 4), from

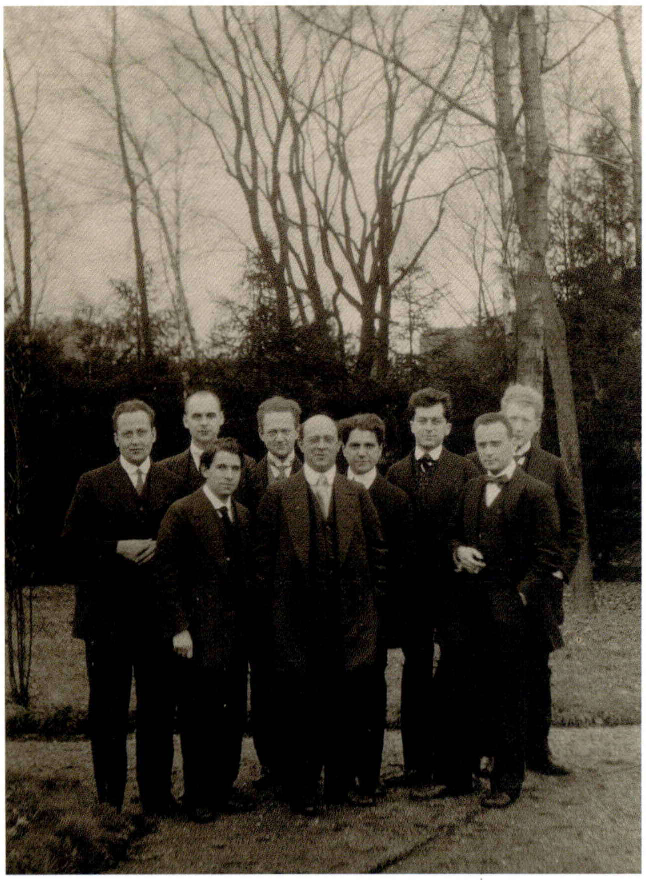

Fig. 5. Schoenberg, with some of his students in Berlin, 1912. Left to right: Paul Königer, Edward Clark, Erwin Stein, Eduard Steuermann, Schoenberg, Hans Nachod (Schoenberg's cousin), Heinrich Jalowetz, Anton Webern, and Josef Polnauer.

the Ballads, op. 12, (1907) to the songs from the *Book of the Hanging Gardens*, op. 15 (1909), from the op. 11 (1909) to the op. 19 (1911) piano pieces.

These were, not incidentally, years of intense self-scrutiny prompted by both public incomprehension and domestic crisis. And as a pendant to the ever-narrowing orbit of his concerns, Schoenberg gathered about him a fiercely loyal following, that first generation of students, including Anton Webern and Alban Berg, who were attracted by his uncompromising public persona (fig. 5). That persona and its prickly entourage formed a bulwark behind which Schoenberg could experiment. Atonality, Schoenberg's "emancipation of dissonance," was but the most obvious manifestation of that experimentation; no less radical were his subversions of conventional notions of phrasing, form, vocal and instrumental writing, and timbre. From the outset there were cracks in the façade and between those cracks the glimmer of Schoenberg's own uncertainties. With irony he sought to ward off or gloss subjective intensity—brazenly in the second movement of the Second String Quartet with the interpolation of the popular ditty "Ach, du lieber Augustin"; more subtly but pervasively with the allusions to tonality in *Pierrot lunaire* (1912).[4] Other distancing strategies, including formal devices ranging from ostinato patterns to strict contrapuntal procedures, begin to reappear, most particularly in his opera *Die glückliche Hand* (The lucky hand; 1910–13) and, again, in *Pierrot lunaire*.

Such devices are also evidence of Schoenberg's growing frustration with the miniature scale imposed upon his music by the absence of large-scale tonal structures. He found release from that frustration by completing *Gurrelieder* in 1911, a huge success at its 1913 premiere, where it was conducted by Schreker (fig. 6). But for Schoenberg it was a work out of its time, not only in its harmonic language but in the very air it breathed. The sultry storm clouds of Waldemar's passion and his Promethean insurrection against earthbound mortality must have been stifling for a composer now craving the thinning atmosphere of the spirit, first inhaled in the finale of the Second String Quartet. Indeed, those sections of *Gurrelieder* revised or orchestrated in 1910 and 1911, above all the passages for the Speaker in Part 3, are already approaching the open spaces of songs like *Herzgewächse* (Heart's foliage; 1911) (fig. 7) and "Mach mich zum Wächter deiner Weiten" (Make me the guardian of thy immensities), of op. 22 (1913–16). Schoenberg's own longing for open spaces and a change of atmosphere certainly contributed to his precipitate move to Berlin in 1911, but his creative breakthrough was the conceptual and compositional work on *Jakobsleiter* (Jacob's ladder; 1912–14, 1917–22), whose structural grandeur dwarfs even *Gurrelieder*. This work of final reckoning, a mixture of Theosophy, mysticism, and biblical moralizing, is impressive even as a torso. The fact that it remained incomplete has more to do with changing times than compositional impasse. *Jakobsleiter* is an artifact of a prewar mentality, and in the sobered environ-

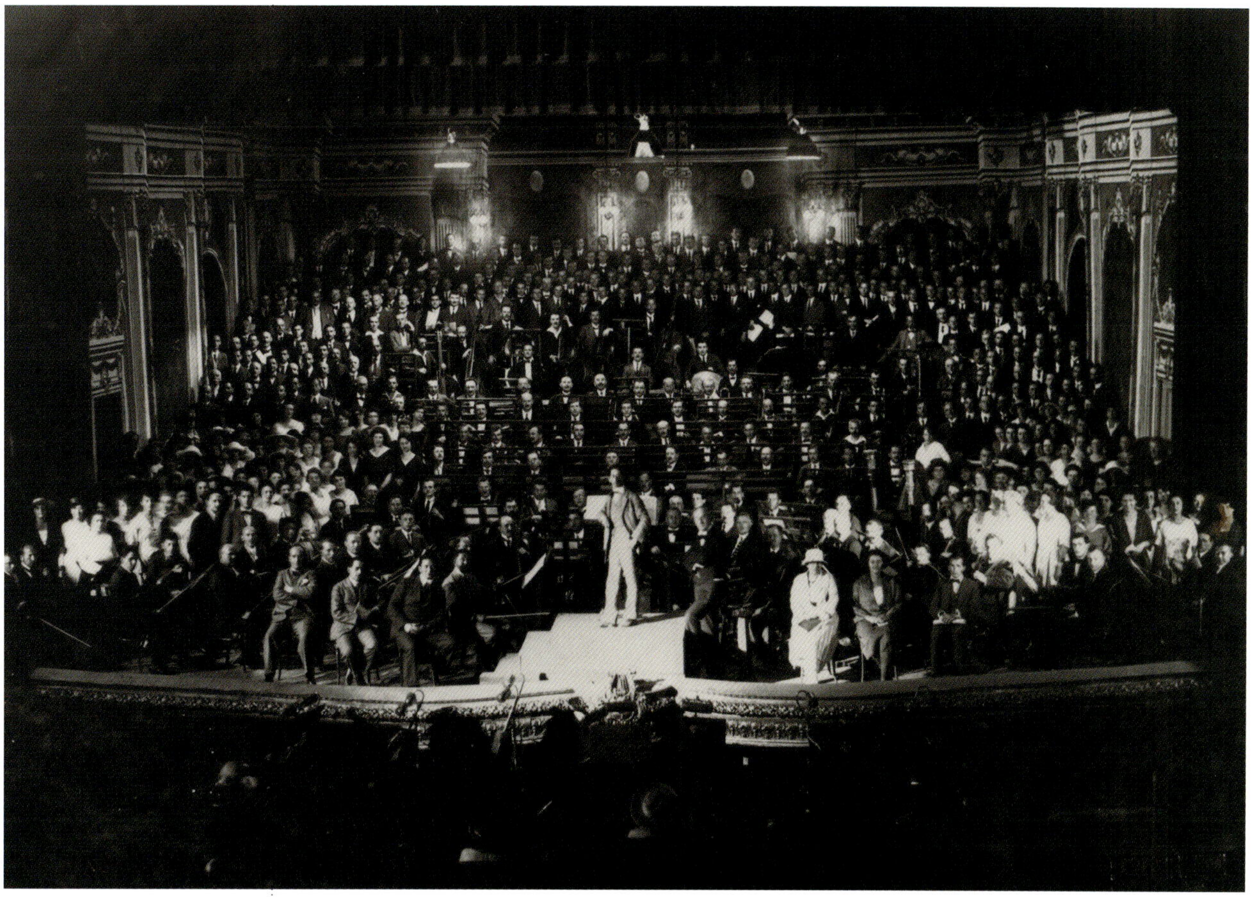

Fig. 6. After its 1913 premiere under Franz Schreker, Schoenberg's *Gurrelieder* enjoyed a number of prominent performances. Here, Alexander Zemlinsky is shown with the work's massive performing forces in Prague in 1921.

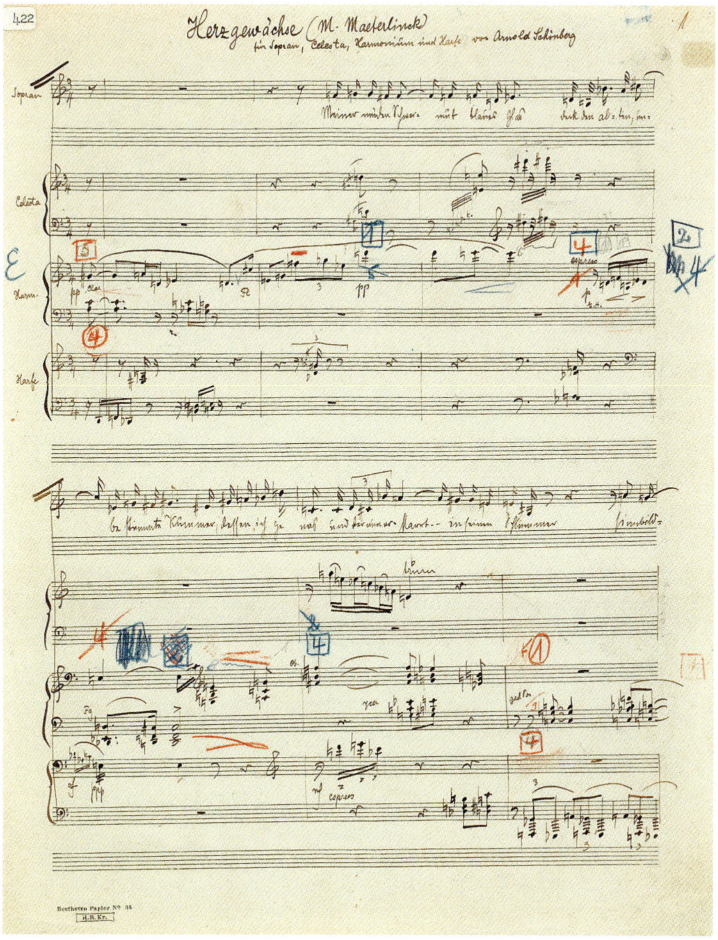

Fig. 7. Autograph score of Schoenberg's *Herzgewächse* (Heart's foliage), op. 20. This 1911 setting of a text by Maurice Maeterlinck for soprano, celesta, harp, and harmonium, was published in the *Blue Rider Almanac* in 1912.

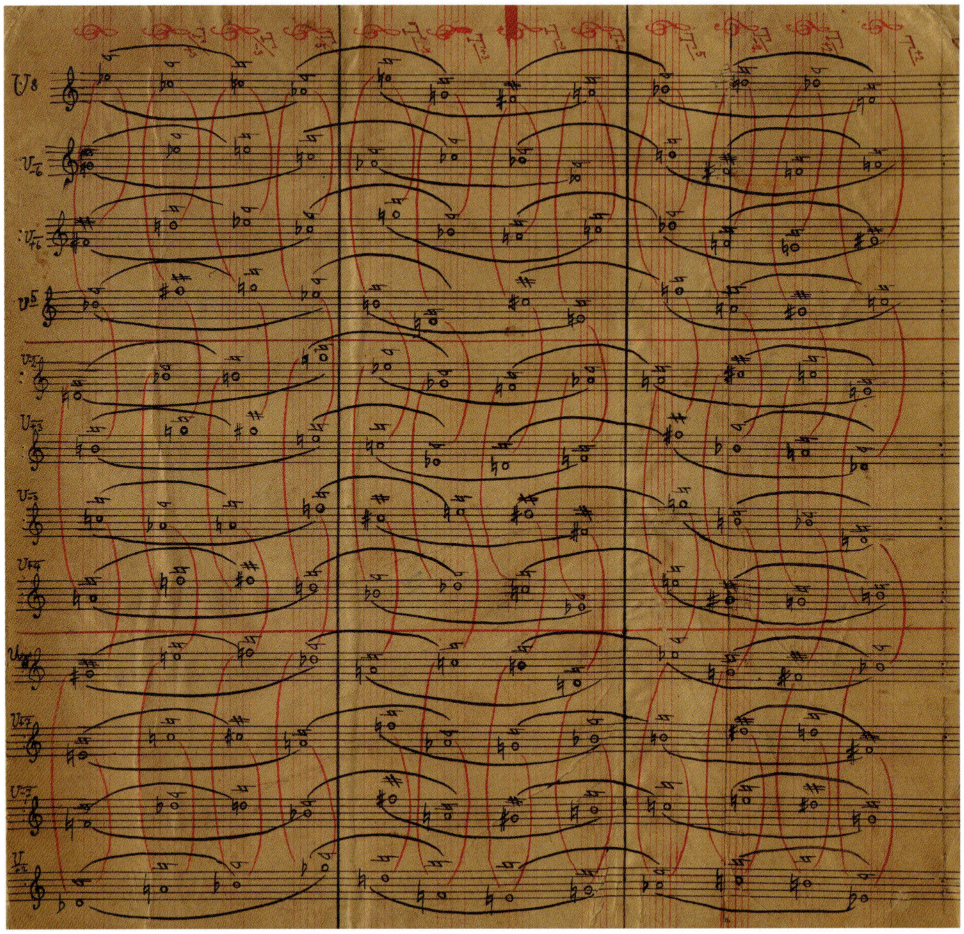

Fig. 8. Schoenberg's row chart for his Suite, op. 29 (1925–26), for E-flat clarinet, clarinet, bass clarinet, violin, viola, violoncello, and piano. This composition is a prime example of Schoenberg's use of the twelve-tone row.

ment that followed the bloodletting of World War I, such exalted pathos seemed manifestly out of place.

Contained within *Jakobsleiter*, however, are the seeds of a pitch organization that would lead Schoenberg to a method of composition in which each of the twelve tones of the chromatic scale would appear in rotation (fig. 8). The so-called twelve-tone row, unique for each work, would serve as a composition's quarry, and operations upon the row, including moving it up or down one or more steps (transposition) and reversing or inverting its order (retrograde; inversion; retrograde inversion), significantly expanded the variety of pitches available to the composer at any given juncture. The twelve-tone method prevents any single tone from asserting dominance over the others, while at the same time creating a network of interrelationships that guide the vertical (harmonic) and horizontal (melodic and contrapuntal) progress of the musical material.

Curiously then, lurking within the structure of *Jakobsleiter* was a rational, "constructivist" compositional approach that seemed far more in keeping with the emerging Neue Sachlichkeit, the "New Objectivity" of the 1920s, than with the more intuitive, prewar Expressionism. Indeed, many of Schoenberg's postwar works, such as the Piano Suite, op. 25, adopted the then popular formal garb of Neoclassicism. Moreover, with his first tentative twelve-tone works, including the piano pieces opp. 23 and 25, Schoenberg returned once again to a smaller scale, although, unlike the piano pieces of opp. 11 and 19, these new works do not represent a collapse into a vortex of expressive intensity, but rather the first steps on the road to a mastery of the material that would, in time, lead to larger structures.

Running through the zigzag course of Schoenberg's development, through the transformations of a quarter century, is a creative trajectory that despite differences in musical syntax is remarkably similar to those of his Viennese contemporaries, who likewise moved from a voracious accumulation of technical and expressive means toward taut intensity. The clarification that followed in the 1920s is often framed as retrenchment or a retreat from the brink, but every climber knows the value of a plateau, every artist the necessity of consolidation.

With the development of the twelve-tone method, Schoenberg had reached such a plateau and found his own natural period of consolidation, which, significantly, coincided with his years of self-imposed exile in Mödling, the small town south of Vienna to which he moved in 1918 (fig. 9). In the immediate postwar years, Schoenberg's works, above all the earlier scores through *Pierrot lunaire*, gradually entered the repertoire of progressive-minded performers and concert organizations, and in 1925 he succeeded Ferruccio Busoni as director of a master class at the Prussian Academy of the Arts in Berlin. Official recognition, however, coincided with diminishing influence, for by this time Schoenberg felt out of touch with a younger generation now fired by the music of Igor Stravinsky, Paul Hindemith, Ernst Krenek, and Kurt Weill, and by American jazz.[5]

Much has been made of Schoenberg's assertion that the twelve-tone method would assure the supremacy of German music for a hundred years to come. It is a pronouncement typical of those inflationary years immediately following the war, a reflection of the insecurities of a defeated nation. It is also a reflection of Schoenberg's own insecurities, which he typically attempted to mask with a pugnacious "me too, only more so." Indeed, as a pivotal 1921 letter to Alma Mahler demonstrates, Schoenberg sought to construe his compositional breakthrough as a defiant assertion of Germanness in the face of blatant anti-Semitism.[6]

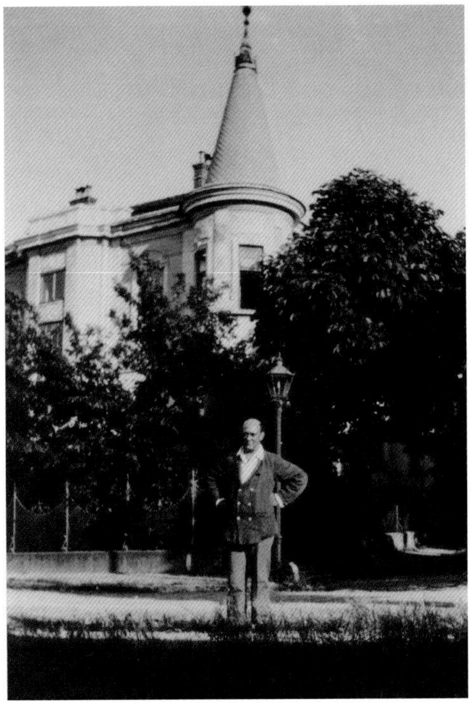

Fig. 9. Schoenberg in front of the house at Bernhardgasse 6 in Mödling, in which he lived from 1918 to 1925.

Schoenberg's claims for the twelve-tone method take on a deeper meaning when measured against the magnetic poles of his own creative personality: the impulse toward extremes, the craving for logical consequence, the drive to balance the concentrated intensity of the moment with transcendent, timeless truth. The isolation imposed by the war, Schoenberg's physical retreat to Mödling, and the experiences of racial and religious discrimination in Mattsee, the Austrian vacation spot where in 1921 Schoenberg confronted anti-Semitism firsthand, led the composer once again to turn inward, but this time not in search of subjective expression. Fifteen years earlier, the self had represented the irreducible core of experiential authenticity; in the unsettled postwar environment, the self was an entity threatened and relativized by a broader range of social, political, and economic contingencies. Schoenberg's new twelve-tone method allowed him to compose no less freely, no less "subjectively" than before, but music's materials were now submitted to sovereign control, made accountable to the "higher authority" of a tone row, an abstract entity in which technical and aesthetic, even moral and religious, dimensions were conflated. If Schoenberg's experience of anti-Semitism at

Mattsee helped focus his self-understanding as a Jew, his new method was a means of reconciling that rediscovered identity with his allegiance to German culture.

In this process, Schoenberg began to revisit his past, and in his postwar writings he was at pains to make sense of his development, smooth out the contradictions, and establish a coherent legacy. That process itself underwent transformation. In an analysis of his Four Orchestral Songs, op. 22 (1913–16), written in 1932, while he was still in Europe, the composer asserted that musical Expressionism arose not from the "logic of its own inherent [musical] resources" but from being led "by a feeling for inner and outer processes, by expressing these processes, adopting and building upon their logic."[7] Two kinds of logic, then: one inherent in the musical materials, the other derived from forces outside music, including the unconscious self. However, by 1937, in an essay entitled "How One Becomes Lonely," Schoenberg, writing of the Stefan George songs of 1909, described his development in terms that minimize extramusical impulses and stress material, that is, purely musical logic:

> It was the first step toward a style which has since been called the style of 'atonality'. Among progressive musicians it aroused great enthusiasm. New sounds were produced, a new kind of melody appeared, a new approach to expression of moods and characters was discovered. In fact, it called into existence a change of such an extent that many people, instead of realizing its evolutionary elements, called it a revolution. . . . I always insisted that the new music was merely a logical development of musical resources.[8]

With such pre-posthumous reckoning, Schoenberg was seeking to disarm critics and guide contemporary response, to encourage his listeners to "understand" to the same degree that he himself was beginning to "understand" where his impulses had been leading him.

Schoenberg's belated arguments notwithstanding, "atonality" was no "logical development," no stepping-stone on an inevitable path to the twelve-tone method. In other words, around 1908, Schoenberg plunged into uncharted waters and began a search for new bearings. With gallows humor and in visionary earnest, with diffident waltzes and learned canons, through spheres absurd and transcendent, Augustin tottering on one side, Jakob hovering on the other, Schoenberg set an exciting but uncertain course. When at last he reached the firm ground of method, he pronounced it, with typical bravado, the high ground of truth. "Atonality" was reduced to a preliminary abstraction of means, and subjective expression recast as a quest for organic integrity. Musical materials assumed an ethical dimension, technique became a category of moral accountability, and tradition, through cautious, logical, evolutionary development, was regenerated through renewal.

It is telling that in his recurring efforts to demonstrate the traditional foundations of his music, Schoenberg usually drew his examples from his earlier tonal works, such as *Verklärte Nacht*, the First String Quartet, the Chamber Symphony, or his later twelve-note compositions, and largely ignored those problematic "atonal" works of 1908 to 1914. In truth, he lacked the vocabulary to describe, let alone justify, what exactly he was doing in this music. For all that hindsight has done to relativize these prewar works as a necessary but passing stage in Schoenberg's development, it remains a period of self-contained significance. What lends this music its special value is its open valence. These are the works that remain least constrained by inherited norms or by any obligation to method, whether inherited or self-imposed; indeed, according to Schoenberg himself, they were the least subject to his conscious control. As a result these works were—and remain—the ones that prove most genuinely available for an unfettered interchange across boundaries of the various arts.

It is no accident that, in January 1911, it was a concert featuring works of this period—in particular the Second String Quartet and the op. 11 piano pieces—that led to the encounter with Kandinsky and his circle. This was a new, unprecedented musical language that seemed to defy established habits of listening. Franz Marc was enthralled by the gestural immediacy of the piano pieces, which he apparently heard as a series of expressive but decontextualized tones. He was reminded, on the one hand, of Kandinsky's "jumping spots" of color, which stand alone, surrounded by white canvas, and, on the other, of the art of the "primitives," who knew nothing of European aesthetic norms of harmony.[9] Kandinsky's response to Schoenberg's music was more sophisticated. As a trained cellist he was drawn to the more difficult string quartets and could appreciate their polyphonic complexity. What is more, he was able to recognize that Schoenberg's dissonance promised a "new" harmony, that emerged from independent voices pursuing their individual "destinies."[10]

Schoenberg was gratified by Kandinsky's initial letter, for it seemed to confirm that, as he had written to Busoni a year and a half earlier, the unconscious, uncalculated creative act would find those "who possess a receiving organ which corresponds to our transmitting organ. As with wireless telegraphy."[11] Such confidence in a communion of like-minded souls was a utopian leap of faith at the very moment when his music was beginning to present insurmountable hurdles to a wider audience. But the composer soon realized the limits of "wireless" communication—less because of what was lost than by what was acquired in the act of transmission. In "The Relationship to the Text," published in the *Blue Rider Almanac* (1912), the very essay that represents the apogee of his aesthetic of unconscious creation, Schoenberg stated at the outset: "There are relatively few people who are capable of understanding, purely in terms of music, what music has to say."[12] Schoenberg's ideal of "pure perception," that is, musical understanding untainted by association or analogy, led him to despair even of his successes. In 1920, following a well-received performance of the First String Quartet in Amsterdam, he complained to Berg that "insofar as it [the audience] is 'well-disposed,' it responds only to 'mood' and 'poetry,' while the modern-minded cling to the abstruse and only enjoy it if it remains unclear to them. The usual fate of my music."[13]

Just when Schoenberg was exploring paths that opened multiple avenues to the other arts, when he himself was painting, designing sets, and writing librettos, and meeting and corresponding with writers, artists, architects, poets, and philosophers, he was at the same time growing skeptical about whether with his own medium—music on and in its own terms—he was capable of reaching any but a chosen few. With his Five Orchestra Pieces, op. 16, for instance, he created an evocative series of character pieces that were given a successful first performance at the London Proms in 1912. And yet he resisted his publisher's request for descriptive titles, and when he relented he sought terms that were either "very obscure" or "highly technical."[14] Similarly, in advising Berg, who was preparing a thematic guide for *Gurrelieder*, he urged his former student to write with detachment and descriptive simplicity. "Nothing philosophical," he cautioned.[15] One would like to think that Schoenberg's aversion to descriptive titles, his reluctance to meet an uninitiated audience halfway, was simply his refusal to make concessions, a sign of uncompromising artistic rectitude, an unwillingness to sully his art by pandering to the public. All this may be true, but Schoenberg, an intensely private man, was also loath to reveal that a number of his purely instrumental works were in fact programmatic in their inspiration, even though such an admission might well have eased the way to broader acceptance. In the diary entry quoted above, Schoenberg wrote of his publisher's request regarding the op. 16 orchestra pieces: "On the whole, unsympathetic to the idea. For the wonderful thing about music is that one can say everything in it, so that he who knows understands everything; and yet one hasn't given away one's secrets—the things one doesn't admit even to oneself. But titles give you away!"[16] Thus, it was during the most radical period of his creative development, when he seemed furthest from his audience, that Schoenberg might arguably have found, with appropriate concessions, access to a broader public. This is the reason why his texted scores, most particularly *Pierrot lunaire*, never generated the scandals that attended early performances of his purely instrumental works.[17] Instead, with stubborn insistence, the composer expected his listeners to appreciate his music as a play of purely musical processes.

A good illustration of Schoenberg's dilemma is his consternation over the success of the 1920 Amsterdam performance of the still tonal First String Quartet. In the letter to Berg cited above, in which Schoenberg bemoaned the audience's attachment to "mood" and "poetry," he went on to reflect that the "audience here seems a long way from grasping the work's 'symphonic' and melodic qualities."[18] By "symphonic and melodic" qualities Schoenberg meant the web of his musical argument, and in a subsequent letter he described a performance ideal in terms that come very close to what Kandinsky had written, nearly a decade before, about independent lines pursuing their individual destinies: "Each voice must have life, be somewhat expressive, and that is only possible if the interpreter has a concept of the total sound. After all, if a composer heard that many voices and if these aren't ornamental, but part of the composition—where now one, now another of these voices has significant influence on the progress of the work—it must be possible at some point to realize it as the composer heard it."[19] One can read this passage as a belated response to Zemlinsky's criticism of motivic density in *Pelleas und Melisande*, but Schoenberg's obsession with clarity and articulation, his goal of making every note audible and graduated according to its significance, is an example of his insistence that the audience hear as he hears, that it understand that

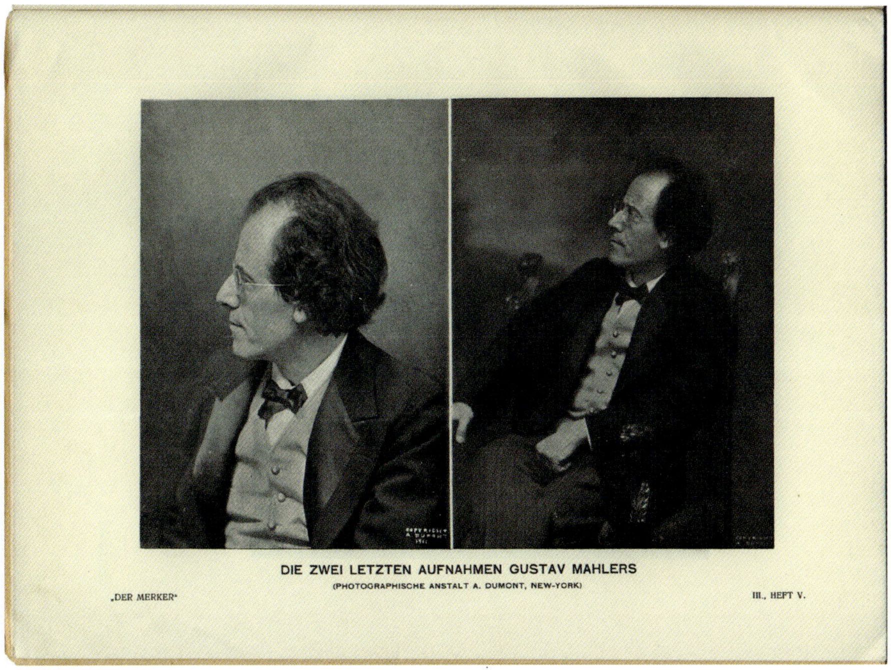

Fig. 10. These portraits of Mahler appeared in a special issue of *Der Merker* (1912), which was devoted to the composer and featured Schoenberg's first article on Mahler.

the independent expressive lines form an organic, coherent whole in which dissonance merges into a higher harmony.

In many ways, Schoenberg's vexed relationship with Gustav Mahler sheds light upon the perplexities of his prewar years (fig. 10). Almost from the beginning of his tenure as director of the Court Opera, Mahler had accomplished the nearly impossible feat of leading the opposition from the very center of power. His support for Schoenberg was unwavering and earned him the younger composer's profound gratitude, but Schoenberg chafed under Mahler's authority, and his deep admiration for the older man was mixed with incomprehension and jealousy. Only after Mahler's death, in May 1911, did Schoenberg begin to address in public the complexity of his feelings, and in terms that clearly reveal his longing to assume the mantle of Mahler's moral leadership.

A short memorial article published in March 1912 is exalted in its praise, but it is all too apparent that the Mahler he describes—a maltreated martyr brought to self-doubt by malicious critics—bears a greater likeness to Schoenberg than to Mahler himself, who, despite his critics, was a powerful, wily, and successful insider.[20] In an extended lecture on Mahler, first delivered in Prague in October 1912, the contours of this self-portrait become still clearer.[21] As in his article, Schoenberg focused upon Mahler's critics, though in the lecture he was candid about his own initial misgivings. But his defense of the older composer—against charges of kitsch, sentimentality, and lack of structural rigor—rests largely on the authority that Schoenberg claimed for his own works of this period: "In reality, there is only one greatest goal toward which the artist strives: *to express himself.*"[22]

Schoenberg's reading of Mahler is not so much a reinterpretation of the composer as an appropriation and instrumentalization of his persona to address his own critics and create a space for the authority of self-expression. This is, however, precisely where Schoenberg betrayed his discomfort with Mahler's symphonies. In his celebration of the self as a guarantor of organic wholeness, Schoenberg was clearly thinking more of the integrative precepts of classical symphonic tradition than of Mahler's more discursive style. Schoenberg's own obsession with organicism made him uneasy with the radical implications of Mahler's penchant for disjunction, including his confrontation of high art with low, of classical heritage with popular culture. Schoenberg's defense of Mahler leaves his own fear of kitsch, sentimentality, and disjunction virtually intact.[23]

Finally, when he revealed his earlier reservations regarding Mahler's music, Schoenberg articulated doubts that might readily apply to his own recent works: "The intellect is sceptical; it does not trust the sensual, and it trusts the supersensual even less."[24] By 1911, the year of Mahler's death, Schoenberg's intellect was beginning to register its alarm that musical materials in the service of the sensual and the supersensual, of visceral immediacy and spiritual transcendence, might lose their integrative coherence and thus forfeit the meaning and authority that are conferred by direct participation in cultural tradition; that personality in and of itself might not be a sufficient guarantor for meaningful musical discourse.

Schoenberg's essay on Mahler shows him torn between impulse and control, between the sway of the unconscious self and the authority of those "acquired" characteristics he identified in his first letter to Kandinsky as "taste . . . upbringing, intelligence, knowledge or skill."[25] It is a conflict of forces similar to that described by Sigmund Freud as existing between the id and the superego, and around 1911 Schoenberg had begun to confront a nagging feeling that he might be squandering the inheritance he had worked so hard to secure. Precisely when he was no longer certain of his course (or feared others might think so), he began a process of defiant public self-accounting––in interviews, published aphorisms and essays, and, most significantly, in his *Theory of Harmony* (*Harmonielehre*) of 1911.[26]

Theory of Harmony reflects the importance teaching had assumed in Schoenberg's creative makeup, but it is more than a textbook, just as his teaching was more than mere instruction. It is, in fact, a sometimes irascible and idiosyncratic debate with established tradition, though less in a spirit of revolt than as an act of appropriation. At the same time, it is a book that was conceived as a demonstration of Schoenberg's sovereign grasp of the very harmonic system that his music seemed to overturn. "Until then," he recalled in 1937, "I had been considered only a destroyer. . . . The *Harmonielehre* endowed me with the respect of many former adversaries who hitherto had considered me a wild man, a savage, an illegitimate intruder into music culture. . . . I was able to show that modern harmony was not developed by an irresponsible fool, but that it was the logical development of the harmony and technique of the masters."[27]

With *Theory of Harmony*, Schoenberg the revolutionary betrayed his profound longing for the kind of deference that in a world of institutional hierarchies might be won by a professorship at the Vienna Academy. That he rejected such a position in 1912 rests less, one suspects, with his stated aversion to Vienna than with the fact that conditions for his acceptance were not yet met. Schoenberg did not crave respect for his intellect and integrity—this he received even from his critics; he craved authority, and that could come only when his music, not his personality, had established its legitimacy. Schoenberg was fifty before the musical world would acknowledge that legitimacy and before he himself had become convinced that, with the development of a method that provided for the renewal of the classical tradition, he had fully earned that authority.

One can argue that Schoenberg's struggle between subjective authenticity and material integrity was the beginning of his own "retreat from the brink." There is much in the music of his so-called atonal period that Schoenberg, in another culture, or given broader horizons, might have developed further. Marc suspected that the composer might have been inspired by the "musical art-means of the Ori-

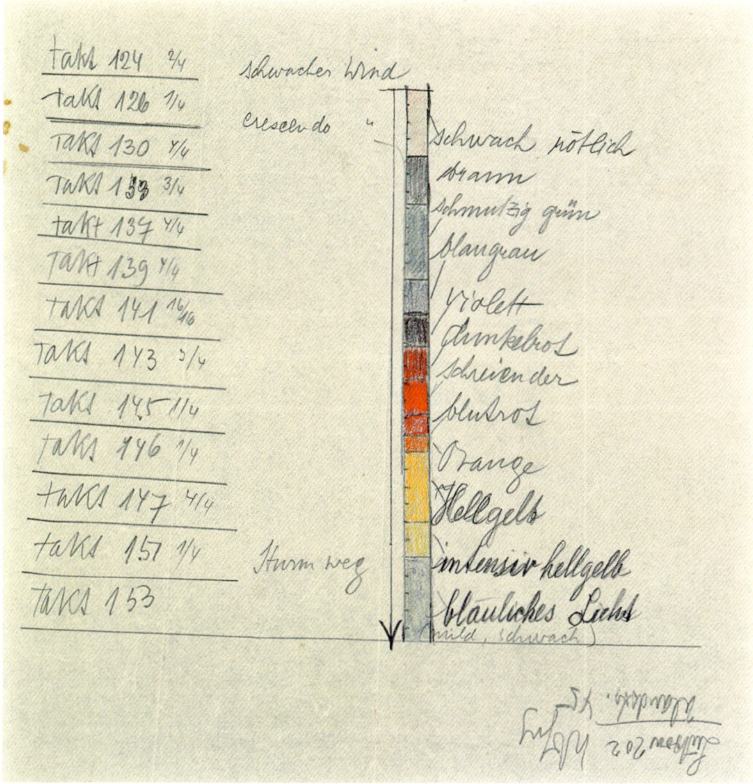

Fig. 11. In the third scene of his opera *Die glückliche Hand* (1910–13), Schoenberg called for a lighting crescendo whose successive colors he illustrated on this sheet.

ent," but Schoenberg had little interest in the non-Western music that so stimulated Debussy, Ravel, and the Russian Orientalists.[28] Schoenberg's innovations were more truly his own, more wholly the product of his individual genius, and the extravagance of his imagination can be gauged by the number of avenues he failed to pursue.

The *Klangfarben*, or timbral colors, explored in the third of the op. 16 Orchestra Pieces and discussed in passing in *Theory of Harmony* remained largely unexplored in subsequent works. Among Schoenberg's Viennese contemporaries, only Franz Schreker would treat timbre with similar sophistication.[29] Likewise, Schoenberg's "color crescendo" in *Die glückliche Hand* (fig. 11), in which a sequence of lighting effects are coordinated with a succession of specific musical gestures, brings to mind Kandinsky's visionary stage directions for *Der gelbe Klang* or the synaesthetic experiments of Alexander Scriabin. In another area, Schoenberg's radical contractions of phrase structure and form in works such as the op. 19 piano pieces and the op. 15 George songs were profitably continued by Webern, while in his own later works Schoenberg returned, in the main, to variations upon classical models. Schoenberg's flirtation with tonal references within an atonal context—so apparent, for instance, in the Second String Quartet and *Pierrot lunaire*—is largely submerged in his later works, but became a central component in Berg's music and even shaped that composer's handling of the twelve-tone method. The fact that "atonal" has become a blanket description for this prewar period of Schoenberg's development and that the twelve-tone method has been seen as its logical consequence have served to delimit his concerns to the realm of pitch and harmony, thus obscuring the incredible wealth of possibilities he actually explored.

But Schoenberg would not have been Schoenberg had he pursued those multiple paths. He needed to make his stand in precisely that area where the tension with his cultural environment was most acute. In other words, his music would not be so taut, energetic, and focused without the background of the integrative Viennese classical tradition from which he was unwilling to stray. His eventual development of the dodecaphonic method was neither a "retreat" nor a triumphant inevitability, but rather a negotiated settlement of that tension between revolutionary impulse and custodial responsibility that so characterized Vienna's turn-of-the-century cultural physiognomy.

The Arnold Schoenberg that Wassily Kandinsky encountered in 1911 was an artist who had set himself free in a sea of possibilities because the harbors he sought lay beyond any known horizon. Schoenberg had transcendent goals, but like any seafarer he came to recognize that his first loyalty was owed to the vessel of his voyage: music, the medium of his art.

Plates

The Concert

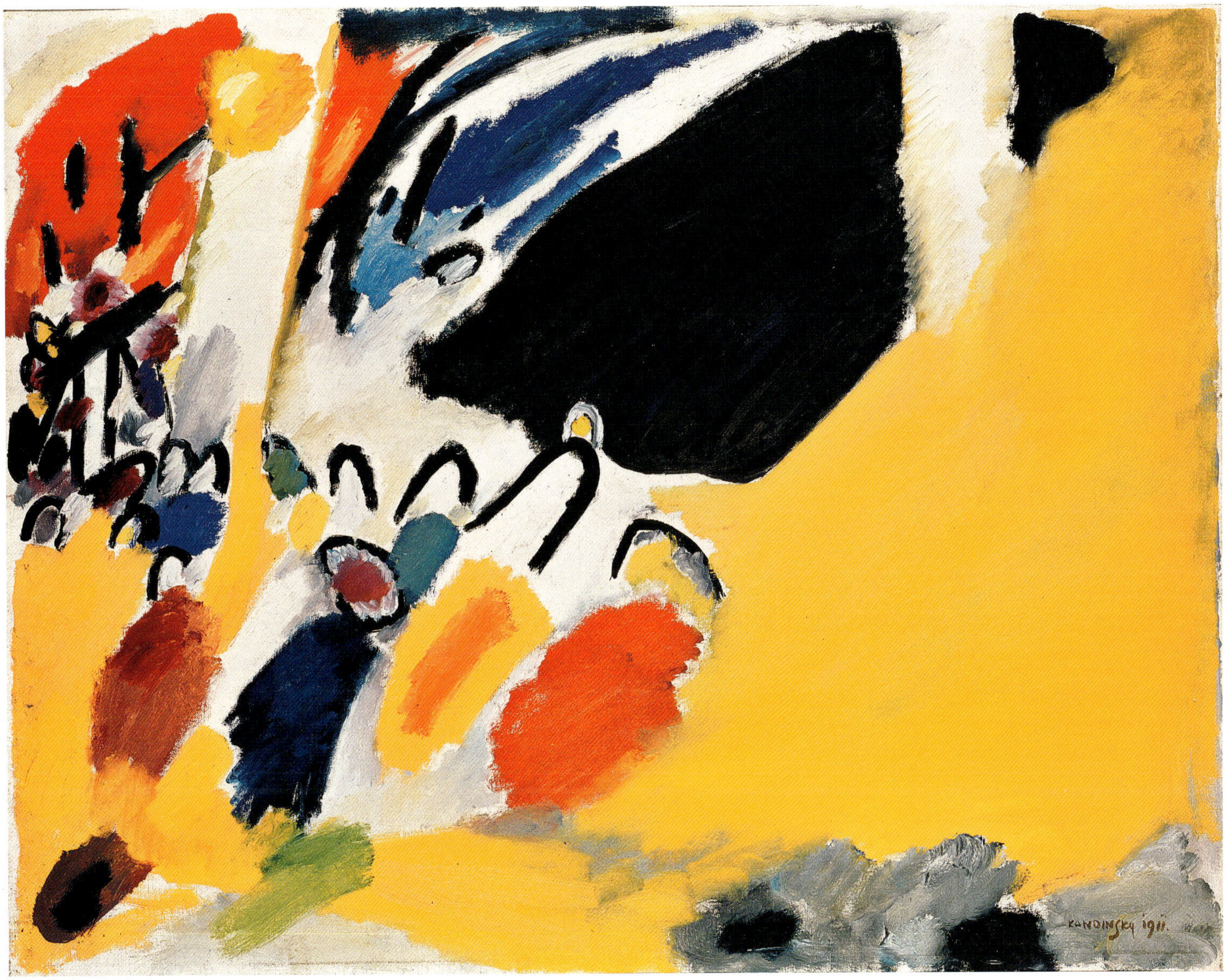

1 **Wassily Kandinsky** (Russian, 1866–1944) *Impression III (Concert)*, 1911. Oil on canvas, 30½ x 39⅜ in. (77.5 x 100 cm). Städtische Galerie im Lenbachhaus, Munich, GMS 78.

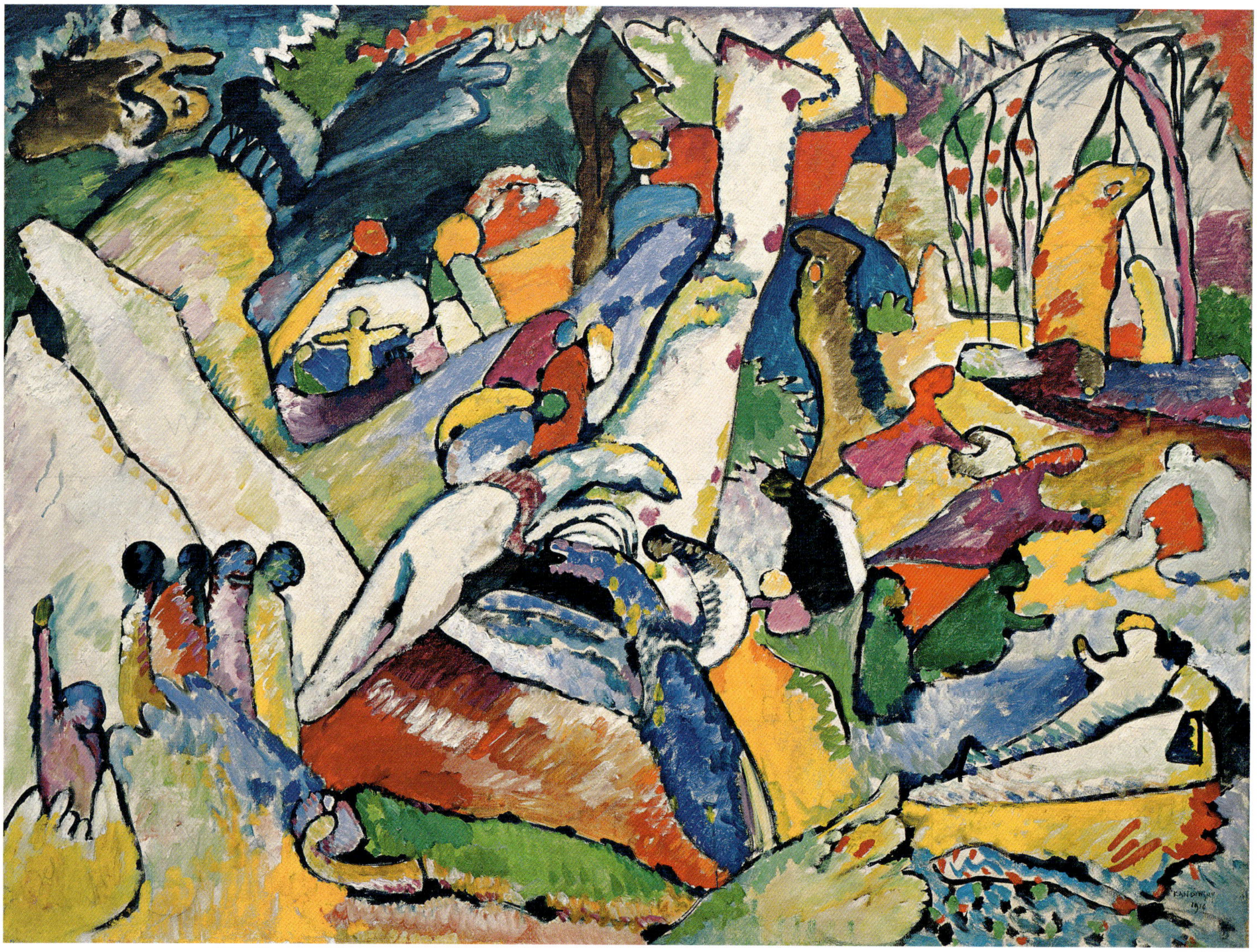

2 **Wassily Kandinsky** *Sketch for Composition II*, 1909–10. Oil on canvas, 38⅜ x 51⅝ in. (97.5 x 131.2 cm). Solomon R. Guggenheim Museum, New York, 45.961.

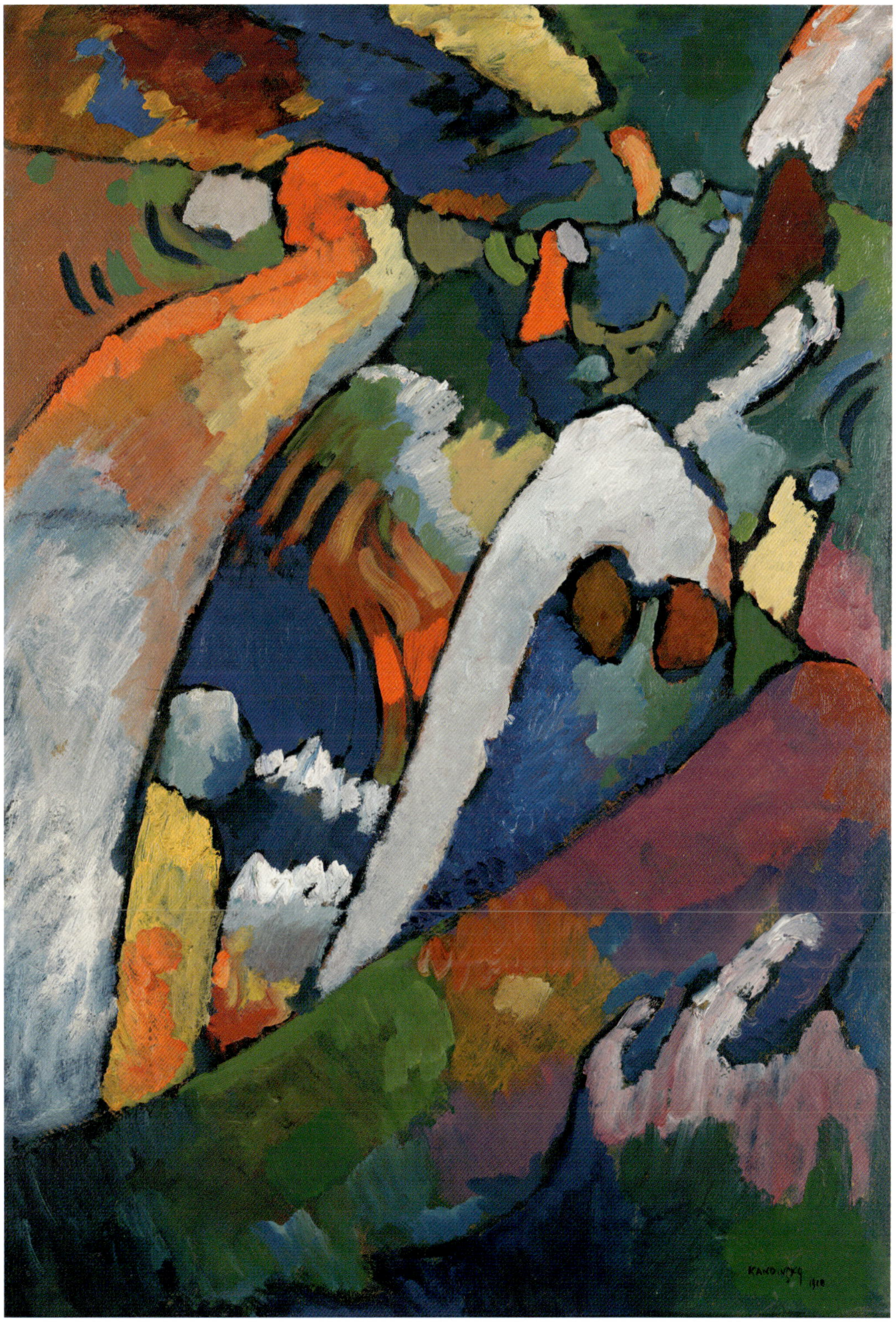

3 **Wassily Kandinsky** *Improvisation 7 (Storm)*, 1910. Oil on pasteboard, 27 9/16 x 19 3/16 in. (70 x 48.7 cm). Yale University Art Gallery, Gift of Collection Société Anonyme, 1941.527.

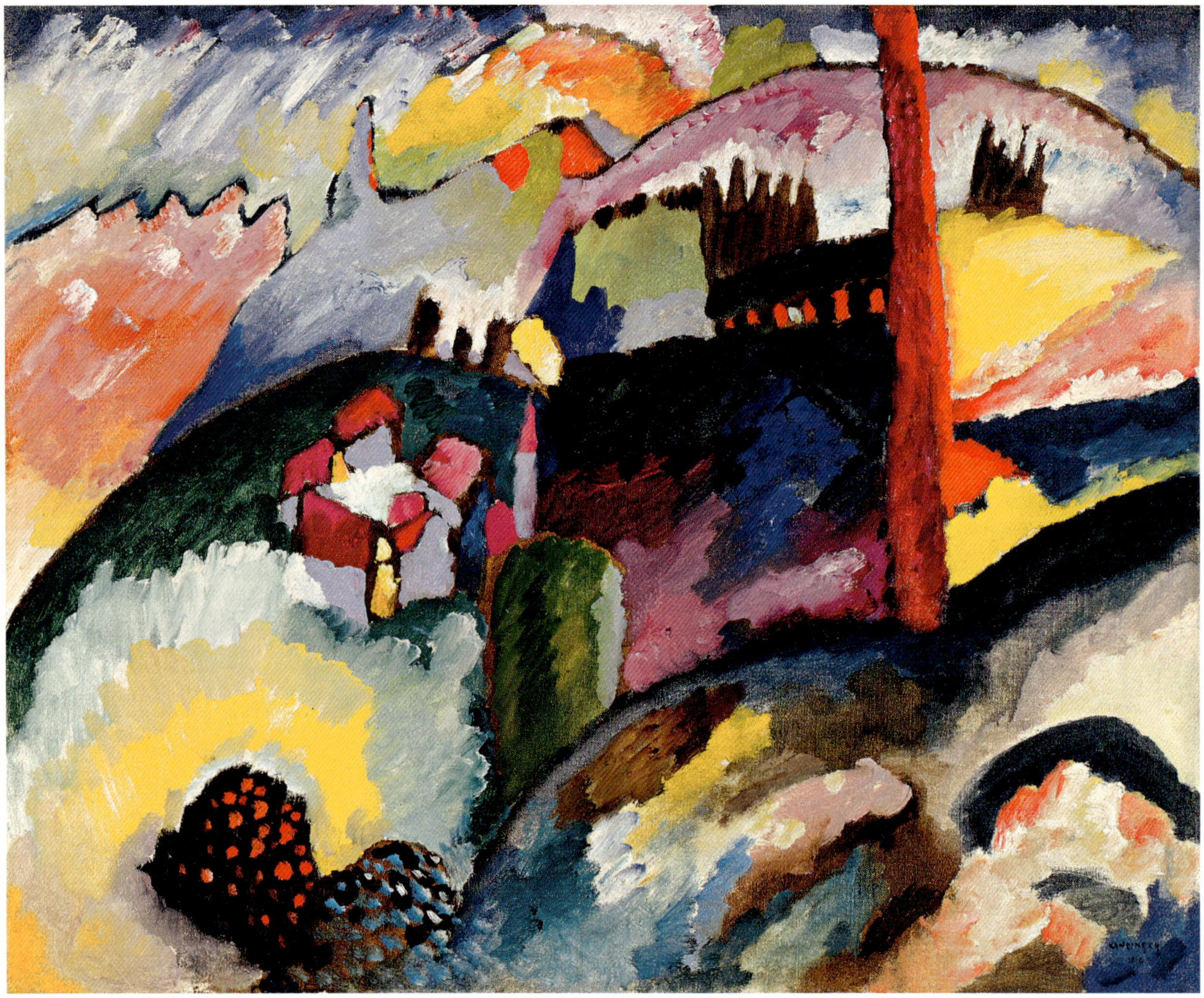

4 **Wassily Kandinsky** *Landscape with Factory Chimney*, 1910. Oil on canvas, 26 x 32¼ in. (66.2 x 82 cm). Solomon R. Guggenheim Museum, New York, Gift of Solomon R. Guggenheim, 1941, 41.504.

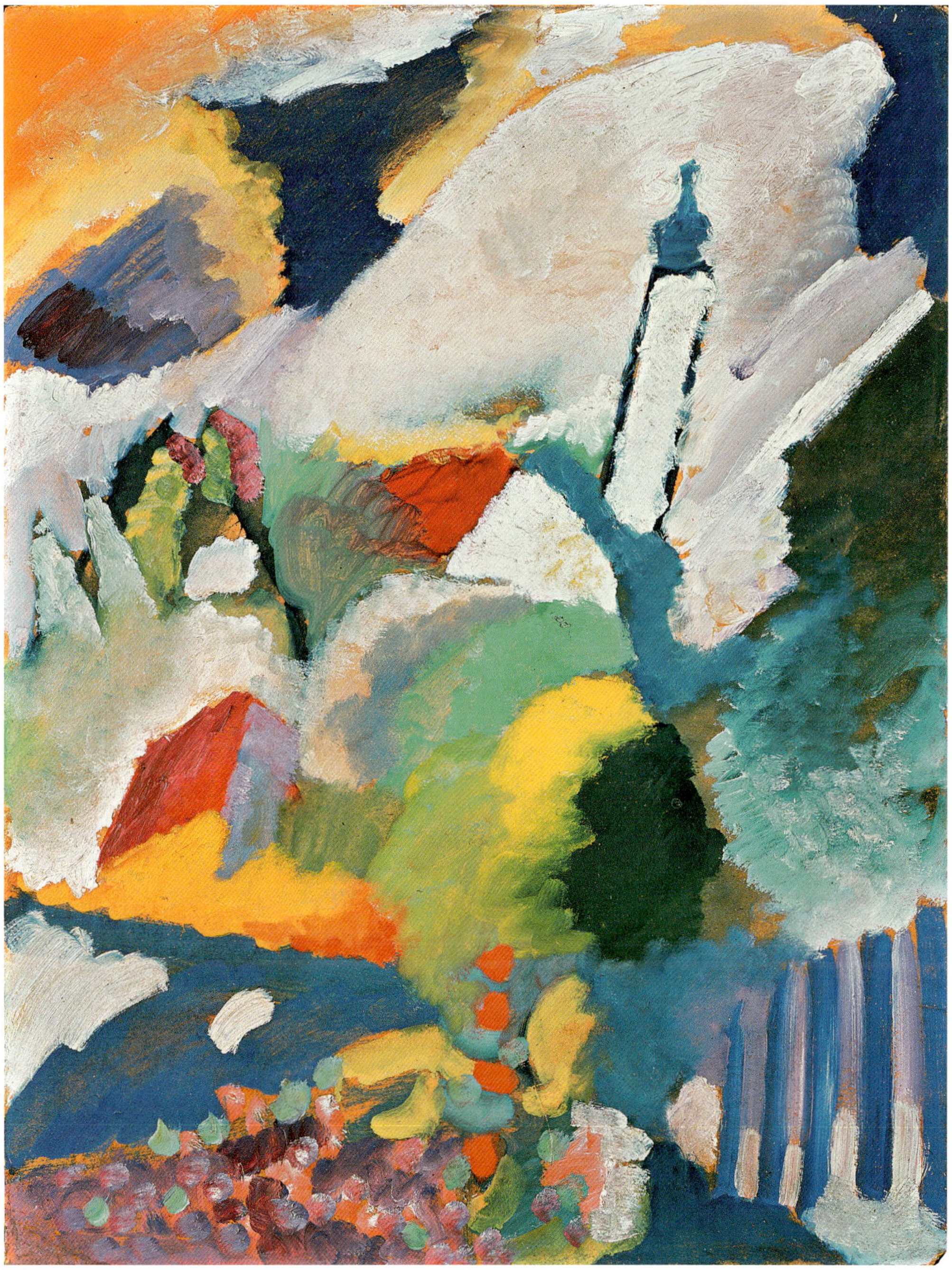

5 **Wassily Kandinsky** *Murnau with Church I*, 1910. Oil and watercolor on cardboard, 25½ x 19¾ in. (64.7 x 50.2 cm). Städtische Galerie im Lenbachhaus, Munich, GMS 59.

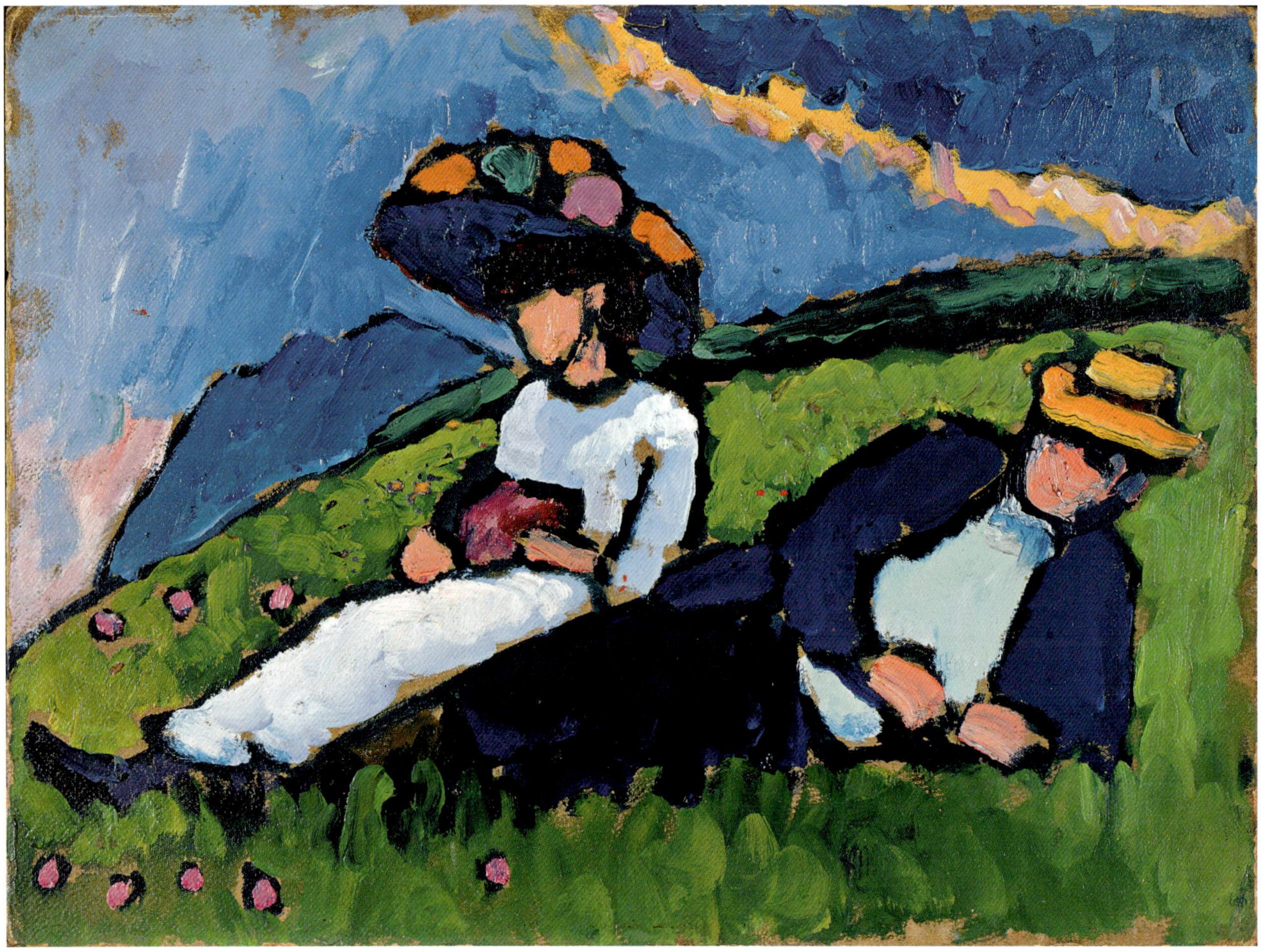

 6 **Gabriele Münter** (German, 1877–1962) *Jawlensky and Werefkin*, 1909. Oil on cardboard, 12⅞ x 17½ in. (32.7 x 44.5 cm). Städtische Galerie im Lenbachhaus, Munich, GMS 655.

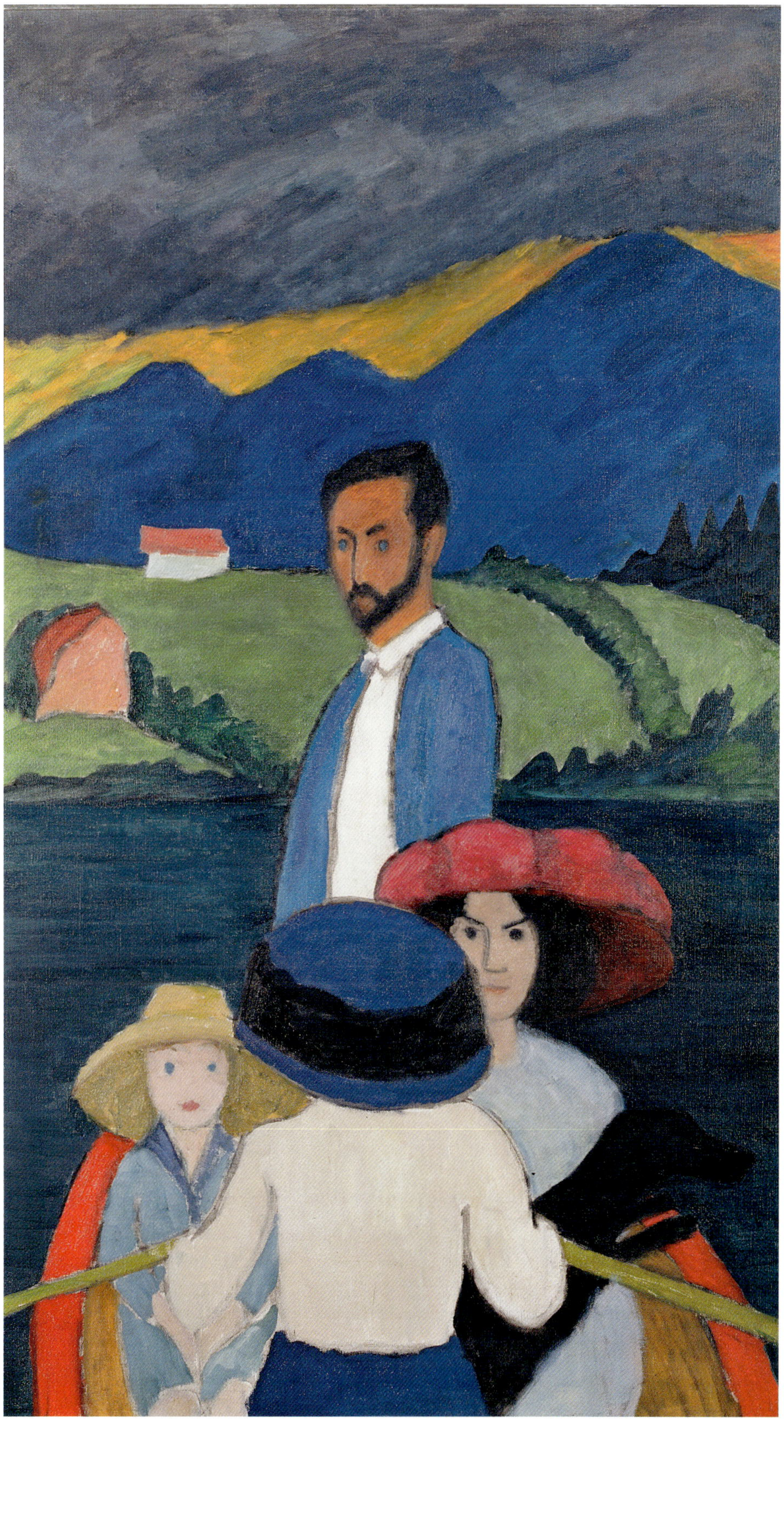

7 **Gabriele Münter** *Boating*, 1910. Oil on canvas, 49¼ x 28⅞ in. (125.1 x 73.3 cm). Milwaukee Art Museum, Gift of Mrs. Harry Lynde Bradley, M1977.128.

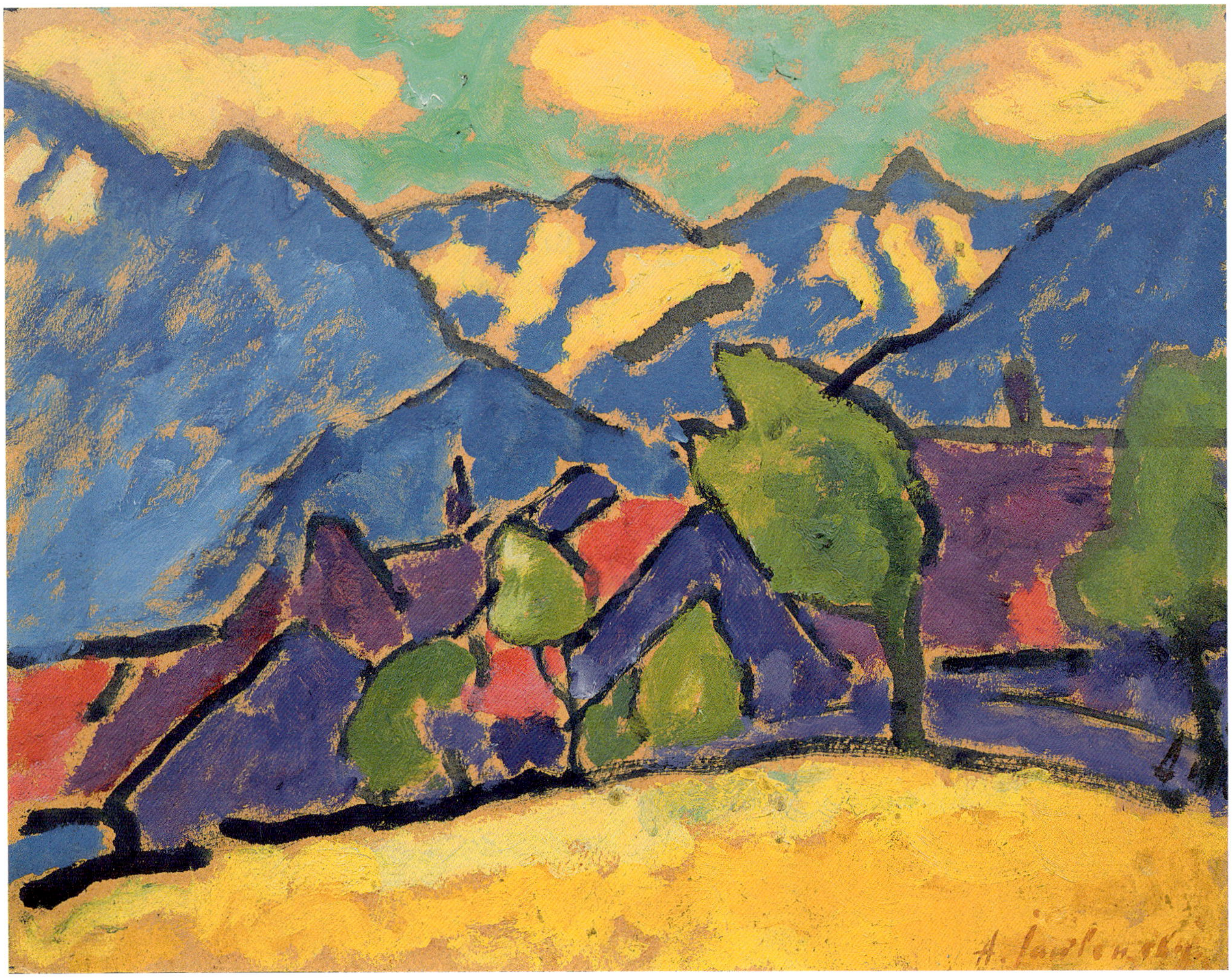

8 **Alexei von Jawlensky** (Russian, 1864–1941) *Gelber Klang* (Yellow sound), 1908. Oil on cardboard, 13 x 17½ in. (33 x 44.5 cm). Private collection.

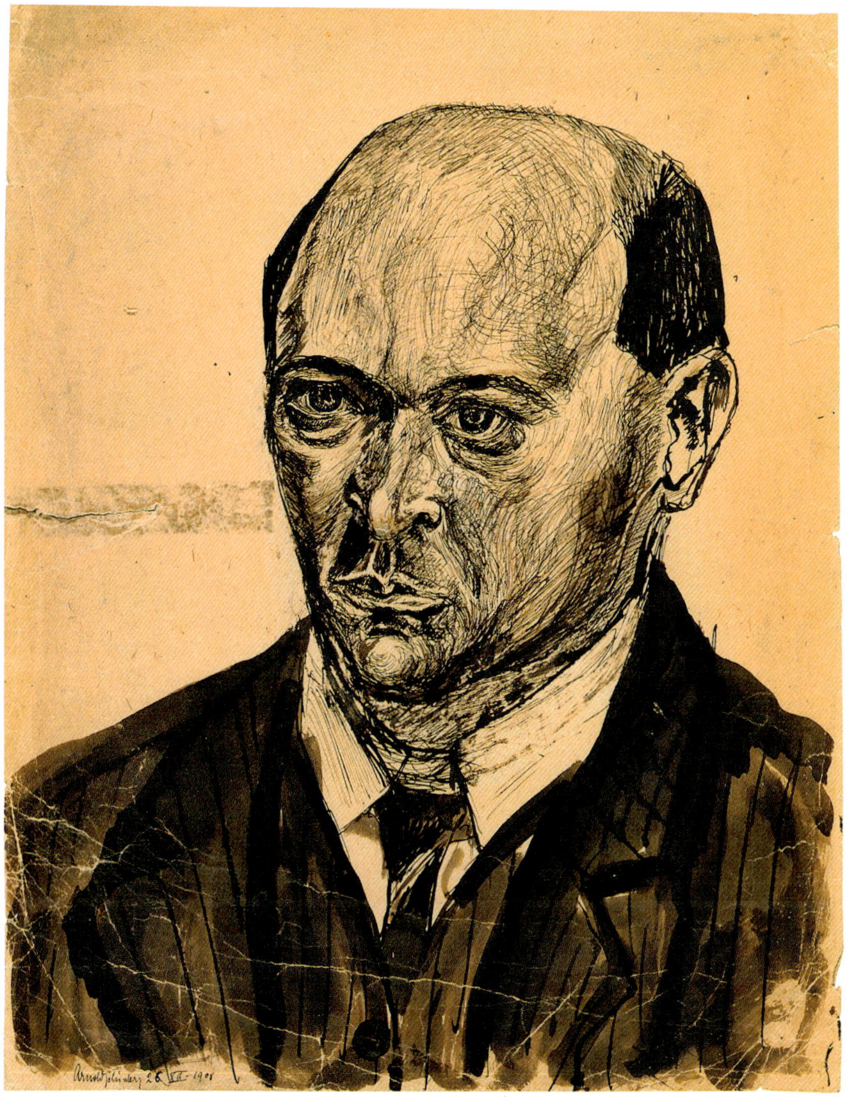

9 **Arnold Schoenberg** (Austrian, 1874–1951) *Self-Portrait*, 1908. Brush, pen, and ink on paper, 15¾ x 12¼ in. (40 x 31 cm). Arnold Schoenberg Center, Vienna.

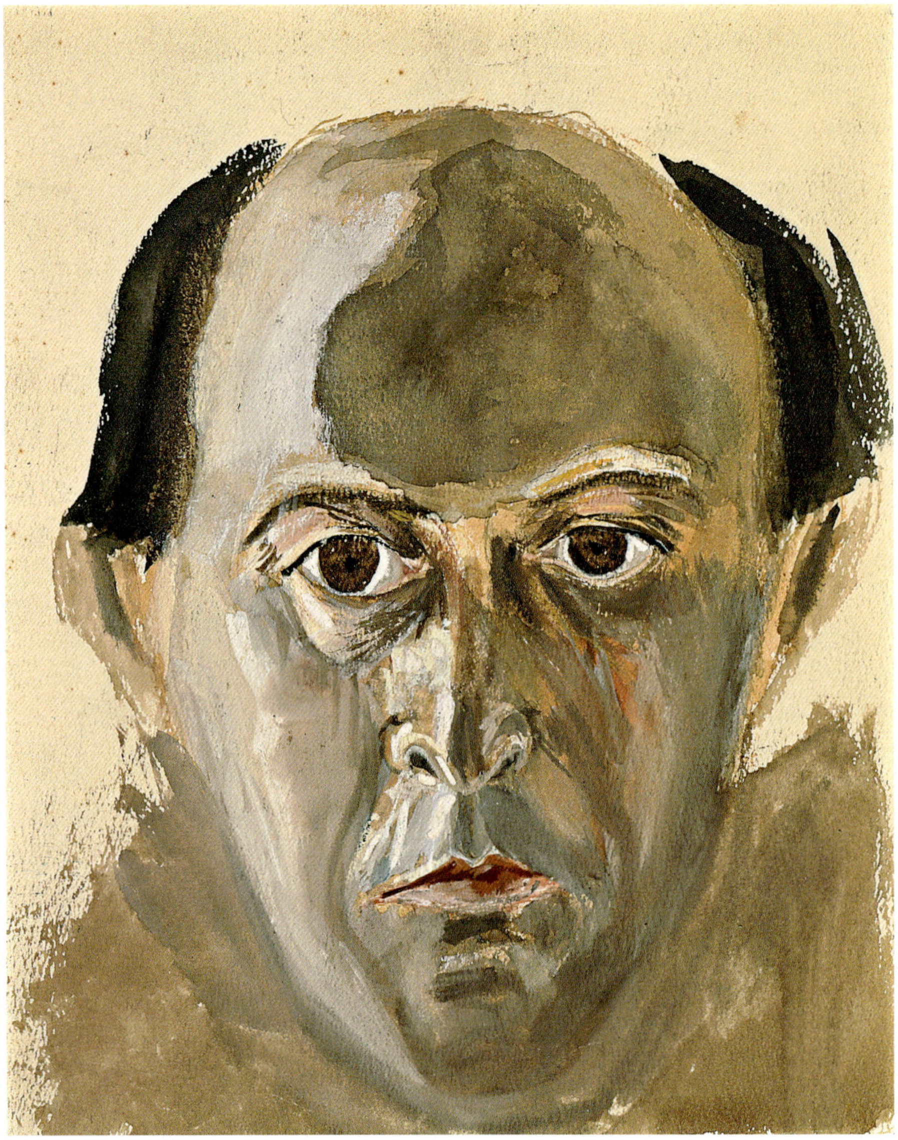

10 **Arnold Schoenberg** *Self-Portrait*, n.d. Gouache on paper, 9 x 7½ in. (23 x 19 cm). Arnold Schoenberg Center, Vienna.

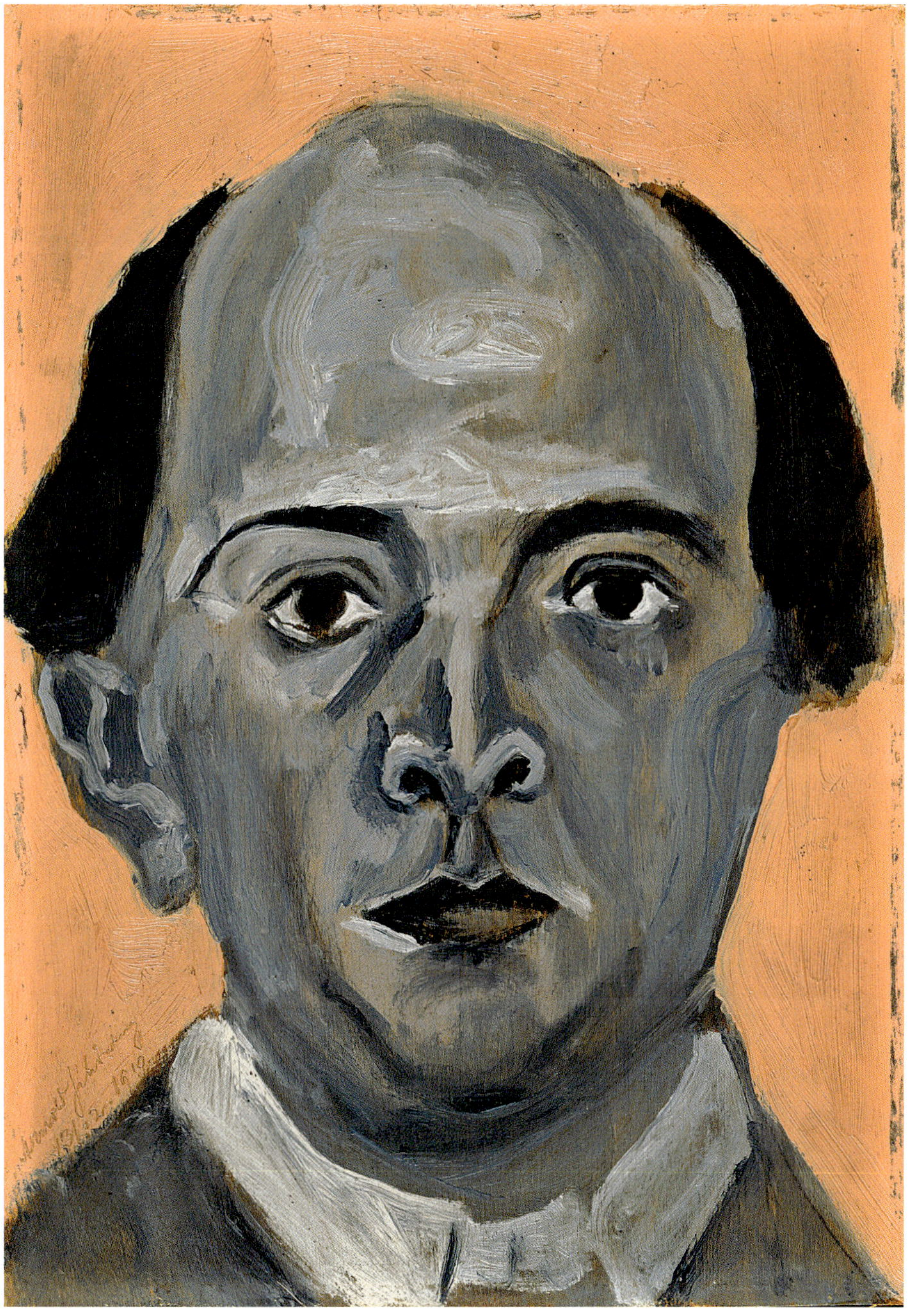

11 **Arnold Schoenberg** *Blue Self-Portrait*, 1910. Oil on wood, 12¼ x 8⅝ in. (31 x 22 cm). Arnold Schoenberg Center, Vienna.

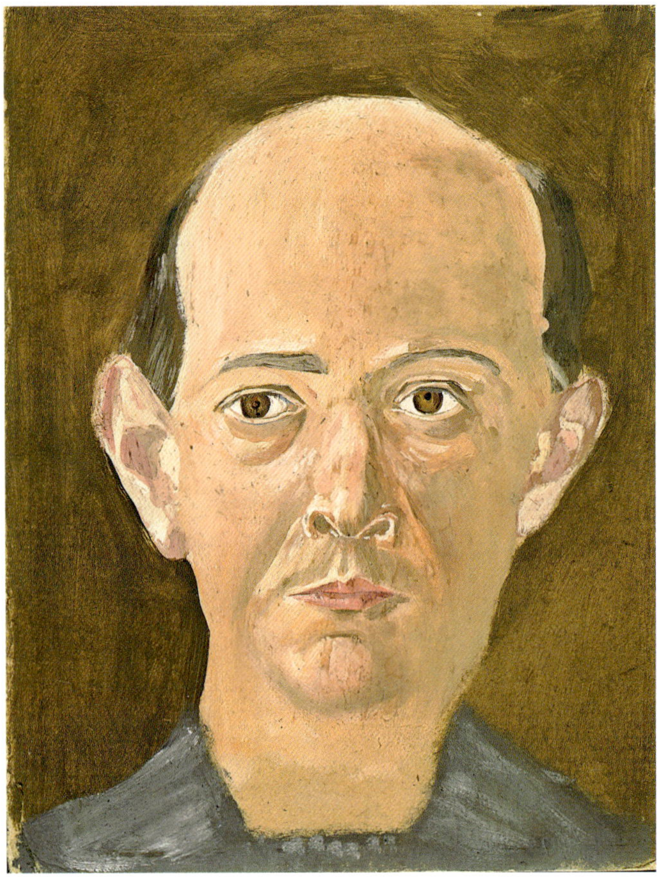

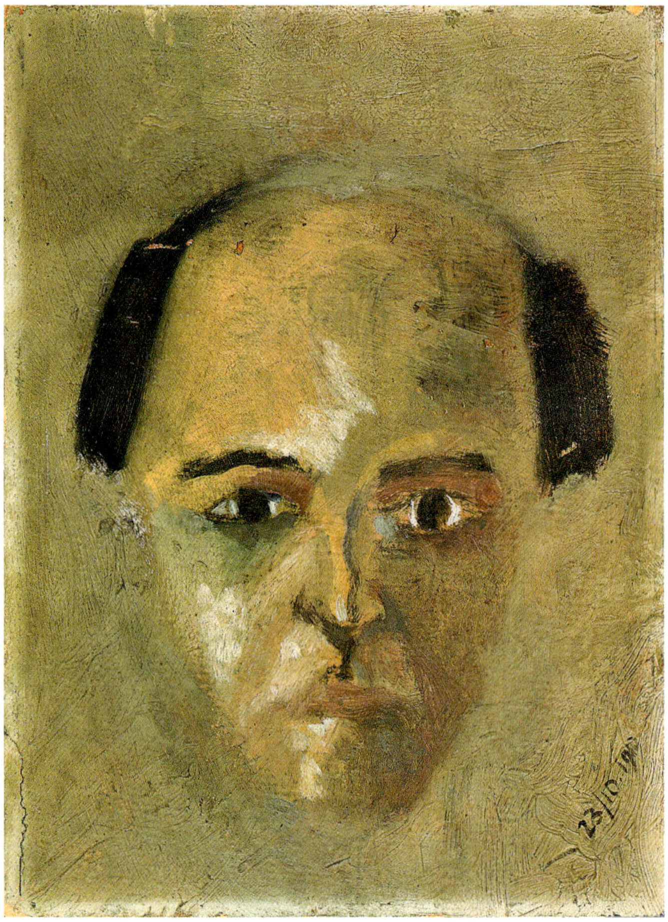

12 **Arnold Schoenberg** *Self-Portrait*, n.d. Oil on cardboard, 12¼ x 9⅝ in. (31 x 24.5 cm). Arnold Schoenberg Center, Vienna.

13 **Arnold Schoenberg** *Green Self-Portrait*, 1910. Oil on wood, 13 x 9½ in. (33 x 24 cm). Arnold Schoenberg Center, Vienna.

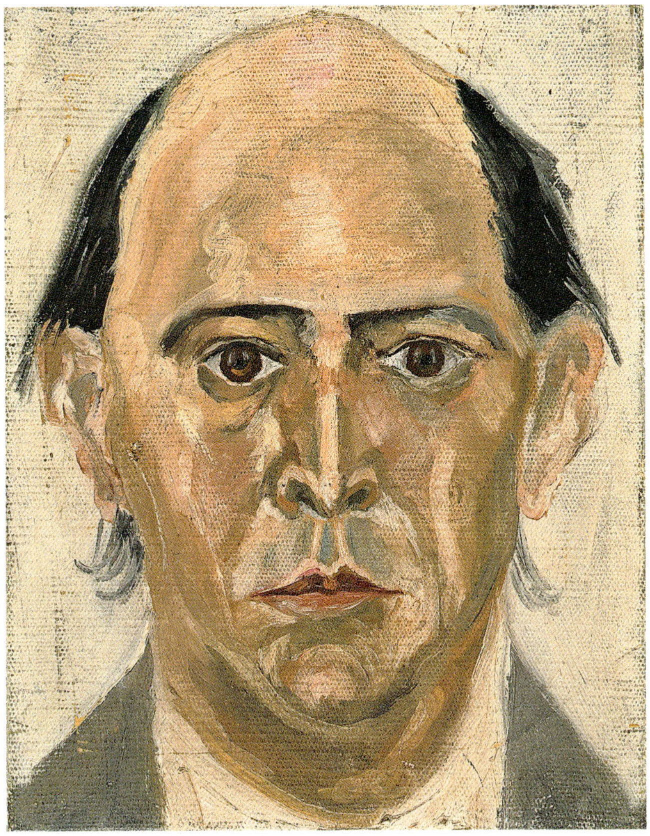

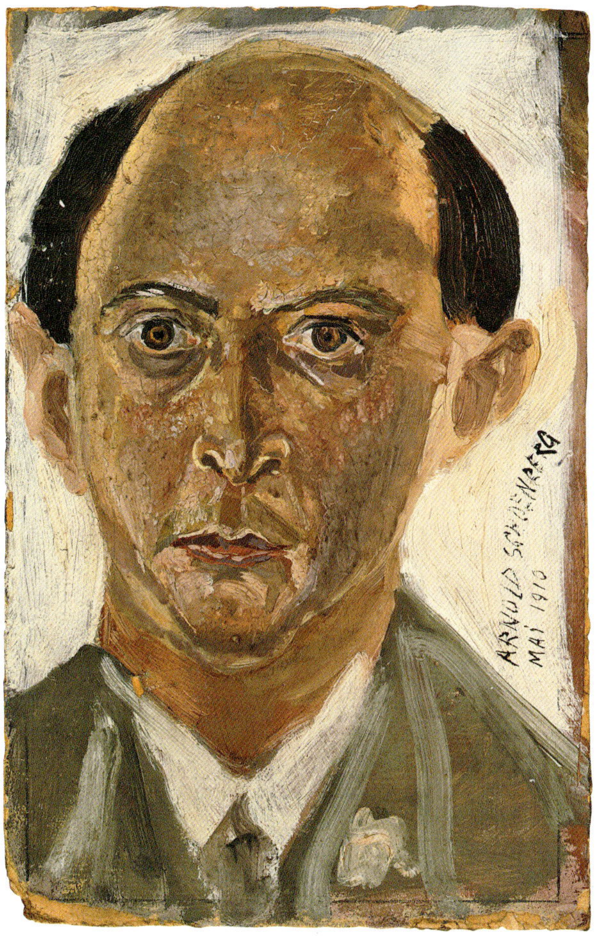

14 **Arnold Schoenberg** *Self-Portrait*, n.d. Oil on canvas, 11⅜ x 9 in. (29 x 23 cm). Arnold Schoenberg Center, Vienna.

15 **Arnold Schoenberg** *Self-Portrait*, 1910. Oil on cardboard, 13 x 8¼ in. (33 x 21 cm). Arnold Schoenberg Center, Vienna.

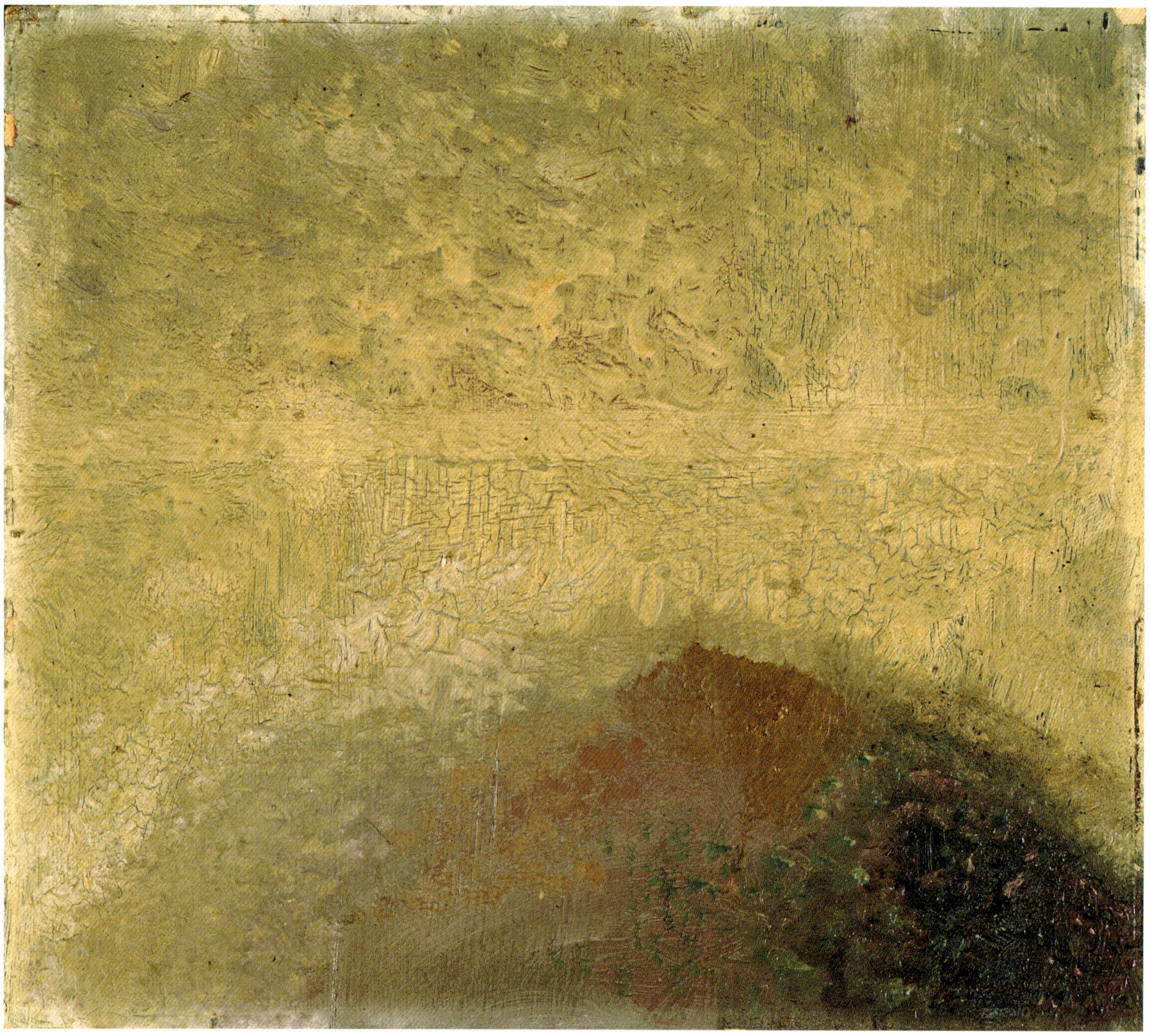

16 **Arnold Schoenberg** *Thinking*, n.d. Oil on cardboard, 8⅝ x 9⅞ in. (22 x 25 cm). Arnold Schoenberg Center, Vienna.

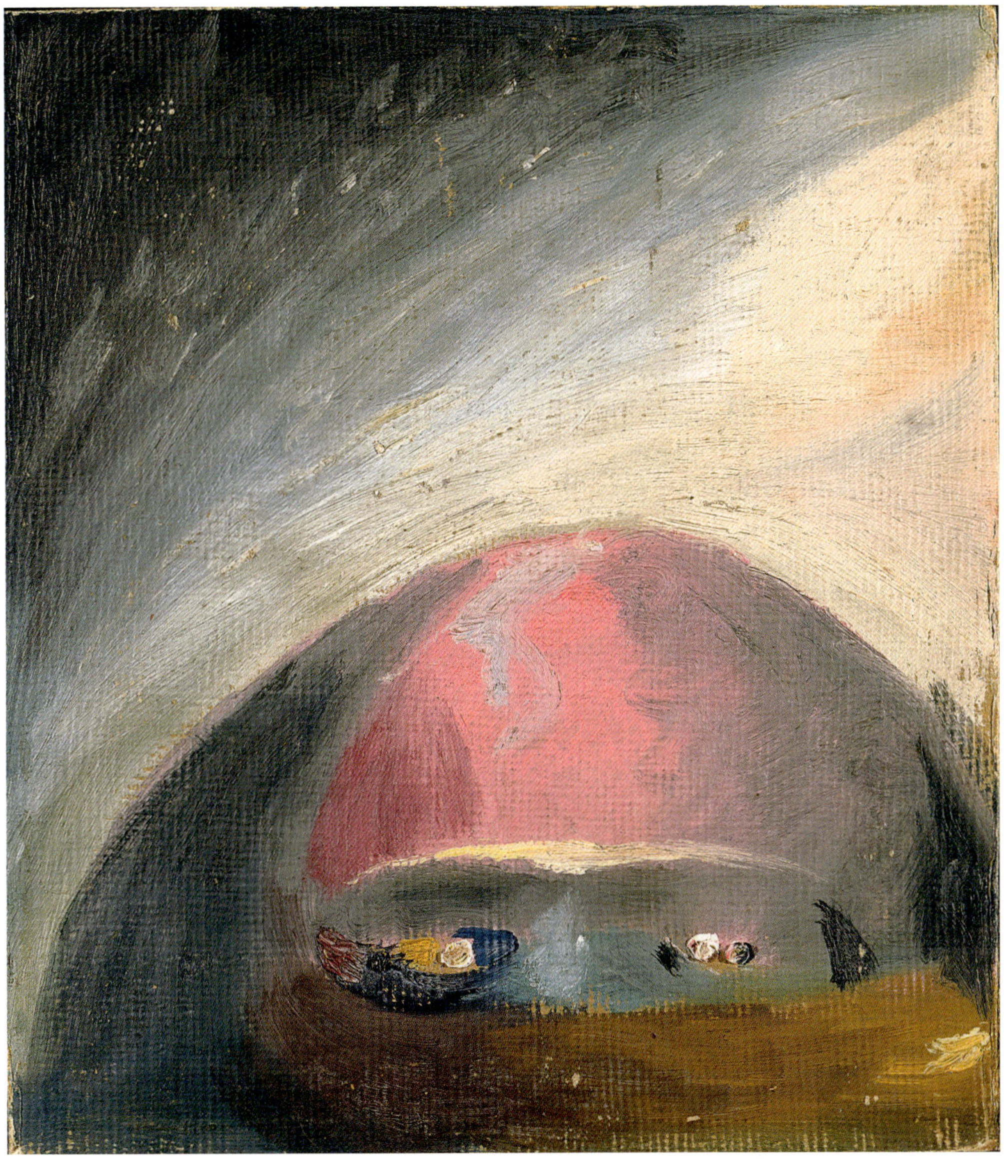

17 **Arnold Schoenberg** *Gaze*, n.d. Oil on cardboard, 12⅜ x 11 in. (31.5 x 28 cm). Arnold Schoenberg Center, Vienna.

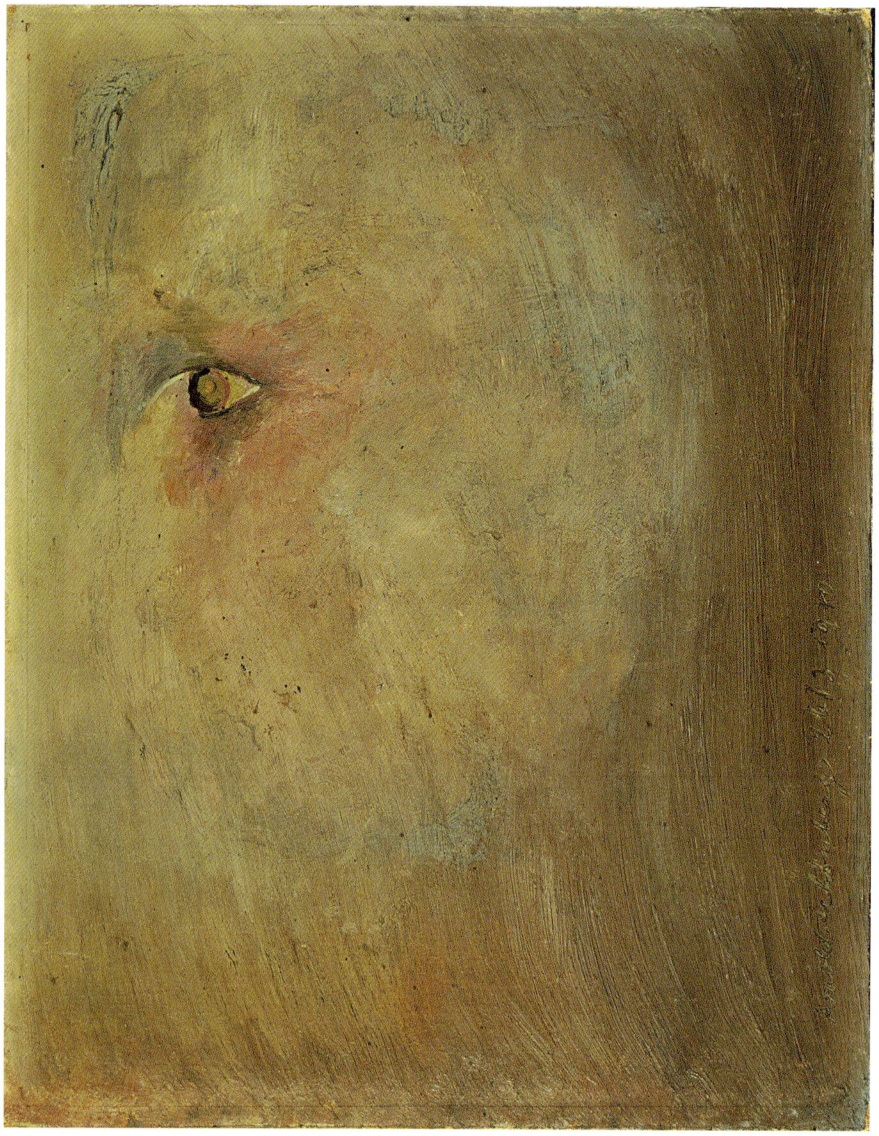

18 **Arnold Schoenberg** *Red Gaze*, 1910. Oil on cardboard, 11 x 8⅝ in. (28 x 22 cm). Arnold Schoenberg Center, Vienna.

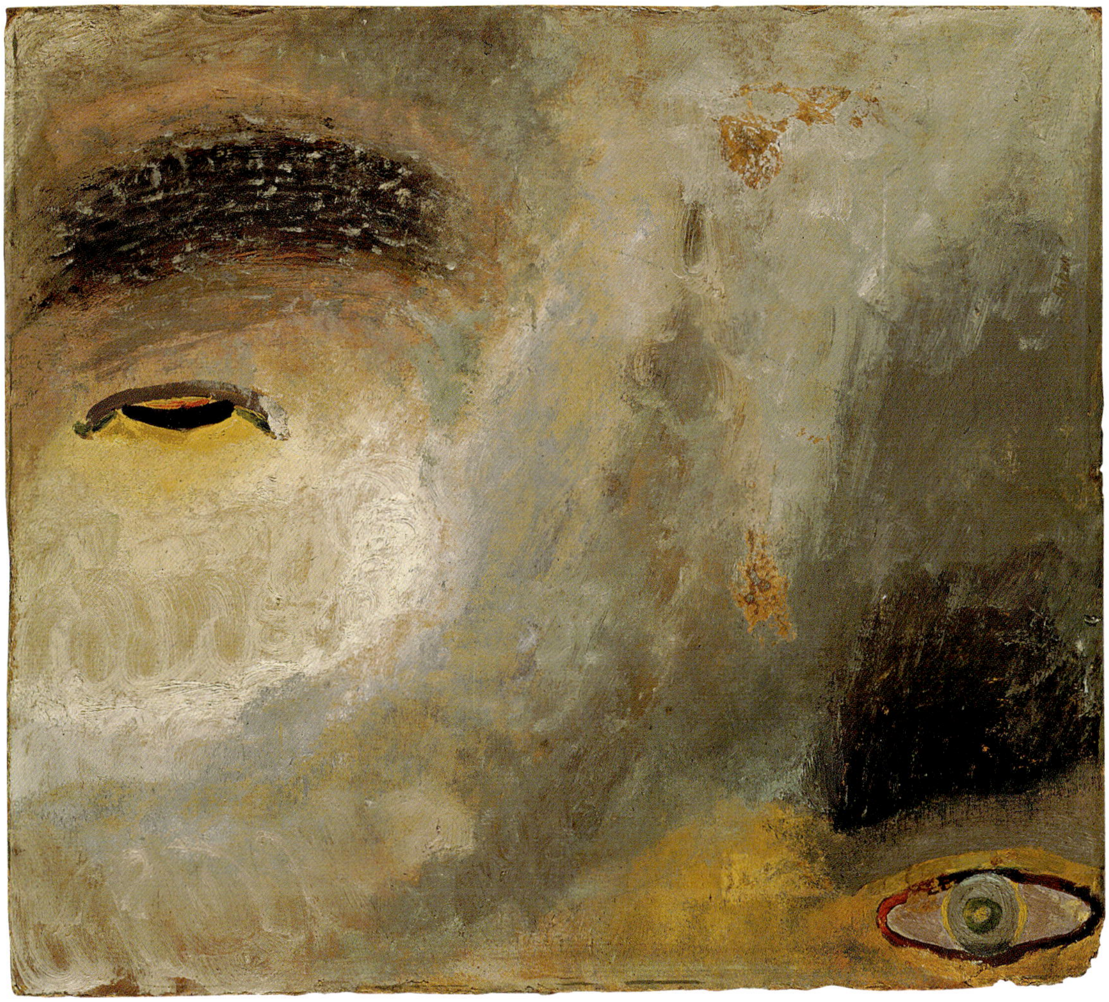

19 **Arnold Schoenberg** *Vision (Eyes)*, 1910. Inscribed: "Erinnerung an Oskar Kokoschka" (Reminiscence of Oskar Kokoschka). Oil on cardboard, 9⅞ x 12¼ in. (25 x 31 cm). Arnold Schoenberg Center, Vienna.

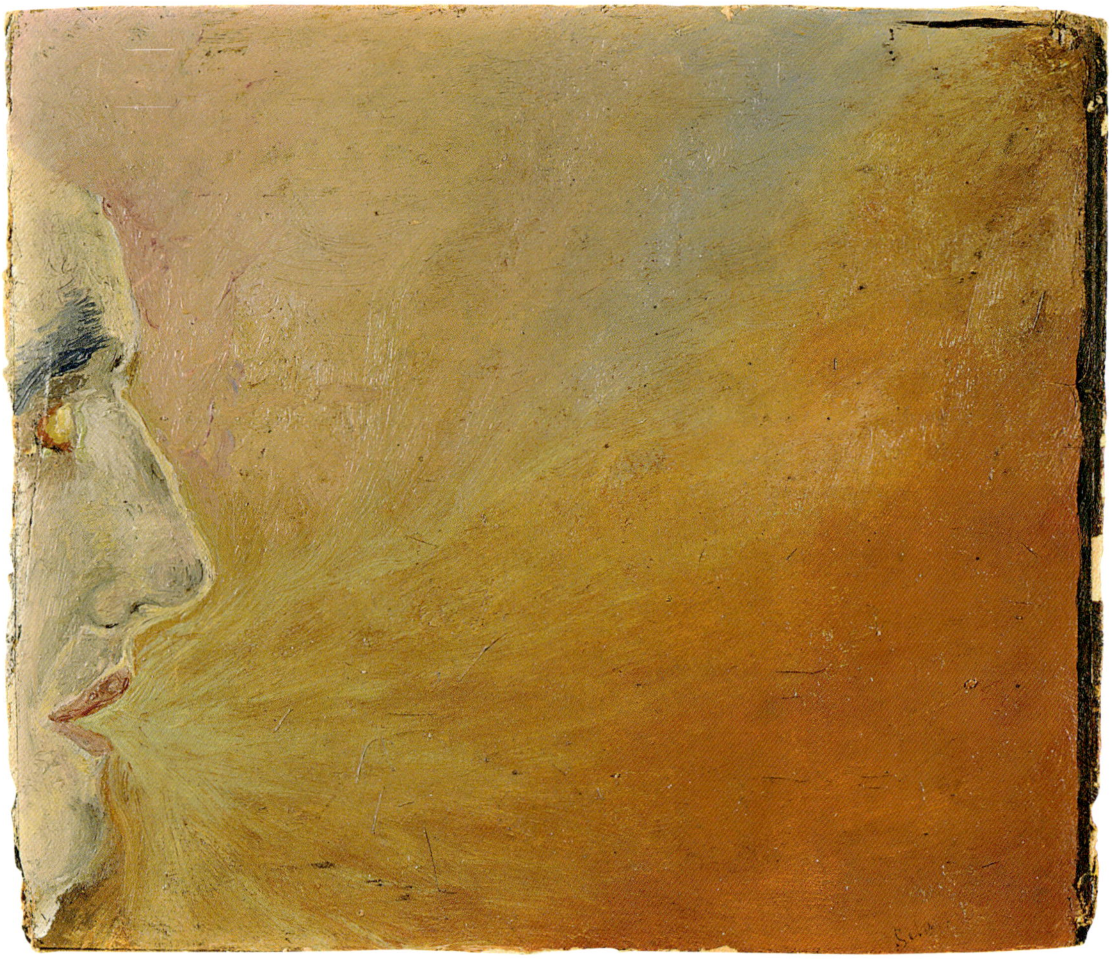

20 **Arnold Schoenberg** *Blue Gaze*, n.d. Oil on cardboard, 7⅞ x 9 in. (20 x 23 cm). Arnold Schoenberg Center, Vienna.

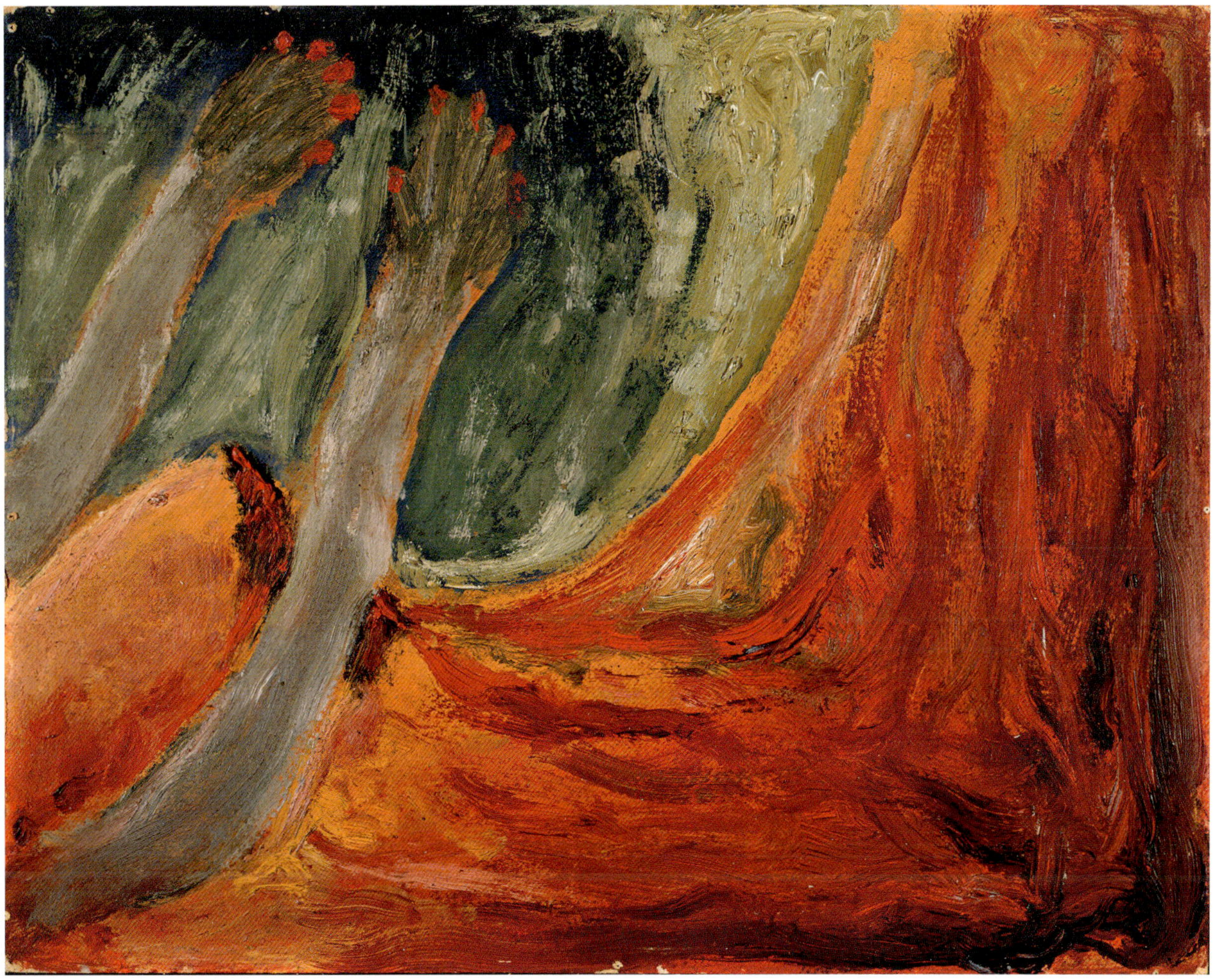

21 **Arnold Schoenberg** *Flesh*, n.d. Oil on cardboard, 8⅝ x 11 in. (22 x 28 cm). Arnold Schoenberg Center, Vienna.

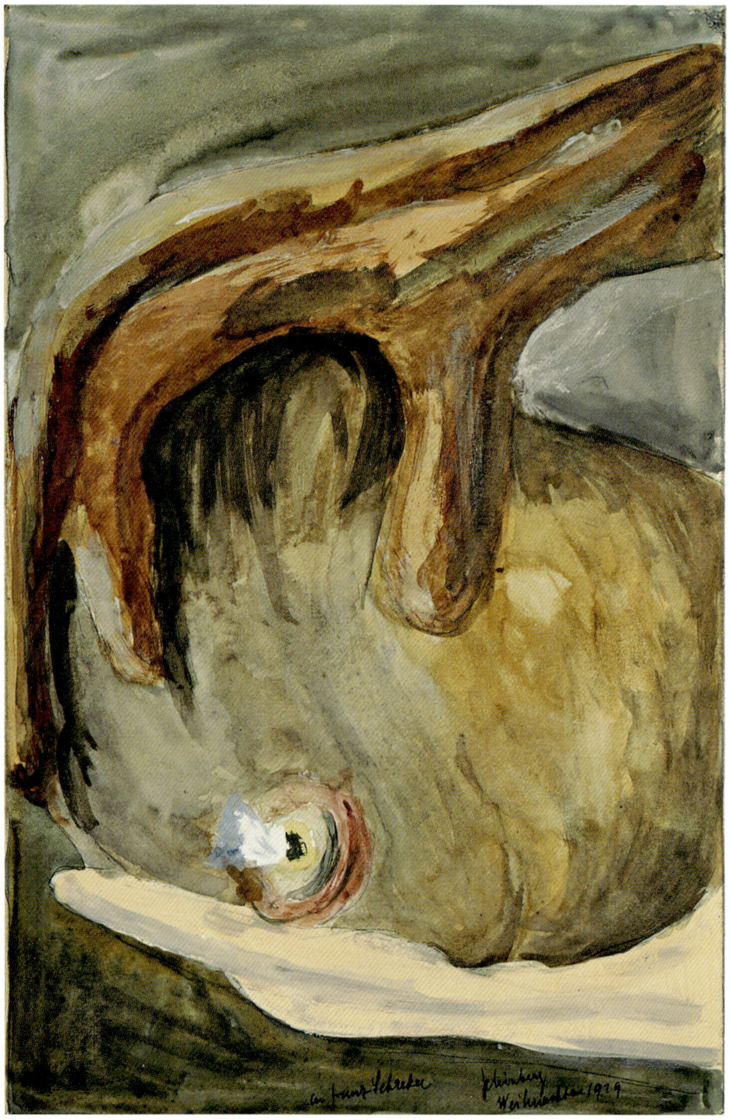

22 **Arnold Schoenberg** *Hands*, n.d. Inscribed: "An Franz Schreker, Schönberg, Weihnachten, 1929" (To Franz Schreker, Schönberg, Christmas, 1929). Watercolor on paper, 12¾ x 8½ in. (32.4 x 21.6 cm). Private collection.

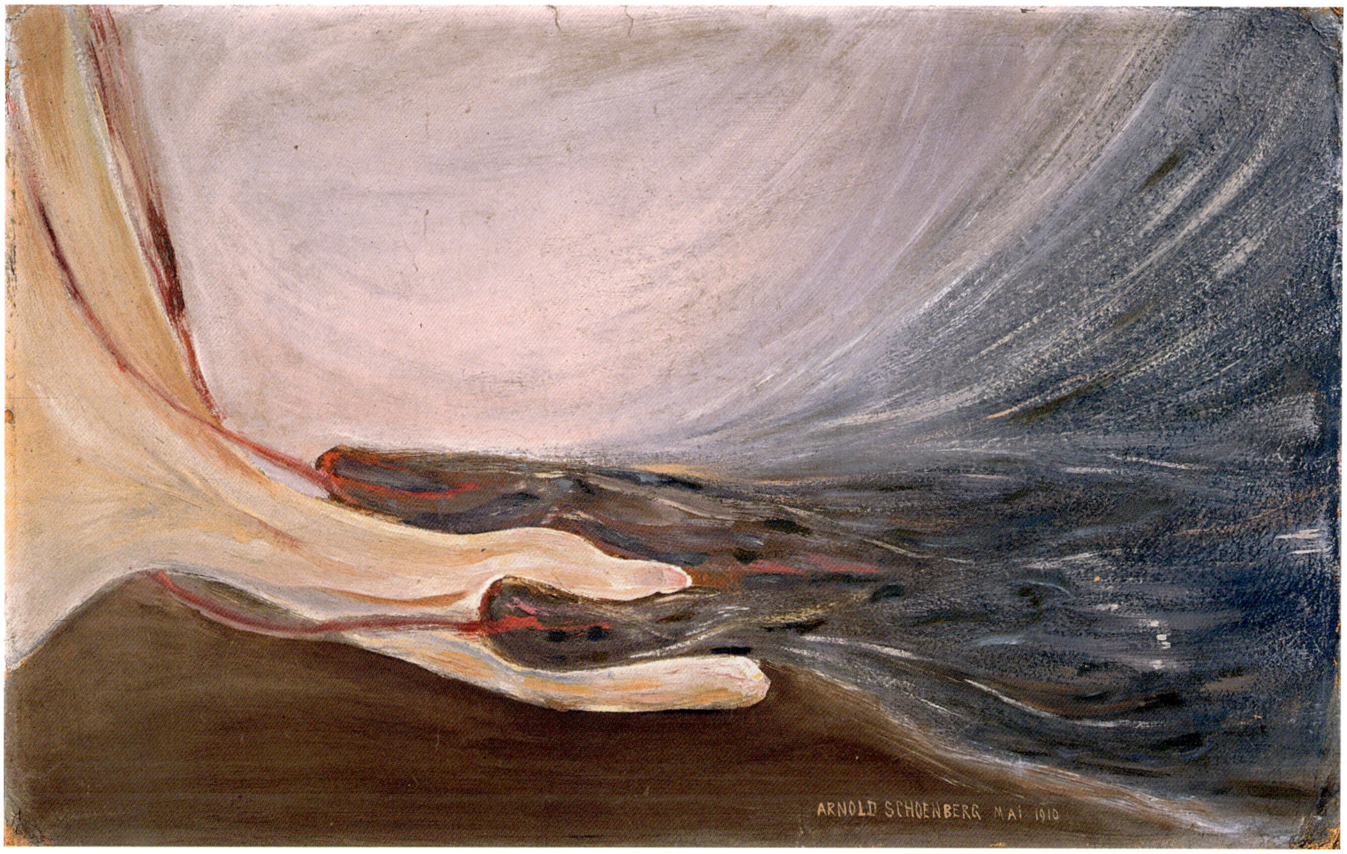

23 **Arnold Schoenberg** *Hands*, 1910. Oil on cardboard, 15⅜ x 24¾ in. (39 x 63 cm). Arnold Schoenberg Center, Vienna.

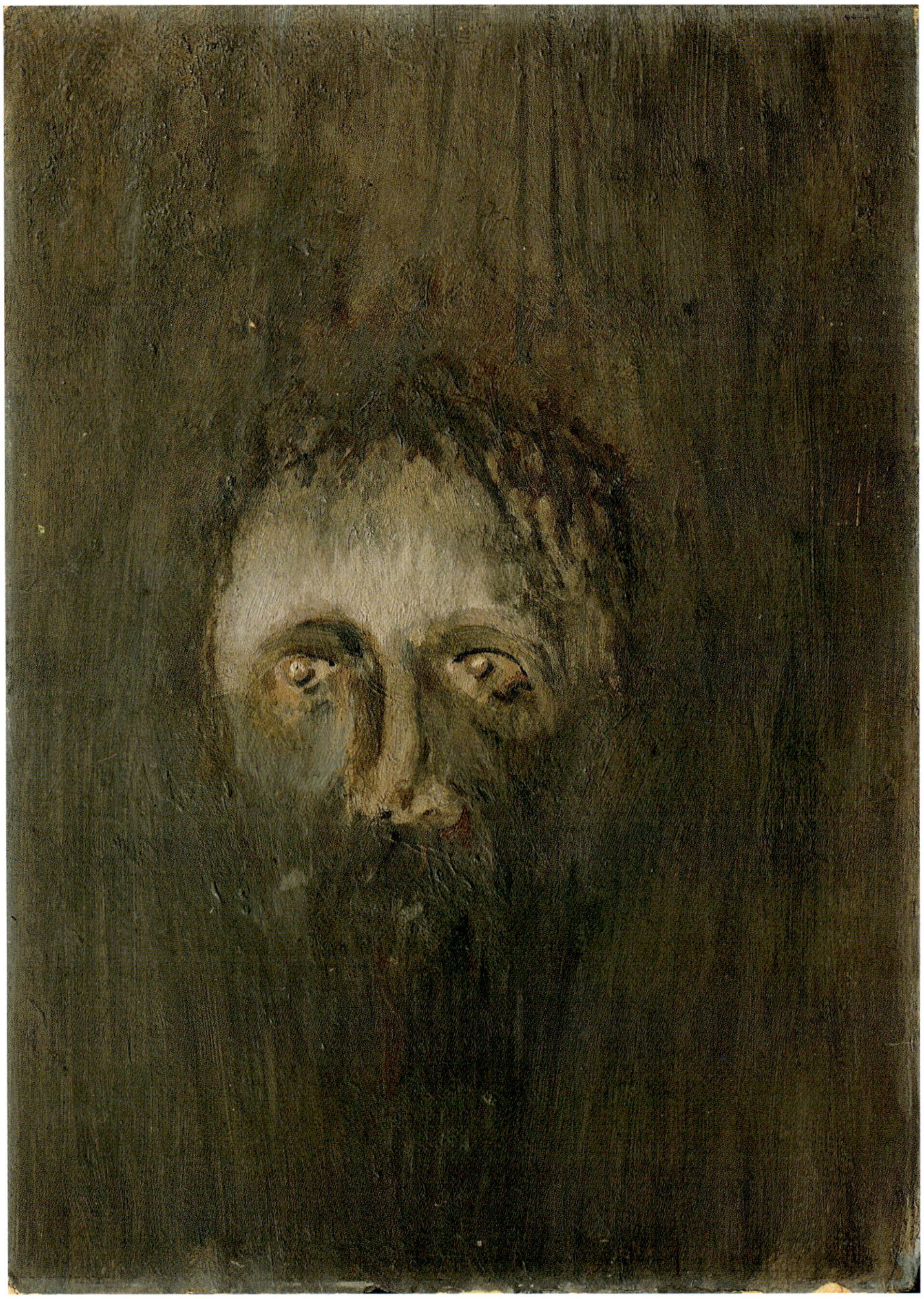

24 **Arnold Schoenberg** *Vision of Christ (Head)*, n.d. Oil on cardboard, $19\frac{11}{16}$ x $14\frac{5}{8}$ in. (50 x 37 cm). Arnold Schoenberg Center, Vienna.

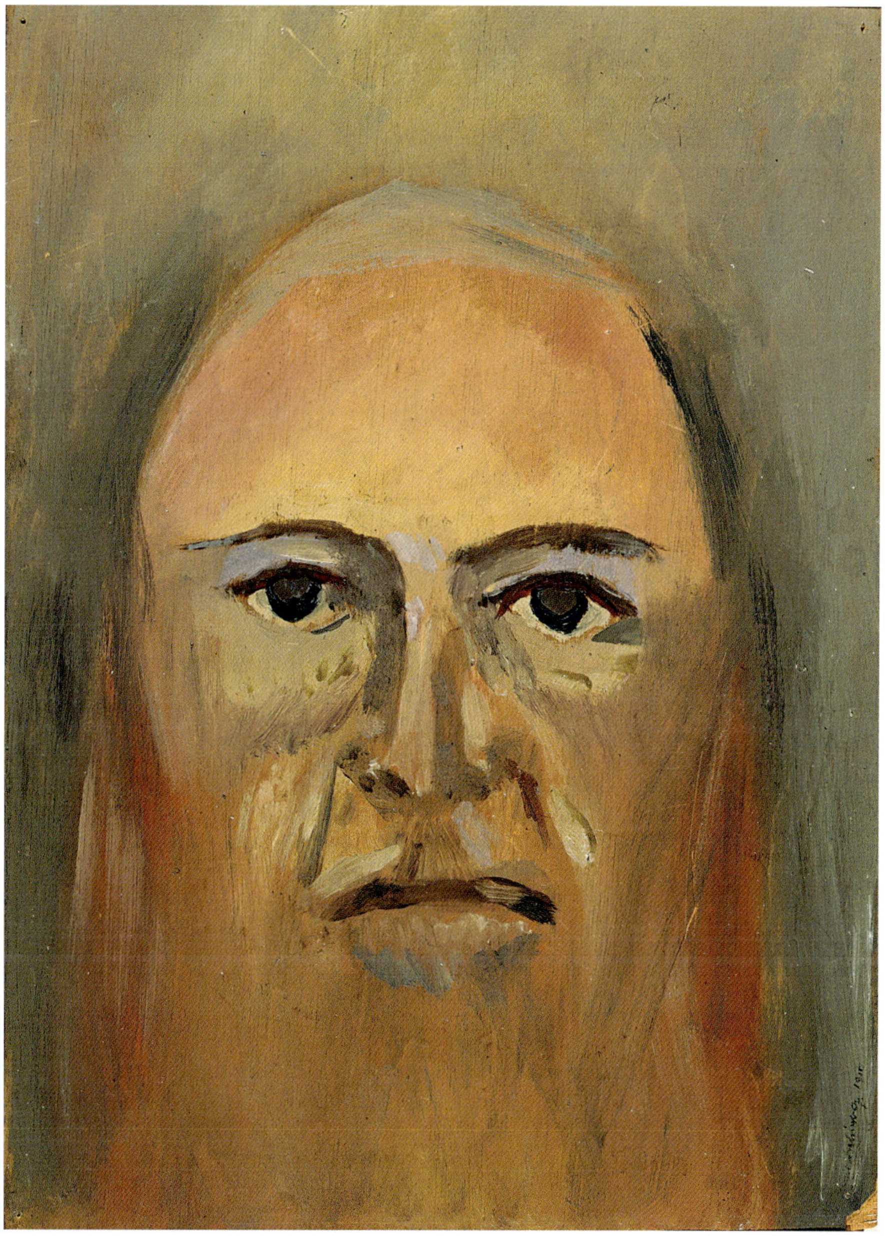

25 **Arnold Schoenberg** *Self-Portrait*, 1910. Oil on wood, 12¼ x 8⅝ in. (31 x 22 cm). Arnold Schoenberg Center, Vienna.

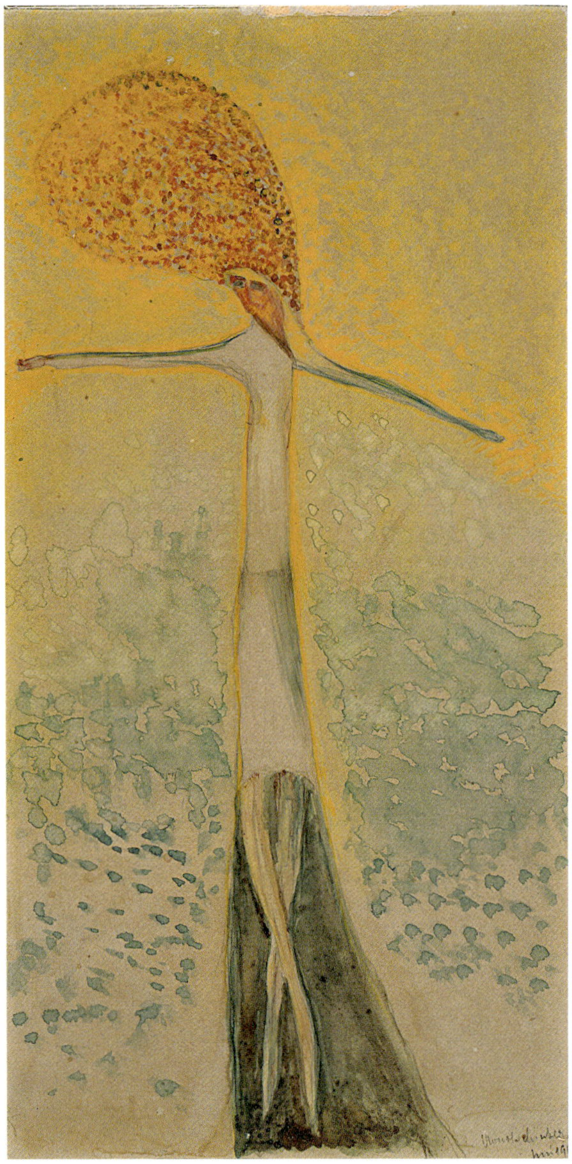

26 **Arnold Schoenberg** *Vision of Christ*, 1919. Watercolor and gouache on paper, $7\frac{7}{8} \times 3\frac{15}{16}$ in. (20 x 10 cm). Arnold Schoenberg Center, Vienna.

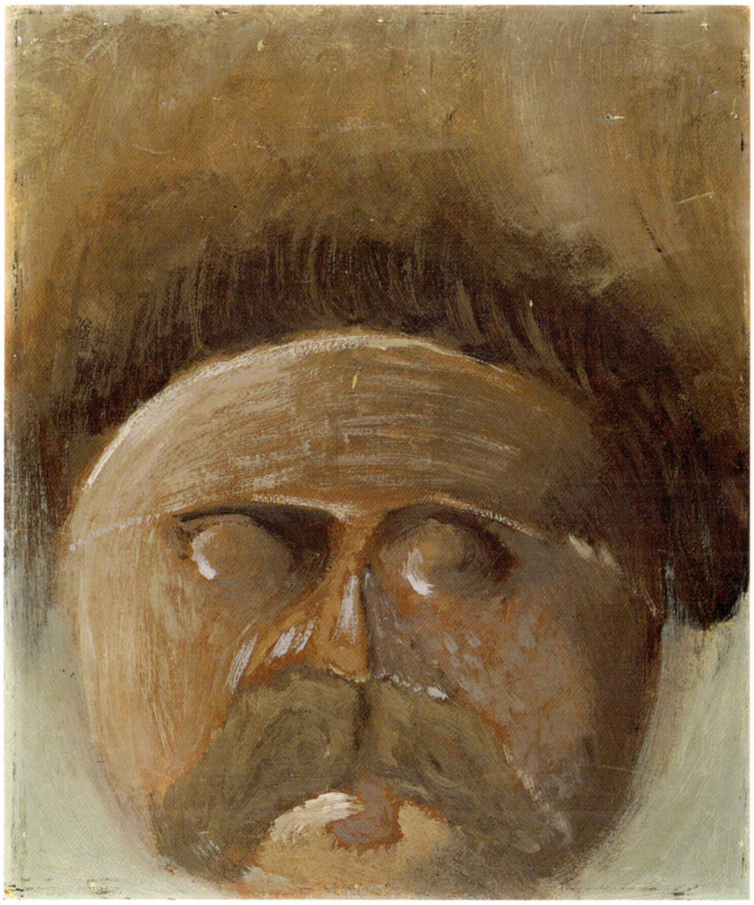

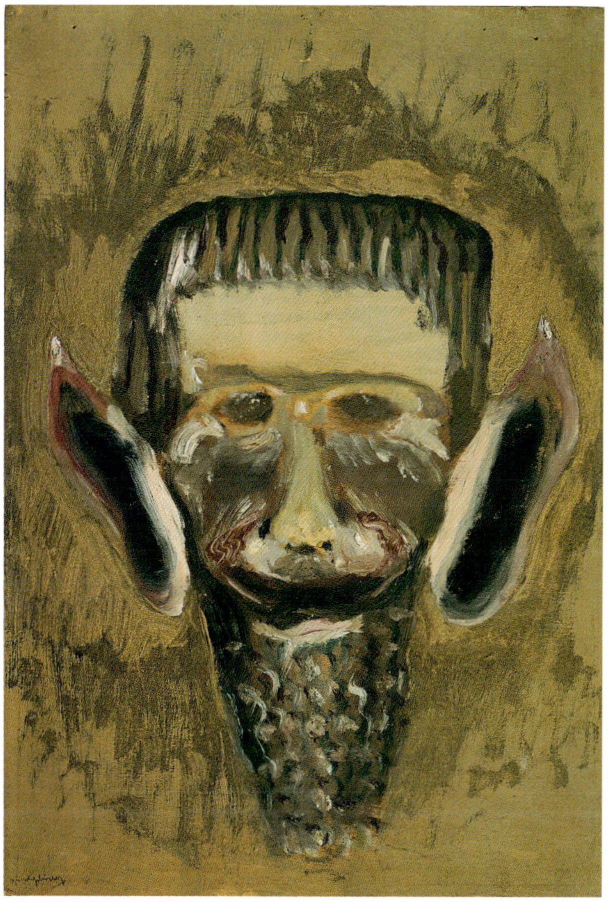

27 **Arnold Schoenberg** *Art Patron*, n.d. Oil on cardboard, 14⅝ x 12⅝ in. (37 x 32 cm). Arnold Schoenberg Center, Vienna.

28 **Arnold Schoenberg** *Critic I*, n.d. Oil on wood, 17 5/16 x 11 13/16 in. (44 x 30 cm). Arnold Schoenberg Center, Vienna.

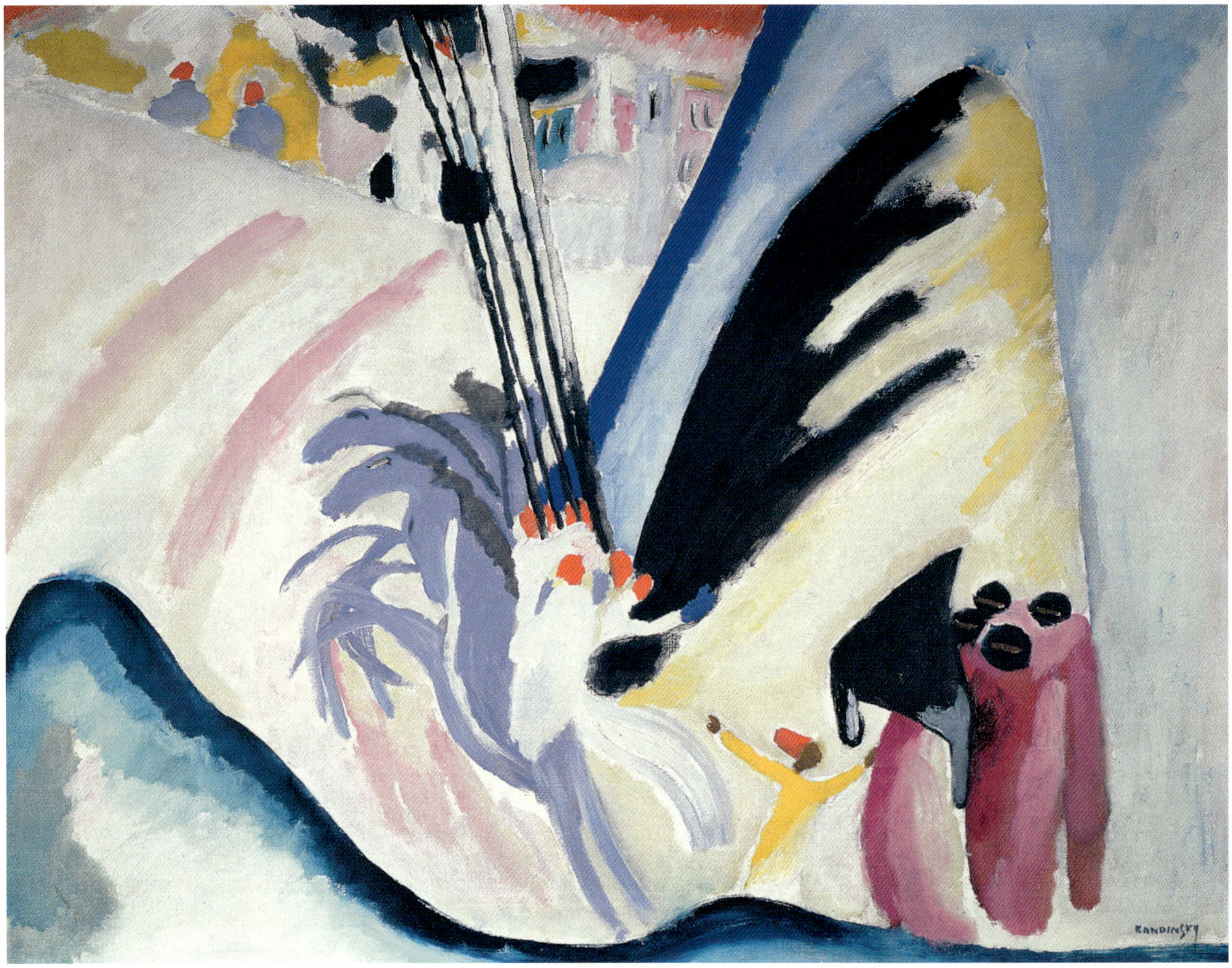

29 **Wassily Kandinsky** *Arabs II*, 1911. Oil on canvas, 27⅝ x 36⅜ in. (70.2 x 92.4 cm). Private collection.

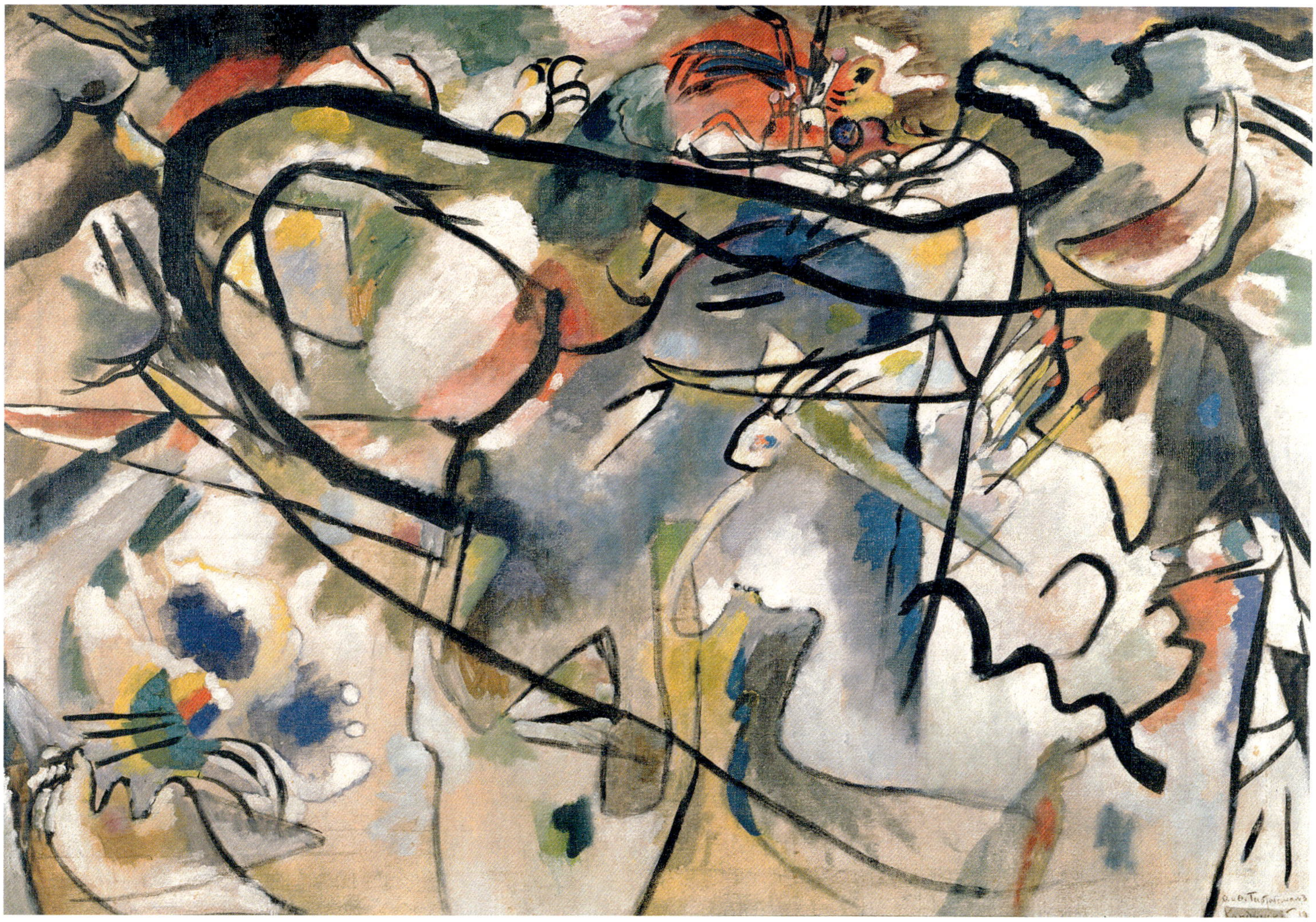

30 **Wassily Kandinsky** *Sketch for Composition V*, 1911. Oil on canvas, 37¼ x 54¾ in. (94.5 x 139 cm). State Hermitage Museum, St. Petersburg.

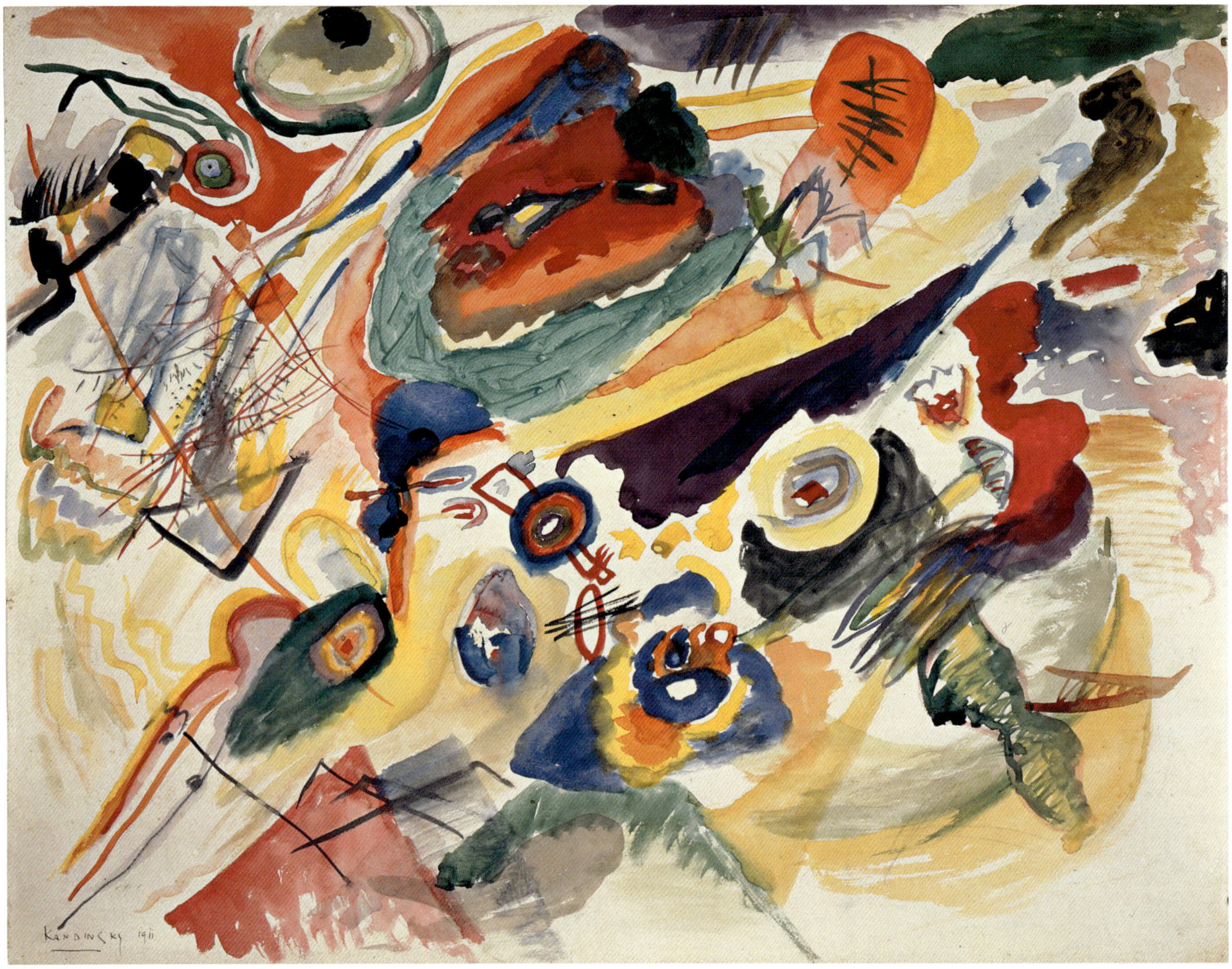

31 **Wassily Kandinsky** *Watercolor with Red Spot (Study for Composition VII)*, 1913. Watercolor and pencil on paper, mounted on cardboard, $19\frac{5}{8} \times 24\frac{7}{8}$ in. (49.8 x 63.3 cm). Collection Deutsche Bank.

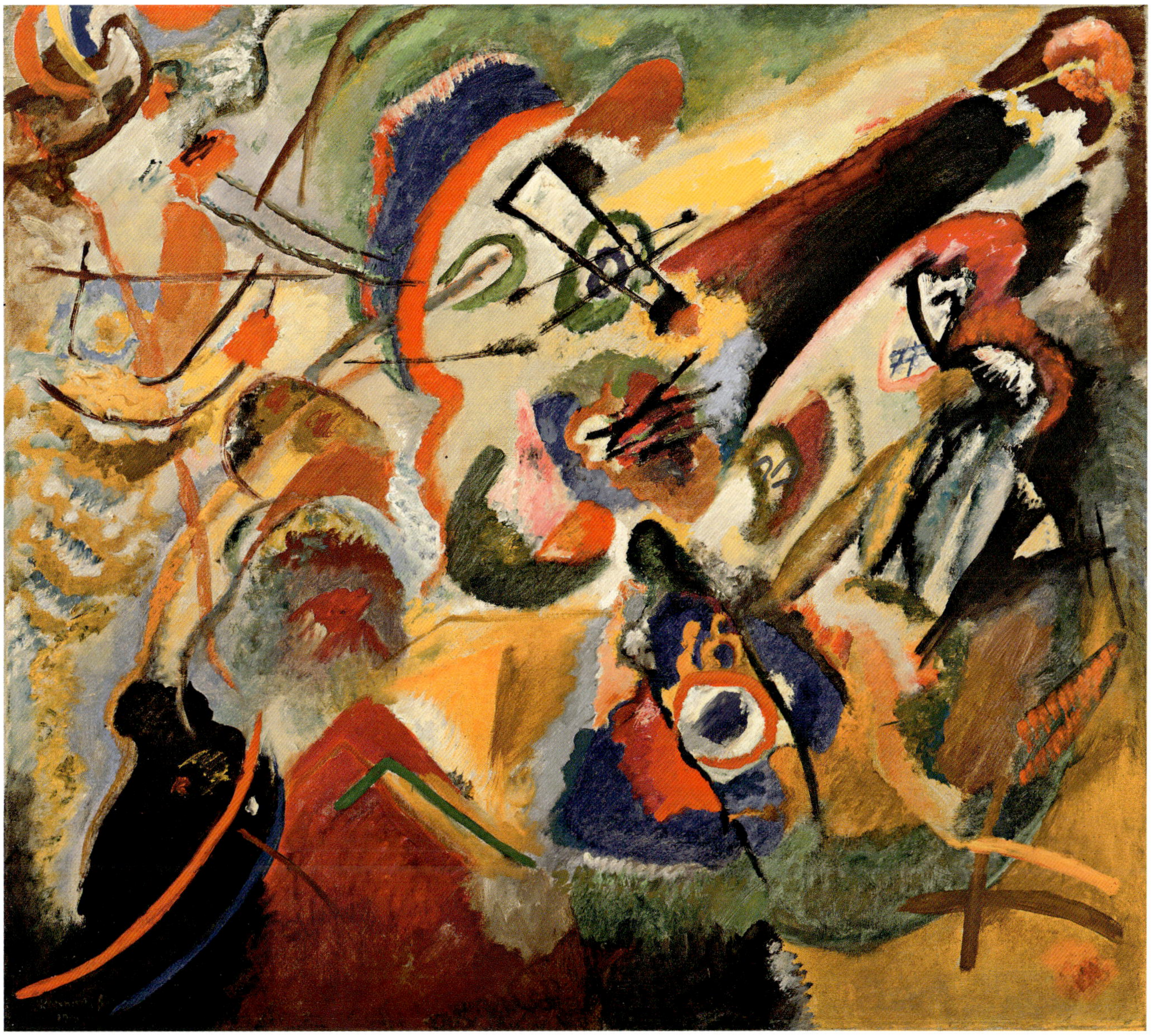

32 **Wassily Kandinsky** *Fragment 2 for Composition VII*, 1913. Oil on canvas, 34½ x 39¼ in. (87.6 x 99.7 cm). Albright-Knox Art Gallery, Buffalo, New York, Room of Contemporary Art Fund, 1947.

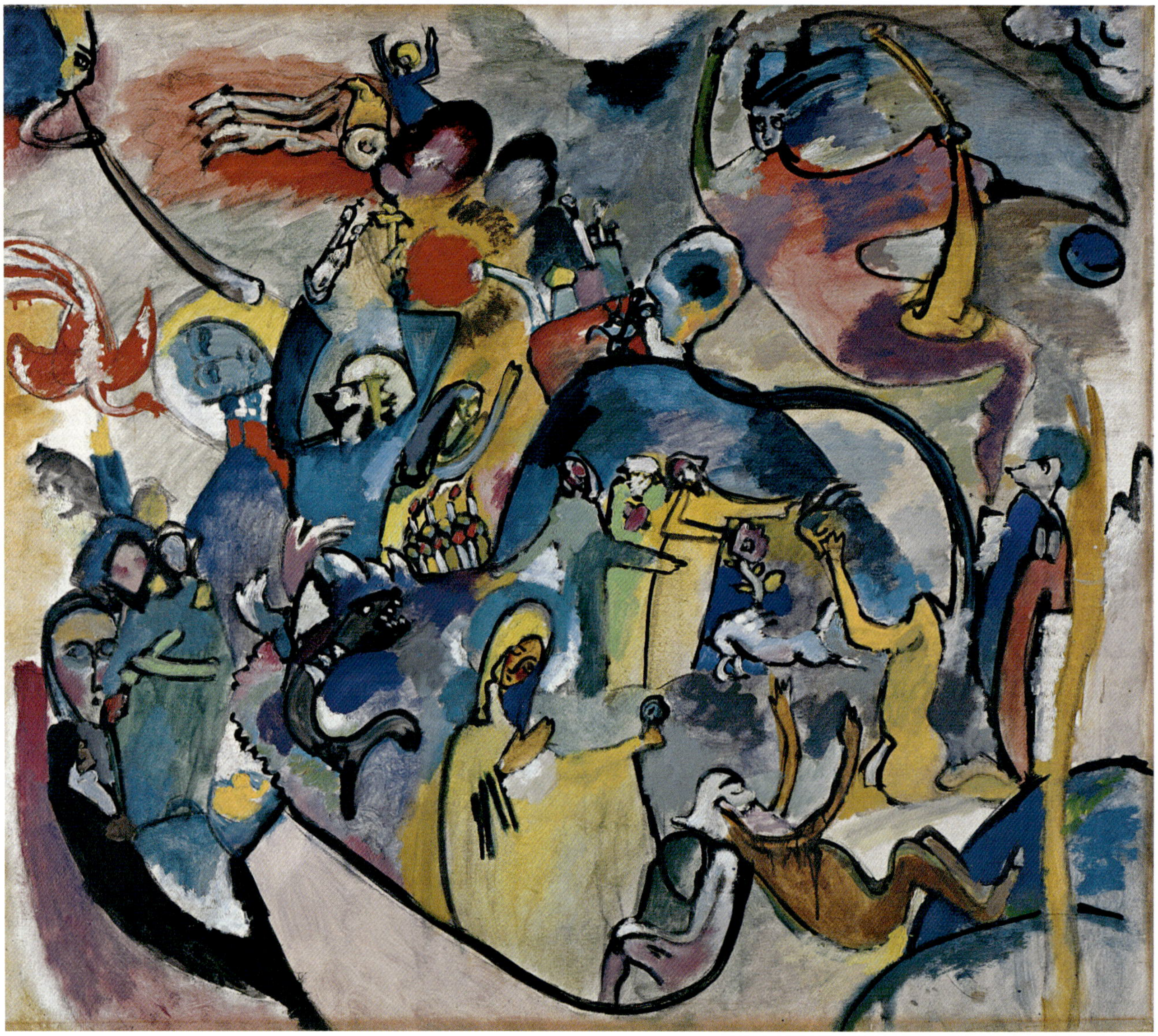

33 **Wassily Kandinsky** *All Saints II*, 1911. Oil on canvas, 33⅞ x 39 in. (86 x 99 cm). Städtische Galerie im Lenbachhaus, Munich, GMS 62.

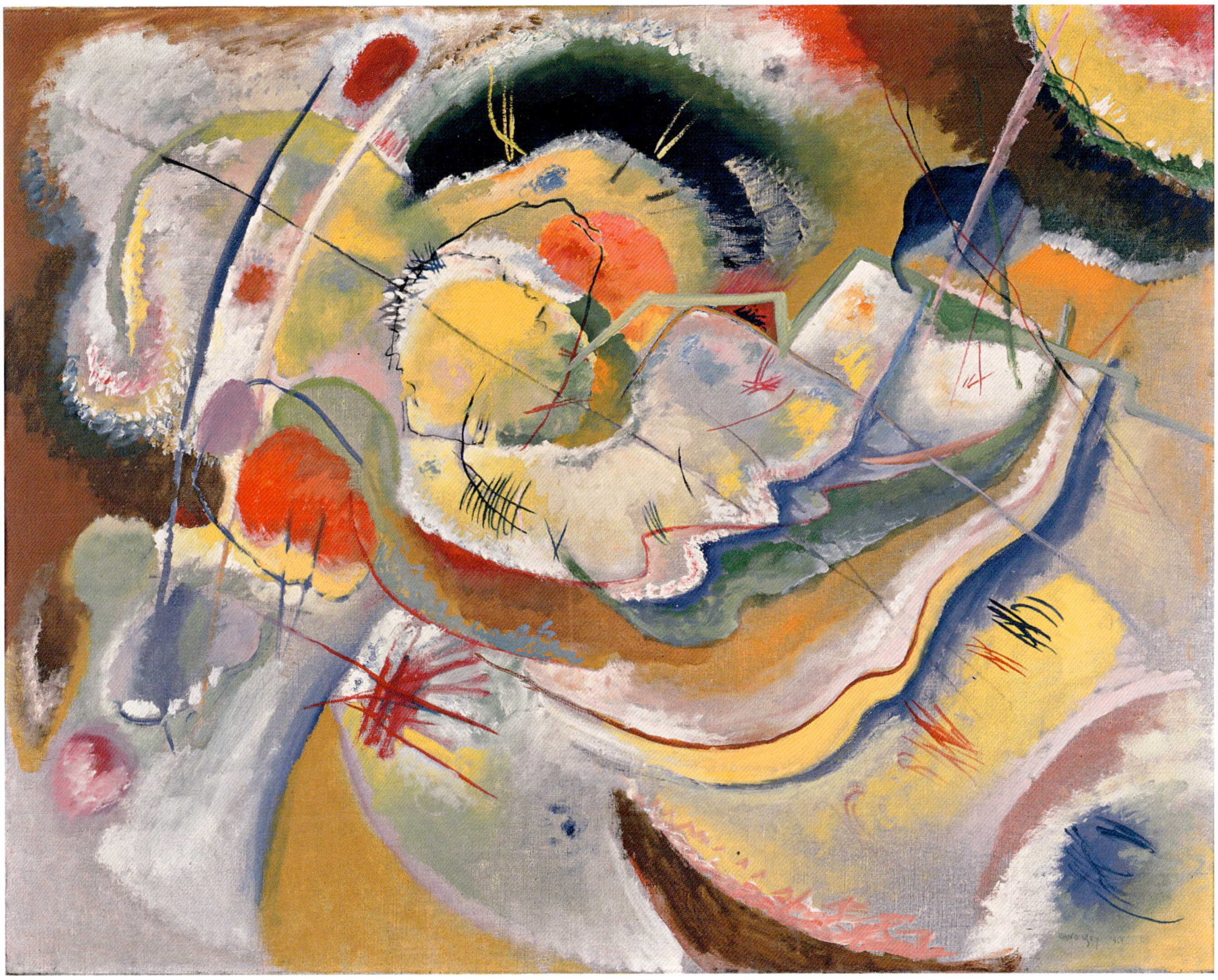

34 **Wassily Kandinsky** *Little Painting with Yellow (Improvisation)*, 1914. Oil on canvas, 31 x 39⅝ in. (78.7 x 100.6 cm).
Philadelphia Museum of Art, The Louise and Walter Arensberg Collection, 1950-134-103.

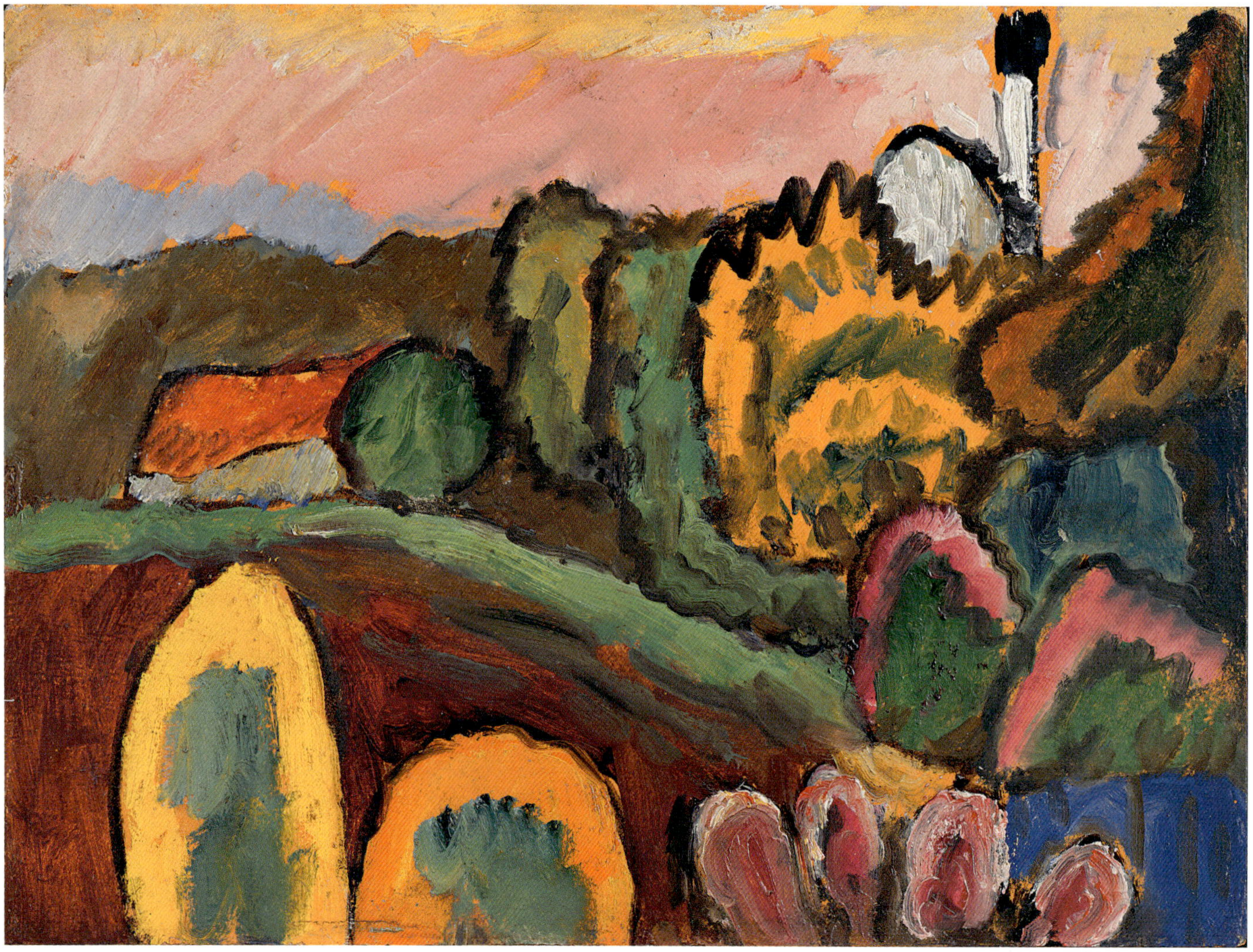

35 **Gabriele Münter** *Landscape with Church*, 1910. Oil on cardboard, 13 x 17⅝ in. (33 x 44.8 cm). Sylvia and Ulrich Ströher Collection, Germany.

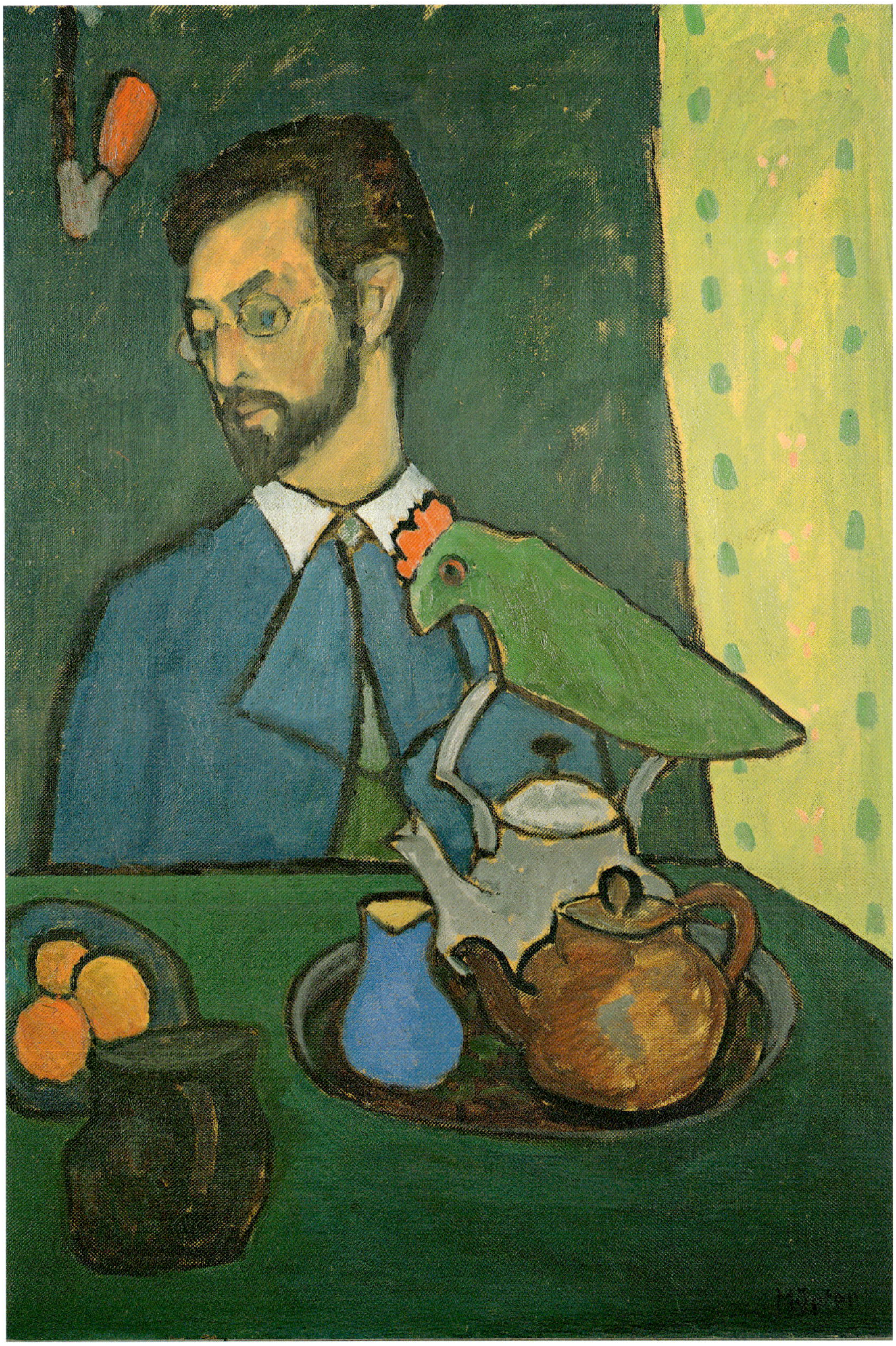

36 **Gabriele Münter** *Kandinsky at Tea*, 1910. Oil on canvas, 26¾ x 18½ in. (68 x 47 cm). Collection The Israel Museum, Jerusalem.

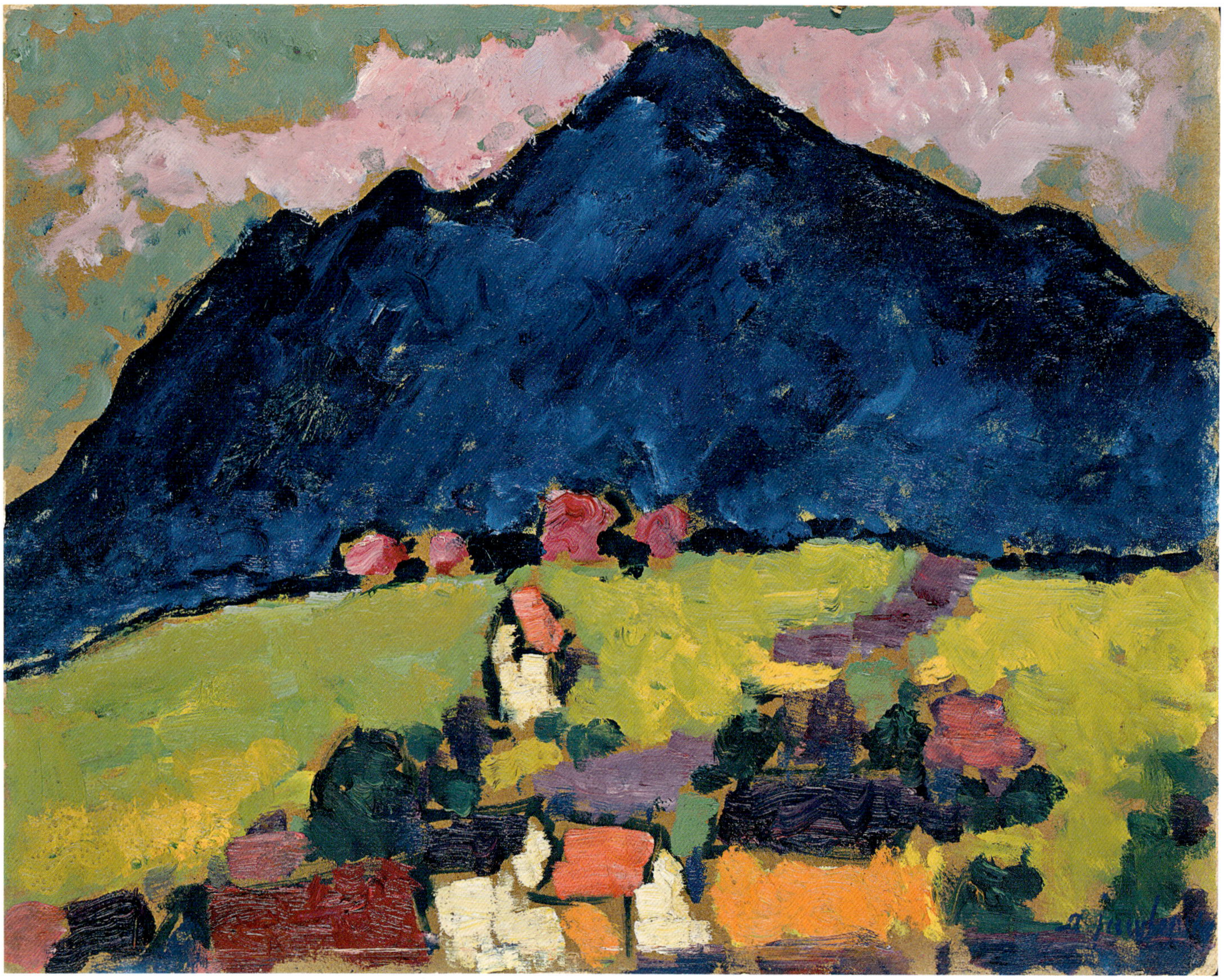

37 **Alexei von Jawlensky** *Murnau*, 1910. Oil on hardboard, 13 x 16⅝ in. (33 x 42 3 cm). National Gallery of Art, Washington, D.C., Gift of Mr. and Mrs. Ralph F. Colin, 1973.69.1.

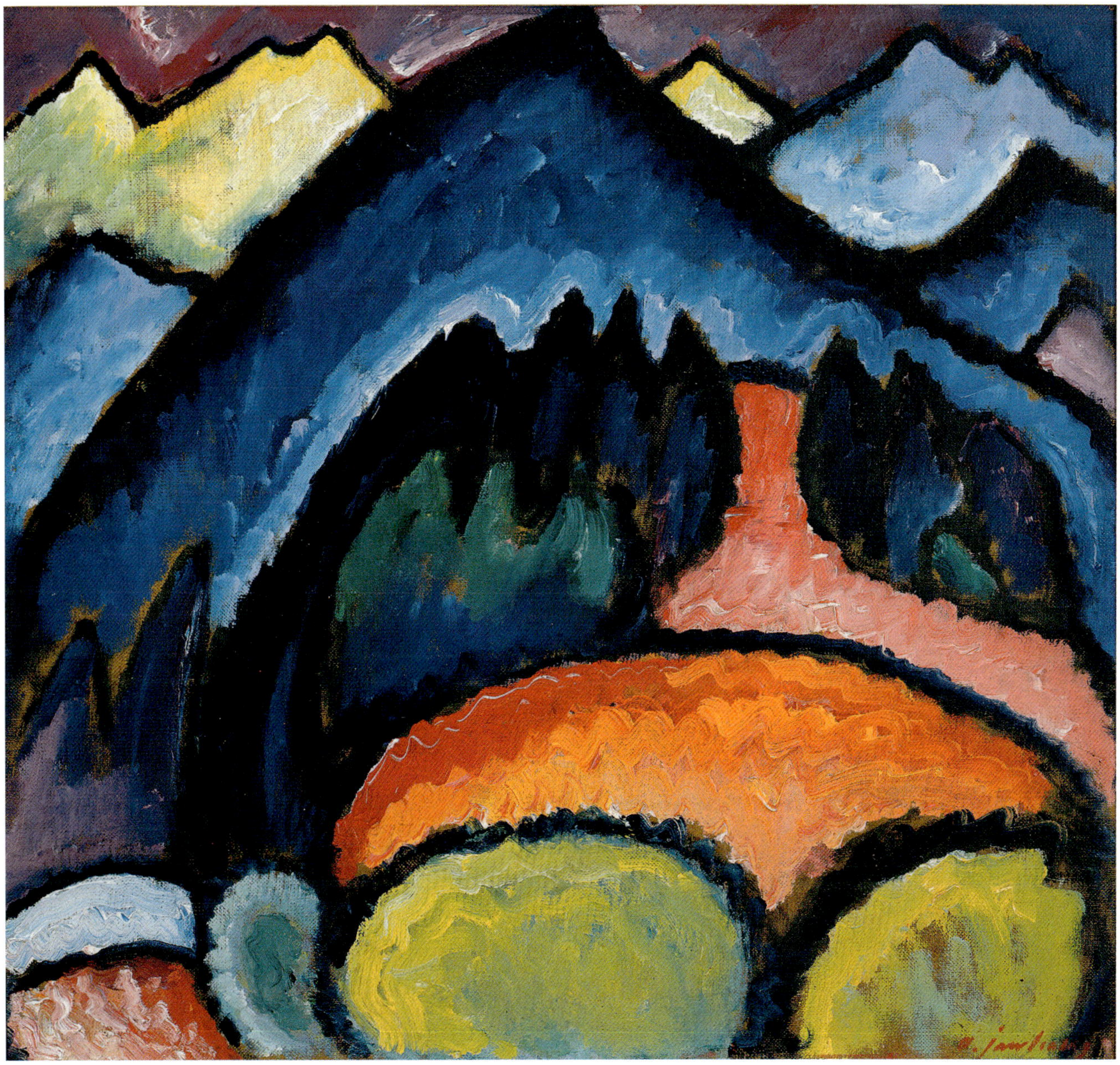

38 **Alexei von Jawlensky** *Oberstdorf (Mountains)*, 1912. Oil on cardboard, 19½ x 21⅛ in. (49.5 x 53.5 cm). Hanna Bekker vom Rath Collection.

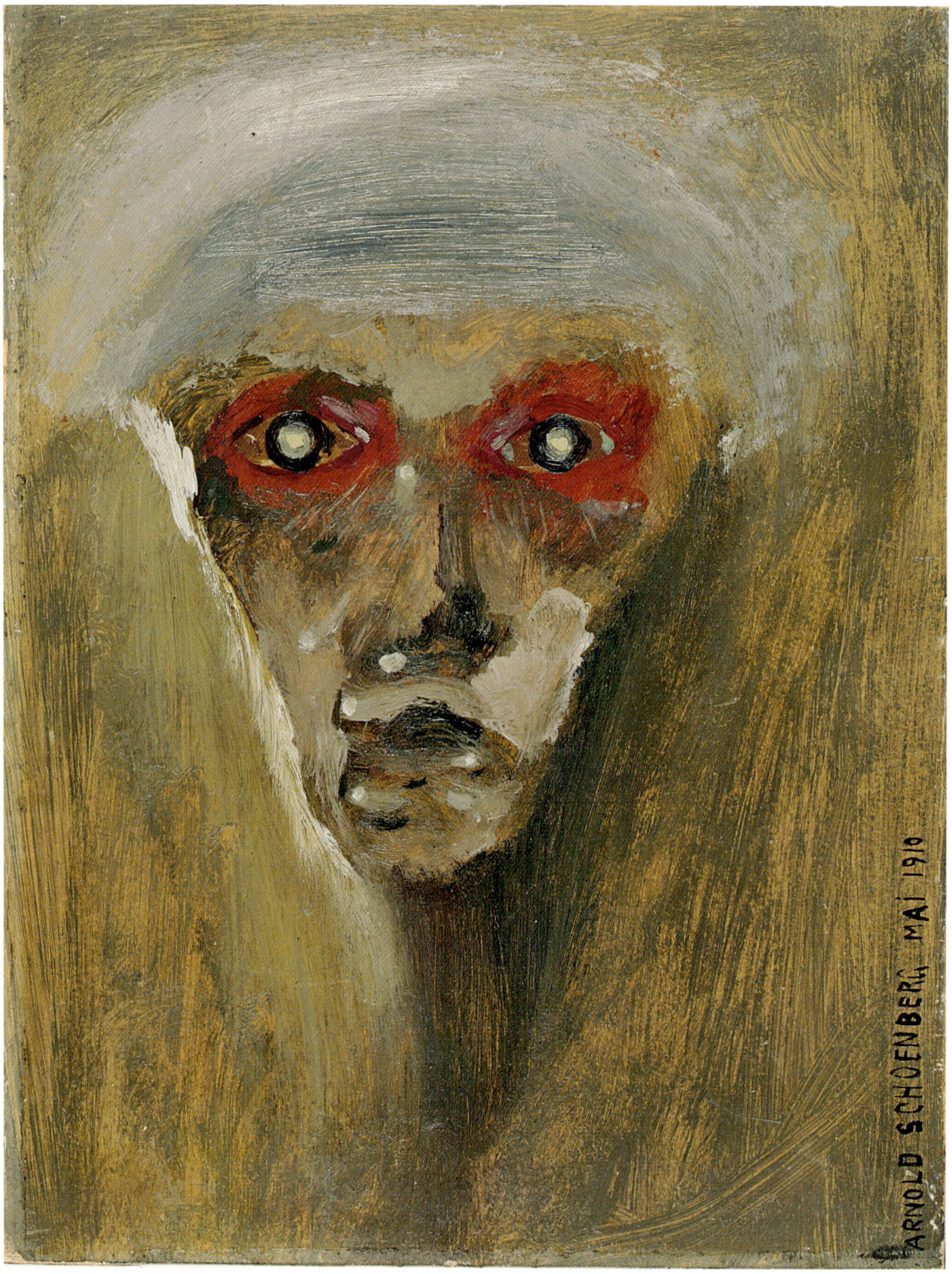

39 **Arnold Schoenberg** *Red Gaze*, 1910. Oil on cardboard, 12⅝ x 9⅞ in. (32 x 25 cm). Arnold Schoenberg Center, Vienna.

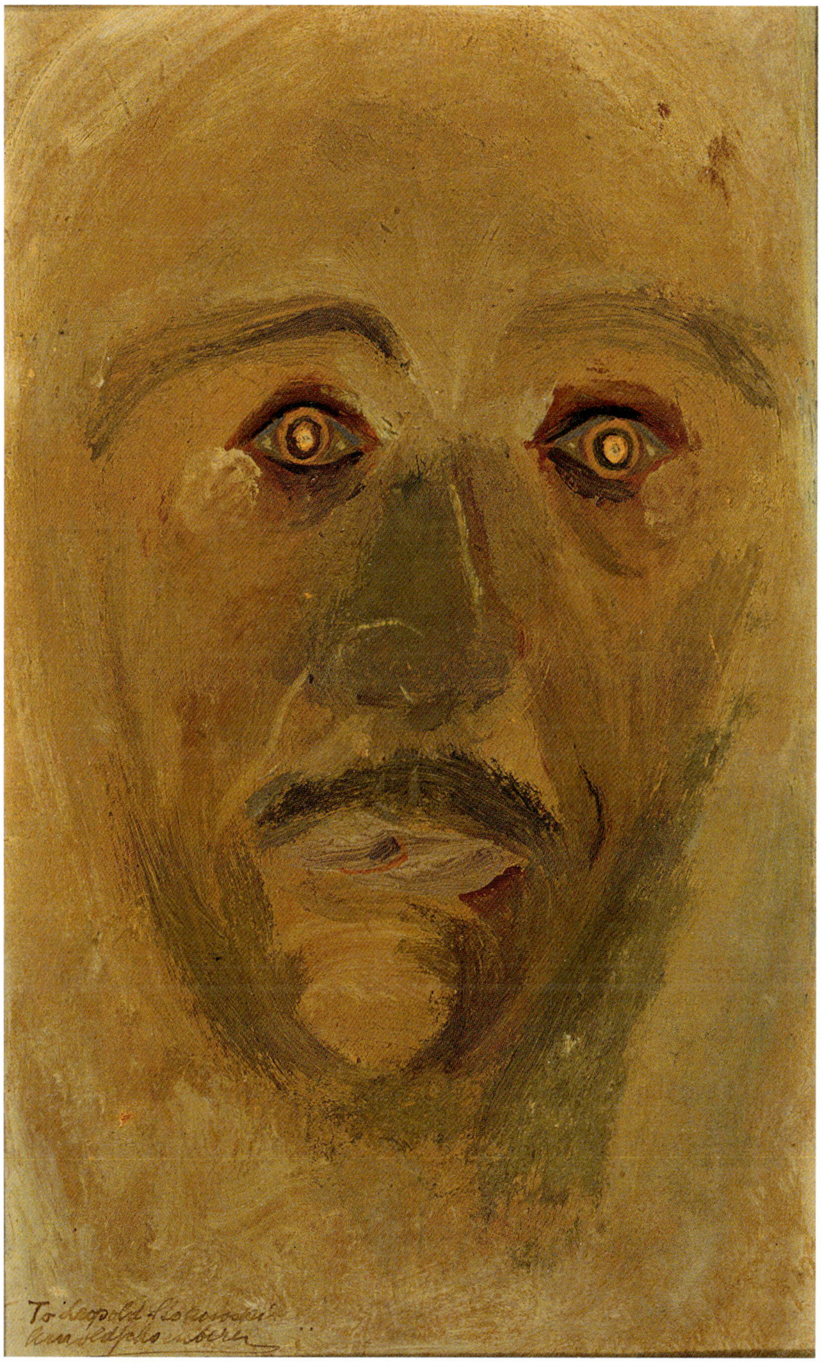

40 **Arnold Schoenberg** *Self-Portrait (Vision)*, 1910. Inscribed: "To Leopold Stokowski. Arnold Schoenberg. September 1944." Oil on canvas, 12⅝ x 7⅞ in. (32 x 20 cm). Music Division, Library of Congress, Washington, D.C.

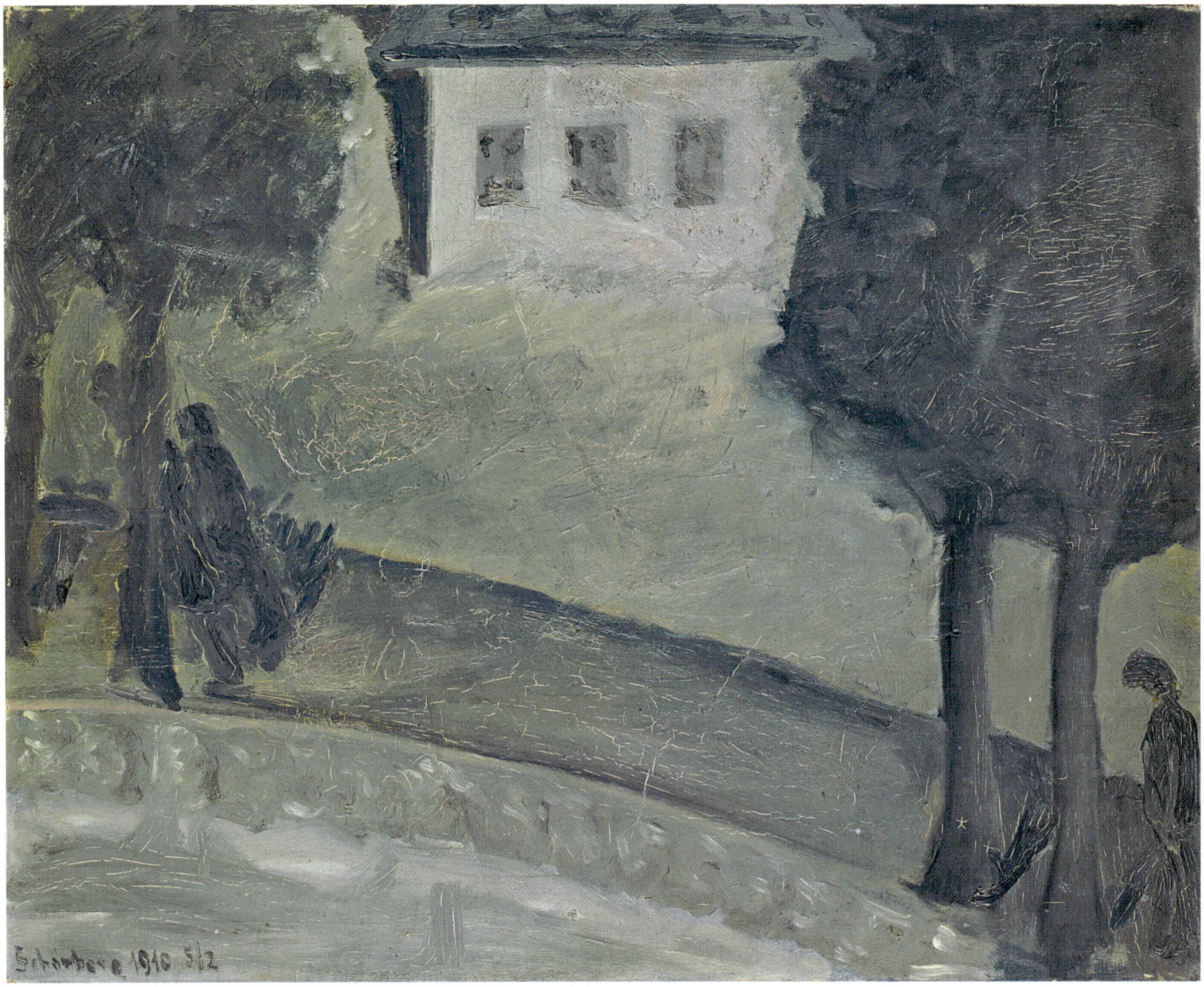

41 **Arnold Schoenberg** *Night Landscape*, 1910. Oil on canvas, $22\frac{13}{16}$ x $28\frac{3}{4}$ in. (58 x 73 cm). Arnold Schoenberg Center, Vienna.

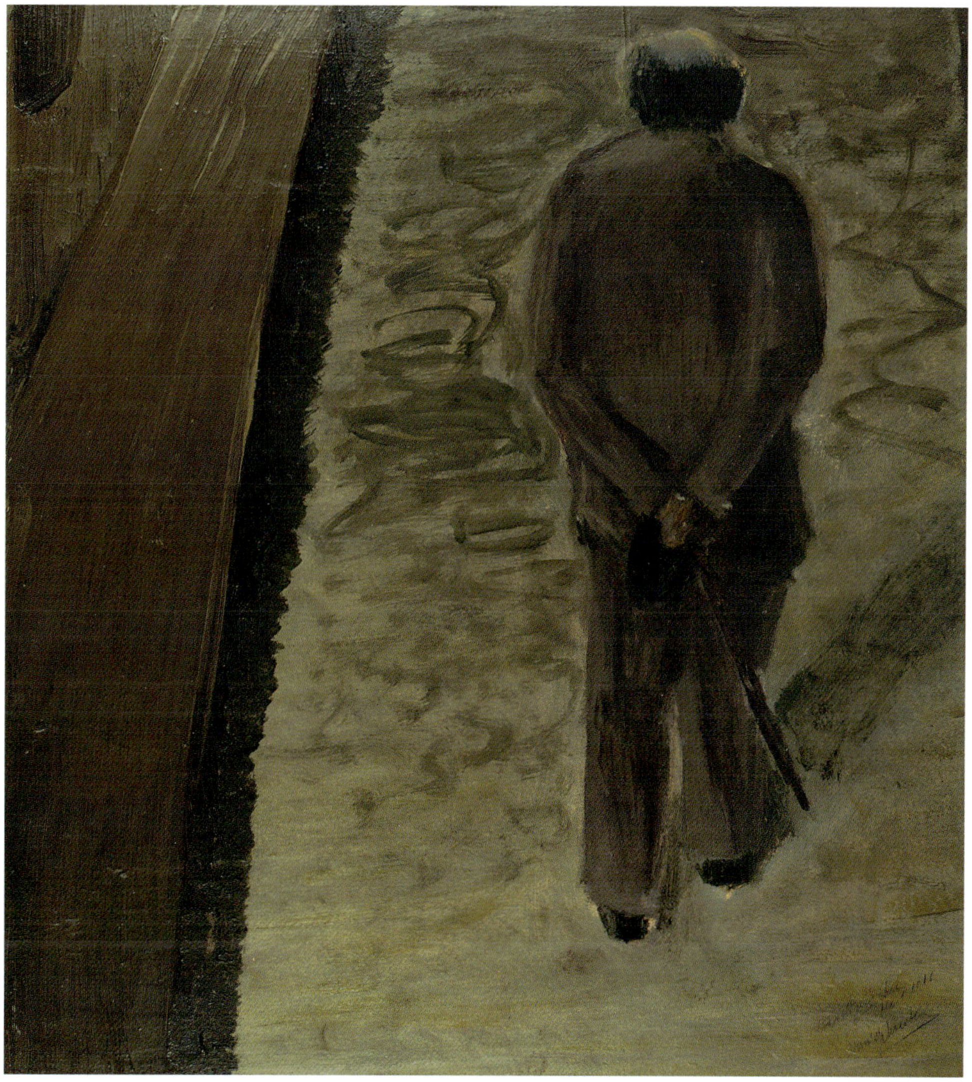

42 **Arnold Schoenberg** *Self-Portrait, Walking*, 1911. Oil on cardboard, 18⅞ x 17¾ in. (48 x 45 cm). Arnold Schoenberg Center, Vienna.

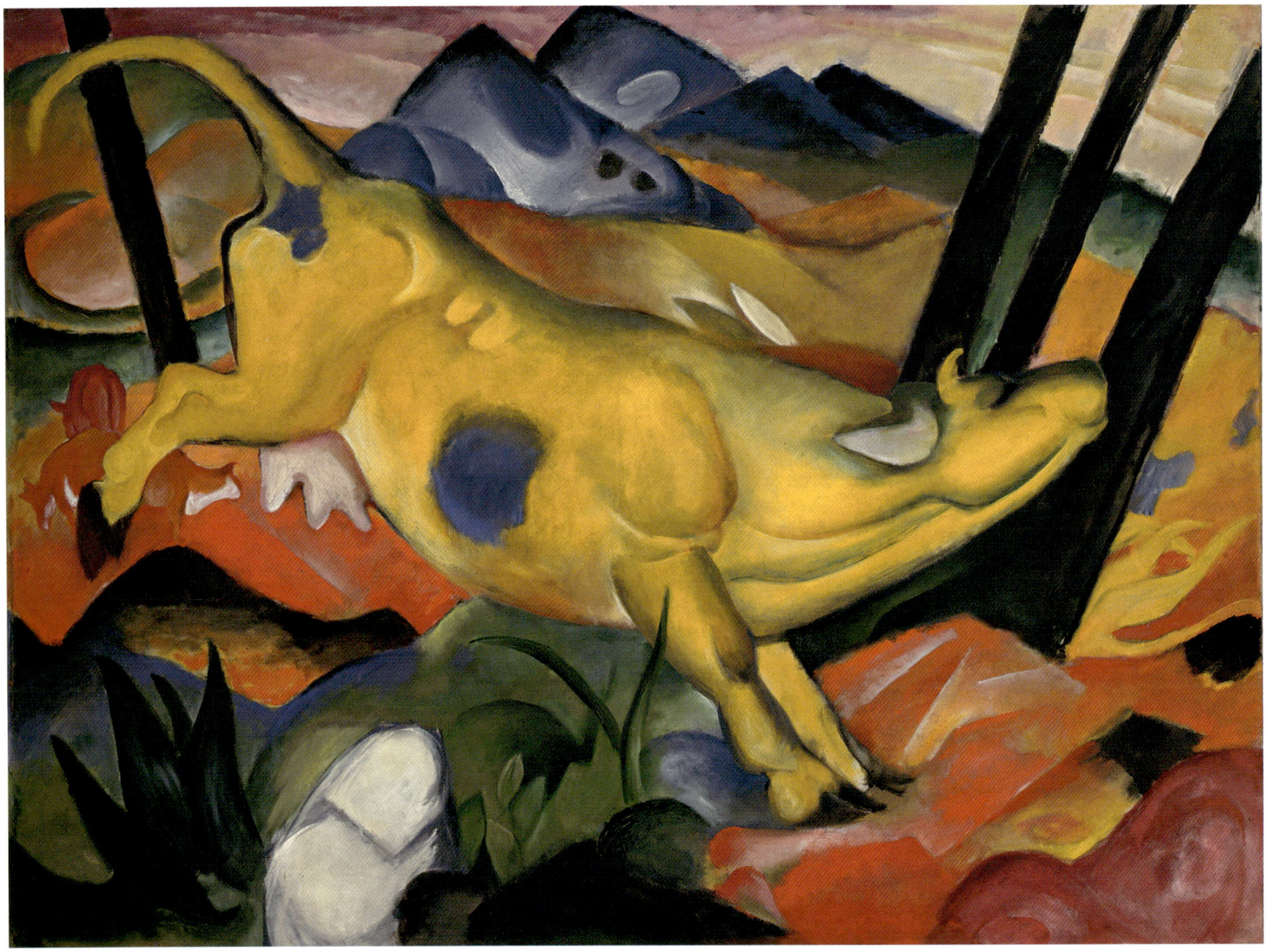

43 **Franz Marc** (German, 1880–1916) *Yellow Cow*, 1911. Oil on canvas, 55⅜ x 74½ in. (140.5 x 189.2 cm). Solomon R. Guggenheim Museum, New York, 49.1210.

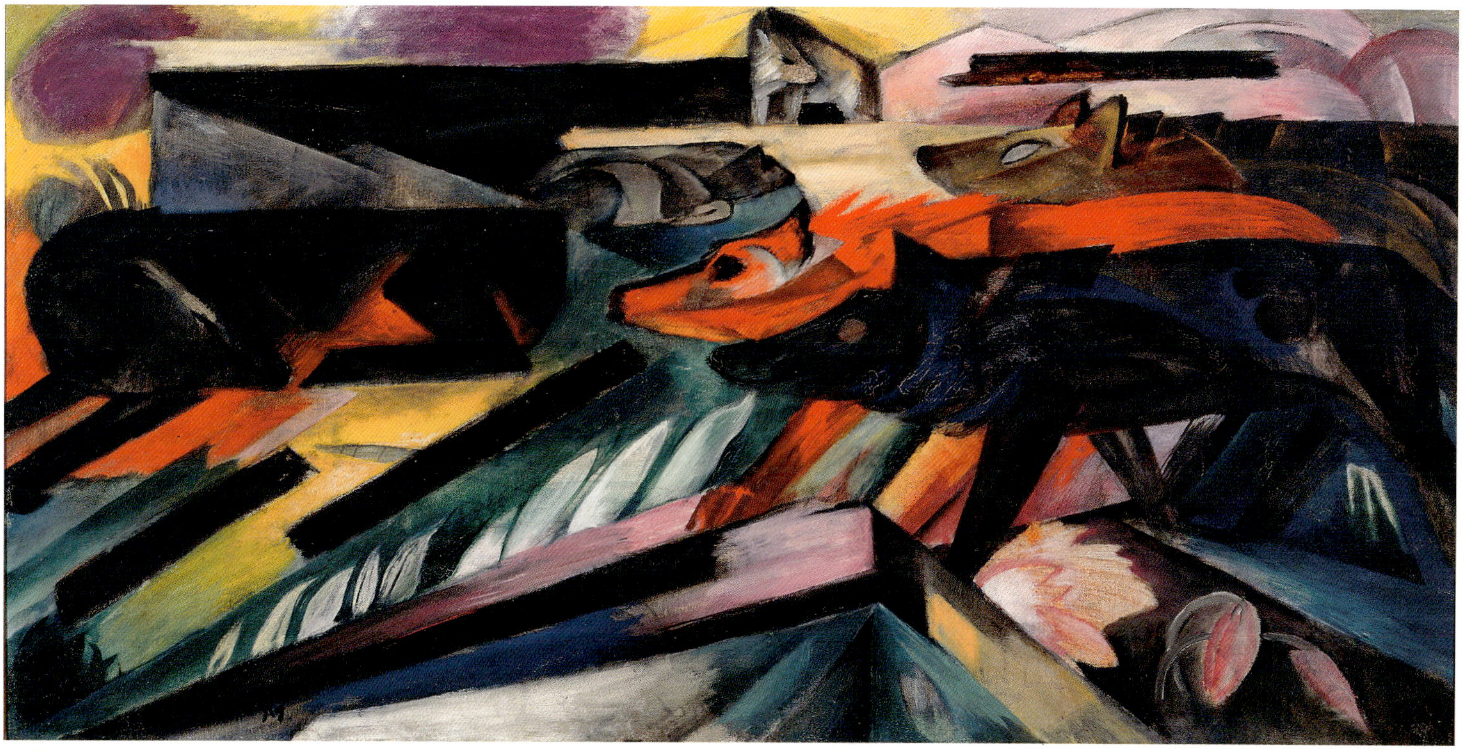

44 **Franz Marc** *The Wolves (Balkan War)*, 1913. Oil on canvas, 27⅞ x 55 in. (70.8 x 139.7 cm). Albright-Knox Art Gallery, Buffalo, New York, Charles Clifton, James G. Forsyth and Charles W. Goodyear Funds, 1951.

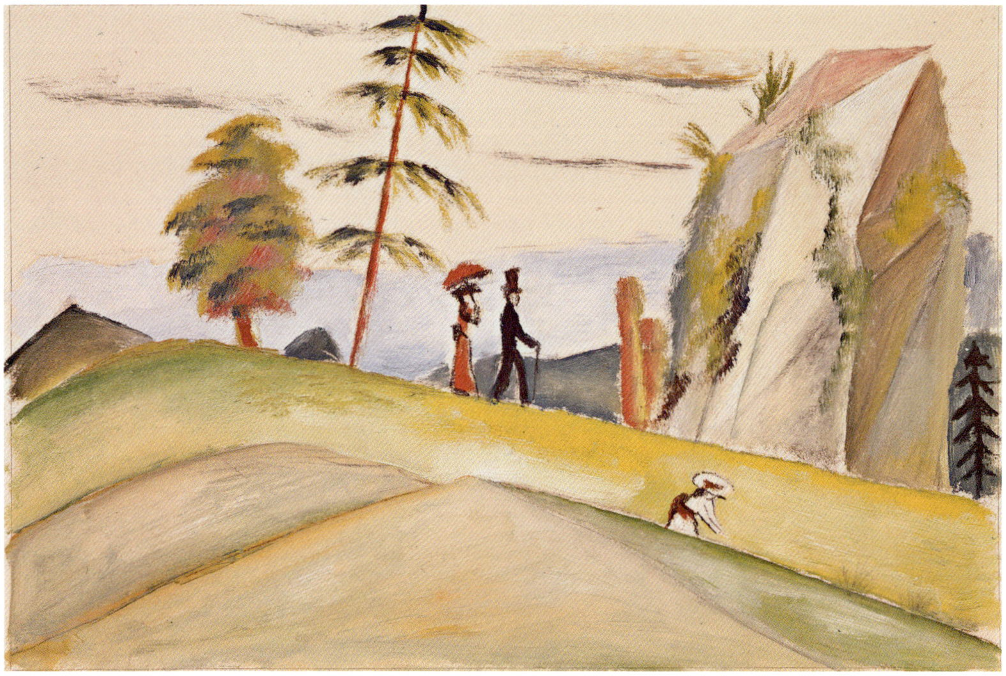

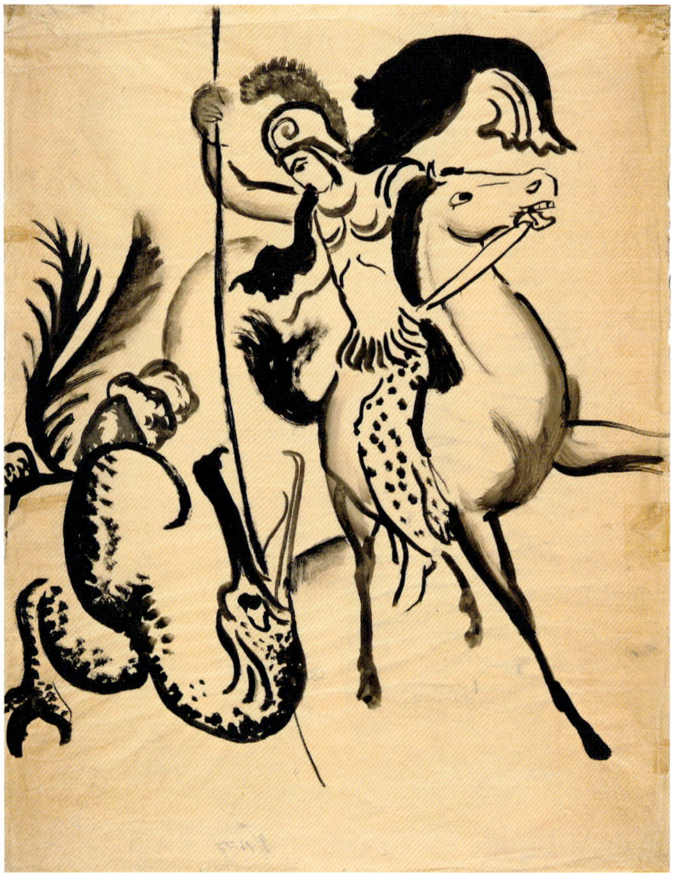

45 **August Macke** (German, 1887–1914) *Strollers in a Rocky Landscape*, 1911. Oil on paper, 10⅞ x 16⅜ in. (27.6 x 41.6 cm). Albright-Knox Art Gallery, Buffalo, New York, Gift of The Seymour H. Knox Foundation, Inc., 1971.

46 **August Macke** *Saint George*, 1912. India ink, brush, 24⅞ x 19½ in. (63.3 x 49.6 cm). Städtische Galerie im Lenbachhaus, Munich, G 12557.

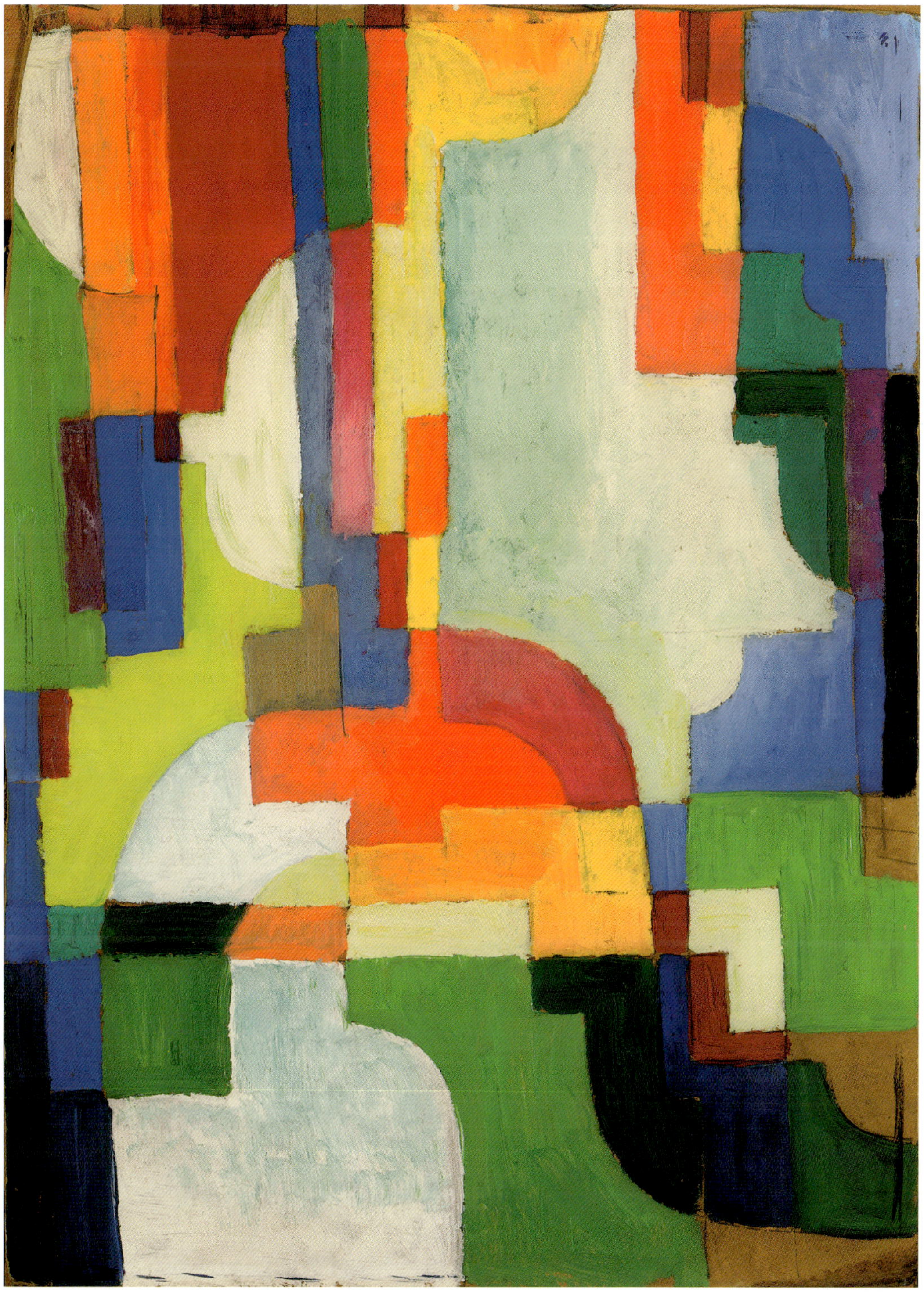

47 **August Macke** *Colored Forms I*, 1913. Oil on pasteboard, mounted on wood, 20⅞ x 15⅛ in. (53.1 x 38.5 cm). Westfälisches Landesmuseum für Kunst und Kulturgeschichte, Münster, Germany, permanent loan from private collection.

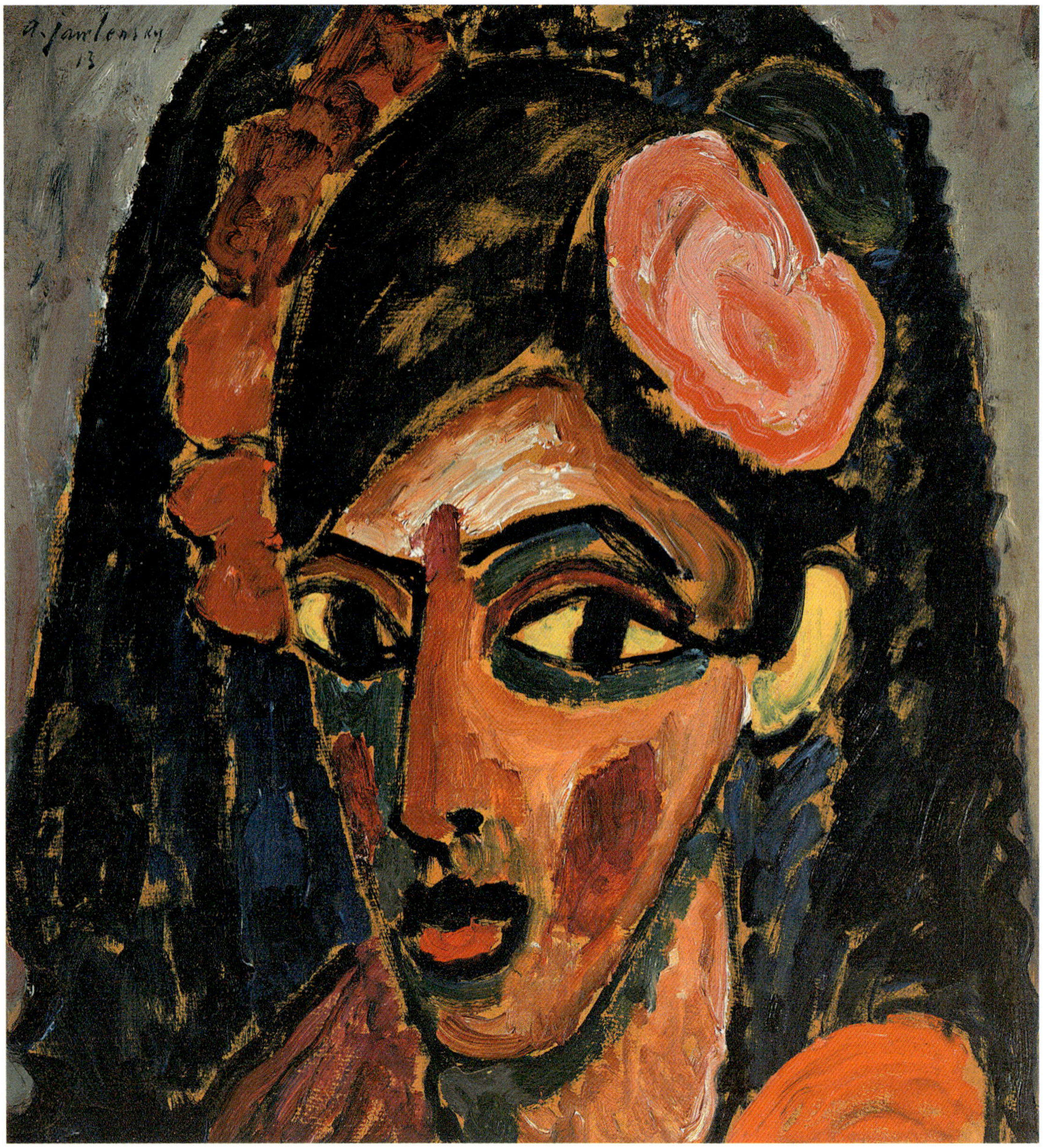

48 **Alexei von Jawlensky** *Egyptian Girl*, 1913. Oil on cardboard, mounted on wood, 21 x 19½ in. (53.3 x 49.5 cm). The Saint Louis Art Museum, Bequest of Morton D. May.

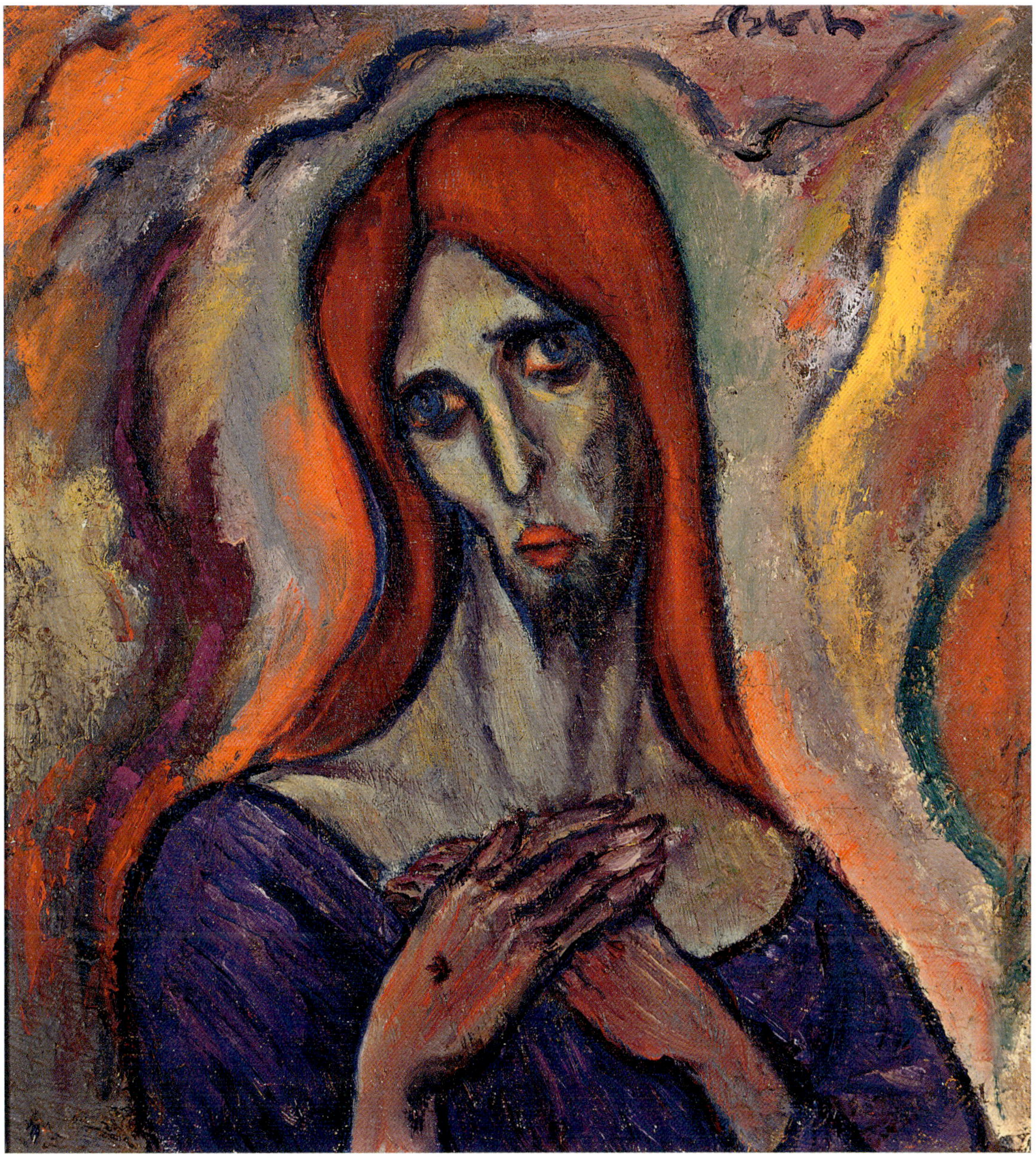

49 **Albert Bloch** (American, 1882–1961) *Head*, 1911. Oil on canvas, 19 1/16 x 17 13/16 in. (48.4 x 45.2 cm). The Albert Bloch Foundation, Lawrence, Kansas.

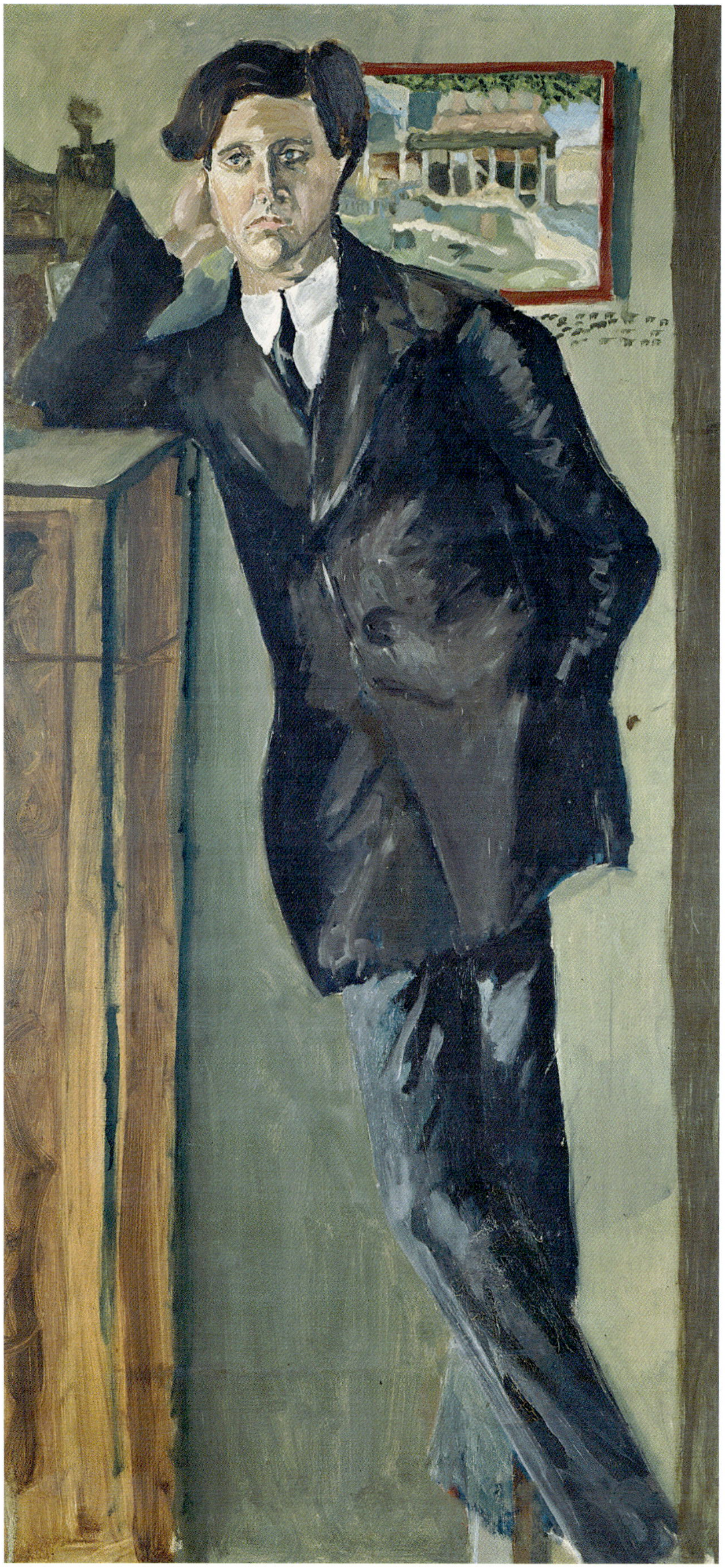

50 **Arnold Schoenberg** *Alban Berg*, n.d. Oil on canvas, 69⅛ x 33½ in. (175.5 x 85 cm). Museen der Stadt Wien.

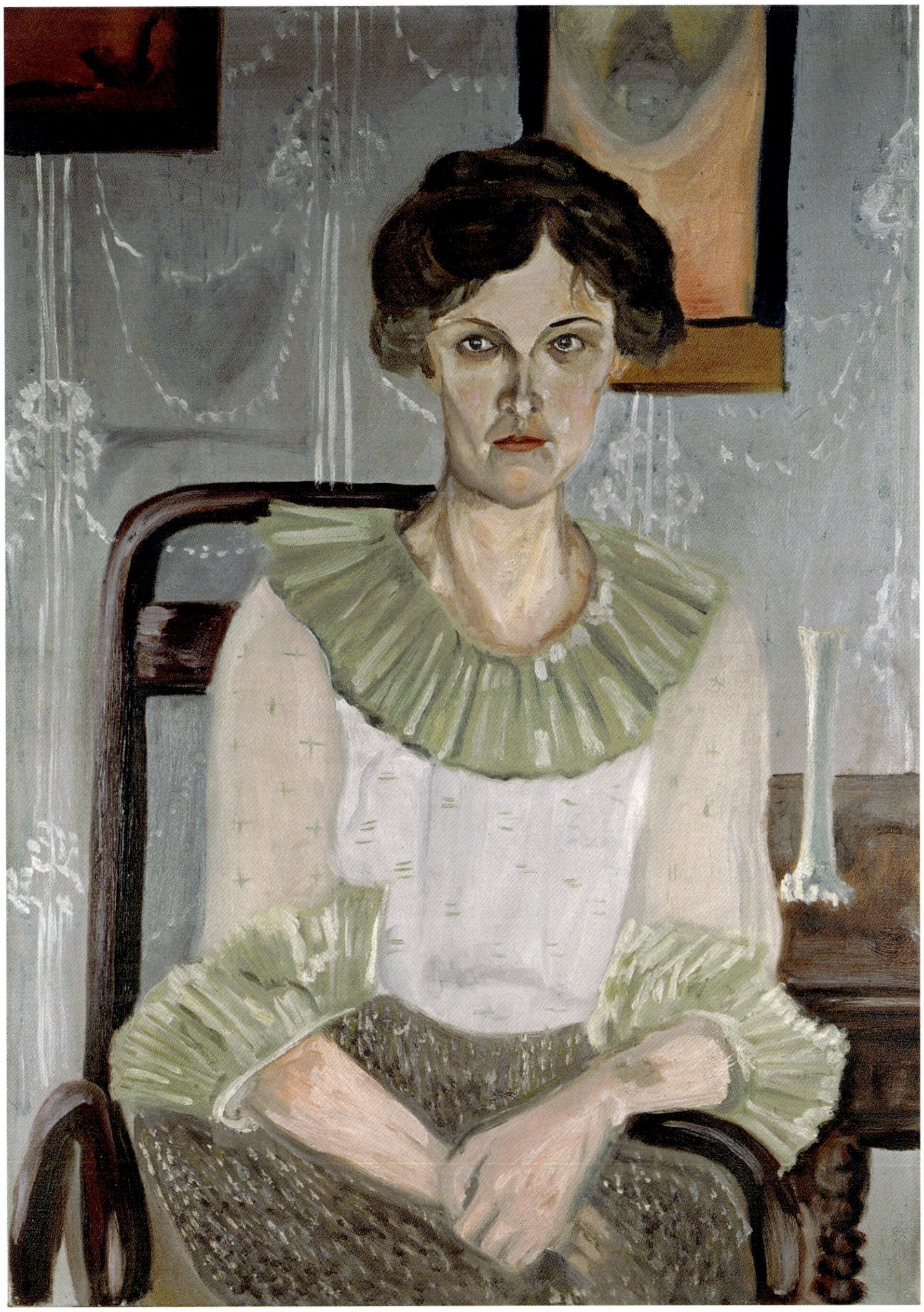

51 **Arnold Schoenberg** *Helene Nahowski*, 1910. Oil on canvas, 39⅜ x 29⅛ in. (100 x 74 cm). Museen der Stadt Wien.

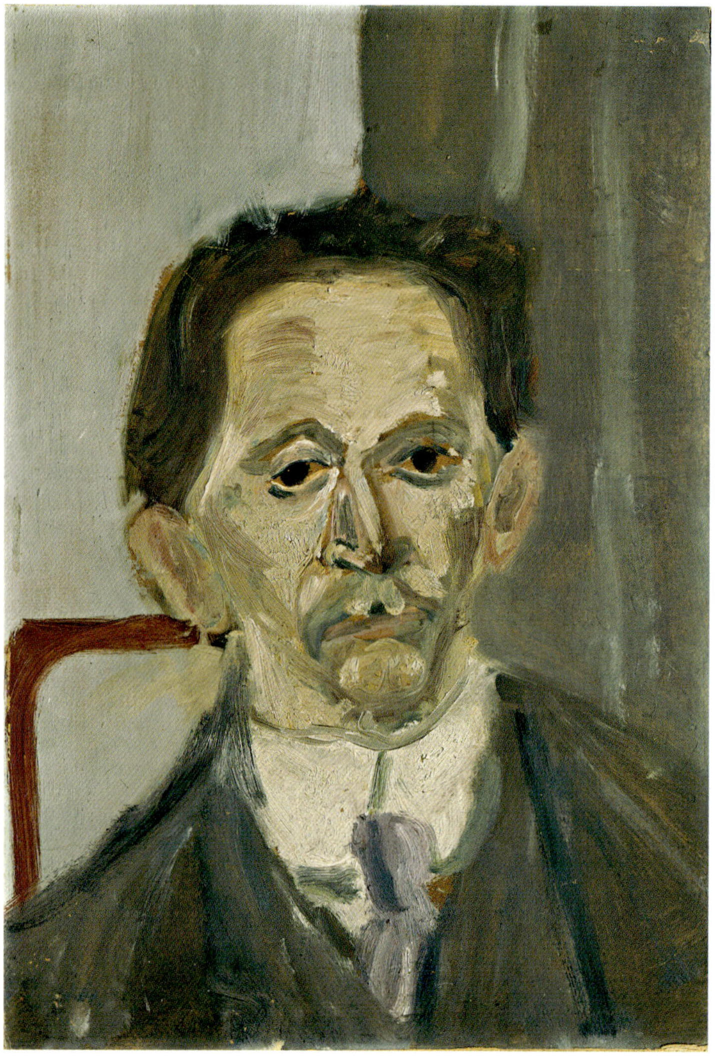

52 **Arnold Schoenberg** *Alexander von Zemlinsky*, n.d. Oil on cardboard, 19¼ x 13⅜ in. (49 x 34 cm). Arnold Schoenberg Center, Vienna.

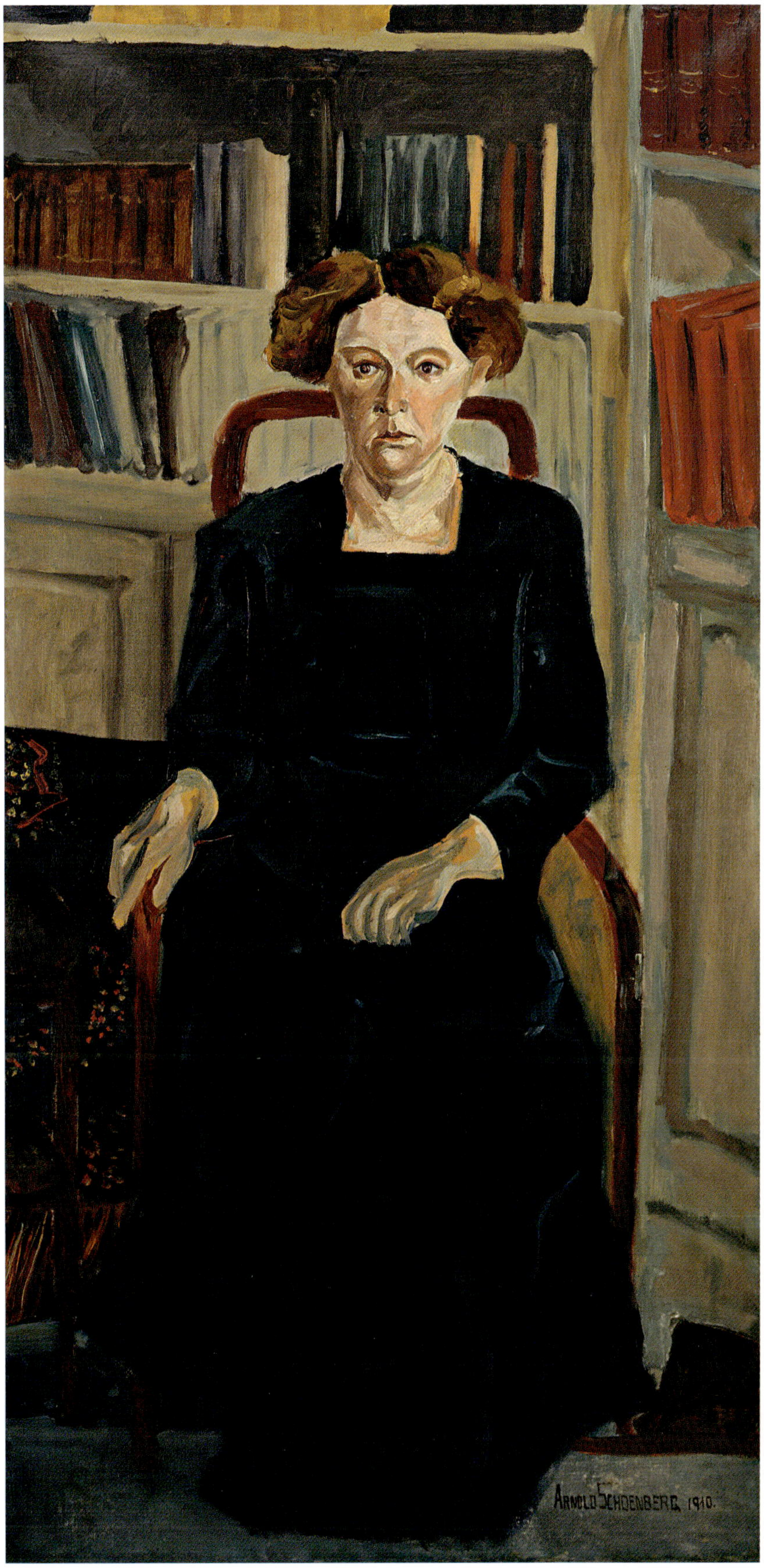

53 **Arnold Schoenberg** *Mathilde Schoenberg*, 1910. Oil on canvas, 63 x 31½ in. (160 x 80 cm). University of Applied Arts Vienna, Collection.

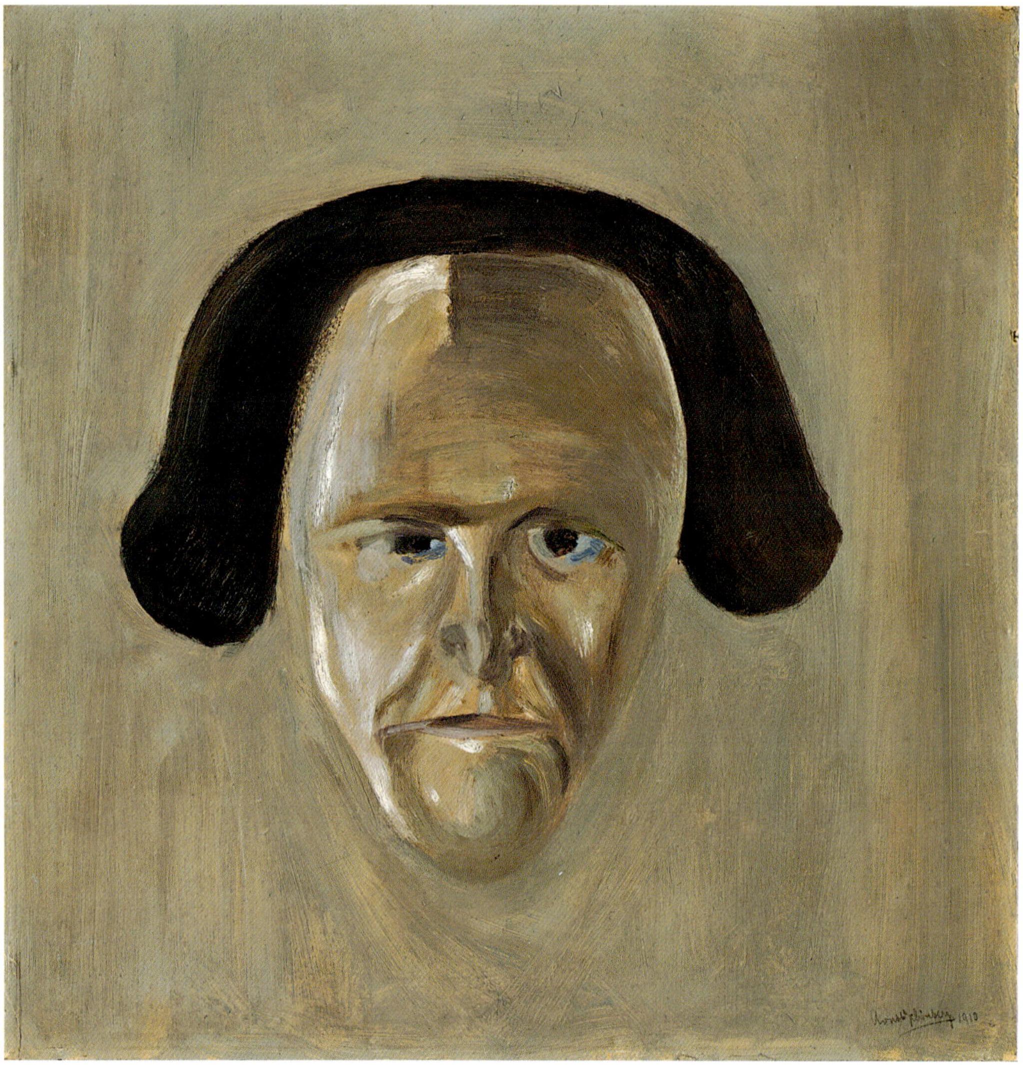

54 **Arnold Schoenberg** *Gustav Mahler*, 1910. Oil on cardboard, 17¾ x 16⅞ in. (45 x 43 cm). Arnold Schoenberg Center, Vienna.

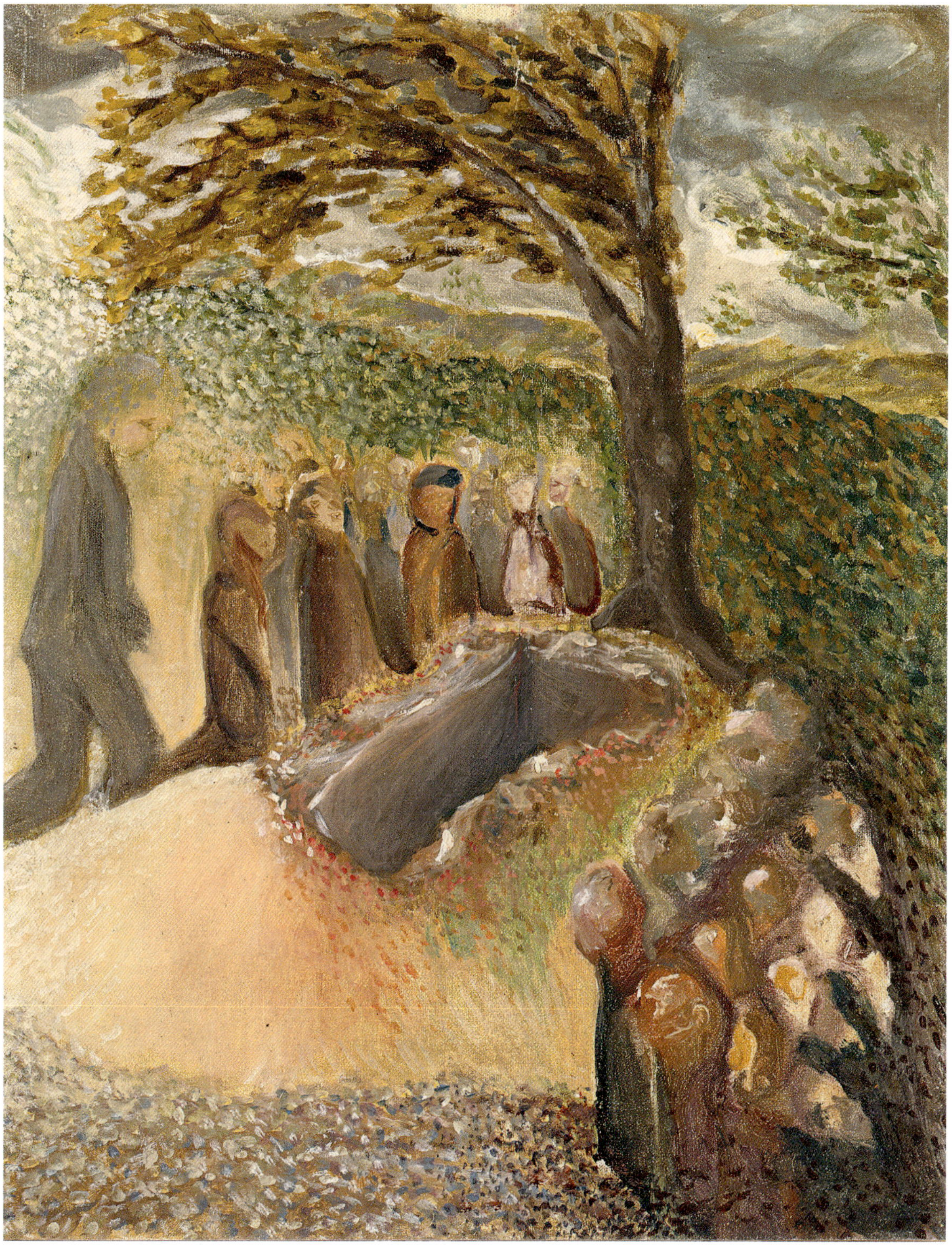

55 **Arnold Schoenberg** *Burial of Gustav Mahler*, 1911. Oil on canvas, 17 x 12 in. (43.2 x 30.5 cm). Estate of Heinrich Jalowetz; Courtesy Galerie St. Etienne, New York.

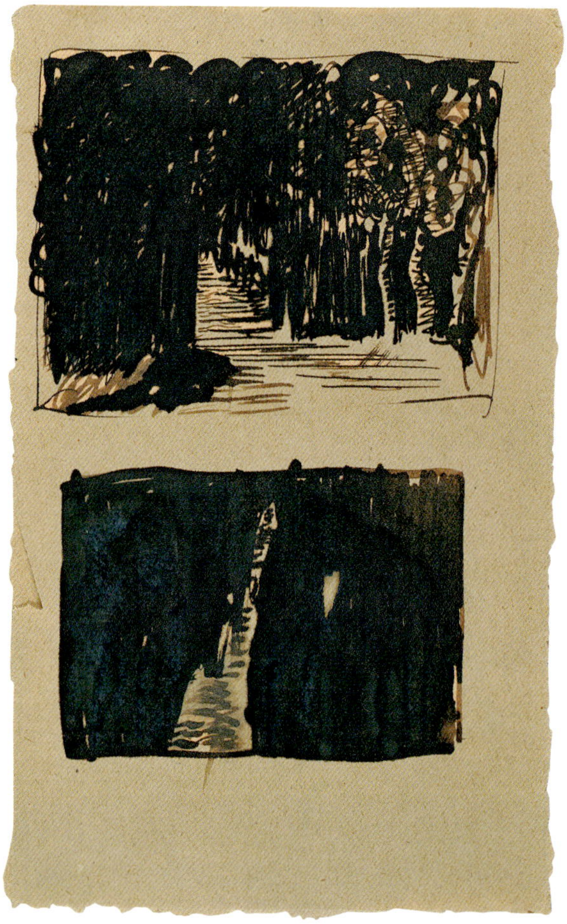

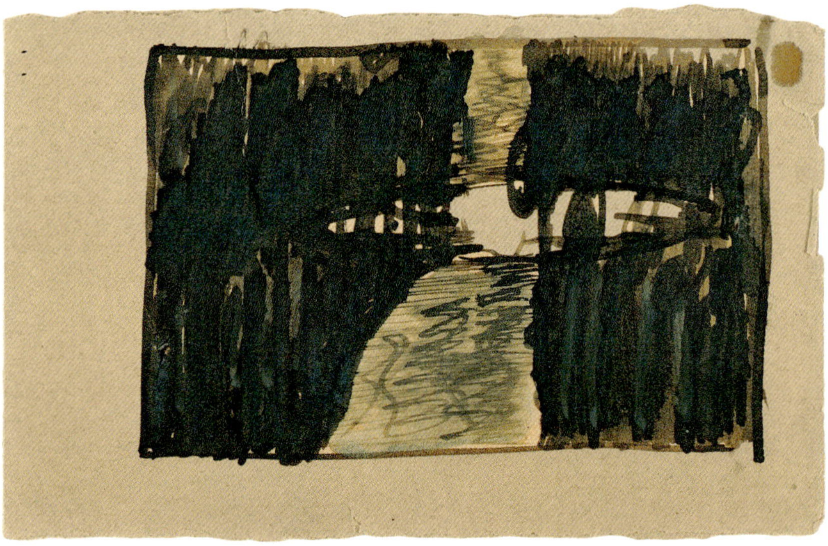

56 **Arnold Schoenberg** *Erwartung (Expectation) (Stage settings)*, n.d. Drawing ink on paper, $6\frac{3}{4} \times 4\frac{3}{8}$ in. (17 x 11 cm). Arnold Schoenberg Center, Vienna.

57 **Arnold Schoenberg** *Erwartung (Stage setting)*, n.d. Watercolor on paper, $3\frac{15}{16} \times 6\frac{3}{4}$ in. (10 x 17 cm). Arnold Schoenberg Center, Vienna.

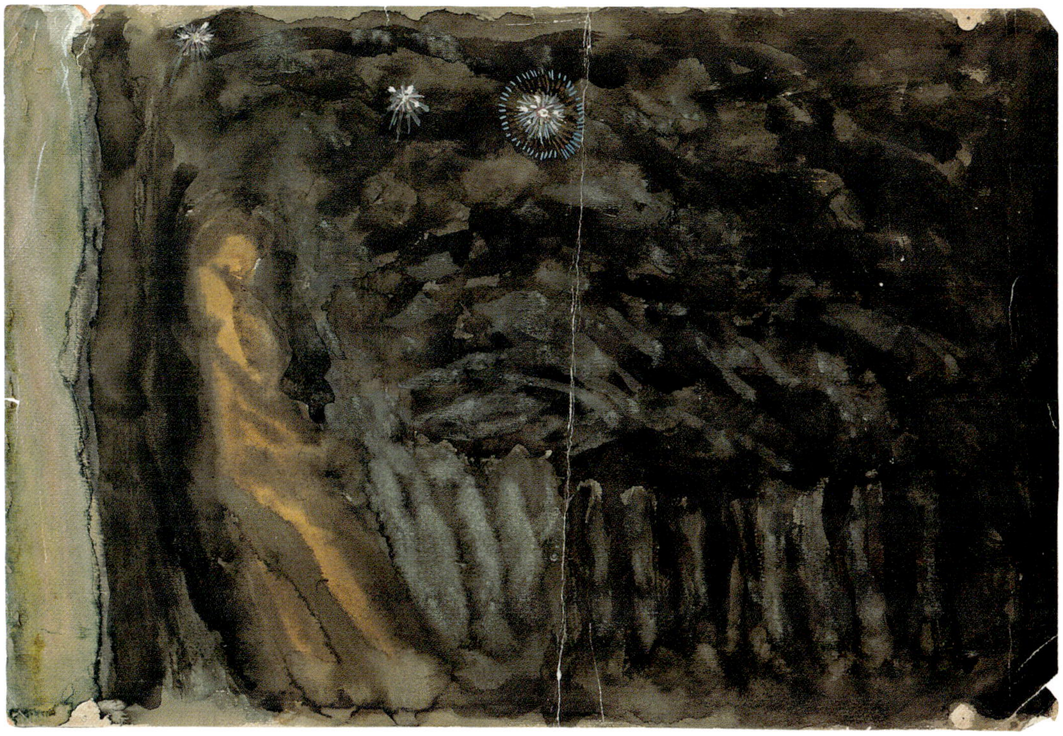

58 **Arnold Schoenberg** *Erwartung (Stage setting)*, n.d. Watercolor and gouache on paper, 13 x 18⅞ in. (33 x 48 cm). Arnold Schoenberg Center, Vienna.

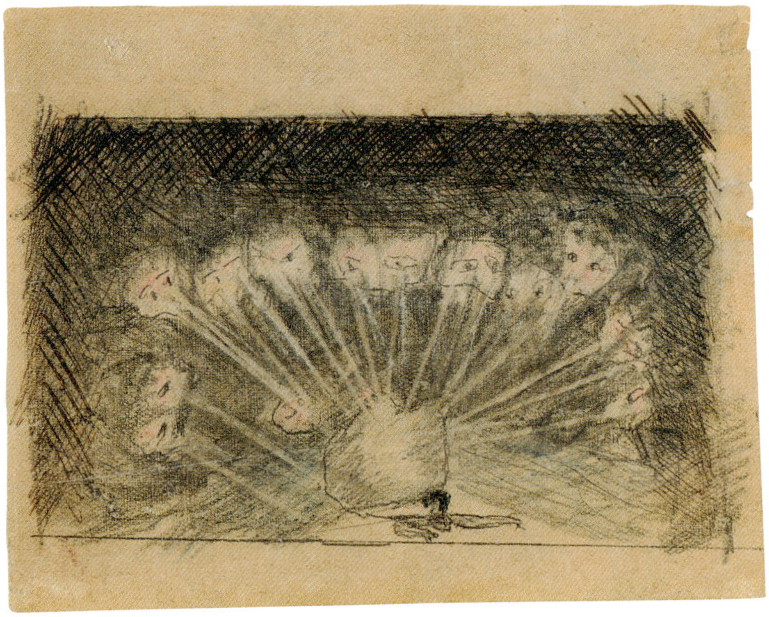

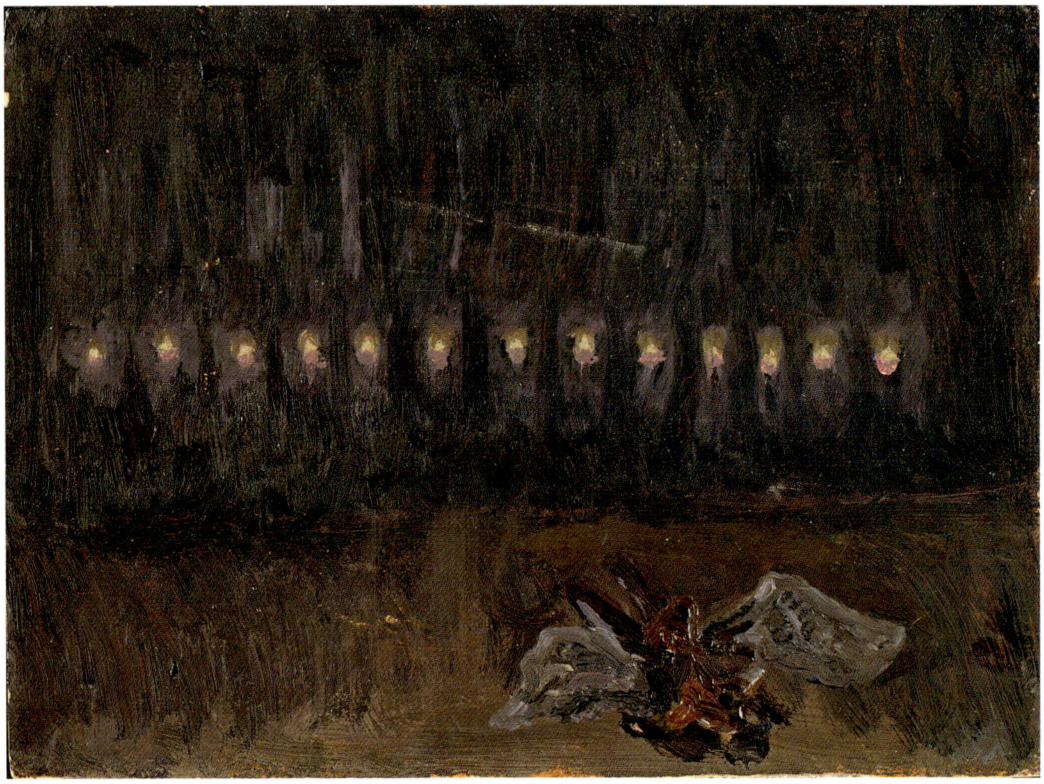

59 **Arnold Schoenberg** *Die glückliche Hand (The lucky hand) (Stage setting, scene 4)*, n.d. Graphite, drawing ink, and colored pencil on paper, 4⅜ x 5½ in. (11 x 14 cm). Arnold Schoenberg Center, Vienna.

60 **Arnold Schoenberg** *Die glückliche Hand (Stage setting, scene 1)*, n.d. Oil on cardboard, 8⅝ x 11¹³⁄₁₆ in. (22 x 30 cm). Arnold Schoenberg Center, Vienna.

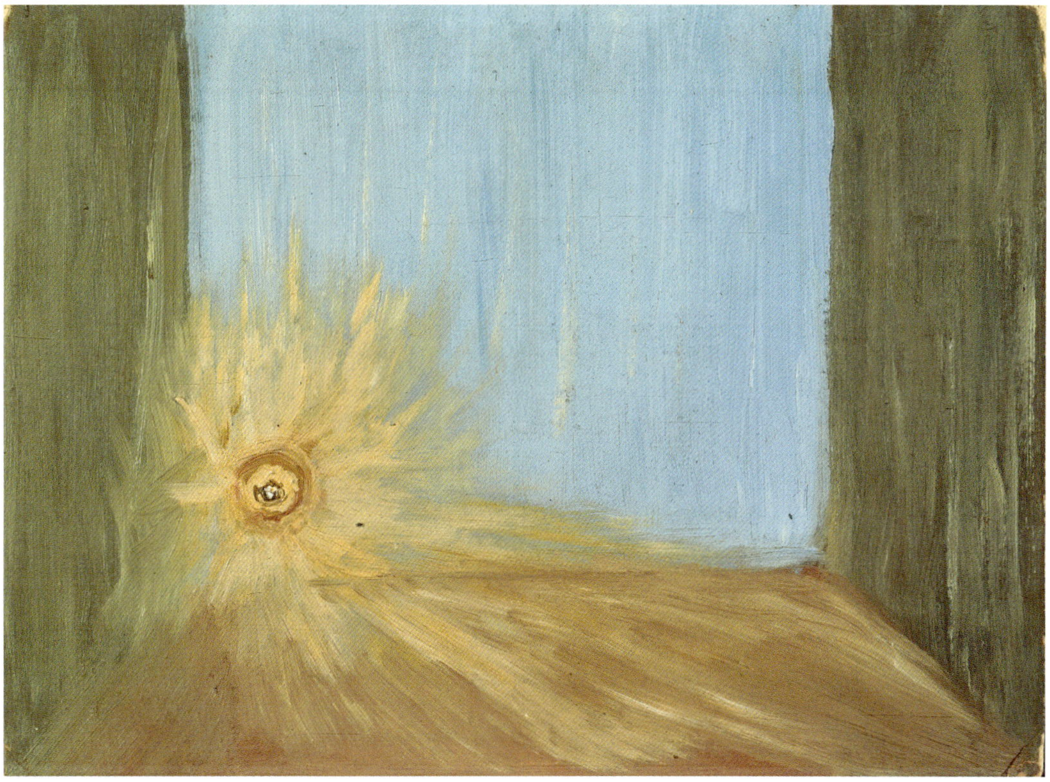

61 **Arnold Schoenberg** *Die glückliche Hand (Stage setting, scene 2)*, n.d. Oil on cardboard, 8⅝ x 11¹³⁄₁₆ in. (22 x 30 cm). Arnold Schoenberg Center, Vienna.

Chronologies of Arnold Schoenberg and Wassily Kandinsky

Gabriel de Guzman

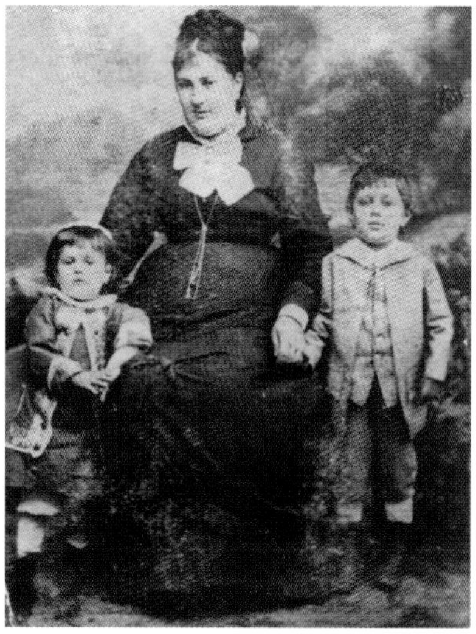

Pauline Schönberg with Ottilie and Arnold, 1879.

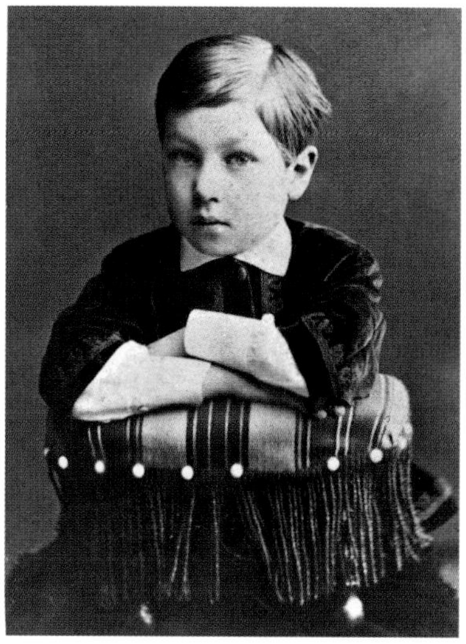

Wassily Kandinsky at age six, 1872.

Arnold Schoenberg
(1874–1951)

1874 Born in Vienna on September 13 to Jewish parents: Samuel Schönberg, a shoemaker, and Pauline Schönberg (née Nachod).

1876 Birth of sister, Ottilie.

1882 Learns to play violin. Birth of brother, Heinrich.

1883 First attempts at musical compositions, primarily violin duets.

1885 Teaches himself to play cello and begins playing chamber music. Composes modest works such as marches and polkas inspired by military band concerts and coffeehouse arrangements of classical music.

1889 Father dies of pneumonia.

1890 Quits school and begins apprenticeship at private bank to help support family.

1893 Composes earliest known complete work, *In hellen Träumen hab ich Dich oft geschaut* (In clear dreams I oft have seen Thee), for voice and piano.

Wassily Kandinsky
(1866–1944)

1866 Born in Moscow on December 4 to Wassily Kandinsky, a tea merchant from East Siberia, and Lydia Kandinsky (née Tikheeva).

1871 Family moves to Odessa. Parents divorce; aunt becomes responsible for raising him. Takes lessons in drawing and music.

1876 Attends humanities grammar school until 1885; learns to play piano and cello there.

1886 Studies law, economics, and ethnography at University of Moscow.

1889 Participates in research expedition to province of Vologda sponsored by Imperial Society for Natural Sciences, Ethnography, and Anthropology. Folk art of northern Russia makes lasting impact on him. Visits Hermitage Museum in Saint Petersburg and sees paintings by Rembrandt for the first time. Travels to Paris.

1892 Concludes studies and passes state

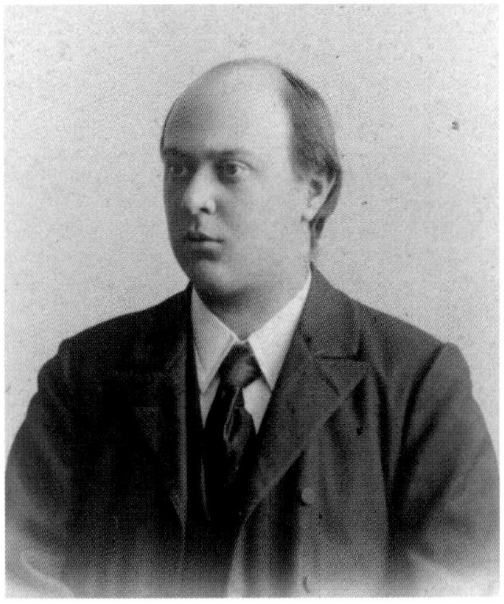

Arnold Schoenberg, Berlin, 1902.

1894 Meets Alexander Zemlinsky, his first composition teacher, musical mentor, and future brother-in-law. Plays in Polyhymnia, an amateur orchestra conducted by Zemlinsky. Receives prize for "Schilflied" (Bulrush song). Composes Three Piano Pieces.

1895 Leaves banking job to dedicate himself exclusively to music. Directs several workers' choirs.

1896 Composes Six Pieces for Piano, Four Hands. Befriends architect Adolf Loos, who provides financial support for many of his early concerts.

1897 Composes String Quartet in D Major.

1898 Converts from Judaism to Protestantism. Composes Two Songs, op. 1, for baritone and piano. Zemlinsky arranges Schoenberg's String Quartet in D Major for performance in December by Fitzner Quartet in Vienna.

1899 Composes Four Songs, op. 2, for voice and piano and string sextet *Verklärte Nacht* (Transfigured night), op. 4. Starts composing Six Songs, op. 3. Begins a relationship with Zemlinsky's sister, Mathilde.

1900 Directs workers' choruses and orchestrates operettas to support himself and his family. Begins composing *Gurrelieder* (Songs of Gurre), which remains incomplete until 1911. Meets Alma Maria Schindler, future wife of composer Gustav Mahler.

1901 Marries Mathilde Zemlinsky on October 18 in Lutheran church in Vienna. They move to Berlin in December.

1902 Birth of daughter Gertrude on August 1. Begins work on symphonic poem *Pelleas und Melisande*, op. 5, based on play of same title by Maurice Maeterlinck. Premiere of *Verklärte Nacht* performed by Rosé Quartet in Vienna. Meets composer Richard Strauss, who recommends him for teaching position at Stern Conservatory, Berlin.

1903 Completes *Pelleas und Melisande* and Six Songs, op. 3. Begins composing Eight Songs, op. 6. Returns to Vienna in late summer. Meets Gustav Mahler. Awarded Liszt Scholarship with Strauss's support. Teaches harmony

law exam. Marries second cousin Ania Chimiakin. Second trip to Paris.

1893 Submits dissertation, "The Legality of Laborers' Wages," and receives Ph.D. Appointed teaching assistant, law faculty of University of Moscow.

1895 Becomes artistic director of art-printing firm in Moscow.

1896 Sees one of Claude Monet's Wheatstacks at French Industrial Exhibition in Moscow. The experience motivates him to become an artist. Declines lecturer position at University of Dorpat (now Tartu, Estonia). Moves to Munich to study painting.

1897 Studies at Anton Ažbè's private art school for two years, where he meets painters Alexei von Jawlensky and Marianne von Werefkin. Visits Munich Secession exhibition and sees Jugendstil art.

1898 Fails entrance exam to Munich Art Academy; continues painting independently.

1900 Second application to Academy is accepted; becomes pupil of Franz von Stuck. Participates in annual exhibition of Moscow Artists' Association, with whom he shows yearly until 1908.

1901 Founds Phalanx artists' association with Rolf Niczky, Waldemar Hecker, Gustav Freytag, and Wilhelm Hüsgen; becomes its president. First Phalanx exhibition held in Munich in August. Travels to Odessa to participate in exhibition of Association of South Russian Artists. Phalanx School of Painting opens in winter under Kandinsky's directorship.

1902 Meets Gabriele Münter, a student in his painting class. Befriends artist and designer Hermann Obrist. Second Phalanx exhibition features artists associated with Darmstadt artists' colony, including Peter Behrens. Writes review of Munich art scene for Russian periodical *Mir Iskusstva* (World of art) and participates in *World of Art* exhibition in Saint Petersburg. Shows his work in sixth exhibition of Berlin Secession. Third Phalanx exhibition features works by Lovis Corinth and Wilhelm Trübner. Produces his first woodcuts. Visits Kochel

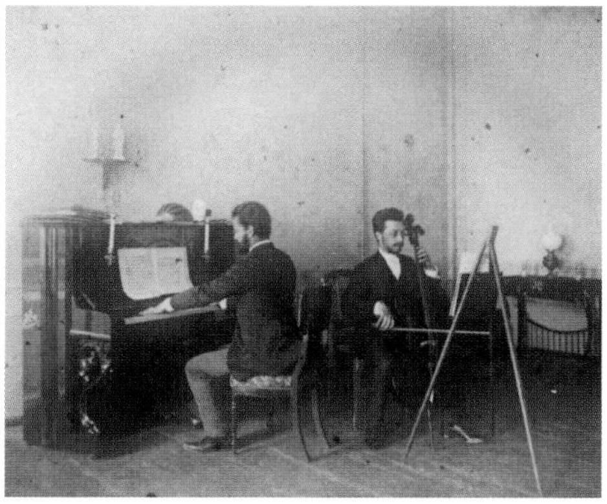

Kandinsky playing the cello, c. 1886.

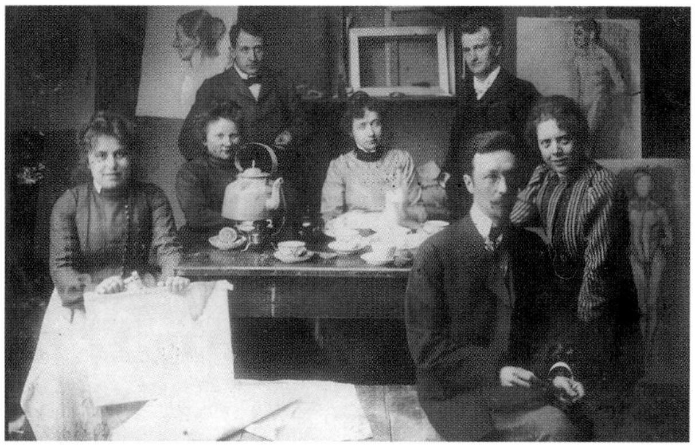

Members of the Phalanx school, Munich, 1902. Clockwise from left: Olga Meerson, Emmy Dresler, Wilhelm Hüsgen, Gabriele Münter, Richard Kothe, Maria Giesler, and Kandinsky.

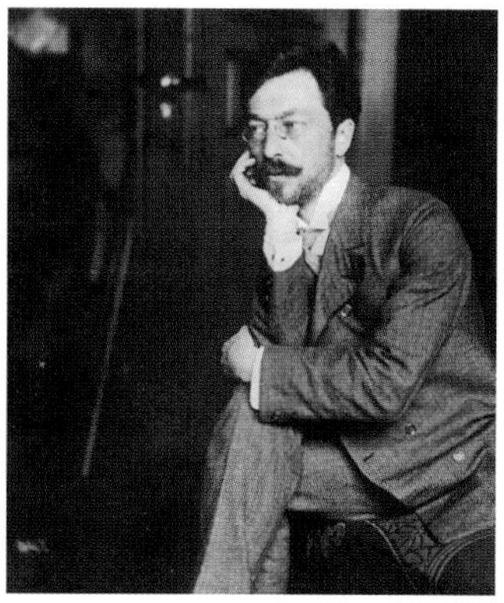

Kandinsky, photographed by Gabriele Münter in Dresden, 1905.

SCHOENBERG

and counterpoint at Schwarzwald School in suburbs of Vienna. Heinrich Jalowetz and Egon Wellesz study composition with Schoenberg.

1904 Founds Society of Creative Composers with Zemlinsky; Mahler named honorary president. Teaches composition privately; Anton Webern, Alban Berg, and Erwin Stein become pupils.

1905 Meets painter Richard Gerstl. Composes First String Quartet in D Minor, op. 7. Conducts premiere of *Pelleas und Melisande* in Vienna. Completes Six Orchestral Songs, op. 8, and Eight Songs, op. 6.

1906 Birth of son Georg on June 22. Completes Chamber Symphony for Fifteen Solo Instruments, op. 9. Starts composing Second Chamber Symphony, which he will not finish until 1939.

1907 Begins to pursue painting seriously. Becomes close friend of Gerstl, who moves into apartment building where Schoenberg and Zemlinsky live. Composes Two Ballads, op. 12, for voice and piano, and *Friede auf Erden* (Peace on earth), op. 13, for mixed chorus. Begins composing Second String Quartet, op. 10, and Two Songs, op. 14, for voice and piano. Premiere of Chamber Symphony, op. 9, in Vienna.

1908 Completes Second String Quartet, op. 10, and Two Songs, op. 14. Begins work on opera *Die glückliche Hand* (The lucky hand), op. 18. Mathilde Schoenberg has brief affair with

KANDINSKY

in German countryside with his students. Meets artist David Burliuk.

1903 Visits Vienna Secession exhibition. Organizes seventh Phalanx exhibition; includes sixteen paintings by Monet. Spends summer visiting German towns with Münter. Phalanx School of Painting closes due to lack of students. Publishes *Poems Without Words* in Moscow. Returns to Munich in October. Meets artist Vladimir Izdebsky in Munich.

1904 Befriends Alfred Kubin, whose work is featured in ninth Phalanx exhibition. Begins working on color theory and "color language." Tenth Phalanx exhibition includes works by Paul Signac, Theo van Rysselberghe, Félix Vallotton, and Henri de Toulouse-Lautrec. Exhibits woodcuts at eleventh Phalanx exhibition. Visits Holland with Münter. Separates from wife, Ania, in September. Participates for the first time in Salon d'Automne and in Les Tendances Nouvelles exhibitions in Paris. Twelfth and last Phalanx exhibition held in Munich in December; the group disbands shortly thereafter. Travels to Tunis with Münter.

1905 Travels through Italy on return to Munich. Spends part of summer with Münter in Dresden. Returns to Munich in mid-August. Exhibits at Salon des Indépendants and Salon d'Automne in Paris. Joins German Artists' Federation. Awarded medal at *XIIe Exposition du Travail* in Paris. First one-man show held at Krause Gallery in Munich.

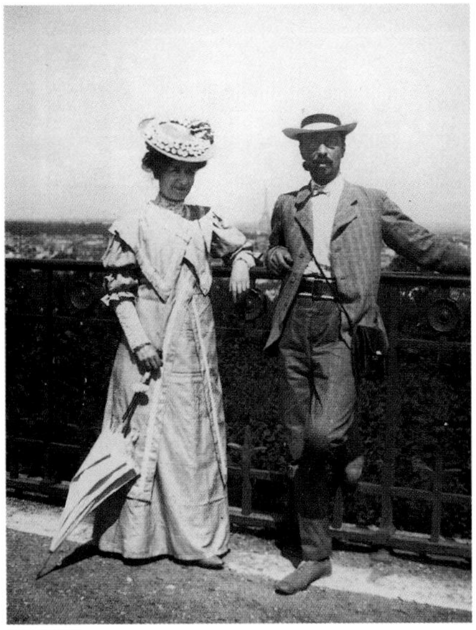

Münter and Kandinsky in Sèvres, 1906.

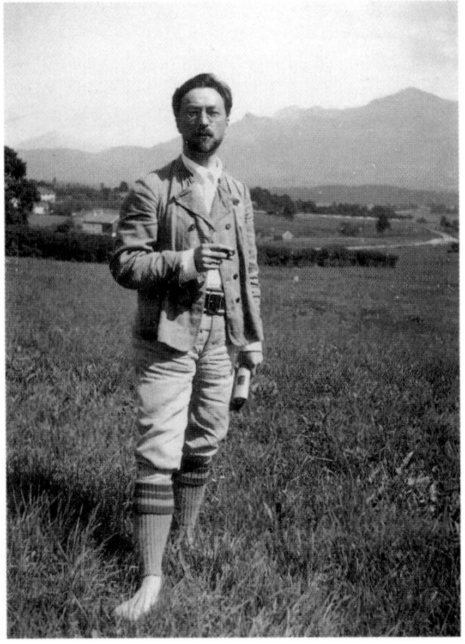

Kandinsky in Murnau, 1910–11.

SCHOENBERG

Gerstl, who commits suicide after affair is exposed. Premiere of Second String Quartet in Vienna causes uproar.

1909 Spends summer in Steinakirchen with his family, Zemlinsky, Berg, Webern, and painter Max Oppenheimer. Composes Five Orchestral Pieces, op. 16, there and meets young doctor and poet Marie Pappenheim, who writes libretto for his opera *Erwartung* (Expectation), op. 17, the score of which is completed in October. Composes Three Piano Pieces, op. 11. Completes song cycle *Fifteen Verses from "The Book of the Hanging Gardens" by Stefan George*, op. 15. Devotes himself to writing and publishes "About Music Criticism," the first of many articles. Signs contract with Universal Editions, Vienna, initiating long professional relationship with its director, Emil Hertzka. Invents a typewriter for musical notes.

1910 First exhibition of his paintings in Hugo Heller's bookshop, Vienna. Lectures on music theory and teaches composition at Vienna's Royal Academy of Music. Writes text for *Die glückliche Hand*.

1911 Begins correspondence with painter Wassily Kandinsky in January. The two meet in mid-September and become friends. Four of Schoenberg's paintings are shown in first Blue Rider exhibition at Moderne Galerie Thannhauser in Munich. Composes Six Little Piano Pieces, op. 19. Publishes *Theory of Harmony* (*Harmonielehre*), his major theoretical work, which he dedicates to Mahler, who died earlier in the year. Completes *Gurrelieder* score and *Herzgewächse* (Heart's foliage), op. 20. Moves to Berlin and teaches at Stern Conservatory.

1912 In February, travels to Prague at Zemlinsky's invitation. Conducts *Pelleas und Melisande* and gives lecture in memory of Mahler. Participates in exhibition *Neukunst Wien* (New Art Vienna) organized by Albert Paris von Gütersloh at Budapest Artists House. Along with Schoenberg's paintings, exhibition includes works by Egon Schiele, Gütersloh, Anton

KANDINSKY

1906 Travels to Paris with Münter in May; they settle in the suburb of Sèvres until June of following year. Works on woodcuts for *Xylographies*. Awarded grand prize at Salon d'Automne in which he shows twenty-one works, including paintings, woodcuts, and craft designs. Exhibits with *Die Brücke* (The bridge) in Dresden.

1907 Shows 109 works at exhibition *Le Musée du Peuple* in Angers, sponsored by Les Tendances Nouvelles. Suffers nervous breakdown and returns to Germany in June. Takes rest cure at Bad Reichenhall in Bavaria. Travels to Berlin in September, where he stays with Münter until spring of 1908.

1908 Attends lecture given by Theosophist Rudolf Steiner in Berlin. Returns to Munich in June. Spends first of several summers in Murnau, a town in foothills of Bavarian Alps, with Münter, Jawlensky, and Werefkin. Begins painting series of Murnau landscapes. Returns to Munich at end of September and moves into apartment with Münter. Meets composer Thomas von Hartmann.

1909 With Jawlensky, Kubin, Münter, Werefkin, and others, founds the Neue Künstlervereinigung München (NKVM) (New Association of Artists Munich) and is elected its president. Begins work on "stage composition" *Der gelbe Klang* (The yellow sound), which is later published in *Blue Rider Almanac*. In summer, Münter buys house in Murnau, where she and Kandinsky stay intermittently until summer of 1914. Kandinsky creates first *Hinterglasmalereien* (reverse glass paintings) inspired by the Bavarian folk art tradition. Begins Improvisations series of paintings. Les Tendances Nouvelles publishes *Xylographies* series of woodcuts in Paris. In December, first exhibition of NKVM is held at Moderne Galerie Thannhauser, Munich, in which Kandinsky shows paintings and woodcuts. Starts work on series of Compositions paintings. Begins *Klänge* (Sounds) prose poems. Participates in Izdeb-

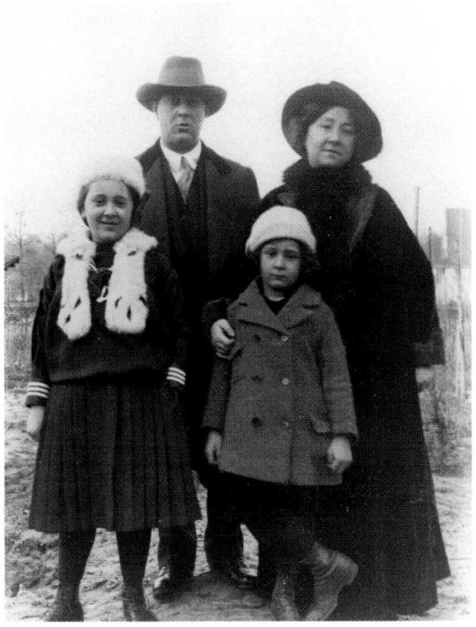

Schoenberg with wife, Mathilde, and children, Gertrude and Georg, in Berlin, 1913.

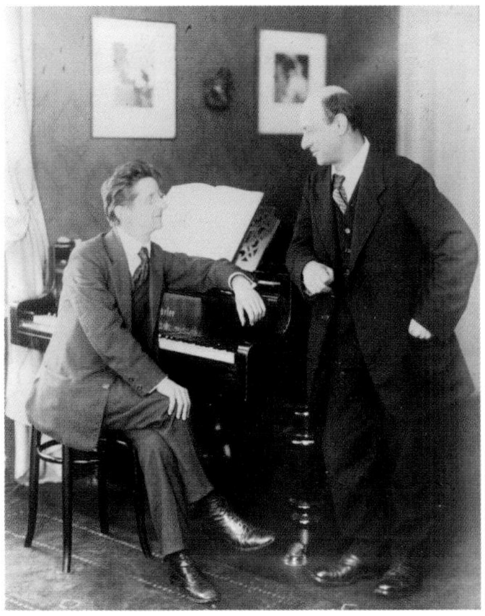

Alexander Zemlinsky and Schoenberg, Prague, 1917.

Kolig, Robin Christian Andersen, and Oskar Kokoschka. Kandinsky and Franz Marc publish *Blue Rider Almanac*, which features Schoenberg's essay "The Relationship to the Text" and score for *Herzgewächse*, as well as reproductions of his *Self-Portrait, Walking* and one of his Vision paintings. Friends and pupils, including Kandinsky, Webern, Jalowetz, and Gütersloh, contribute to Festschrift, *To Arnold Schoenberg: In Highest Admiration*, published by R. Piper, Munich. Composes *Pierrot lunaire*, op. 21, based on poems by Albert Giraud; conducts premiere in Berlin in October. Travels to Saint Petersburg in December to conduct *Pelleas und Melisande* as part of Alexander Siloti's concert series. Through Kandinsky, meets Nikolai Kulbin, Russian Futurist and founder of ARS Art Association.

1913 Successful premiere of *Gurrelieder* in February under direction of Franz Schreker in Vienna. However, scandal erupts five weeks later during Vienna performance of works by Schoenberg, Berg, Webern, Mahler, and Zemlinsky. Receives first of three stipends awarded to him from Mahler Foundation. Begins work on Four Songs for voice and orchestra, op. 22. Completes *Die glückliche Hand*.

1914 Conducts *Gurrelieder* in Leipzig and Five Pieces for Orchestra, op. 16, in London. Spends summer near Murnau, close to Kandinsky and Münter's house. Outbreak of World War I.

1915 Begins work on libretto and score for oratorio *Die Jakobsleiter* (Jacob's ladder). Drafted into Austro-Hungarian army in December.

1916 As a result of requests from Viennese Composers' Union and with Béla Bartók's help, Schoenberg receives honorable discharge from army due to asthma. Inspired by wartime experience, composes *Die eiserne Brigade* (The iron brigade), a march for string quartet and piano. Completes Four Songs for voice and orchestra, op. 22.

1917 Recalled to active duty in September, but receives another medical dis-

sky's first International Salon, Odessa, which travels to Kiev, Saint Petersburg, and Riga during 1910.

1910 Completes *Composition II* in March, and shows this painting in second NKVM exhibition at Moderne Galerie Thannhauser in September. In the fall, travels to Russia, where he spends time with older avant-garde artists Izdebsky, Nikolai Kulbin, and Vladimir Markov. In December, shows in *Bubnovnyi valet* (Jack of diamonds) exhibition in Moscow. Shows fifty-four works, including *Improvisation III*, at Izdebsky's second International Salon, Odessa; catalogue of touring versions of exhibition includes Kandinsky's Russian translation of Schoenberg's essay, "On Parallel Octaves and Fifths" (1910). Returns to Munich at year's end. Meets Franz Marc and August Macke at New Year's Eve party hosted by Jawlensky and Werefkin.

1911 On January 2, attends concert of Arnold Schoenberg's music with Jawlensky, Marc, Münter, and Werefkin. Deeply moved by the experience, Kandinsky sketches two drawings and paints large canvas *Impression III (Concert)*. Shortly thereafter, initiates correspondence with the composer that will continue through 1914. Resigns position as NKVM president. Marc joins NKVM in February. Writes to Marc in June about plans for *Blue Rider Almanac*. Meets Schoenberg in mid-September. Finalizes divorce from wife, Ania, in the fall. Meets Paul Klee and Emil Nolde. Befriends Hans Arp and Heinrich Campendonk. Corresponds with Robert Delaunay, Natalia Goncharova, and Mikhail Larionov. Completes *Composition V*, which is rejected by NKVM jury, prompting Kandinsky, Marc, Münter, and Kubin to resign from the group. First Blue Rider exhibition opens on December 18 at Moderne Galerie Thannhauser, where third NKVM exhibition shows concurrently. Also in December, first edition of *On the Spiritual in Art* is published by R. Piper, Munich, excerpts of which

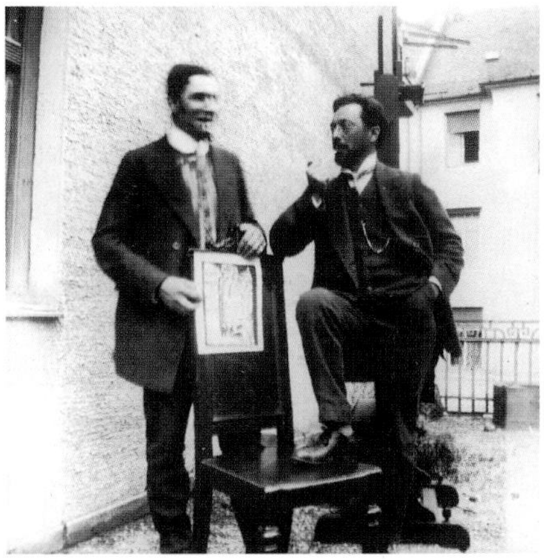

Franz Marc and Kandinsky on the balcony of Kandinsky and Münter's Munich apartment, with a woodcut print cover of the *Blue Rider Almanac*, 1911/12.

charge in December because of poor physical health.

1918 World War I ends. Teaches composition at Schwarzwald School. Moves to Mödling near Vienna. Founds Society for Private Musical Performances with Erwin Ratz and others.

1919 Hanns Eisler, Rudolf Kolisch, and Karl Rankl begin studying composition with him.

1920 Attends Mahler Festival in Amsterdam; named first president of International Mahler Society. Begins working on Five Piano Pieces, op. 23, and Serenade, op. 24.

1921 In June, travels with family and several pupils to Mattsee health spa, where local government demands that he provide proof that he is not Jewish; he refuses and leaves town. Spends rest of summer in Traunkirchen. Formulates twelve-tone method of composition, in which twelve serial notes are related only to one another. Death of mother, Pauline, on October 12. Publication of first biography of Schoenberg by Egon Wellesz. Final concert of Society for Private Musical Performances in December.

1922 Conducts *Pierrot lunaire* in Prague. Interrupts composition of *Die Jakobsleiter*, which remains unfinished. Completes arrangements of two Bach chorale preludes, which premiered in New York with Josef Stransky and New York Philharmonic; concert is first performance of Schoenberg's work in the United States. Renews correspondence with Kandinsky.

1923 Completes Five Piano Pieces, op. 23, and Suite for Piano, op. 25. Gives full realization to his twelve-tone method with completion of Serenade, op. 24. In April, Kandinsky, who had joined faculty of Bauhaus in Weimar, writes to Schoenberg inviting him to direct music school there. Schoenberg declines offer and eventually cuts off contact with Kandinsky, after hearing from Alma Mahler that Kandinsky had made anti-Semitic remarks. Death of wife, Mathilde, in October.

1924 Composes Wind Quintet, op. 26.

are read by Nikolai Kulbin at Second All-Russian Congress of Artists in Saint Petersburg.

1912 First Blue Rider exhibition travels to Cologne, Bremen, Zurich, Hagen and Frankfurt during 1912. Second Blue Rider exhibition opens at Galerie Hans Goltz, Munich, on February 12. In April, second edition of *On the Spiritual in Art* published by R. Piper; third edition published in the fall. First edition of the *Blue Rider Almanac*, edited by Kandinsky and Marc, published in May by R. Piper, with contributions by the editors, Burliuk, Macke, Schoenberg, Hartmann, and French critic Roger Allard. Kandinsky participates in *Sonderbund International Art Exhibition* in Cologne. In July, excerpts from *On the Spiritual in Art* published by Alfred Stieglitz in *Camera Work*, New York. First solo exhibition in Berlin held in October at Herwarth Walden's Der Sturm Gallery. *Klänge* (Sounds) prose poems and woodcuts published by R. Piper in December.

1913 In February, exhibits at Armory Show, New York, which travels to Chicago and Boston. Participates in *Erster Deutscher Herbstsalon* (First German autumn salon) at Der Sturm Gallery in Berlin. Publication of *Der Sturm* album in Berlin, which includes Kandinsky's autobiographical text, "Reminiscences." Final version of the monumental canvas *Composition VII* completed in November.

1914 Solo exhibition at Moderne Galerie Thannhauser in January. Second edition of *Blue Rider* almanac published in March. *On the Spiritual in Art* published as *The Art of Spiritual Harmony* in London and Boston. Flees to Switzerland with Münter at outbreak of World War I. Returns to Moscow, where he resides until 1921.

1915 Alexander Rodchenko and Varvara Stepanova live temporarily in Kandinsky's apartment. Burliuk rents studio next to Kandinsky's. Participates in *Exhibition of Painting: 1915* in Moscow with Natan Altman, Burliuk and his brother Vladimir Burljuk, Goncharova, Larionov, and others.

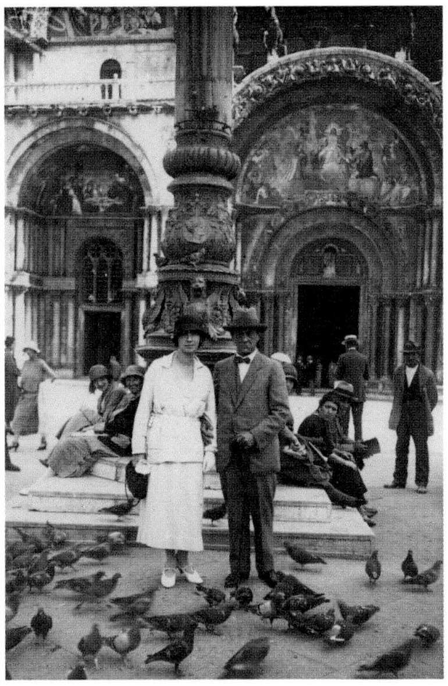

Schoenberg and his wife, Gertrud, St. Mark's Square, Venice, 1924.

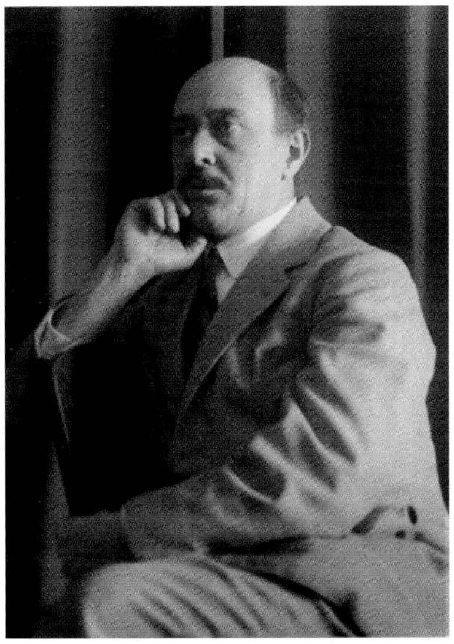

Arnold Schoenberg, 1925.

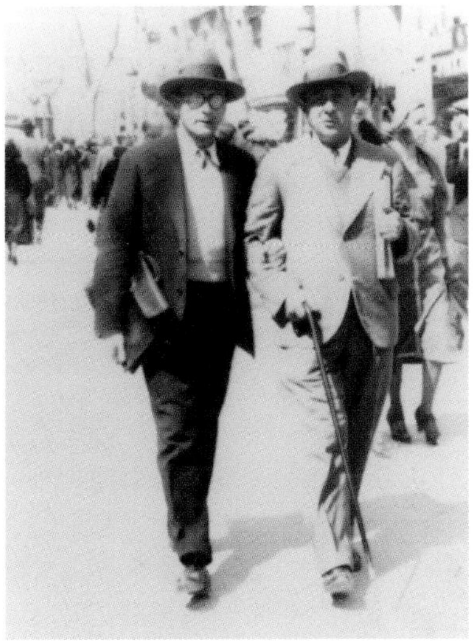

Anton Webern and Schoenberg walking on a street in Berlin, c. 1926-29.

Marries Gertrud Kolisch, sister of pupil Rudolf Kolisch, in Mödling Lutheran Parish Church on August 28. Special concerts performed and publication released in celebration of his fiftieth birthday. Publication of Paul Stefan's biography of Schoenberg. Zemlinsky conducts premiere of *Erwartung* in Prague. World premiere of *Die glückliche Hand* under Fritz Stiedry's direction at Vienna Volksoper in October. Begins composing Suite for Piano, Woodwinds, and Strings, op. 29.

1925 Appointed director of music master class at Prussian Academy of Arts in Berlin, which prompts anti-Semitic protests in the periodical *Zeitschrift für Musik*. Composes Four Pieces for Mixed Chorus, op. 27, and Three Satires for Mixed Chorus, op. 28.

1926 Arrives in Berlin at beginning of year. Completes Suite, op. 29. Several visits to Vienna between July and November. Resumes teaching in Berlin in November.

1927 Conducts performance of *Pelleas und Melisande* on Berlin radio. Composes Third String Quartet, op. 30, commissioned by American arts patron Elizabeth Sprague Coolidge. Spends summer in Pörtschach, where Kandinsky and his wife, Nina, are also staying. After several years of estrangement, the two artists renew their friendship. Completes Zionist drama, *Der biblische Weg* (The biblical way), Schoenberg's first artistic exploration of his Jewish identity, beliefs, and politics, and attempt to deal with his own experiences of anti-Semitism. Premiere of Third String Quartet in September performed by Kolisch Quartet in Vienna.

1928 Composes Variations for Orchestra, op. 31. Writes libretto for *Moses und Aron*, in which Schoenberg again explores his Jewish identity. Premiere of Variations for Orchestra in Berlin with Wilhelm Furtwängler and Berlin Philharmonic.

1929 Completes Piano Piece, op. 33a, and one-act opera *Von Heute auf Morgen* (From today till tomorrow), op. 32, considered first stage work to employ

From December to March, visits Münter for last time in Stockholm.

1916 Solo exhibition held at Galerie Gummeson, Stockholm. Returns to Moscow in March. Works by Kandinsky are shown at Galerie Dada in Zurich. *Klänge* poems read by Hugo Ball at Cabaret Voltaire, Zurich; the poem "Sehen" (See) is published in *Cabaret Voltaire* review. Meets Nina von Adreevskaia in September.

1917 Marries Nina von Andreevskaia in Moscow on February 11. Birth of son, Volodia, in September. Narkompros (People's Commissariat for Enlightenment) established in Moscow shortly after October Revolution.

1918 At Vladimir Tatlin's invitation, joins Department of Visual Arts (IZO) of Narkompros (NKP). Appointed editor of periodical *Visual Art*, published by IZO NKP. Teaching appointment at Svomas (Free State Art Studios), Moscow. IZO NKP publishes *Text of the Artist*, a Russian translation of his "Reminiscences." As part of committee in charge of International Bureau of IZO, initiates contact with German artists and architect Walter Gropius.

1919 Helps found Museum of Pictorial Culture in Moscow; becomes its first director. With Rodchenko and others, helps organize system of twenty-two provincial museums. Exhibits with Kazimir Malevich, El Lissitsky, Marc Chagall, and others in First Free State Exhibition in Moscow.

1920 Foundation of Institute of Artistic Culture (Inkhuk) in Moscow. Death of son, Volodia, on June 16 at less than three years old. Named Honorary Professor of Aesthetics at University of Moscow. Teaches at Vkhutemas (Higher State Art–Technical Studios), which replaces Svomas. *Composition VII* and more than fifty other works displayed in *Nineteenth Exhibition of All-Russian Central Exhibition Commission*, Moscow. In December, reports on activities of Inkhuk at All-Russian Conference of Heads of Art Sections, which operates under NKP. When teaching program is rejected, leaves Inkhuk at end of year.

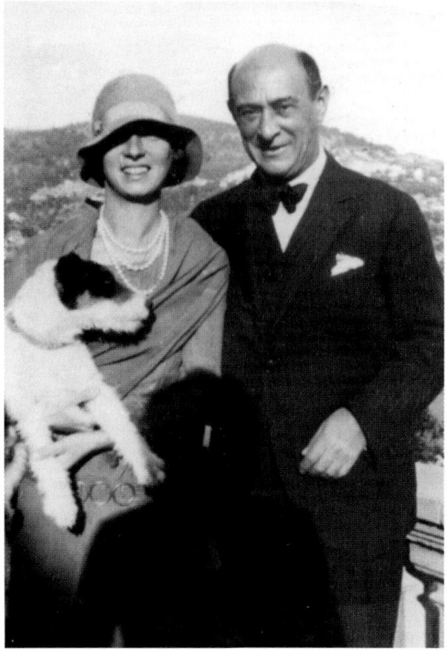

Gertrud and Arnold Schoenberg with their dog, Witz, standing on a balcony in Roquebrune-Cap Martin, France, c. 1928-29.

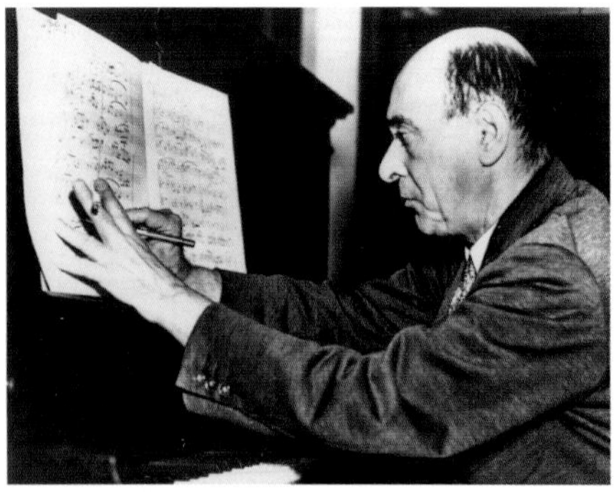

Schoenberg, composing in Los Angeles, c. 1935.

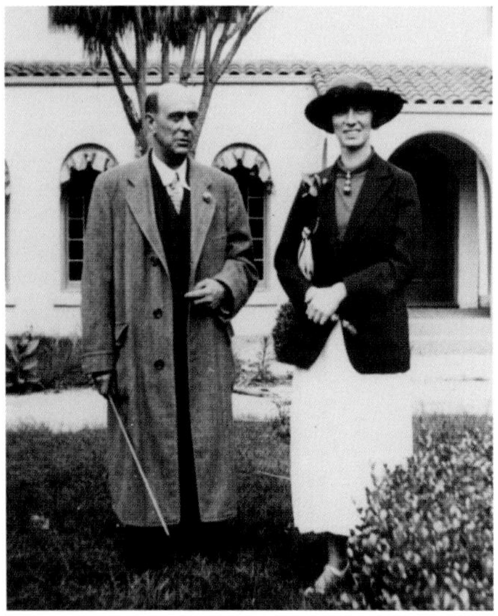

Arnold and Gertrud Schoenberg outside their house in Brentwood Park, Los Angeles, 1935.

twelve-tone method. Begins Accompaniment to a Cinematic Scene, op. 34, and Six Pieces for Male Chorus, op. 35.

1930 Premiere of *Von Heute auf Morgen* in Frankfurt. Completes Six Pieces for Male Chorus, op. 35. Oskar Schlemmer designs stage set for performance of *Die glückliche Hand* at Kroll Opera in Berlin. Finishes composition of Accompaniment to a Cinematic Scene. Begins correspondence with author Thomas Mann.

1931 Lectures on Berlin radio in March. Travels to Barcelona in the fall. Composes Piano Piece, op. 33b.

1932 Remains in Barcelona due to anti-Semitic opposition to his professorship at Art Academy, Berlin. Finishes second act of *Moses und Aron* in March; third act remains incomplete. Birth of daughter Nuria on May 7. Returns to Berlin in June. Writes short essays throughout the year on wide-ranging topics, including tonality, language, politics, power, morals, and Fascism, attesting to his growing awareness of political situation in Germany, particularly in regard to anti-Jewish sentiment.

1933 Delivers lecture "Brahms, the Progressive" on Berlin radio in February. Composes Three Songs, op. 48, for voice and piano. Nazis bar him from Academy; leaves Berlin in May. While in exile in Paris, reconverts to Judaism with artist Marc Chagall serving as a witness. Changes spelling of name from "Schönberg" to "Schoenberg" following his religious conversion. Travels to United States with his wife and daughter, arriving in New York on October 31. Teaches in Boston at Malkin Conservatory and gives private lessons in New York.

1934 Conducts *Pelleas und Melisande* in Boston. Delivers lectures at University of Chicago, and on radio. Composes Suite for String Orchestra, his first work written in the United States. Moves from East Coast to Los Angeles, where he writes and lectures about plight of the Jews. Meets Albert Einstein. Participates in concert to

1921 Helps establish Russian Academy of Artistic Sciences; becomes its vice-director. Leaves Russia for Berlin in December. Meets Lyonel Feininger.

1922 In March, receives invitation from Gropius to teach at Bauhaus in Weimar. Solo exhibition at Galerie Goldschmidt-Wallerstein, Berlin. Moves to Weimar in June; reunited with Klee. Teaches preliminary course and wall-painting workshop at Bauhaus. Publication of series of graphic works, *Small Worlds*, by Propyläen-Verlag, Berlin.

1923 First solo exhibition in New York, organized by Société Anonyme opens in March; Kandinsky becomes the society's honorary vice-president. In April, invites Schoenberg to direct music school at Bauhaus. Schoenberg rejects offer, accusing Kandinsky of anti-Semitism. The two sever ties as a result. Completes *Composition VIII* in July. Publishes three essays ("The Basic Elements of Form," "Color Course Seminar," and "Abstract Synthesis on the Stage") in anthology *Bauhaus Weimar 1919–1923.*

1924 Blue Four exhibition group, comprised of Kandinsky, Feininger, Jawlensky, and Klee, formed by art patron Galka Scheyer, who becomes Kandinsky's representative in the United States.

1925 Under pressure from right-wing circles, and due to cuts in funding from government of Thuringia, Bauhaus leaves Weimar and moves to Dessau in April. Kandinsky exhibits *Composition VIII* and other works in one-man exhibition at Neues Museum, Wiesbaden. Completes manuscript of *Point and Line to Plane* in November.

1926 *Point and Line to Plane* published by Albert Langen, Munich. Father dies in Odessa. Kandinsky's sixtieth-birthday exhibition opens in Braunschweig and travels to Dresden, Berlin, Dessau, and other European cities. Participates in *An International Exhibition of Modern Art*, organized by Société Anonyme at The Brooklyn Museum. First issue of periodical *Bauhaus* published in

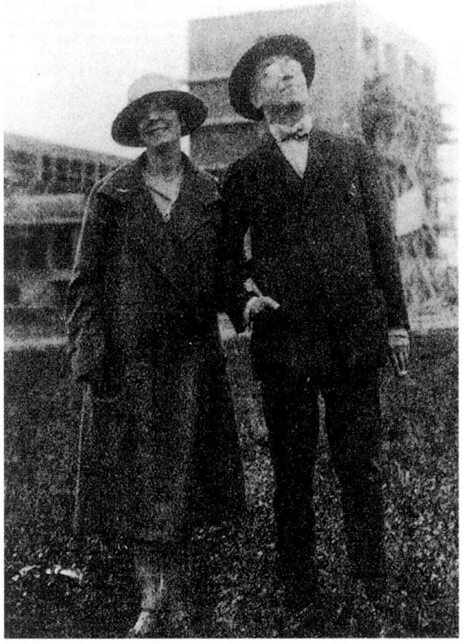

Nina and Wassily Kandinsky at the Bauhaus construction site, Dessau, 1926.

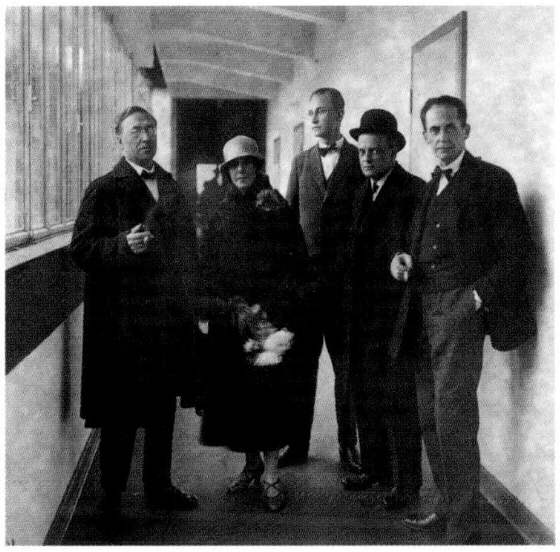

Wassily and Nina Kandinsky with Georg Muche, Paul Klee, and Walter Gropius at the Bauhaus, Dessau, 1926.

benefit Zionist Organization of New York given in Einstein's honor.

1935 Lectures at University of Southern California. Gives private lessons; John Cage is among his pupils. Arranges First Chamber Symphony for Orchestra, which he numbers op. 9b; conducts premiere in Los Angeles in December. Death of Alban Berg.

1936 Completes Concerto for Violin and Orchestra, op. 36, begun the year before. Composes Fourth String Quartet, op. 37. Appointed Professor of Music at University of California, Los Angeles (UCLA). Settles in Brentwood Park in West Los Angeles, where he lives for the rest of his life. Befriends George Gershwin. Receives final letter from Kandinsky.

1937 Premiere of Fourth String Quartet performed by Kolisch Quartet in Los Angeles in January. Birth of son Ronald on May 26. Begins writing *Fundamentals of Musical Composition.*

1938 Composes choral work *Kol Nidre*, op. 39, in which Schoenberg creates his own melody for the Jewish prayer recited on Yom Kippur; conducts premiere in Los Angeles the night before the High Holiday. Helps elder daughter, Gertrude, and her husband, Felix Greissle, flee Austria and immigrate to the United States. Schoenberg's music targeted in *Degenerate Art* exhibition in Düsseldorf. Zemlinsky and his wife, Louise, immigrate to New York.

1939 World War II begins. Completes Second Chamber Symphony, op. 38, begun in 1906.

1940 Conducts *Pierrot lunaire* for a recording. Premiere of Second Chamber Symphony in New York. Reconnects with Alma Mahler-Werfel, who has moved with her third husband, dramatist Franz Werfel, to Beverly Hills. Premiere of Violin Concerto in Philadelphia.

1941 Birth of son Lawrence on January 27. Arnold, Gertrud, and Nuria are granted U.S. citizenship in April. Death of brother, Heinrich, in Salzburg. Composes Variations on a Recitative, op. 40, for organ.

1942 Composes *Ode to Napoleon*

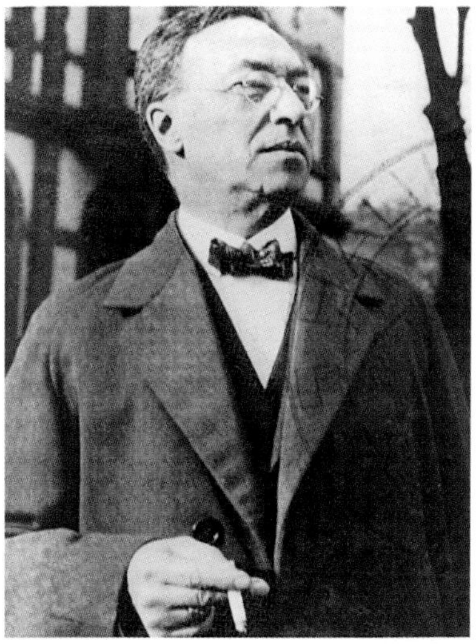

Photograph of Kandinsky used on his Bauhaus identity card, Dessau, 1927.

December, dedicated to Kandinsky in honor of his sixtieth birthday.

1927 Vacations in Austria and Switzerland. Meets Schoenberg for the first time in several years in Pörtschach, Austria, where the composer and his wife Gertrud are spending the summer. The two artists rekindle their friendship.

1928 Becomes German citizen in March. Directs and designs scenery and costumes for Modest Mussorgsky's *Pictures at an Exhibition*, which opens in April at Friedrich Theater, Dessau.

1929 In January, first solo exhibition in Paris of watercolors and gouaches at Galerie Zak; show travels to The Hague and Brussels. Marcel Duchamp and Katherine Dreier, co-founders of Société Anonyme, visit Kandinsky at Bauhaus. Meets Hilla Rebay and Mr. and Mrs. Solomon R. Guggenheim in the summer. Visits artist James Ensor in Belgium. In November, visits architect Erich Mendelsohn in Berlin.

1930 Works by Kandinsky, Klee, and Schlemmer removed from Weimar museum by Nazi architect Paul Schultze-Naumburg. Kandinsky exhibition held at Galerie de France, Paris, in March. Shows works at Venice Biennale and with artist group Cercle et Carré in Paris.

1931 In May, edits issue of *Bauhaus*, which includes his tribute to Klee. In the fall,

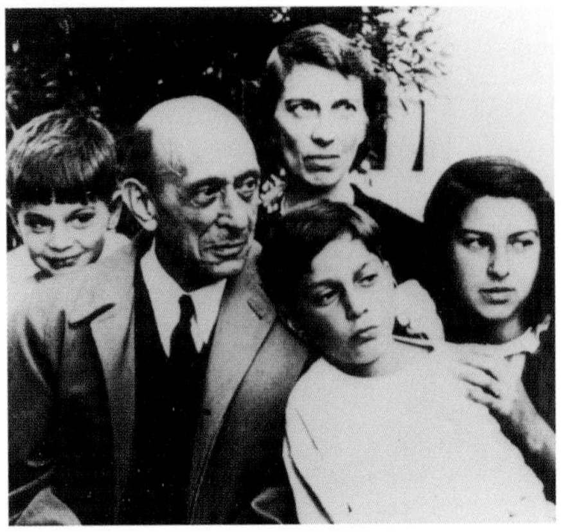

Arnold and Gertrud Schoenberg with their children, Lawrence, Ronald and Nuria (left to right), in Los Angeles, 1940s.

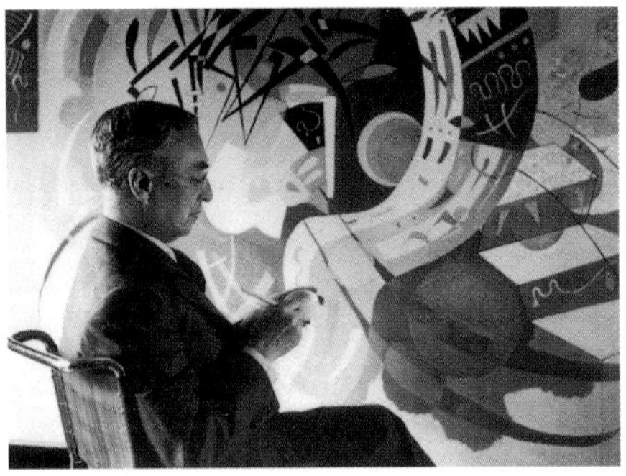

Kandinsky in his studio in Neuilly-sur-Seine, 1939.

Buonaparte, op. 41, for string quartet, piano, and narrator, and Concerto for Piano and Orchestra, op. 42. Writes textbook *Models for Beginners in Composition*.

1943 Composes Theme and Variations for Band, op. 43; version for symphony orchestra, op. 43b, completed a few months later.

1944 Named Professor Emeritus at UCLA. Continues to teach privately.

1945 World War II ends. Rejection of application for Guggenheim Fellowship to complete *Moses und Aron, Die Jakobsleiter*, and music textbooks. Composes Prelude for Orchestra and Mixed Chorus, op. 44. Death of Anton Webern.

1946 Appointed Honorary President of International Society for Contemporary Music. Suffers heart attack and nearly dies on August 2. Composes String Trio, op. 45; writes into its musical texture his experience of having a heart attack. Princeton University grants honorary doctorate, but Schoenberg is unable to attend ceremony. Writes textbook *Structural Functions of Harmony*.

1947 Elected member of American Academy of Arts and Letters. Health improves. Composes and writes text for cantata *A Survivor from Warsaw*, op. 46. Death of elder daughter, Gertrude.

1948 Controversy with Thomas Mann over parallels between Schoenberg and Adrian Leverkühn, protagonist and "inventor of twelve-tone music" in Mann's novel *Dr. Faustus*. Composes Three Folk Songs, op. 49. Completes textbook *Fundamentals of Musical Composition*. Premiere of *A Survivor from Warsaw* in Albuquerque, New Mexico.

1949 Poor health prevents composer from traveling to Europe for festival in honor of his seventy-fifth birthday. Composes choral work, *Dreimal tausend Jahre* (Three times a thousand years), op. 50a, and Fantasy for Violin with Piano Accompaniment, op. 47, which is premiered in Los Angeles by Adolf Koldofsky and Leonard Stein. Becomes honorary

contributes for the first time to Christian Zervos's magazine *Cahiers d'Art*.

1932 National Socialists close down Bauhaus in Dessau in August; school relocates to Berlin in October. Kandinsky moves to Berlin in December, where he lives for the next year.

1933 Final closing of Bauhaus on July 20. Spends summer in Paris and near Toulon, France. Returns briefly to Berlin in November. In late December, emigrates to Neuilly-sur-Seine near Paris.

1934 In March, meets artists Joan Miró, Piet Mondrian, and Alberto Magnelli and is reacquainted with Arp. Exhibits at Galerie Cahiers d'Art, Paris. In June, visits Man Ray, Fernand Léger, Constantin Brancusi, and Robert and Sonia Delaunay. Max Ernst visits Kandinsky.

1935 Exhibits with Max Weber and Klee at J. B. Neumann's New Art Circle in New York; the show is his first with Neumann, who becomes his eastern U.S. representative in July.

1936 Participates in *Abstract and Concrete* exhibition at Lefèvre Gallery, London, and *Cubism and Abstract Art* at The Museum of Modern Art, New York. Publishes memoir of Marc in *Cahiers d'Art*.

1937 Art dealer Karl Nierendorf mounts solo exhibition of Kandinsky's work in New York in March. Many of his works in German museums confiscated by Nazis; several included in *Degenerate Art* exhibition, Munich, in July. At end of July, participates in *Origines et Développement de l'Art International Indépendent* exhibition at Jeu de Paume, Paris.

1938 Participates in *Abstract Art* exhibition at Stedelijk Museum in Amsterdam. Essay "Concrete Art" published in first issue of *XXe siècle*.

1939 Completes *Composition X*, his last painting in the series. *Composition IX* purchased by French state. Granted French citizenship. World War II begins.

1940 Paris invaded by German troops; Kandinsky spends two months in Pyrenees.

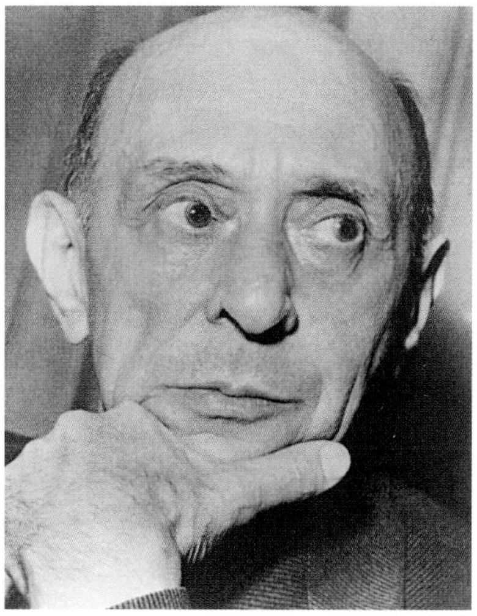

Arnold Schoenberg, Los Angeles, 1940s.

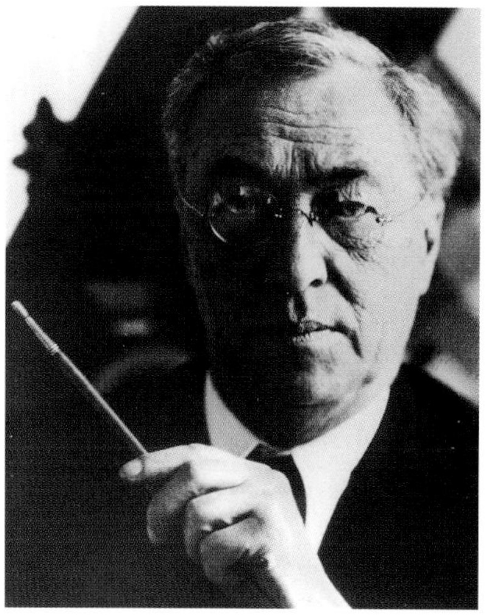

Kandinsky in Berlin, 1933.

citizen of city of Vienna.

1950 Mann agrees to add postscript to all future copies of *Dr. Faustus* clarifying that Schoenberg invented twelve-tone method and thereby ending their dispute. Composes *Psalm 130 "De Profundis,"* op. 50b, for mixed chorus a cappella, which he contributes to Chemjo Vinaver's *Anthology of Jewish Music.* Writes texts for *Psalms, Prayers, and Other Conversations with God,* excerpts of which he uses in his composition for *Modern Psalm,* op. 50c, for speaker, mixed chorus, and orchestra. Sells manuscripts of *Verklärte Nacht, Pierrot lunaire,* and Second String Quartet to Library of Congress. The Philosophical Library in New York publishes *Style and Idea,* a collection of Schoenberg's essays edited by pupil Dika Newlin.

1951 Premiere of "The Dance around the Golden Calf" from *Moses und Aron* in Darmstadt with Hermann Scherchen conducting. Named Honorary President of Israeli Academy of Music in Jerusalem. Donates his correspondence to Library of Congress. Dies at home on July 13 in Los Angeles.

1941 Through arrangement made by Varian Fry, on behalf of Centre Américain de Secours, Kandinskys invited to emigrate to United States, but they decline.

1942 Solo exhibition at Galerie Jeanne Bucher in Paris. Paints last large canvas, but continues to work, mostly in watercolor and gouache.

1944 Completes last catalogued painting, *Tempered Elan,* in March. Plans to design set for film comedy and ballet set to music by Hartmann. Becomes ill, but continues to work until June. In August, liberation of Paris by the Allies. Last solo exhibition held during his lifetime opens in November at Galerie l'Esquisse. Dies on December 13 in Neuilly-sur-Seine from sclerosis of the cerebellum.

The author wishes to thank the Arnold Schoenberg Center in Vienna for permission to include some previously published material.

Exhibition Checklist

Paintings and Works on Paper

Arnold Schoenberg

SELF-PORTRAITS

Arnold Schoenberg (Austrian, 1874–1951)
Self-Portrait, n.d.
Gouache on paper
9 x 7½ in. (23 x 19 cm)
Arnold Schoenberg Center, Vienna
Plate 10

Arnold Schoenberg
Self-Portrait, n.d.
Oil on cardboard
12¼ x 9⅝ in. (31 x 24.5 cm)
Arnold Schoenberg Center, Vienna
Plate 12

Arnold Schoenberg
Self-Portrait, n.d.
Oil on canvas
11⅜ x 9 in. (29 x 23 cm)
Arnold Schoenberg Center, Vienna
Plate 14

Arnold Schoenberg
Self-Portrait, 1908
Brush, pen, and ink on paper
15¾ x 12¼ in. (40 x 31 cm)
Arnold Schoenberg Center, Vienna
Plate 9

Arnold Schoenberg
Blue Self-Portrait, 1910
Oil on wood
12¼ x 8⅝ in. (31 x 22 cm)
Arnold Schoenberg Center, Vienna
Plate 11

Arnold Schoenberg
Green Self-Portrait, 1910
Oil on wood
13 x 9½ in. (33 x 24 cm)
Arnold Schoenberg Center, Vienna
Plate 13

Arnold Schoenberg
Self-Portrait, 1910
Oil on cardboard
13 x 8¼ in. (33 x 21 cm)
Arnold Schoenberg Center, Vienna
Plate 15

Arnold Schoenberg
Self-Portrait, 1910
Oil on wood
12¼ x 8⅝ in. (31 x 22 cm)
Arnold Schoenberg Center, Vienna
Plate 25

Arnold Schoenberg
Self-Portrait (Vision), 1910
Inscribed: "To Leopold Stokowski.
Arnold Schoenberg. September 1944"
Oil on canvas
12⅝ x 7⅞ in. (32 x 20 cm)
Music Division, Library of Congress,
Washington, D.C.
Plate 40

Arnold Schoenberg
Self-Portrait, Walking, 1911
Oil on cardboard
18⅞ x 17¾ in. (48 x 45 cm)
Arnold Schoenberg Center, Vienna
Plate 42

GAZES/VISIONS

Arnold Schoenberg
Thinking, n.d.
Oil on cardboard
8⅝ x 9⅞ in. (22 x 25 cm)
Arnold Schoenberg Center, Vienna
Plate 16

Arnold Schoenberg
Gaze, n.d.
Oil on cardboard
12⅜ x 11 in. (31.5 x 28 cm)
Arnold Schoenberg Center, Vienna
Plate 17

Arnold Schoenberg
Blue Gaze, n.d.
Oil on cardboard
$7\frac{7}{8}$ x 9 in. (20 x 23 cm)
Arnold Schoenberg Center, Vienna
Plate 20

Arnold Schoenberg
Red Gaze, 1910
Oil on cardboard
11 x $8\frac{5}{8}$ in. (28 x 22 cm)
Arnold Schoenberg Center, Vienna
Plate 18

Arnold Schoenberg
Vision (Eyes), 1910
Inscribed: "Erinnerung an Oskar Kokoschka" (Reminiscence of Oskar Kokoschka)
Oil on cardboard
$9\frac{7}{8}$ x $12\frac{1}{4}$ in. (25 x 31 cm)
Arnold Schoenberg Center, Vienna
Plate 19

Arnold Schoenberg
Red Gaze, 1910
Oil on cardboard
$12\frac{5}{8}$ x $9\frac{7}{8}$ in. (32 x 25 cm)
Arnold Schoenberg Center, Vienna
Plate 39

HANDS

Arnold Schoenberg
Flesh, n.d.
Oil on cardboard
$8\frac{5}{8}$ x 11 in. (22 x 28 cm)
Arnold Schoenberg Center, Vienna
Plate 21

Arnold Schoenberg
Hands, n.d.
Inscribed: "An Franz Schreker, Schönberg, Weihnachten, 1929" (To Franz Schreker, Schönberg, Christmas, 1929)
Watercolor on paper
$12\frac{3}{4}$ x $8\frac{1}{2}$ in. (32.4 x 21.6 cm)
Private collection
Plate 22

Arnold Schoenberg
Hands, 1910
Oil on cardboard
$15\frac{3}{8}$ x $24\frac{3}{4}$ in. (39 x 63 cm)
Arnold Schoenberg Center, Vienna
Plate 23

IMAGES OF CHRIST

Arnold Schoenberg
Vision of Christ (Head), n.d.
Oil on cardboard
$19\frac{11}{16}$ x $14\frac{5}{8}$ in. (50 x 37 cm)
Arnold Schoenberg Center, Vienna
Plate 24

Arnold Schoenberg
Vision of Christ, 1919
Watercolor and gouache on paper
$7\frac{7}{8}$ x $3\frac{15}{16}$ in. (20 x 10 cm)
Arnold Schoenberg Center, Vienna
Plate 26

CARICATURES

Arnold Schoenberg
Art Patron, n.d.
Oil on cardboard
$14\frac{5}{8}$ x $12\frac{5}{8}$ in. (37 x 32 cm)
Arnold Schoenberg Center, Vienna
Plate 27

Arnold Schoenberg
Critic I, n.d.
Oil on wood
$17\frac{5}{16}$ x $11\frac{13}{16}$ in. (44 x 30 cm)
Arnold Schoenberg Center, Vienna
Plate 28

PORTRAITS

Arnold Schoenberg
Alban Berg, n.d.
Oil on canvas
$69\frac{1}{8}$ x $33\frac{1}{2}$ in. (175.5 x 85 cm)
Museen der Stadt Wien
Plate 50

Arnold Schoenberg
Alexander von Zemlinsky, n.d.
Oil on cardboard
$19\frac{1}{4}$ x $13\frac{3}{8}$ in. (49 x 34 cm)
Arnold Schoenberg Center, Vienna
Plate 52

Arnold Schoenberg
Helene Nahowski, 1910
Oil on canvas
$39\frac{3}{8}$ x $29\frac{1}{8}$ in. (100 x 74 cm)
Museen der Stadt Wien
Plate 51

Arnold Schoenberg
Mathilde Schoenberg, 1910
Oil on canvas
63 x $31\frac{1}{2}$ in. (160 x 80 cm)

University of Applied Arts Vienna,
Collection
Plate 53

Arnold Schoenberg
Gustav Mahler, 1910
Oil on cardboard
$17\frac{3}{4}$ x $16\frac{7}{8}$ in. (45 x 43 cm)
Arnold Schoenberg Center, Vienna
Plate 54

Arnold Schoenberg
Burial of Gustav Mahler, 1911
Oil on canvas
17 x 12 in. (43.2 x 30.5 cm)
Estate of Heinrich Jalowetz;
Courtesy Galerie St. Etienne, New York
Plate 55

LANDSCAPE

Arnold Schoenberg
Night Landscape, 1910
Oil on canvas
$22\frac{13}{16}$ x $28\frac{3}{4}$ in. (58 x 73 cm)
Arnold Schoenberg Center, Vienna
Plate 41

STAGE SETTINGS

Arnold Schoenberg
Erwartung (Expectation) *(Stage settings)*, n.d.
Drawing ink on paper
$6\frac{3}{4}$ x $4\frac{3}{8}$ in. (17 x 11 cm)
Arnold Schoenberg Center, Vienna
Plate 56

Arnold Schoenberg
Erwartung (Stage setting), n.d.
Watercolor on paper
$3\frac{15}{16}$ x $6\frac{3}{4}$ in. (10 x 17 cm)
Arnold Schoenberg Center, Vienna
Plate 57

Arnold Schoenberg
Erwartung (Stage setting), n.d.
Watercolor and gouache on paper
13 x $18\frac{7}{8}$ in. (33 x 48 cm)
Arnold Schoenberg Center, Vienna
Plate 58

Arnold Schoenberg
Die glückliche Hand (The lucky hand) *(Stage setting, scene 1)*, n.d.
Oil on cardboard
$8\frac{5}{8}$ x $11\frac{13}{16}$ in. (22 x 30 cm)
Arnold Schoenberg Center, Vienna
Plate 60

Arnold Schoenberg
Die glückliche Hand (Stage setting, scene 2), n.d.
Oil on cardboard
$8\frac{5}{8}$ x $11\frac{13}{16}$ in. (22 x 30 cm)
Arnold Schoenberg Center, Vienna
Plate 61

Arnold Schoenberg
Die glückliche Hand (Stage setting, scene 4), n.d.
Graphite, drawing ink, and colored pencil on paper
$4\frac{3}{8}$ x $5\frac{1}{2}$ in. (11 x 14 cm)
Arnold Schoenberg Center, Vienna
Plate 59

Wassily Kandinsky

Wassily Kandinsky (Russian, 1866–1944)
Sketch for Composition II, 1909–10
Oil on canvas
$38\frac{3}{8}$ x $51\frac{5}{8}$ in. (97.5 x 131.2 cm)
Solomon R. Guggenheim Museum,
New York, 45.961
Plate 2

Wassily Kandinsky
Improvisation 7 (Storm), 1910
Oil on pasteboard
$27\frac{9}{16}$ x $19\frac{3}{16}$ in. (70 x 48.7 cm)
Yale University Art Gallery, Gift of
Collection Société Anonyme, 1941.527
Plate 3

Wassily Kandinsky
Landscape with Factory Chimney, 1910
Oil on canvas
26 x $32\frac{1}{4}$ in. (66.2 x 82 cm)
Solomon R. Guggenheim Museum, New York,
Gift of Solomon R. Guggenheim, 1941, 41.504
Plate 4

Wassily Kandinsky
Murnau with Church I, 1910
Oil and watercolor on cardboard
$25\frac{1}{2}$ x $19\frac{3}{4}$ in. (64.7 x 50.2 cm)
Städtische Galerie im Lenbachhaus,
Munich, GMS 59
Plate 5

Wassily Kandinsky
Impression III (Concert), 1911
Oil on canvas
$30\frac{1}{2}$ x $39\frac{3}{8}$ in. (77.5 x 100 cm)
Städtische Galerie im Lenbachhaus,
Munich, GMS 78
Plate 1

Wassily Kandinsky
Arabs II, 1911
Oil on canvas
$27\frac{5}{8}$ x $36\frac{3}{8}$ in. (70.2 x 92.4 cm)
Private collection
Plate 29

Wassily Kandinsky
Sketch for Composition V, 1911
Oil on canvas
$37\frac{1}{4}$ x $54\frac{3}{4}$ in. (94.5 x 139 cm)
State Hermitage Museum,
St. Petersburg
Plate 30

Wassily Kandinsky
All Saints II, 1911
Oil on canvas
$33\frac{7}{8}$ x 39 in. (86 x 99 cm)
Städtische Galerie im Lenbachhaus,
Munich, GMS 62
Plate 33

Wassily Kandinsky
Watercolor with Red Spot (Study for Composition VII), 1913
Watercolor and pencil on paper,
mounted on cardboard
$19\frac{5}{8}$ x $24\frac{7}{8}$ in. (49.8 x 63.3 cm)
Collection Deutsche Bank
Plate 31

Wassily Kandinsky
Fragment 2 for Composition VII, 1913
Oil on canvas
$34\frac{1}{2}$ x $39\frac{1}{4}$ in. (87.6 x 99.7 cm)
Albright-Knox Art Gallery, Buffalo, New York,
Room of Contemporary Art Fund, 1947
Plate 32

Wassily Kandinsky
Little Painting with Yellow (Improvisation), 1914
Oil on canvas
31 x $39\frac{5}{8}$ in. (78.7 x 100.6 cm)
Philadelphia Museum of Art, The Louise
and Walter Arensberg Collection,
1950-134-103
Plate 34

Albert Bloch

Albert Bloch (American, 1882–1961)
Head, 1911
Oil on canvas
$19\frac{1}{16}$ x $17\frac{13}{16}$ in. (48.4 x 45.2 cm)
The Albert Bloch Foundation
Plate 49

Alexei von Jawlensky

Alexei von Jawlensky (Russian, 1864–1941)
Gelber Klang (Yellow sound), 1908
Oil on cardboard
13 x 17½ in. (33 x 44.5 cm)
Private collection
Plate 8

Alexei von Jawlensky
Murnau, 1910
Oil on hardboard
13 x 16⅝ in. (33 x 42.3 cm)
National Gallery of Art, Washington, D.C., Gift of Mr. and Mrs. Ralph F. Colin, 1973.69.1
Plate 37

Alexei von Jawlensky
Oberstdorf (Mountains), 1912
Oil on cardboard
19½ x 21 1/16 in. (49.5 x 53.5 cm)
Hanna Bekker vom Rath Collection
Plate 38

Alexei von Jawlensky
Egyptian Girl, 1913
Oil on cardboard, mounted on wood
21 x 19½ in. (53.3 x 49.5 cm)
The Saint Louis Art Museum, Bequest of Morton D. May
Plate 48

August Macke

August Macke (German, 1887–1914)
Strollers in a Rocky Landscape, 1911
Oil on paper
10⅞ x 16⅜ in. (27.6 x 41.6 cm)
Albright-Knox Art Gallery, Buffalo, New York, Gift of The Seymour H. Knox Foundation, Inc., 1971
Plate 45

August Macke
Saint George, 1912
India ink, brush
24⅞ x 19½ in. (63.3 x 49.6 cm)
Städtische Galerie im Lenbachhaus, Munich, G 12557
Plate 46

August Macke
Colored Forms I, 1913
Oil on pasteboard, mounted on wood
20⅞ x 15⅛ in. (53.1 x 38.5 cm)
Westfälisches Landesmuseum für Kunst und Kulturgeschichte, Münster, Germany, permanent loan from private collection
Plate 47

Franz Marc

Franz Marc (German, 1880–1916)
Yellow Cow, 1911
Oil on canvas
55⅜ x 74½ in. (140.5 x 189.2 cm)
Solomon R. Guggenheim Museum, New York, 49.1210
Plate 43

Franz Marc
The Wolves (Balkan War), 1913
Oil on canvas
27⅞ x 55 in. (70.8 x 139.7 cm)
Albright-Knox Art Gallery, Buffalo, New York, Charles Clifton, James G. Forsyth and Charles W. Goodyear Funds, 1951
Plate 44

Gabriele Münter

Gabriele Münter (German, 1877–1962)
Jawlensky and Werefkin, 1909
Oil on cardboard
12⅞ x 17½ in. (32.7 x 44.5 cm)
Städtische Galerie im Lenbachhaus, Munich, GMS 655
Plate 6

Gabriele Münter
Boating, 1910
Oil on canvas
49¼ x 28⅞ in. (125.1 x 73.3 cm)
Milwaukee Art Museum, Gift of Mrs. Harry Lynde Bradley, M1977.128
Plate 7

Gabriele Münter
Landscape with Church, 1910
Oil on cardboard
13 x 17⅝ in. (33 x 44.8 cm)
Sylvia and Ulrich Ströher Collection, Germany
Plate 35

Gabriele Münter
Kandinsky at Tea, 1910
Oil on canvas
26¾ x 18½ in. (68 x 47 cm)
Collection The Israel Museum, Jerusalem
Plate 36

Archival Materials

The Concert

Program of the Schoenberg concert
in Munich, January 2, 1911
8¾ x 6⅛ in. (22.2 x 15.5 cm)
Arnold Schoenberg Center, Vienna
Page 16, fig. 1

Arnold Schoenberg
First String Quartet, op. 7 (1905), sketch
First sketchbook MS 75
One leaf from the sketchbook
5¾ x 13¾ in. (14.5 x 35 cm)
Arnold Schoenberg Center, Vienna
Page 97, fig. 3

Arnold Schoenberg
Second String Quartet, op. 10 (1907–8), sketch
One sheet with four pages (Inv. Nr. 992)
11⅜ x 14½ in. (29 x 36.7 cm)
Arnold Schoenberg Center, Vienna
Page 97, fig. 4

Arnold Schoenberg
Three Piano Pieces, op. 11 (1909), sketch
One leaf (Inv. Nr. 3a)
5 13/16 x 14⅜ in. (14.8 x 36.5 cm)
Arnold Schoenberg Center, Vienna
Page 19, fig. 2

Rosé Quartet, c. 1905
Photograph (reproduction)
From *Schönberg, Kandinsky, Blauer Reiter und die Russische Avantgarde* (see bibliography)
Page 21, fig. 3

Marie Gutheil-Schoder, n.d.
Photograph (reproduction)
From *Schönberg, Kandinsky, Blauer Reiter und die Russische Avantgarde* (see bibliography)
Page 21, fig. 4

"Münchener Konzerte"
Concert review from *Münchener Post*, no. 6, January 8, 1911
9 x 7⅝ in. (22.9 x 19.4 cm)
Arnold Schoenberg Archives, Music Division, Library of Congress, Washington, D.C.

Friendship and Correspondence

Wassily Kandinsky
Letter to Arnold Schoenberg, January 18, 1911
11¼ x 8⅝ in. (28.6 x 21.9 cm)
Arnold Schoenberg Archives, Music Division, Library of Congress, Washington, D.C.
Page 25, fig. 7

Arnold Schoenberg
Letter to Wassily Kandinsky, January 24, 1911
7½ x 9⅞ in. (19 x 25 cm)
Gabriele Münter und Johannes Eichner Stiftung, Munich
Page 27, fig. 16

Wassily Kandinsky, 1911
Inscribed on verso: "To Arnold Schönberg, with feelings of profound affinity. Kandinsky, Munich, 9 April 1911"
Photograph (mounted)
6⅞ x 4½ in. (17.4 x 11.5 cm)
Arnold Schoenberg Center, Vienna
Page 28, fig. 17

Arnold Schoenberg, 1911
Inscribed: "Dear Mr. Kandinsky, I am discharging in musical tones—an obligation I have long wished to fulfill. 12 December 1911. Arnold Schönberg."
Photograph (reproduction)
Musée National d'Art Moderne, Centre Georges Pompidou, Paris
Page 29, fig. 18

Wassily Kandinsky's *Improvisation 7*, 1910
Photograph, gift of the painter to Arnold Schoenberg
6 x 4½ in. (15.2 x 11.3 cm)
Arnold Schoenberg Center, Vienna
Page 26, fig. 14

Wassily Kandinsky's *Improvisation 16*, 1910
Photograph, gift of the painter to Arnold Schoenberg
4 x 4⅜ in. (10.2 x 11 cm)
Arnold Schoenberg Center, Vienna
Page 26, fig. 15

Wassily Kandinsky
Xylographies, 1909
Title page
Inscribed on verso: "Prof. Arnold Schönberg, with affinity, Kandinsky, Munich, 18 January 1911"
12⅝ x 12⅝ in. (32 x 32 cm)
Arnold Schoenberg Center, Vienna
Page 26, fig. 8

Wassily Kandinsky
Xylographies, 1909
Rider
Woodcut, photo engraving
12⅝ x 12⅝ in. (32 x 32 cm)
Arnold Schoenberg Center, Vienna
Page 26, fig. 9

Wassily Kandinsky
Xylographies, 1909
Birds
Woodcut, photo engraving
12⅝ x 12⅝ in. (32 x 32 cm)
Arnold Schoenberg Center, Vienna
Page 26, fig. 10

Wassily Kandinsky
Xylographies, 1909
Church
Woodcut, photo engraving
12⅝ x 12⅝ in. (32 x 32 cm)
Arnold Schoenberg Center, Vienna
Page 26, fig. 11

Wassily Kandinsky
Xylographies, 1909
Birches
Woodcut, photo engraving
12⅝ x 12⅝ in. (32 x 32 cm)
Arnold Schoenberg Center, Vienna
Page 26, fig. 12

Wassily Kandinsky
Xylographies, 1909
Women in the Woods
Woodcut, photo engraving
12⅝ x 12⅝ in. (32 x 32 cm)
Arnold Schoenberg Center, Vienna
Page 26, fig. 13

Catalogue of the Second International Art Exhibition ("Salon 2") in Odessa, 1910/11
Cover illustrated by Wassily Kandinsky
Handwritten annotations by Kandinsky
10¾ x 9⅛ x ⅛ in. (27.2 x 23.3 x .3 cm)
Arnold Schoenberg Center, Vienna
Page 32, fig. 23

Arnold Schoenberg
Letter to Wassily Kandinsky, December 14, 1911
9¼ x 11⅝ in. (23.5 x 29.5 cm)
Gabriele Münter und Johannes Eichner Stiftung, Munich

Wassily Kandinsky
Über das Geistige in der Kunst (On the spiritual in art) (Munich: R. Piper, 1912)
Inscribed: "My dear Mr. Schönberg, in expression of sympathy, Kandinsky, Munich, 9 December [19]11"
8¼ x 7¼ x ⅜ in. (21 x 18.3 x 1 cm)
Arnold Schoenberg Center, Vienna
Page 30, figs. 19-20

Gabriele Münter and Wassily Kandinsky
Telegram to Arnold Schoenberg, February 1912
Message reads, "Herzlich mit ihnen – Muenter

Kandinsky" (Thinking of you warmly)
$7\frac{1}{8}$ x $9\frac{1}{4}$ in. (18.1 x 23.5 cm)
Arnold Schoenberg Archives, Music Division, Library of Congress, Washington, D.C.
Page 32, fig. 25

Arnold Schoenberg in St. Petersburg, December 1912
Photograph (mounted)
$6\frac{7}{8}$ x $4\frac{1}{2}$ in. (17.4 x 11.5 cm)
Arnold Schoenberg Center, Vienna
Page 32, fig. 24

Gabriele Münter
Woodcut ("1913 bring euch Gluck!" [1913 brings you luck!]), 1912
Sent to Schoenberg
$7\frac{1}{8}$ x $10\frac{5}{8}$ in. (18 x 27 cm)
Arnold Schoenberg Center, Vienna
Page 33, fig. 26

Gabriele Münter and Wassily Kandinsky
Letter to Arnold Schoenberg, June 4, 1914
Includes a hand-drawn map of Murnau by Kandinsky
9 x $11\frac{1}{4}$ in. (22.9 x 28.6 cm)
Arnold Schoenberg Archives, Music Division, Library of Congress, Washington, D.C.
Page 34, fig. 27

Schoenberg as Painter

Catalogue of Arnold Schoenberg's first exhibition at Kunstsalon Heller, Vienna, October 1910
9 x $6\frac{1}{4}$ in. (23 x 16 cm)
Arnold Schoenberg Center, Vienna
Page 38, fig. 2

The Blue Rider

Gabriele Münter
On the balcony of Kandinsky and Münter's apartment in Munich, 1911
Photograph (reproduction)
Left to right: Maria and Franz Marc, Bernhard Koehler, Heinrich Campendonk, Thomas von Hartmann, sitting: Wassily Kandinsky
Gabriele Münter und Johannes Eichner Stiftung, Munich
Page 62, fig. 1

Wassily Kandinsky, Gabriele Münter, Maria Franck, August Macke, and Elisabeth Macke
Postcard of Murnau am Staffelsee addressed to Arnold Schoenberg, c. October 1911
$3\frac{5}{8}$ x $5\frac{1}{2}$ in. (9.2 x 14 cm)
Arnold Schoenberg Archives, Music Division, Library of Congress, Washington, D.C.
Page 31, figs. 21-22

Wassily Kandinsky and Franz Marc
Catalogue for the first Blue Rider exhibition, Munich, 1911
Paperbound book (cover: woodcut on gray wove paper)
$5\frac{7}{8}$ x $4\frac{3}{4}$ x $\frac{1}{8}$ in. (15 x 12 x .4 cm)
Arnold Schoenberg Center, Vienna
Page 74, fig. 10

Wassily Kandinsky and Franz Marc
Blue Rider Almanac, 1st ed. (Munich: R. Piper, 1912)
Paperbound book (cover: relief print on cream card)
12 x 9 x $\frac{3}{4}$ in. (30.5 x 22.9 x 1.9 cm)
Rare Book and Special Collections Division, Library of Congress, Washington, D.C.
Page 72, fig. 8

Gabriele Münter
View into the first Blue Rider exhibition, Moderne Galerie Thannhauser, Munich, December 1911
Room 1 (from left to right): Jean Bloé Niestlé, *Birds* (top left), Albert Bloch, *Head* (bottom), Wassily Kandinsky, *Impression Moscow*
Photograph (reproduction)
Gabriele Münter und Johannes Eichner Stiftung, Munich
Page 75, fig. 12

Gabriele Münter
View into the first Blue Rider exhibition, Moderne Galerie Thannhauser, Munich, December 1911
Room 1 (from left to right): Robert Delaunay, *La Ville No. 2*, Arnold Schoenberg, *Night Landscape* (top), Gabriele Münter, *Frosty Landscape* (bottom), August Macke, *Still Life of Flowers with Agave*, Gabriele Münter, *Evening* (top), Albert Bloch, *Houses and Chimneys*
Photograph (reproduction)
Gabriele Münter und Johannes Eichner Stiftung, Munich
Page 41, fig. 6

Gabriele Münter
View into the first Blue Rider exhibition, Moderne Galerie Thannhauser, Munich, December 1911
Room 1 (from left to right): Gabriele Münter, *Dark Still Life (Mystery)*, Wassily Kandinsky, *Composition V* (in adjacent room), Albert Bloch, *Three Pierrots No. 2*, Heinrich Campendonk, *Leaping Horse*, Henri Rousseau, *La Basse-Cour*, Franz Marc, *Portrait of Henri Rousseau*, Robert Delaunay, *La Ville No. 2*

Photograph (reproduction)
Gabriele Münter und Johannes Eichner Stiftung, Munich
Page 75, fig. 11

Gabriele Münter
View into the first Blue Rider exhibition, Moderne Galerie Thannhauser, Munich, December 1911
Room 2 (from left to right): Franz Marc, *Yellow Cow*, Arnold Schoenberg, *Self-Portrait, Walking*, Wassily Kandinsky, *Saint George II*, Vladimir Burljuk, *Portrait Study* (top), Gabriele Münter, *Country Road in Winter* (bottom), Franz Marc, *Deer in the Forest I*, Wassily Kandinsky, *Composition V*
Photograph (reproduction)
Gabriele Münter und Johannes Eichner Stiftung, Munich
Page 41, fig. 5

Gabriele Münter
View into the first Blue Rider exhibition, Moderne Galerie Thannhauser, Munich, December 1911
Room 2 (from left to right): Gabriele Münter, *Still Life (Pink)*, August Macke, *Indians on Horseback* (top), Robert Delaunay, *St. Severin No. 1* (below), David Burliuk, *Horses* (over the door), Franz Marc, *Landscape with Animals and Rainbow* (top), Wassily Kandinsky, *With Sun* (bottom), Wassily Kandinsky, *Improvisation 22*
Photograph (reproduction)
Gabriele Münter und Johannes Eichner Stiftung, Munich
Page 75, fig. 13

Gabriele Münter
View into the first Blue Rider exhibition, Moderne Galerie Thannhauser, Munich, December 1911
Room 3 (from left to right): Franz Marc, *Landscape*, Robert Delaunay, *Tour Eiffel*, Elizabeth Epstein, *Portrait* (top), Heinrich Campendonk, *Woman and Animal* (bottom)
Photograph (reproduction)
Gabriele Münter und Johannes Eichner Stiftung, Munich
Page 75, fig. 14

Musical Interludes

Wassily Kandinsky
Klänge (Sounds) (Munich: R. Piper, 1912)
Limited first edition clothbound book; color woodcut prints and text on paper
11¼ x 11¼ x 11/16 in. (28.5 x 28.5 x 1.7 cm)
Arnold Schoenberg Center, Vienna

Alban Berg et al.
Arnold Schoenberg—im höchster Verehrung (in highest admiration), Munich, 1912
Festschrift
9½ x 6¼ x ½ in. (24 x 16 x 1.2 cm)
Arnold Schoenberg Center, Vienna
Page 94, fig. 1

Arnold Schoenberg
Die glückliche Hand (The lucky hand), op. 18, "Color crescendo" (scene 3), n.d.
Sketch
9 x 8⅞ in. (23 x 22.5 cm)
Arnold Schoenberg Center, Vienna
Page 107, fig. 11

Arnold Schoenberg
Erwartung (Expectation), op. 17, 1909
One leaf from the condensed score (Inv. Nr. 2386)
11⅜ x 14⅜ in. (28.8 x 36.5 cm)
Arnold Schoenberg Center, Vienna

Marie Pappenheim
Libretto for *Erwartung*
One manuscript page
8¼ x 6½ in. (21 x 16.5 cm)
Arnold Schoenberg Center, Vienna

Arnold Schoenberg
Herzgewächse (Heart's foliage), op. 20
Autograph score
13⅜ x 10⅝ in. (34 x 27 cm)
Arnold Schoenberg Center, Vienna
Page 99, fig. 7

Postscript

Arnold Schoenberg
Letter to Wassily Kandinsky (carbon copy), April 19, 1923
11½ x 9 in. (29.2 x 22.9 cm)
Arnold Schoenberg Archives, Music Division, Library of Congress, Washington, D.C.

Wassily Kandinsky
Letter to Arnold Schoenberg, April 24, 1923
10½ x 8⅝ in. (26.7 x 21.9 cm)
Arnold Schoenberg Archives, Music Division, Library of Congress, Washington, D.C.

Wassily and Nina Kandinsky, Gertrud and Arnold Schoenberg, Pörtschach, 1927
Photograph (reproduction)
From *Schönberg, Kandinsky, Blauer Reiter und die Russische Avantgarde* (see bibliography)
Page 35, fig. 28

Notes

Fred Wasserman, "Schoenberg and Kandinsky in Concert," pp. 17–35

I would especially like to thank Allen Ellenzweig, Donna Harkavy, Gilbert High, and T. Kaori Kitao for their insightful suggestions; and translators Katharina Garrelt, Henning Grentz, Eric Gabriel Lehman, Marcus Patka, and Walter Weil. Unless otherwise noted, all translations are new.

1. Franz Marc to Maria Franck, January 1, 1911, in Günter Meissner, *Franz Marc: Briefe, Schriften und Aufzeichnungen* (Leipzig and Weimar: Gustav Kiepenheuer Verlag, 1989), p. 38.

2. Ibid., p. 39.

3. Marc to August Macke, January 14, 1911, in *August Macke–Franz Marc: Briefwechsel*, ed. Wolfgang Macke (Cologne: M. DuMont Schauberg, 1964), p. 40.

4. Jane Kallir, *Arnold Schoenberg's Vienna*, exh. cat. (New York: Galerie St. Etienne and Rizzoli, 1984), p. 22.

5. H. H. Stuckenschmidt, *Arnold Schoenberg: His Life, World and Work*, trans. Humphrey Searle (New York: Schirmer Books, 1977), pp. 90, 105. Also see Paul Stefan's contemporaneous report on the February 5, 1907, premiere in Willi Reich, *Schoenberg: A Critical Biography*, trans. Leo Black (New York: Da Capo Press, 1981), pp. 20–21. Mahler similarly defended Schoenberg's Chamber Symphony, op. 9, at its premiere three days later on February 8, 1907 (Stuckenschmidt, *Life, World and Work*, p. 105). Schoenberg later wrote, "This First String Quartet played an important role in the history of my life. On the one hand, the scandals provoked by it were so widely reported the world over that I was known at once to a considerable part of the public. Of course, I was primarily regarded as the Satan of modernistic music; but, on the other hand, many of the progressive musicians became interested in my music and wanted to know more about it." This quotation comes from Arnold Schoenberg, "How One Becomes Lonely," in *Style and Idea: Selected Writings of Arnold Schoenberg*, ed. Leonard Stein, trans. Leo Black (New York: St. Martin's Press, 1975), p. 42.

6. At the Second String Quartet premiere, the critic Ludwig Karpath stood up and screamed, "Stop it! That's enough!" while another critic, Richard Specht, shouted back, "Quiet! Go on playing!" For a full account of the incident by Richard Batka, writing for a Prague newspaper, see Reich, *Schoenberg*, p. 36. Also see Kallir, *Arnold Schoenberg's Vienna*, p. 29. For an extended discussion of the critical response to Schoenberg during the years 1904–8, see Leon Botstein, "Music and Its Public: Habits of Listening and the Crisis of Musical Modernism in Vienna, 1870–1914" (Ph.D. diss., Harvard University, 1985), pp. 1184–231.

7. Iris Pfeiffer, "Introduction," in *Schönberg, Kandinsky, Blauer Reiter und die Russische Avantgarde*, exh. cat. [*Journal of the Arnold Schoenberg Center* 1] (Vienna: Arnold Schoenberg Center, 2000), pp. 89–91. Gutmann favored a program including the String Sextet *Verklärte Nacht* (Transfigured night), op. 4; two lieder; and the Second String Quartet.

8. *Arnold Schoenberg–Wassily Kandinsky: Letters, Pictures and Documents*, ed. Jelena Hahl-Koch, trans. John C. Crawford (London: Faber and Faber, 1984), p. 24. Hahl-Koch published the complete extract that appeared on the poster on pp. 24–25. "On Parallel Octaves and Fifths" was published in the Berlin periodical *Die Musik* (October 1910): 97–105. *Theory of Harmony* (*Harmonielehre*) was published in 1911.

9. Concerning "emancipation of the dissonance," see Arnold Schoenberg, "Composition with Twelve Tones (1)" (1941), in *Style and Idea*, pp. 216–17. Concerning his renunciation of a "tonal center," see Arnold Schoenberg, "My Evolution" (1949), in ibid., p. 86.

10. The information about Schoenberg's painting at the Munich concert can be found in Pfeiffer, "Introduction," pp. 91–92. It is unknown which of Schoenberg's self-portraits was displayed in the Jahreszeitensaal at the January 2, 1911, concert.

11. *Allgemeine Musik-Zeitung* 3 (January 20[?], 1911). Transcription of review on stationery of Konzert-Bureau Emil Gutmann, München, Arnold Schoenberg Collection, Music Division, Library of Congress, Box 32, "1911" folder.

12. Arthur Hahn, "Münchener Musikleben," n.d. Unidentified clipping, Arnold Schoenberg Collection, Music Division, Library of Congress, Box 32, "Not Yet Dated" folder (annotated "Schönberg: Münch Ztg. No. 2, 3/I").

13. "Münchener Konzerte," *Münchener Post* 6 (January 8, 1911).

14. Emil Gutmann to Schoenberg, January 3, 1911, quoted in Pfeiffer, "Introduction," p. 93. Gutmann observed that the piano pieces "really need to be heard more than once to be understood."

15. Marc to Macke, January 14, 1911, in Stuckenschmidt, *Life, World and Work*, pp. 141–42.

16. "Münchener Konzerte," *Münchener Post* 6 (January 8, 1911).

17. *Allgemeine Musik-Zeitung* 3 (January 20[?], 1911).

18. Otto Keller, "Ein Arnold Schönberg-Abend

in München," *Chemnitzer Tageblatt*, January 8, 1911. Transcription of review on stationery of Konzert-Bureau Emil Gutmann, München, Arnold Schoenberg Collection, Music Division, Library of Congress, Box 32, "1911" folder.

19. Ibid.

20. "Münchener Konzerte," *Münchener Post* 6 (January 8, 1911).

21. Hahn, "Münchener Musikleben."

22. Ibid.

23. Keller, "Ein Arnold Schönberg-Abend in München." This summary indictment is fairly typical of Schoenberg's reception. For a fuller discussion of this subject, see Leon Botstein, "Schoenberg and the Audience: Modernism, Music, and Politics in the Twentieth Century," in Walter Frisch, ed., *Schoenberg and His World* (Princeton: Princeton University Press, 1999), p. 39.

24. Friedrich Keyfel, "München, Ende Januar," *Signale für die musikalische Welt*, February 8, 1911, p. 221.

25. Pfeiffer, "Introduction," p. 93.

26. Marc to Franck, January 4, 1911, in Helmut Friedel and Annegret Hoberg, *The Blue Rider in the Lenbachhaus, Munich* (Munich: Prestel, 2000), p. 42. Concerning the rathskeller, see *August Macke–Franz Marc: Briefwechsel*, p. 41.

27. Marc to Macke, January 14, 1911, in *Schoenberg–Kandinsky*, p. 136. Emphasis in original. According to Peg Weiss, the "large *Composition*" that Marc refers to is Kandinsky's *Composition II*, which Marc had seen when it created an uproar at the second NKVM exhibition in September 1910. This painting was what first drew Marc's attention to Kandinsky. See Peg Weiss, "Evolving Perceptions of Kandinsky and Schoenberg: Toward the Ethnic Roots of the 'Outsider,'" in Juliane Brand and Christopher Hailey, eds., *Constructive Dissonance: Arnold Schoenberg and the Transformations of Twentieth-Century Culture* (Berkeley and Los Angeles: University of California Press, 1997), p. 36. Marc's last line about dissonance suggests that he had read the excerpt from Schoenberg's *Theory of Harmony* in the concert's program notes. On the impact of Schoenberg's concept of dissonance on Marc's ideas about painting, see Karin von Maur, "'. . . from looking at the world to looking through the world': Franz Marc and *Der Blaue Reiter* in the Struggle for Modernism," in Christian von Holst, ed., *Franz Marc: Horses*, exh. cat. (Ostfildern-Ruip: Hatje Cantz Publishers; Cambridge, Mass.: Busch-Reisinger Museum, 2000), p. 198.

28. I would especially like to thank T. Kaori Kitao for our fruitful discussions, which opened up new avenues of thought on the sketches and their relationship to the final painting.

29. For a good description of Kandinsky's working method by Thomas von Hartmann, the Russian composer who collaborated with Kandinsky on his opera, *Der gelbe Klang*, see Hartmann's "The Indecipherable Kandinsky" (1913), quoted in *Schoenberg–Kandinsky*, p. 141. Notably, in discussing Kandinsky's movement away from the representational, Hartmann wrote, "Painting is put on the same level as music, which seeks only the purity and appropriateness of sound combinations."

30. Peg Weiss mentions both the singer and the other musicians; see Weiss, "Evolving Perceptions," p. 52 n. 4.

31. For a discussion of Kandinsky and synaesthesia, see Rose-Carol Washton Long, *Kandinsky: The Development of an Abstract Style* (Oxford: Oxford University Press, 1980), pp. 53–54.

32. Wassily Kandinsky, *On the Spiritual in Art*, in Kenneth C. Lindsay and Peter Vergo, eds., *Kandinsky: Complete Writings on Art* (New York: Da Capo Press, 1994), p. 157.

33. Ibid., pp. 180–81. In the same text, Kandinsky noted, "The correspondence between color and musical tones is of course only relative. Just as a violin can produce very different tones, so, e.g., can yellow in its various shades be expressed by the sounds of different instruments" (p. 181).

34. Ibid., p. 185. Kandinsky went on to caution, "It is clear that all the descriptions employed for these quite simple colors are extremely provisional and clumsy. So too are the emotions we have used to characterize these colors (joy, sorrow, etc.). These emotions are no more than material states of the soul. The different tones of the colors, like those of music, are of a much subtler nature and awaken far subtler vibrations in the soul than can be described in words" (pp. 189–90).

35. Ibid., p. 193.

36. Wassily Kandinsky, "Institut Khudozhestvennoi Kul'tury v Moskve" [1920], *Sovetskoe iskusstvo* 15 (1933): 126–43, quoted in Weiss, "Evolving Perceptions," p. 44. This also appears in Wassily Kandinsky, "Program for the Institute of Artistic Culture [*Programma Instituta Khudozhestvennoi Kultury*]" (Moscow, 1920); reprinted in I. Matsa et al., eds., *Sovetskoe iskusstvo za 15 let* (Moscow and Leningrad, 1933), in Lindsay and Vergo, *Complete Writings on Art*, pp. 469–70.

37. Kandinsky, *On the Spiritual in Art*, p. 154.

38. Gabriele Münter is the one who actually obtained Schoenberg's address. See Jelena Hahl-Koch, "Kandinsky, Schönberg and Their Parallel Experiments," in Konrad Boehmer, ed., *Schönberg and Kandinsky: An Historic Encounter* (Amsterdam: Harwood Academic Publishers, 1997), p. 68.

39. Kandinsky to Schoenberg, January 18, 1911, in *Schoenberg–Kandinsky*, p. 21. Emphasis in original. Kandinsky did not mention in this letter, nor in any of the subsequent letters, that he had painted *Impression III (Concert)*. It is unknown whether Kandinsky told Schoenberg about the painting when they met in person. *Impression III (Concert)* was in the *Jack of Diamonds* exhibition in Moscow in February–March 1912 (no. 64). See Hans K. Roethel and Jean K. Benjamin, *Kandinsky: Catalogue Raisonné of the Oil Paintings, Volume One, 1900–1915* (Ithaca, N.Y.: Cornell University Press, 1982), p. 354.

40. *Improvisation 7* was first shown in the Second International Art Exhibition at the Salon Izdebsky, Odessa, December 1910 (cat. no. 214). *Improvisation 16* was first shown in the *Jack of Diamonds* exhibition, Moscow, December 1910, as well as in the Second International show in Odessa (unnumbered). See Roethel and Benjamin, *Catalogue Raisonné*, pp. 313, 341.

41. Schoenberg to Kandinsky, January 24, 1911, in *Schoenberg–Kandinsky*, pp. 23–24. Emphasis in original.

42. Hahl-Koch does not find the use of "Sie" surprising, since the familiar "Du" form of address was much less common at the time and, with only one exception (Thomas von Hartmann), Kandinsky used the formal "Sie" with all of his friends (*Schoenberg–Kandinsky*, pp. 137–38). Kandinsky's salutation in his first few letters to Schoenberg was "Dear Professor," and the composer's first letter to the artist began "Dear Sir." Thereafter they used "Dear Mr. Schoenberg" and "Dear Mr. Kandinsky" and closed with "Your Kandinsky" and "Your Schoenberg." Notably, when Kandinsky renewed contact with Schoenberg in 1922, he affectionately wrote, "My dear Schoenberg," and the artist responded, "My dear Kandinsky." Kandinsky's invitation to Schoenberg to come to the Bauhaus was addressed to "Dear friend," but when things became strained between the two friends, Kandinsky reverted to "Dear Mr. Schoenberg," and the composer similarly reverted to "Dear Mr. Kandinsky," or, in his most heated letter, that of May 4, 1923, simply "Dear Kandinsky."

43. On October 7, 1911, Kandinsky chided the composer: "Don't forget that you still owe me your picture, I mean your photographic portrait. I can wait still longer, but I must have it!" (ibid., p. 34).

44. Ibid., p. 172.

45. Kandinsky to Schoenberg, February 6, 1911, in ibid., pp. 26–27. Although Schoenberg had been concerned that Kandinsky would not be able to appreciate the importance of color in the black-and-white images, Kandinsky indicated that he could do without color, describing such black-and-white photographs as "a kind of piano reduction" (Kandinsky to Schoenberg, January 26, 1911, in ibid., p. 26).

46. Kandinsky to Schoenberg, November 16, 1911, in ibid., p. 36. Emphasis in original.

47. Wassily Kandinsky first wrote to Franz Marc with the idea of such an almanac on June 19, 1911. In a letter to Marc on September 1, 1911, Kandinsky wrote: "Schönberg *must* write on German music. . . . There should also be a few scores. Schönberg, e.g., has lieder." See Wassily Kandinsky and Franz Marc, eds., *The Blaue Reiter Almanac*, documentary edition by Klaus Lankheit (New York: Viking Press, 1974), pp. 16–17.

48. Postcard to Arnold Schoenberg, n.d., from Maria Marc, August Macke, Elisabeth Macke, Münter, and Kandinsky," in *Schoenberg-Kandinsky*, pp. 31–32. Hahl-Koch says that the card was probably written at the end of September 1911, but an annotation on the original in the Arnold Schoenberg Collection at the Library of Congress indicates a date of "[24 Oct. 1911]." Based on when the *Blue Rider Almanac* meetings were known to have occurred, the October date seems more likely. Maria Franck signed her name "Maria Marc" although she did not actually marry Franz Marc until 1913.

49. Kandinsky to Schoenberg, November 16, 1911, in *Schoenberg–Kandinsky*, p. 35.

50. Kandinsky, *On the Spiritual in Art*, p. 149. Kandinsky's treatise was published in December 1911 with a 1912 date, but most of it was completed in 1909. The references to Schoenberg were added in 1911.

51. Schoenberg to Kandinsky, November 11, 1911, in *Schoenberg–Kandinsky*, p. 35.

52. Ibid. On November 16, 1911, Kandinsky wrote Schoenberg, "I was actually always sure that *you* would understand and be sensitive to Münter. In general, very few people are sensitive to her work" (ibid., p. 36). Schoenberg thought Münter's works were "really extremely original and of salutary simplicity. Absolute naturalness" (Schoenberg to Kandinsky, December 14, 1911, in ibid., p. 39). The composer's favorite work by Kandinsky was *Romantische Landschaft* (Romantic landscape), coincidentally, a work that the artist had painted on January 3, the same day that he had made *Impression III (Concert)* (Schoenberg to Kandinsky, December 14, 1911, in ibid., p. 38).

53. Schoenberg to Kandinsky, December 14, 1911, in ibid., p. 39.

54. Schoenberg to Kandinsky, August 19, 1912, in ibid., p. 54.

55. Schoenberg to Kandinsky, September 28, 1913, in ibid., p. 59.

56. Kandinsky and Münter spent a few months in Switzerland and effectively separated as a couple when Kandinsky (a "hostile alien" who could not go back to Germany) returned to Russia in November 1914. For more on this subject, see *Wassily Kandinsky and Gabriele Münter: Letters and Reminiscences, 1902–1914*, ed. Annegret Hoberg, trans. Ian Robson (Munich: Prestel, 2001), pp. 26–28.

57. Kandinsky to Schoenberg, July 3, 1922, in *Schoenberg–Kandinsky*, p. 73.

58. Schoenberg to Kandinsky, July 20, 1922, in ibid., pp. 73–74.

59. Kandinsky to Schoenberg, April 15, 1923, in ibid., p. 75.

60. Schoenberg to Kandinsky, April 19, 1923, in ibid., p. 76. The details of Alma Mahler's role in this incident are sketchy. However, there is a letter from Schoenberg to Mahler dated May 11, 1923, in which he wrote, "In my view you should not tell Kandinsky and Gropius that I've heard from you whose spiritual brothers they now are." See *Arnold Schoenberg: Letters*, ed. Erwin Stein, trans. Eithne Wilkins and Ernst Kaiser (New York: St. Martin's Press, 1965), p. 94. The names of both Kandinsky and Gropius were omitted in the published version but are in the carbon copy of the letter in the Arnold Schoenberg Collection at the Library of Congress.

61. Kandinsky to Schoenberg, April 24, 1923, in *Schoenberg–Kandinsky*, p. 77.

62. Schoenberg to Kandinsky, May 4, 1923, in ibid., pp. 78, 81–82. Schoenberg spelled Hitler's name with two *t*s ("Hittler") in his original letter.

63. Kandinsky to Schoenberg, July 1, 1936, in ibid., pp. 84–85.

Esther da Costa Meyer, "Schoenberg's Echo: The Composer as Painter," pp. 37–61

I wish to thank Stanley Corngold, Lionel Gossman, Christopher Hailey, Arno Mayer, and Leonard Stein for their many helpful suggestions.

Unless otherwise noted, all translations are my own.

1. Gerstl's friend and fellow painter Victor Hammer claimed that Gerstl taught Schoenberg how to wield a brush. Victor Hammer, "Memories of Richard Gerstl," in Jane Kallir, *Richard Gerstl, Oskar Kokoschka* (New York: Galerie St. Etienne, 1992), p. 28.

2. For Gerstl, see Klaus Albrecht Schröder, *Richard Gerstl, 1883–1908* (Vienna: Kunstforum der Bank Austria, 1993), and Otto Breicha, *Gerstl und Schönberg. Eine Beziehung* (Salzburg: Galerie Welz, 1993); see also Jane Kallir, "Arnold Schönberg et Richard Gerstl," in *Vienne 1880–1938: L'Apocalypse joyeuse*, ed. Jean Clair (Paris: Éditions du Centre Pompidou, 1986), pp. 454–70.

3. *Arnold Schoenberg: Letters*, ed. Erwin Stein, trans. Eithne Wilkins and Ernst Kaiser (Berkeley: University of California Press, 1987), pp. 25–26.

4. The checklist actually itemizes forty-four works, but two numbers were unaccountably left out, and the final tally seems to be forty-two or forty-one. As this catalogue was going to press, several hitherto unknown paintings by Schoenberg were found on the verso of his canvases. As the investigations are not yet complete, we were not given access to the new information. The current catalogue raisonné, on which our exhibition is based, is currently being drastically revised. See *Arnold Schoenberg: Paintings and Drawings*, ed. Thomas Zaunschirm (Klagenfurt: Ritter Verlag, 1991).

5. Entry for October 14, 1910. Arthur Schnitzler, *Arthur Schnitzler, Tagebuch, 1909–1912* (Vienna: Verlag der Österreichischen Akademie der Wissenschaften, 1981), p. 184.

6. Quoted in Hans Heinz Stuckenschmidt, *Schoenberg: His Life, World and Work*, trans. Humphrey Searle (London: John Calder, 1977), p. 143; originally published as *Schönberg, Leben, Umwelt, Werk* (Zurich: Atlantis, 1974), p. 133. Emphasis in original; translation slightly modified.

7. R. R. [pseud.], "Der Komponist als Maler," *Illustriertes Wiener Extrablatt* 277 (October 9, 1910): 2.

8. R. von Enderes, *Neuigkeits Welt-Blatt*, October 11, 1910, p. 12.

9. Adalbert Franz Seligman, "Aus der Wiener Kunstleben," *Neue Freie Presse*, morning edition, October 13, 1910, p. 2.

10. Elsa Bienenfeld, "Eine Bilderausstellung von Arnold Schönberg," *Neues Wiener Journal*, October 9, 1910, p. 14. Bienenfeld, a highly respected music critic, died at Auschwitz. See also Richard Specht, "Arnold Schönberg. Eine Vorbemerkung," and Karl Linke, "Gedanken zu Schönberg," both in *Der Merker* 17, no. 2 (June 1911): 697–700 and 710–14, respectively.

11. Quoted in Patrick Werkner, *Austrian Expressionism*, trans. Nicholas T. Parsons (Palo Alto, Calif.: Society for the Promotion of Science and Scholarship, 1993), p. 179.

12. The Rosé Quartet premiered many of Schoenberg's important works, including the two string quartets in question, as well as *Verklärte Nacht*. Arnold Rosé, founder of the ensemble, was married to Gustav Mahler's sister, Justine. For the opening concert, and the show in general, see Paul Stefan, "Schönberg-Abend," *Der Merker* 2 (October 25, 1910): 79.

13. Franz Marc to August Macke, January 14, 1911, in *August Macke–Franz Marc: Briefwechsel*, ed. Wolfgang Macke (Cologne: DuMont Schauberg, 1964), p. 40. Emphasis in original.

14. Wassily Kandinsky to Arnold Schoenberg, January 18, 1911, in *Arnold Schoenberg–Wassily Kandinsky: Letters, Pictures and Documents*, ed. Jelena Hahl-Koch, trans. John C. Crawford (London: Faber and Faber, 1984), p. 21.

15. Musicologists no longer see atonality and abstraction as parallel movements. Abstraction is closer to serialism than to atonality, which more closely resembles Expressionism. See Carl Dahlhaus, "La Construction du disharmonique: À propos des théories artistiques de Schoenberg et Kandinsky," *Contrechamps* 2 (April 1984): 137.

16. *The Berg–Schoenberg Correspondence*, ed. Juliane Brand, Christopher Hailey, and Donald Harris (New York: W. W. Norton, 1987), p. 23. For the checklist, see *Die erste Ausstellung der Redaktion der blaue Reiter* (Munich: Moderne Galerie Thannhauser, 1911).

17. Schoenberg to Kandinsky, December 18, 1911; quoted in Klaus Kropfinger, "Latent Structural Power versus the Dissolution of Artistic Material," in Konrad Boehmer, ed. *Schönberg and Kandinsky* (Amsterdam: Harwood Academic Publishers, 1997), p. 61 (English translation on p. 63).

18. Arnold Schoenberg, "The Relationship to the Text," in Wassily Kandinsky and Franz Marc, eds. *The Blaue Reiter Almanac*, documentary edition by Klaus Lankheit (New York: Viking Press, 1974), pp. 90–102; originally published as "Das Verhältnis zum Text," in Kandinsky and Marc, eds. *Der Blaue Reiter* (Munich: Piper Verlag, 1912).

19. Schoenberg, "The Relationship to the Text," p. 102.

20. Paris von Gütersloh was the pseudonym of the artist and actor Albert Konrad Kiehtreiber, a student of Klimt. For the Budapest show, see János Breuer, "Schoenberg's paintings," *New Hungarian Quarterly* 29, no. 3 (Autumn 1988): 215–21.

21. Quoted in ibid., p. 219. Breuer points out, interestingly, that the German-speaking newspapers of Budapest were much more clement toward Schoenberg.

22. Quoted in Werkner, *Austrian Expressionism*, p. 171.

23. In this case, however, it was Schoenberg who did not think highly of the young artist: "Marc is quite friendly [*sympathischer*]. Somewhat nebulous and insignificant. He won't last long with Kandinsky." Arnold Schoenberg, *Berliner Tagebuch, mit einer Hommage à Schönberg*, ed. Josef Rufer (Berlin: Propyläen, 1974), p. 15.

24. Quoted in Stuckenschmidt, *Life, World and Work*, p. 205.

25. *Tagebücher von Paul Klee, 1898–1918*, ed. Felix Klee (Cologne: DuMont Schauberg, 1957). See entry no. 917 (1913), p. 276.

26. Kandinsky to Schoenberg, January 13, 1912, in *Schoenberg–Kandinsky*, p. 42. Kandinsky had made his reactions clear before. On December 15, 1911, he informed Schoenberg that he wanted to exhibit two or three Visions, "which make a strong impression on everyone, just as they do on me (but I *love* the realistic ones)." Ibid., p. 40. Emphasis in the original.

27. Schoenberg to Kandinsky, March 8, 1912, in ibid., p. 48. Emphasis in the original.

28. *Der Sturm* 37 (October 10, 1910): 295; quoted in

Schoenberg–Kandinsky, p. 193.

29. Quoted in Robert Fleck, "Ahnenfigur und Innovationsmodell—Reflexionen über die Aktualität Schönbergs," in *Die Visionen des Arnold Schönberg. Jahre der Malerei* (Frankfurt: Schirn Kunsthalle, 2002), p. 37; originally in Paul Wilhelm, "Bei Arnold Schönberg," in *Neues Wiener Journal*, January 10, 1909, p. 3.

30. See Schoenberg, "Malerische Einflüsse" (1938), in *Journal of the Arnold Schoenberg Institute* 2, no. 3 (June 1978): 238 (hereafter cited as *JASI*).

31. Halsey Stevens, "A Conversation with Schoenberg About Painting," *JASI* 2, no. 3 (June 1978): 179.

32. See O., *Wiener Abendpost* (*Beilage zur Wiener Zeitung*) 230 (October 8, 1910): 3; and Bienenfeld, "Eine Bilderausstellung von Arnold Schönberg," p. 14.

33. Anton Webern to Alban Berg, September 6, 1921, Berg-Fonds, Musiksammlung, Österreichische Nationalbibliothek. My thanks to Therese Muxeneder for bringing this letter to my attention. Berg and Webern subsequently sent their former teacher a portfolio of lithographs by Klimt as a birthday present.

34. Joseph Auner makes this point with regard to Schoenberg's compositions, but it is equally applicable to his art: "A corollary to the ideal of spontaneous creation is a prohibition of any sketching, revision or other 'conscious' intervention in the compositional process." Auner, "Schoenberg's Aesthetic Transformations and the Evolution of Form in *Die glückliche Hand*," *JASI* 12, no. 2 (November 1989): 106–7.

35. Liebermann had exhibited at the Hagenbund in 1905, Corinth at the Miethke Gallery in 1906, and Van Gogh at the Secession in 1904 and the Miethke Gallery in 1906. At least one critic compared Schoenberg's painting to Van Gogh's and, less plausibly, to Gauguin's. See O., *Wiener Abendpost*, p. 3.

36. Arnold Schoenberg, "Gustav Mahler" (1912, rev. 1948), in *Style and Idea*, ed. Leonard Stein, trans. Leo Black (Berkeley: University of California Press, 1984), p. 456. Translation slightly modified. See Arnold Schoenberg, *Stil und Gedanke*, ed. Ivan Vojtech (Frankfurt: Fischer, 1992), p. 22, for the original version in German.

37. Schoenberg, "Relationship to the Text," p. 102.

38. "Curiously, the forehead had become higher; the brain obviously takes up more room," wrote Schoenberg of photographs of Mahler. Schoenberg, "Gustav Mahler," p. 468.

39. Schoenberg to Mahler, July 5, 1910, in *Life, World and Work*, p. 100.

40. See Sigrid Wiesmann, ed., *Gustav Mahler in Vienna*, trans. Anne Shelley (New York: Rizzoli, 1976), p. 113. The Mahler Foundation, established after the composer's death by Alma Mahler, continued to help Schoenberg financially.

41. Willi Reich, *Schoenberg: A Critical Biography* (New York: Praeger, 1971), pp. 44–45; and Schoenberg, "Gustav Mahler," pp. 447–48. Toward the end of 1912, Berg sent Schoenberg a postcard of the house in which Mahler was born, in Kalischt, Bohemia. Berg wrote: "Doesn't this resemble the shelter in which Christ was born?" *Berg–Schoenberg*, p. 139.

42. In 1907–8, Schoenberg had composed a lied in honor of Mahler, just after a wrenching farewell when Mahler had left Vienna for New York: "Ich darf nicht dankend an dir niedersinken" (I may not sink down before you with gratitude), op. 14, no. 1. Alexander L. Ringer, *Arnold Schoenberg: The Composer as Jew* (Oxford: Clarendon Press, 1990), p. 41.

43. Schoenberg to Berg, August 5, 1930, in Schoenberg, *Letters*, p. 143.

44. "Practically expressed: I feel these colorweights less, because they disappear too much from my field of vision. (A few escape me entirely.) I had to stand far away, *and then of course the picture is smaller, the equation 'reduced.'* Perhaps I have for this reason less of an impression of the very large pictures, because I could not take them in as a whole." Schoenberg to Kandinsky, December 14, 1911, in *Schoenberg–Kandinsky*, p. 39. Emphasis in original. Kandinsky disagreed: "It is precisely my intention (sometimes) to prevent, by means of the dimensions, the pictures being taken in at a glance." Ibid., p. 42. Kandinsky painted *Romantische Landschaft* just after he heard Schoenberg's concert in Munich in 1911.

45. For Pappenheim, see Elizabeth Lorraine Keathley, "Revisioning Musical Modernism: Arnold Schoenberg, Marie Pappenheim, and *Erwartung*'s New Woman" (Ph.D. diss., State University of New York at Stony Brook, 1999); and Eva Weissweiler, "Frau und Musik: 'Schreiben Sie mir doch einen Operntext, Fräulein,'" *Neue Zeitschrift für Musik* 145 (June 1984): 4–8.

46. Lewis Wickes, "Schoenberg, *Erwartung*, and the Reception of Psychoanalysis in Musical Circles in Vienna Until 1910/1911," *Studies in Music* 23 (1989): 96. Josef Breuer and Sigmund Freud, *Studien über Hysterie* (Leipzig and Vienna: Deuticke, 1895). For the English translation, see *Studies on Hysteria*, trans. James Strachey (New York: Basic Books, 1999). It was Bertha Pappenheim who came up with the expression "talking cure," which Freud used before coining the term "psychoanalysis."

47. In 1971, when Schoenberg's biographer Hans Heinz Stuckenschmidt searched his home in Brentwood Park, California, no books on psychoanalysis or even on psychology were found in his library. Stuckenschmidt, *Life, World and Work*, p. 183.

48. In a letter to Berg written on January 19, 1932, Schoenberg apologized for not having acknowledged Berg's birthday gift earlier, adding: "I have put off my thank-you letter through abreaction [*abreagiert*] or suppression or some other such psychoanalytically expressible means." *Berg–Schoenberg*, p. 429. The notion of abreaction, first published by Freud in 1893, was popularized in *Studies on Hysteria* (1895). Berg had been acquainted with Freud for years, and mentions him in a letter to Schoenberg in 1911. Ibid., p. 9.

49. Wickes, "Schoenberg, *Erwartung*, and the Reception of Psychoanalysis," p. 101. Freud's only lecture to a nonacademic audience, "Der Dichter und das Phantasieren" (The relation of the poet to day-dreaming), had taken place in 1907 at Heller's bookshop, where Schoenberg would later have his one-man exhibition. Ibid, pp. 94–95.

50. Sigmund Freud, "Analysis of a Phobia in a Five-Year-Old Boy" (1909), in *The Standard Edition of the Complete Psychological Works of Sigmund Freud*, ed. and trans. James Strachey, 24 vols. (London: Hogarth Press, 1953–73), 10:3–149. Wickes points out that in the first edition of the case study, Freud does not appear as the author, since it was Graf who analyzed his own son: the case was "mitgeteilt von" (communicated by) Freud. Wickes, "Schoenberg, *Erwartung*, and the Reception of Psychoanalysis," p. 91.

51. For a psychoanalytical interpretation of frontality in Schoenberg's work, see Mary Mathews Gedo, *Psychoanalytical Perspectives on Art* (London: Hillsdale, 1985), p. 185.

52. Indeed, the portrait appears to succeed only at the expense of the face. Sabine Melchior-Bonnet, *Histoire du miroir* (Paris: Imago, 1994), p. 156.

53. Quoted in Joseph Leo Koerner, "Rembrandt and the Epiphany of the Face," *Res* 12 (Autumn 1986): 9.

54. See Robert Rosenblum, *Modern Painting and the Northern Romantic Tradition: Friedrich to Rothko* (London: Thames and Hudson, 1975), p. 63.

55. This is the case in *Die glückliche Hand*. See John Crawford, "*Die glückliche Hand*: Schoenberg's *Gesamtkunstwerk*," *Musical Quarterly* 60, no. 4 (October 1974): 600.

56. Mirror construction appears as a principle of composition in the mirror canons that Schoenberg penned as gifts for friends such as Thomas Mann. It also occurs in both the libretto and the score of *Glückliche Hand*. Ibid., p. 597. For mirror writing, see Clara Steuermann, "From the Archives: Schoenberg at Play," *JASI* 2, no. 3 (June 1978): 246; and Arnold Schoenberg, *Thirty Kanons*, ed. Josef Rufer (Kassel and New York: Bärenreiter, 1963), pp. 64–65.

57. Stuckenschmidt, *Life, World and Work*, p. 199.

58. For Schoenberg and the *Rückenfiguren*, see

Georg Eisler (son of Schoenberg's student Hanns Eisler), "Observations on Schoenberg as Painter," *JASI* 2, no. 3 (June 1978): 175; and Werner Hofmann, "Les trois regards de Schoenberg," in *Arnold Schoenberg: Regards* (Paris: Musée d'Art Moderne de la Ville de Paris, 1995), p. 34.

59. Eberhard Freitag, "German Expressionism and Schoenberg's Self-Portraits," *JASI* 2, no. 3 (June 1978): 171.

60. Bahr took the phrase from Mach's *Analysis of Sensations*. Jacques Le Rider, *Modernity and the Crises of Identity*, trans. Rosemary Morris (New York: Continuum, 1993), pp. 41–42.

61. Kallir, "Arnold Schönberg et Richard Gerstl," p. 457.

62. "Kandinsky when he saw them, called them 'Visions,' while I had named them 'Gazes.'" Arnold Schoenberg, "About Kandinsky" (1934), *JASI* 2, no. 3 (June 1978): 239.

63. Oskar Kokoschka, "On the Nature of Visions," trans. Hedi Modlinger and John Thwaites, in Edith Hoffmann, *Kokoschka: Life and Work* (London: Faber and Faber, 1947), p. 287. Originally delivered in 1912, Kokoschka's lecture was published in 1921 ("Von der Natur der Gesichte").

64. *Ferruccio Busoni: Selected Letters*, ed. and trans. Antony Beaumont (London: Faber and Faber, 1987), p. 396. Emphasis in original.

65. Schoenberg to Kandinsky, January 24, 1911, in *Schoenberg–Kandinsky*, p. 23. Emphasis in original.

66. Schoenberg, "About Music Criticism" (1909), in *Style and Idea*, p. 193.

67. For the history of this pictorial form, see Sixten Ringbom, *Icon to Narrative: The Rise of the Dramatic Close-up in Fifteenth-Century Devotional Painting* (Turku, Finland: Åbo Akademi, 1965).

68. Eisler, "Observations on Schoenberg as Painter," p. 174.

69. In 1885, Brahms's publisher, Fritz Simrock, commissioned Klinger to do the title pages for Brahms's compositions. Klinger took the project to heart, and followed it with the *Brahms-Phantasien* (1886–94), a cycle of forty-one drawings and engravings inspired by Brahms. Schoenberg's use of the title *Phantasien* may reflect his acquaintance with Klinger's work.

70. Pierre Boulez, "Schoenberg, le Mal-Aimé," in *Points de repère*, ed. Jean-Jacques Nattier (Paris: Christian Bourgois et Seuil, 1985), p. 304. Originally in *Die Welt*, September 7, 1974. This connection is all the more plausible because Redon had exhibited at the Secession in 1903.

71. Claudia Baumbusch, "Betrachtungen zur Ikonographie Schönbergs am Beispiel der *Hände*," in *Zu Arnold Schönberg als Maler* (Klagenfurt: Ritter, 1991), p. 56.

72. Schreker, *Die Gezeichneten*, act 2, scene 2. See Christopher Hailey, *Franz Schreker, 1878–1934: A Cultural Biography* (Cambridge, U.K.: Cambridge University Press, 1993), pp. 65–66. Schreker taught at the Prussian Academy of the Arts in Berlin with Schoenberg, and like him was dismissed from his post in 1933 for being Jewish.

73. Roland Barthes, "The Third Meaning: Research Notes on Some Eisenstein Stills," in *Image Music Text*, trans. Stephen Heath (New York: Farrar, Straus and Giroux, 1990), p. 67.

74. Charles Rosen, *Arnold Schoenberg* (Chicago: University of Chicago Press, 1996), p. 53.

75. Darius Milhaud, "To Arnold Schoenberg on His Seventieth Birthday," *Musical Quarterly* 30, no. 4 (1944): 383.

76. Bienenfeld, "Eine Bilderausstellung von Arnold Schönberg," p. 14.

77. Rosenblum, *Modern Painting and the Northern Romantic Tradition*, p. 171.

78. Schoenberg, "Gustav Mahler," p. 471. For Schoenberg and Theosophy, see Walther Klein, "Das theosophische Element in Schönbergs Weltanschauung," in *Musikblätter des Anbruch (Sonderheft zu Schönbergs 50. Geburtstag)* 6, no. 7/8 (August–September 1924): 273–74; and for the connection between Theosophy and eyes, see Suzanne Neuberger, "Gazes, Visions and Images," in *Arnold Schoenberg: Paintings and Drawings*, p. 103.

79. Rosenblum, *Modern Painting and the Northern Romantic Tradition*, p. 212.

80. Schoenberg, who discussed abstraction with Kandinsky, may have heard of Wilhelm Worringer's seminal *Abstraktion und Einfühlung* (Abstraction and empathy), published in 1908. Both Kandinsky and Marc were acquainted with Worringer, and frequented the salon of his sister Emmy in Berlin. See Kandinsky's letter to Schoenberg of January 16, 1912, mentioning her, in *Schoenberg–Kandinsky*, p. 43.

81. Schoenberg to Kandinsky, January 24, 1911, in *Schoenberg–Kandinsky*, pp. 23–24. Translation amended.

82. Paul Claudel, *L'Oeil écoute* (Paris: Gallimard, 1946). In an undated letter to Hertzka, probably written in 1913, Schoenberg also had mentioned "sounds for the eye." Schoenberg, *Letters*, p. 44.

83. A third image, showing Christ kneeling on the Mount of Olives, which was probably executed around 1910, appears on the back of one of the night landscapes. According to the catalogue raisonné, there is no proof that Schoenberg actually painted this piece. *Arnold Schoenberg: Paintings and Drawings*, p. 390. But the brushwork and the fact that it is painted on the verso of a landscape signed and dated by the artist make other authorship highly unlikely. The depiction of Christ alone, abandoned by his disciples, fits in with the persona of the revolutionary artist.

84. Ziva Amishai-Maisels, "The Jewish Jesus," *Journal of Jewish Art*, no. 9 (1982): 103–4. See also

Ziva Amishai-Maisels, "Origins of the Jewish Jesus," in *Complex Identities: Jewish Consciousness and Modern Art*, ed. Matthew Baigell and Milly Heyd (New Brunswick, N.J.: Rutgers University Press, 2001), pp. 51–86.

85. Annegret Hoberg, "Albert Bloch in Munich, 1909–21," in *Albert Bloch: The American Blue Rider*, ed. Henry Adams, Margaret C. Conrads, and Annegret Hoberg (Munich: Prestel Verlag, 1997), p. 61. See also Reinhold Kauenhoven Janzen, "Albert Bloch's Images of Christ," in *Albert Bloch: Artistic and Literary Perspectives*, ed. Frank Baron, Helmut Arntzen, and David Cateforis (Munich: Prestel Verlag, 1997), pp. 55–64.

86. G. Tobias Natter, *Max Oppenheimer, 1885–1954*, exh. cat. (Vienna: Jüdisches Museum der Stadt Wien, 1994), p. 17.

87. For Schoenberg's use of this poem, see Walter Frisch, "Schoenberg and the Poetry of Richard Dehmel," *JASI* 9, no. 2 (November 1986): 151–52.

88. CD booklet for *Pierrot lunaire* (Harmonia Mundi, 1992), text by Albert Giroud, trans. James O. Wooton, p. 33. For the identification of Christ with the artist in *Pierrot lunaire*, see Carl Schorske, *Fin-de-Siècle Vienna: Politics and Culture* (New York: Vintage Books, 1981), pp. 355–57.

89. Henry Adams, "Albert Bloch: The Invisible Blue Rider," in Adams, Conrads, and Hoberg, *American Blue Rider*, p. 33.

90. Karin von Maur, "Arnold Schönberg oder die Vereinigung von Musik und Malerei," in *Die Visionen des Arnold Schönberg. Jahre der Malerei* (Frankfurt: Schirn Kunsthalle, 2002), p. 27.

91. E. H. Gombrich, "The Cartoonist's Armoury," in *Meditations on a Hobby Horse* (London: Phaidon, 1978), p. 130.

92. Sigmund Freud, *Jokes and Their Relation to the Unconscious*, ed. and trans. James Strachey (New York: W. W. Norton, 1963). Freud was followed by Theodor Reik, "Lust und Leid in Witz," *Imago* 15 (1929), and then by the art historian Ernst Kris, "The Psychology of Caricature," *International Journal of Psychoanalysis* (July 1936): 285–303.

93. Schoenberg to Amadeo De Filippi, May 13, 1949, in Schoenberg, *Letters*, pp. 271–72.

94. Schoenberg, words added to the margins of a letter to Berg, dated January 16, 1921, in *Berg–Schoenberg*, p. 312.

95. Marc to Franck, February 10, 1911; quoted in Iris Pfeiffer, "Introduction," *Schönberg, Kandinsky, Blauer Reiter, und die Russische Avantgarde*, exh. cat. [*Journal of the Arnold Schoenberg Center* 1] (Vienna: Arnold Schoenberg Center, 2000), p. 95.

96. *Schoenberg–Kandinsky*, p. 162. John Crawford and Joseph Auner have shown that Kandinsky's ideas were crucial for Schoenberg's opera. See Crawford, "*Die glückliche Hand*," pp. 583–601; and Joseph Henry Auner, "Schoenberg's Compositional and Aesthetic Transformations, 1910–1913: The Genesis of *Die glückliche Hand*" (Ph.D. diss., University of Chicago, 1991).

97. See Schoenberg's letter to Kandinsky, December 14, 1911, in *Schoenberg–Kandinsky*, pp. 38–39. For Redon and his interest in Wagner, see Douglas W. Druick, ed., *Odilon Redon: Prince of Dreams, 1840–1916*, exh. cat. (Chicago: Art Institute of Chicago; New York: Harry N. Abrams, 1994), p. 203.

98. Aphorism of 1910, quoted in Reich, *Critical Biography*, pp. 56–57.

99. Quoted in Ringer, *Composer as Jew*, p. 199.

100. At the time, the number of Jewish converts never exceeded 10 percent of the Jewish community, and only one-quarter of these became Protestants. Le Rider, *Modernity and the Crises of Identity*, p. 187.

101. This last theme played a crucial role in his art; see his "Heart and Brain in Music" (1946), in *Style and Idea*, pp. 53–61.

102. Schoenberg, "Gustav Mahler," p. 455.

103. Stuckenschmidt, *Life, World and Work*, p. 107.

104. Ringer, *Composer as Jew*, p. 7.

105. The incident was widely reported in the press, as in this account: "A significant summer experience of the well-known composer, Arnold Schoenberg, is reported by our correspondent in Graz. He had chosen Mattsee as a place to spend the summer and had recently been asked by the local town council to give documentary proof that he is not a Jew. Should he be one, he would have to leave the place at once, as by a decision of the Council, Jews are not permitted to stay there. Although Schoenberg could provide proof that he is a Protestant, he has decided to leave Mattsee." "Composer's Certificate of Baptism," *Neue Freie Presse*, June 30, 1921, in Alban Berg, *Letters to His Wife*, ed. and trans. Bernard Grun (New York: St. Martin's Press, 1971), p. 292.

106. Leon Botstein, "Schoenberg and the Audience: Modernism, Music and Politics in the Twentieth Century," in Walter Frisch, ed., *Schoenberg and His World* (Princeton, N.J.: Princeton University Press, 1999), p. 39.

107. James Huneker, "Schoenberg, Musical Anarchist, Who Has Upset Europe," *New York Times*, January 19, 1913, sec. 5, p. 9.

108. Schoenberg to Alma Mahler, July 26, 1921, Arnold Schoenberg Center, Vienna.

109. Schoenberg to Kandinsky, April 19, 1923, in Schoenberg, *Letters*, p. 88. The date of this letter is erroneously given as April 20 in this volume.

110. Schoenberg to Kandinsky, May 4, 1923, in ibid., p. 93. "To survive in exile, uncorrupted and unbroken," was to be the theme of his great opera *Moses und Aron* (1930–32).

111. Schoenberg to Berg, September 23, 1932, in *Berg–Schoenberg*, p. 436.

Reinhold Heller, "The Blue Rider," pp. 63–77

Unless otherwise noted, all translations are my own.

1. Thomas Mann, "Gladius Dei," in *Die Erzählungen*, 1 (Frankfurt: Fischer Bücherei, 1967), pp. 149–50. Among the first to recognize the significance of Mann's description was Peg Weiss, *Kandinsky in Munich: The Formative Jugendstil Years* (Princeton, N.J.: Princeton University Press, 1979), p. 3.

2. Wassily Kandinsky, "The *Blaue Reiter* [Recollection]," in Kenneth C. Lindsay and Peter Vergo, eds., *Kandinsky: Complete Writings on Art* (New York: Da Capo Press, 1994), p. 745.

3. Gabriele Münter to Kenneth Lindsay, May 7, 1950, in Reinhold Heller, *Gabriele Münter: The Years of Expressionism, 1903–1920* (Munich and New York: Prestel, 1997), p. 53.

4. Quoted in Władysława Jaworska, *Paul Gauguin and the School of Pont-Aven*, trans. Patrick Evans (Greenwich, Conn.: New York Graphic Society, 1972), p. 129.

5. The significance of the simultaneous presence of Ślewiński, Verkade, and Sérusier in Munich, as well as their acquaintance with Jawlensky and Werefkin during 1907–8, remains little explored and undervalued. Bernd Fäthke, *Marianne Werefkin: Leben und Werk* (Munich: Prestel Verlag, 1988), pp. 99–105, is mistaken about the dates of the artists' stay in Munich, but otherwise provides the most extensive discussion of the significance of the presence of these followers of Gauguin there for Jawlensky and Werefkin. Also see Armin Zweite, "'Nur das Notwendige stark zum Ausdruck bringen,'" in *Expressionistische Bilder: Sammlung der Firmengruppe Ahlers*, exh. cat. (Stuttgart: Verlag Gerd Hatje and the Käthe Kollwitz Museum, Berlin, 1993), pp. 11–14. Concerning Verkade's studies in Munich and his association with Jawlensky, see Caroline Boyle-Turner, *Jan Verkade: Ein holländischer Schüler Gauguins* (Zwolle: Waanders Verlag; Amsterdam: Rijksmuseum Vincent van Gogh, 1989), pp. 53–57.

6. On Murnau's attraction for the artists, and the motivation and significance of that attraction, compare Heller, *Münter*, pp. 70–78.

7. Gabriele Münter, entry dated May 17, 1911, in ibid., p. 16.

8. Wassily Kandinsky to Alexei von Jawlensky, April 24, 1934, in Jelena Hahl-Koch, "Der frühe Jawlensky," in Armin Zweite, ed., *Alexej Jawlensky, 1864–1941*, exh. cat. (Munich: Städtische Galerie im Lenbachhaus, 1983), p. 43.

9. The most extensive discussion of the NKVM is provided in Annegret Hoberg and Helmut Friedel, eds., *Der Blaue Reiter und das Neue Bild: Von der "Neuen Künstlervereinigung München"* zum "Blauen Reiter," exh. cat. (Munich, London, and New York: Prestel Verlag and Städtische Galerie im Lenbachhaus, 1999). Unless otherwise indicated, I have derived my information concerning the NKVM from this exemplary source.

10. Münter to Lindsay, May 7, 1950, in Heller, *Münter*, p. 17.

11. The initial membership, according to Gabriele Münter's handwritten list in the Gabriele Münter–Johannes Eichner Archive, Munich, is published in Hoberg and Friedel, *Der Blaue Reiter und das Neue Bild*, p. 30. Compare the membership compiled by Otto Fischer in *Das Neue Bild: Veröffentlichung der Neuen Künstlervereinigung München* (Munich: Delphin Verlag, 1912), p. 22. As Annegret Hoberg, "'Neue Künstlervereinigung München' und 'Blauer Reiter,'" in *Der Blaue Reiter und das Neue Bild*, p. 17, points out, it is noteworthy that the NKVM was the first German artists' association to include a significant number of women as members and as artists invited to exhibit.

12. Reproduced in Hoberg and Friedel, *Der Blaue Reiter und das Neue Bild*, p. 30.

13. Compare Franz Marc's comments concerning the NKVM core group: "Characteristic of the artists of the 'Association' was their strong emphasis on their program; the one learned from the other; there was a general competition as to who best understood the ideas. One heard, sometimes probably too frequently, the word 'synthesis.'" Franz Marc, "Die Wilden Deutschlands," in Wassily Kandinsky and Franz Marc, eds., *Der Blaue Reiter*, rev. documentary edition by Klaus Lankheit (Munich: Piper Verlag, 1984), p. 30. (Cf. an alternate English translation in Kandinsky and Marc, eds.,*The Blaue Reiter Almanac*, documentary edition by Lankheit [New York: Viking Press, 1974], p. 64.) On the concept of "synthesis," as applied by Jawlensky, Münter, and Kandinsky, see Reinhold Heller, "Innenräume: Erlebnis, Erinnerung und Synthese in der Kunst Gabriele Münters," in Annegret Hoberg and Helmut Friedel, eds., *Gabriele Münter 1877–1962: Retrospektive*, exh. cat. (Munich: Prestel Verlag and Städtische Galerie im Lenbachhaus, 1992), pp. 53–54, pp. 64–65 nn. 20, 21.

14. The NKVM's affiliation with French Symbolist art is further apparent in the short essay by Odilon Redon that appeared in the catalogue for the group's second touring exhibition. There were also texts by Kandinsky, Le Fauconnier, and the brothers David Burliuk and Vladimir Burljuk, and an excerpt from the catalogue of a "Douanier" Rousseau exhibition in Paris; reprinted in Hoberg and Friedel, *Der Blaue Reiter und das Neue Bild*, pp. 393–400. The Symbolist influence is also overtly retained in the theories of Marianne Werefkin, *Briefe an einen Unbekannten, 1901–1905*, ed. Clemens Weiler (Cologne: DuMont Schauberg, 1960).

15. The typescript of Kandinsky's manuscript in the Gabriele Münter–Johannes Eichner Archive, Munich, is dated August 3, 1909. The book was published at Christmastime 1911 by Reinhard Piper Verlag, Munich. Cf. Hans Konrad Röthel, *Kandinsky: Das graphische Werk* (Cologne: DuMont Schauberg, 1970), pp. 443–45, for the documentation and publication history of *Über das Geistige in der Kunst* (On the spiritual in art).

16. Wassily Kandinsky, *Über das Geistige in der Kunst*, 10th ed. (Bern: Benteli Verlag, 1952), p. 79. My translation here varies from that provided by Lindsay and Vergo in Wassily Kandinsky, *On the Spiritual in Art*, in *Complete Writings on Art*, p. 173.

17. Kandinsky, *Über das Geistige*, pp. 85–86; *On the Spiritual in Art*, p. 177.

18. Kandinsky, *Über das Geistige*, p. 80; *On the Spiritual in Art*, p. 173.

19. On Hugo von Tschudi and his efforts to fundamentally transform German collecting and exhibition practices, see Barbara Paul, *Hugo von Tschudi und die moderne französische Kunst* (Mainz: P. von Zabern, 1993), and Johann Georg Prinz von Hohenzollern and Peter-Klaus Schuster, eds., *Manet bis Van Gogh: Hugo von Tschudi und der Kampf um die Moderne* (Berlin: Nationalgalerie, Staatliche Museen zu Berlin; Munich: Prestel Verlag, 1996).

20. The exhibition brochure is reproduced in Hoberg and Friedel, *Der Blaue Reiter und das Neue Bild*, pp. 356–57.

21. Franz Marc, "Zur Ausstellung der 'Neuen Künstlervereinigung' bei Thannhauser," in the pamphlet *Zwei Kritiken. Zweite Ausstellung der Neuen Künstlervereinigung München* (Munich: Neue Künstlervereinigung München, 1910), reprinted in Hoberg and Friedel, *Der Blaue Reiter und das neue Bild*, pp. 36–38. The pamphlet was inserted into the catalogue of the exhibition in 1910–11.

22. The catalogue of the second NKVM exhibition is reprinted in Hoberg and Friedel, *Der Blaue Reiter und das neue Bild*, pp. 356–62.

23. The international emphasis, however, could also be turned against the NKVM, as when the artist-members were identified as predominantly Russian, thus not representative of Munich's or Germany's art, or else were criticized for adapting their art to fleeting Parisian art fashions.

24. The main proponents of these readings of Kandinsky's compositions are Klaus Brisch, "Wassily Kandinsky (1866–1944): Untersuchungen zur Entstehung der gegenstandslosen Malerei an seinem Werk von 1900–1921" (Ph.D. diss., University of Bonn, 1955); Rose-Carol Washton Long, *Kandinsky: The Development of an Abstract Style* (Oxford: Clarendon Press, 1980);

and Weiss, *Kandinsky in Munich*, and *Kandinsky and Old Russia: The Artist as Ethnographer and Shaman* (New Haven, Conn.: Yale University Press, 1995). For a summary of the evolution of the painting and the various interpretations of *Composition II*, see Magdalena Dabrowski, *Kandinsky: Compositions*, exh. cat. (New York: The Museum of Modern Art, 1995), pp. 25–29.

25. These contradictory views were presented, for example, in the NKVM's 1910 brochure. In it, Marc's positive evaluation ("What artistic insight is harbored in this rare painter! The grand consequence of his color holds his freedom of drawing in balance—is this not simultaneously a definition of painting?") countered the negative response of the Munich journalist and critic Maximilian Karl Rohe: "There are only two ways to explain this absurd exhibition: one assumes either that the majority of the members and guests of the Association are incurably insane, or else that here one is confronted with shameless charlatans" ("Zwei Kritiken," pp. 36–38).

26. For a study of how Kandinsky's contemporaries responded to his paintings and the difficulty they had in "seeing" them, see Riccardo Marchi, "'Pure Painting' in Berlin, 1912–1913: Boccioni, Kandinsky and Delaunay at 'Der Sturm'" (Ph.D. diss., University of Chicago, 2002).

27. In a probably exaggerated and pointedly sarcastic recollection, Kandinsky reported that "the gallery owner complained that after closing every day he had to dry off the paintings because the public had spit on them," and that "the press demanded the immediate closing of this 'anarchistic' exhibition . . . put together by foreign artists, who were endangering the good old Bavarian culture." Wassily Kandinsky, "Franz Marc," in Andreas Hünecke, ed., *Der Blaue Reiter: Dokumente einer Bewegung* (Leipzig: Reclam-Verlag, 1991), p. 34.

28. Kandinsky to Münter, December 4, 1910, in Hoberg and Friedel, *Der Blaue Reiter und das neue Bild*, p. 38.

29. Kandinsky to Alexei von Jawlensky, January 10, 1911, in ibid., p. 39.

30. Marc to Maria Franck, January 21, 1911, in Hünecke, *Dokumente einer Bewegung*, pp. 42–43.

31. Alexander Kanoldt to Walter Riezler, December 11, 1911, in Hoberg, "'Neue Künstlervereinigung München' und 'Blauer Reiter,'" p. 25.

32. Carl Vinnen, comp., *Ein Protest deutscher Künstler* (Jena: Eugen Diederichs Verlag, 1911), quoted in Hünecke, *Dokumente einer Bewegung*, p. 413.

33. Franz Marc, in *Im Kampf um die Kunst: Die Antwort auf den "Protest deutscher Künstler"* (Munich: R. Piper, 1911), quoted in Hünecke, *Dokumente einer Bewegung*, pp. 425–26. For an extensive discussion of the *Protest* and *Response*, see Ron Manheim, *"Im Kampf um die Kunst": De discussie van 1911 over contemporaine Kunst in Duitsland* (Hamburg: Sautter and Lachmann, 1987).

34. Kandinsky to Marc, June 19, 1911, in Wassily Kandinsky and Franz Marc, *Briefwechsel*, ed. Klaus Lankheit (Munich and Zurich: R. Piper, 1983), pp. 39–40, n. 17.

35. The best summary of the *Blue Rider Almanac*'s history remains Klaus Lankheit, "A History of the Almanac," in Kandinsky and Marc, *Der Blaue Reiter*, pp. 11–48.

36. Marc to Reinhard Piper, September 10, 1911, in Kandinsky and Marc, *Der Blaue Reiter*, pp. 244–45.

37. Kandinsky, "The Blue Rider [Recollection]," p. 747.

38. Kandinsky and Marc, *Der Blaue Reiter*, p. 250.

39. For a reproduction of the catalogue, see Hoberg and Freidel, *Der Blaue Reiter und das Neue Bild*, pp. 364–65.

40. *Die I. Ausstellung der Redaktion des Blauen Reiters*, reproduced in Hoberg and Freidel, *Der Blaue Reiter und das Neue Bild*, p. 51.

42. Wassily Kandinsky, "Unsere Freundschaft," in Klaus Lankheit, comp., *Franz Marc im Urteil seiner Zeit*, rev. ed. (Munich and Zurich: R. Piper, 1989), p. 51.

Magdalena Dabrowski, "Kandinsky and Schoenberg: Abstraction as a Visual Metaphor for Emancipated Dissonance," pp. 79–93

1. See Kandinsky's first letter to Schoenberg in *Arnold Schoenberg–Wassily Kandinsky: Letters, Pictures and Documents*, ed. Jelena Hahl-Koch, trans. John C. Crawford (London: Faber and Faber, 1984), p. 21.

2. This treatise, dated in its German typescript version "3 August 1909," encompassed, according to Kandinsky himself, the ideas he had developed over the preceding ten years. The first German edition, *Über das Geistige in der Kunst*, was published by Reinhard Piper, Munich, in December 1911, to coincide with the first *Blue Rider* exhibition. Also in December 1911, excerpts of the Russian version were read by members of the Russian avant-garde, including a friend of Kandinsky's, Nikolai Kulbin, at the Pan-Russian Congress of Artists, held in Saint Petersburg. The second edition, expanded by two passages, was published by Piper in Munich in 1912. The quotations used throughout this essay come from the second edition, as found in Wassily Kandinsky, *On the Spiritual in Art*, in Kenneth C. Lindsay and Peter Vergo, eds., *Kandinsky: Complete Writings on Art* (New York: Da Capo Press, 1994), pp. 114–219.

3. Kandinsky, *On the Spiritual in Art*, pp. 131–52. For Kandinsky's background and the evolution of his theories, see Peg Weiss, *Kandinsky in Munich: The Formative Jugendstil Years* (Princeton, N.J.: Princeton University Press, 1979), and Magdalena Dabrowski, *Kandinsky: Compositions*, exh. cat. (New York: The Museum of Modern Art, 1995), pp. 11–23.

4. See Esther de Costa Meyer, "Schoenberg and Kandinsky: Emancipations," in *Schönberg, Kandinsky, Blauer Reiter und die Russische Avantgarde*, exh. cat. [*Journal of the Arnold Schoenberg Center* 1] (Vienna: Arnold Schoenberg Center, 2000), p. 33.

5. For a detailed discussion of the falling-out between Kandinsky and Schoenberg, see Hahl-Koch, *Schoenberg–Kandinsky*, pp. 73–85, 138–40.

6. Schoenberg to Kandinsky, January 24, 1911, in ibid., p. 24.

7. The phrase "blue rider," Kandinsky wrote some twenty years later, originated from the fact that he and Marc "both loved blue, Marc—horses, I—riders." Wassily Kandinsky, "The Blue Rider [Recollection]," in Lindsay and Vergo, *Complete Writings on Art*, p. 747.

8. On "emancipation of the dissonance," see Arnold Schoenberg, "Composition with Twelve Tones (1)," in *Style and Idea: Selected Writings of Arnold Schoenberg*, ed. Leonard Stein, trans. Leo Black (New York: St. Martin's Press, 1975), pp. 216–17.

9. In his sonnet "Correspondances," in *Les Fleurs du mal* (1855), Baudelaire propounded a theory of correspondences among nature, poetry, visual and literary symbols, smells, sounds, and colors. See Charles Baudelaire, *Oeuvres Complètes*, ed. Marcel A. Ruff (Paris: Éditions du Seuil, 1968), pp. 13, 46. This theory was later expanded and popularized by the French Symbolists in the last decade of the nineteenth century. For an in-depth discussion, see Robert Goldwater, *Symbolism* (New York: Harper and Row, 1979).

10. See Wassily Kandinsky, "Reminiscences," in Lindsay and Vergo, *Complete Writings on Art*, pp. 363–64.

11. Franz Marc to August Macke, January 14, 1911, in *Schoenberg–Kandinsky*, pp. 136–37. The Composition that Marc was referring to was, according to scholar Peg Weiss, *Composition II*, which was shown at a Neue Künstlervereinigung München (New Association of Artists Munich) exhibition in October 1910. See Weiss, "Evolving Perceptions of Kandinsky and Schoenberg: Toward the Ethnic Roots of the 'Outsider,'" in Juliane Brand and Christopher Hailey, eds., *Constructive Dissonance: Arnold Schoenberg and the Transformations of Twentieth-Century Culture* (Berkeley and Los Angeles: University of California Press, 1997), p. 36. But the painting that Marc had in mind could also have been Kandinsky's *Composition IV*, begun in 1910, completed in February 1911, and reproduced in the *Blue Rider Almanac*. For an analysis of the work, see Rose-Carol Washton Long, *Kandinsky: The Development of an Abstract Style* (Oxford: Clarendon Press, 1975), and Dabrowski, *Compositions*, pp. 31–34.

12. Marc to Macke, February 14, 1911, in *Schoenberg–Kandinsky*, p. 137.

13. Kandinsky to Schoenberg, January 18, 1911, in ibid., p. 21.

14. The "passages" characteristic of Paul Cézanne's paintings result from opening the contours of forms situated on different planes and making them "bleed" into one another to create a single, continuous planar pictorial surface.

15. For a discussion of the developments in Russian avant-garde art during the Revolutionary period, see Christina Lodder, *Russian Constructivism* (New Haven, Conn.: Yale University Press, 1983); Camilla Gray, *The Russian Experiment in Art, 1863–1922*, rev. ed. (London: Thames and Hudson, 1986); and Magdalena Dabrowski, "The Russian Contribution to Modernism: 'Construction' as Realization of Innovative Aesthetic Concepts of the Russian Avant-Garde" (Ph.D. diss., Institute of Fine Arts, New York University, 1990), pp. 1–43.

16. For the full quotation, see Hahl-Koch, *Schoenberg–Kandinsky*, p. 23.

17. See Kandinsky, "Reminiscences," p. 373.

18. See Kandinsky, *On the Spiritual in Art*, pp. 179–201.

19. Ibid, p. 218.

20. Ibid.

21. Ibid., p. 165.

22. Ibid., p. 159.

23. Ibid., p. 218.

24. The cycle of Kandinsky's Compositions was the subject of an exhibition at The Museum of Modern Art, New York, in 1995; the catalogue provides an extensive discussion of the subject. See Dabrowski, *Compositions*.

25. See Kandinsky, *On the Spiritual in Art*, p. 218.

26. Dabrowski, *Compositions*, pp. 25–29.

27. Kandinsky, *On the Spiritual in Art*, p. 160.

28. The painting achieved something of a succès de scandale when Kandinsky submitted it for the Neue Künstlervereinigung München exhibition in Munich in December 1911. As a result of the controversy, Kandinsky, Münter, Marc, and Alfred Kubin resigned from the society. For details, see Long, *Development of an Abstract Style*, pp. 112–13.

29. For the text of the lecture, which Kandinsky never delivered because he did not attend the opening of his exhibition, see Lindsay and Vergo, *Complete Writings on Art*, pp. 393–400.

30. For a broad analysis of the iconography of *Composition V*, see Long, *Development of an Abstract Style*, pp. 114–15, and Dabrowski, *Compositions*, pp. 34–37.

31. For an in-depth discussion of *Composition VII*, see Long, *Development of an Abstract Style*, pp. 118–22, and Dabrowski, *Compositions*, pp. 40–45.

32. See Long, *Development of an Abstract Style*, pp. 118–22, and Dabrowski, *Compositions*, pp. 40–45.

33. Kandinsky had harbored this aim since his 1889 trip to the northeastern Siberian province of Vologda, where he traveled to study the laws and customs of the local Zyrian tribes. The peasant huts he visited were profusely decorated with icons, colorful carvings, and other decorative objects and ornaments, which gave him the impression of having entered a painting and been surrounded by it on all sides. For the details of this trip, see Kandinsky, "Reminiscences," pp. 368–69; Peg Weiss, *Kandinsky and Old Russia: The Artist as Ethnographer and Shaman* (New Haven, Conn.: Yale University Press, 1995); and Dabrowski, *Compositions*, pp. 15–17.

34. James Leggio, "Kandinsky, Schoenberg, and the Music of the Spheres," in *Music and Modern Art*, ed. James Leggio (New York: Routledge, 2002), pp. 97–127, is a very thorough and enlightening discussion of this subject.

35. Kandinsky, *On the Spiritual in Art*, p. 373.

36. Wassily Kandinsky, *Point and Line to Plane* (New York: Dover Publications, 1979), pp. 99–100.

37. Leggio, "Kandinsky, Schoenberg, and the Music of the Spheres," pp. 97–127.

38. Kandinsky, *Point and Line to Plane*, pp. 99–100.

39. Leggio, "Kandinsky, Schoenberg, and the Music of the Spheres," pp. 105–19.

Christopher Hailey, "First Loyalties: Schoenberg and Vienna's Classical Tradition," pp. 95–107

Unless otherwise noted, all translations are my own.

1. The varied backgrounds of these composers serve to illustrate the wide spectrum of Jewish identities and the accordingly varied paths to assimilation. Mahler was raised in the Jewish faith; in 1897 he converted to Catholicism, ostensibly for strategic reasons, though he seems to have felt deep ties to the religion. On the other hand, Schreker, whose Jewish father had converted to Protestantism in order to marry a Catholic bride of minor Austrian nobility, was raised a Catholic, though by temperament he seems to have been an agnostic. Zemlinsky was actually only one-quarter Jewish, as his mother was of Jewish/Muslim parentage and his father was a Catholic by birth who had converted to Judaism and became a leading figure in Vienna's Sephardic

(Turkish-Israelite) community. Zemlinsky's conversion to Protestantism, like that of Schoenberg, sprang from considerations more pragmatic than confessional. Schoenberg alone reconverted to Judaism (1933).

2. Alexander Zemlinsky to Arnold Schoenberg, April 1903, in *Zemlinskys Briefwechsel mit Schönberg, Webern, Berg und Schreker* (Briefwechsel der Wiener Schule 1), ed. Horst Weber (Darmstadt: Wissenschaftliche Buchgesellschaft, 1995), pp. 42–43.

3. In 1914, a Leipzig critic complained in a similar vein that the sound collage of the second act of Schreker's *Der ferne Klang* (The distant sound) strained the limits of intelligibility: "There are not very many who can hear and absorb polyphonically to the high degree the composer requires. For the rest this great fractured whole will only represent a sea of sound which they are incapable of disentangling." F., "*Der ferne Klang*" (review), *Leipziger Volkszeitung*, February 10, 1913.

4. The shock of Schoenberg's bald quotation of this tune within a highly dissonant context is underscored by the song's unspoken text, with which Schoenberg's Viennese audience would have been very familiar: "Ach, du lieber Augustin, alles ist hin" (O, dear Augustine, it's all over now). In *Pierrot lunaire* the multiple tonal references are likewise linked to its text, as in the final number, "O alter Duft aus Märchenzeit" (O ancient scent from far-off days), in which parallel thirds evoke the lost paradise of a *Märchenzeit* (literally, "fairytale age").

5. This sense of generational displacement is a frequent topic of Schoenberg's music and writing during the 1920s. "The young composers find my way a blind alley," he wrote in 1926. See Arnold Schoenberg, "My Blind Alley," in *Style and Idea: Selected Writings of Arnold Schoenberg*, ed. Leonard Stein (Berkeley: University of California Press, 1984), p. 95. In his *Three Satires*, op. 28 (1925), Schoenberg directly parodied both Stravinsky and Ernst Krenek.

6. In and around 1921, Schoenberg made this assertion to several students, friends, and acquaintances. The first documented instance of his claim came in a letter to Alma Mahler, quoted on page 60 in the present volume.

7. Arnold Schoenberg, "Analyse der 4 Orchesterlieder op. 22," in *Arnold Schönberg: Stil und Gedanken: Aufsätze zur Musik*, ed. Ivan Vojtěch (Frankfurt: S. Fischer, 1976), p. 286.

8. Schoenberg first presented this essay as a lecture at the Colorado Consistory Auditorium in Denver on October 11, 1937. It is published in Schoenberg, *Style and Idea*, pp. 49–50.

9. Franz Marc to August Macke, January 14 and February 14, 1911, quoted in *Arnold Schoenberg–Wassily Kandinsky: Letters, Pictures, and Documents*, ed. Jelena Hahl-Koch, trans. John C. Crawford (London: Faber and Faber, 1984), pp. 136–37.

10. Wassily Kandinsky to Arnold Schoenberg, January 18, 1911, in ibid., p. 21.

11. Schoenberg to Ferruccio Busoni, July 20, 1909, in Ferruccio Busoni, *Selected Letters*, ed. and trans. Antony Beaumont (New York: Columbia University Press, 1987), p. 383.

12. Schoenberg, *Style and Idea*, p. 141.

13. Schoenberg to Alban Berg, December 6, 1920, in *The Berg–Schoenberg Correspondence*, ed. Juliane Brand, Christopher Hailey, and Donald Harris (New York: W. W. Norton, 1987), p. 295. A well-known anecdote underscores this point. When told that his Wind Quintet, op. 26, had met with an enthusiastic response, Schoenberg replied laconically, "Then they didn't understand it."

14. Diary entry of January 27, 1912, quoted in Josef Rufer, *The Works of Arnold Schoenberg: A Catalogue of His Compositions, Writings and Paintings*, trans. Dika Newlin (London: Faber and Faber, 1962), p. 34. Schoenberg made a note that the printed score should reflect that the titles were added "for technical reasons of publication and not to give a 'poetic' content."

15. Schoenberg to Berg, December 4, 1912, in *Berg–Schoenberg*, p. 132.

16. Rufer, *Works of Arnold Schoenberg*, p. 34. It is interesting to note that the First String Quartet is among those works for which there is a suppressed "program" consisting of a series of words and phrases relating to a succession of psychological states that can be said to correspond to individual themes and sections within the piece. See Christian Martin Schmidt, "Schönberg's 'Very Definite—but Private' Programm zum Streichquartett op. 7," in *Bericht über den 2. Kongress der Internationalen Schönberg—Gesellschaft "Die Wiener Schule in der Musikgeschichte des 20. Jahrhunderts,"* ed. Rudolf Stephan and Sigrid Wiesmann (Vienna: Verlag Elisabeth Lafite, 1986), pp. 230–34.

17. It was naturally far more likely that new works in genres with established expectations would provoke greater opposition than in those, such as songs or program music with more fluid boundaries of form and content. Thus, the Schoenberg premieres that generated the most vociferous response were *Verklärte Nacht*, op. 4 (1903); the First String Quartet, op. 7 (1907); the Chamber Symphony, op. 9 (1907); and the Second String Quartet, op. 10 (1908). The tumultuous premiere of this final piece is somewhat more complicated. Compared to the First String Quartet, the Second is more classically balanced, its thematic material is clear and concise, and its four movements are relatively brief and follow a traditional ordering of First Movement Sonata—Allegro, Scherzo, Adagio, and Finale. However, the unexpected quotation of "Ach, du lieber Augustin" in the second movement and the soprano soloist in the last two were perceived as an assault upon the well-defined formal and aesthetic parameters of chamber music. In another context, Schoenberg's two movements with soprano would have aroused little opposition, particularly as ensemble songs enjoyed a certain popularity at this time.

18. Schoenberg to Berg, December 6, 1920, in *Berg–Schoenberg*, p. 295.

19. Ibid. The Kandinsky citation is quoted above, p. 103.

20. Schoenberg's article "Gustav Mahler—In Memoriam" was first published in the Viennese cultural journal *Der Merker* 3, no. 5 (March 1, 1912): 182–83. Schoenberg reworked the essay in 1948, and it is translated in Schoenberg, *Style and Idea*, pp. 447–48.

21. Schoenberg's lecture "Gustav Mahler" was delivered in Prague on October 13, 1912, and was given again in Vienna on November 3, 1912. An English translation (with revisions Schoenberg added in 1948) appears in Schoenberg, *Style and Idea*, pp. 449–72.

22. Schoenberg, "Gustav Mahler," p. 454.

23. Ibid., p. 462. It is significant that Schoenberg's favorite Mahler symphony was the Sixth, which is the most rigorous in its adherence to classical form.

24. Ibid., p. 450.

25. Schoenberg to Kandinsky, January 24, 1911, in *Schoenberg–Kandinsky*, p. 23.

26. Arnold Schoenberg, *Harmonielehre* (Leipzig: Universal-Edition, 1911). An expanded edition was published in Vienna in 1922.

27. Arnold Schoenberg, "How One Becomes Lonely," in Schoenberg, *Style and Idea*, p. 50.

28. Marc to Macke, January 14, 1911, quoted in *Schoenberg–Kandinsky*, p. 137. It is noteworthy that around the turn of the century the non-Western impulse that had such an impact in Parisian cultural circles evoked great interest among Vienna's Secessionist artists but little response from its composers, with the notable exception, perhaps, of Mahler in *Das Lied von der Erde* (The song of the earth; 1911).

29. The Munich critic Alexander Berrsche recognized as much in his 1914 review of *Der ferne Klang* when he wrote, "Arnold Schoenberg's speculations about 'Klangfarbenmelodien' [timbral colors] have here become a reality. During the performance of Schreker's work one hears harmonic and melodic configurations one knows by heart only as color." See Berrsche, "München," review of the Munich premiere of Schoenberg's *Der ferne Klang*, *Die Musik* 13 (April 1914): 50.

Bibliography

Adams, Henry, Margaret C. Conrads, and Annegret Hoberg, eds. *Albert Bloch: The American Blue Rider.* Munich and New York: Prestel, 1997.

Arnold Schoenberg Center. *Schönberg, Kandinsky, Blauer Reiter und die Russische Avantgarde.* Exh. cat. *Journal of the Arnold Schoenberg Center* 1. Vienna: Arnold Schoenberg Center, 2000.

Arnold Schoenberg–Wassily Kandinsky: Letters, Pictures and Documents. Ed. Jelena Hahl-Koch. Trans. John C. Crawford. London: Faber and Faber, 1984.

Barnett, Vivian Endicott. *Kandinsky at the Guggenheim.* New York: Abbeville Press, 1983.

——. *Kandinsky Watercolours: Catalogue Raisonné.* 2 vols. Ithaca, N.Y.: Cornell University Press, 1992–94.

——. *Vasily Kandinsky: A Colorful Life.* Ed. Helmut Friedel. Cologne: Dumont, 1995.

Boehmer, Konrad, ed. *Schönberg and Kandinsky: An Historic Encounter.* Amsterdam: Harwood Academic Publishers, 1997.

Brand, Juliane, and Christopher Hailey, eds. *Constructive Dissonance: Arnold Schoenberg and the Transformations of Twentieth-Century Culture.* Berkeley and Los Angeles: University of California Press, 1997.

Dabrowski, Magdalena. *Kandinsky: Compositions.* Exh. cat. New York: The Museum of Modern Art, 1995.

Fondation Beyeler. *Farben–Klänge: Wassily Kandinsky, Bilder 1908 bis 1914: Arnold Schönberg, Konzerte und Dokumentation.* Exh. cat. Riehen/Basel: Fondation Beyeler, 1998.

Friedel, Helmut, and Annegret Hoberg. *The Blue Rider in the Lenbachhaus, Munich.* Munich and New York: Prestel, 2000.

Frisch, Walter, ed. *Schoenberg and His World.* Princeton, N.J.: Princeton University Press, 1999.

Heiderich, Ursula. *August Macke Aquarelle: Werkverzeichnis.* Exh. cat. Ostfildern-Ruit: Hatje Cantz, 1997.

Heller, Reinhold. *Gabriele Münter: The Years of Expressionism, 1903–1920.* Munich and New York: Prestel, 1997.

Hoberg, Annegret, ed. *Wassily Kandinsky and Gabriele Münter: Letters and Reminiscences, 1902–1914.* Trans. Ian Robson. Munich: Prestel, 1994.

——, and Helmut Friedel. *Der Blaue Reiter und das Neue Bild.* Munich and New York: Prestel, 1999.

——, and Helmut Friedel, eds. *Gabriele Münter, 1877–1962: Retrospektive.* Exh. cat. Münich: Städtische Galerie im Lenbachhaus and Prestel, 1992.

Holst, Christian von, et al. *Franz Marc: Horses.* Exh. cat. Trans. Elizabeth Clegg and Claudia Spinner. Cambridge, Mass.: Busch-Reisinger Museum, Harvard University Art Museums; Ostfildern-Ruit: Hatje Cantz, 2000.

Jawlensky, Maria, Lucia Pieroni-Jawlensky, and Angelica Jawlensky. *Alexej von Jawlensky: Catalogue Raisonné of the Oil Paintings.* 4 vols. London: Sotheby's Publications, 1991–98.

Kallir, Jane. *Arnold Schoenberg's Vienna.* Exh. cat. New York: Galerie St. Etienne and Rizzoli, 1984.

Kandinsky, Wassily. *The Complete Writings on Art.* Ed. Kenneth C. Lindsay and Peter Vergo. New York: Da Capo Press, 1994.

———. *On the Spiritual in Art.* In *Kandinsky: The Complete Writings on Art.* Ed. Kenneth C. Lindsay and Peter Vergo. New York: Da Capo Press, 1994. Pp. 114–219.

———. *Point and Line to Plane.* New York: Dover Publications, 1979.

———. *Sounds.* Trans. Elizabeth R. Napier. New Haven, Conn., and London: Yale University Press, 1981.

———, and Franz Marc, eds. *The Blaue Reiter Almanac.* Documentary edition by Klaus Lankheit. New York: Viking Press, 1974.

Leggio, James. "Kandinsky, Schoenberg, and the Music of the Spheres." In *Music and Modern Art.* Ed. James Leggio. New York: Routledge, 2002. Pp. 97–127.

Long, Rose-Carol Washton. *Kandinsky: The Development of an Abstract Style.* Oxford: Clarendon Press; New York: Oxford University Press, 1980.

Musée d'Art Moderne de la Ville de Paris. *Arnold Schoenberg: Regards.* Exh. cat. Paris: Musée d'Art Moderne de la Ville de Paris, 1995.

Reich, Willi. *Schoenberg: A Critical Biography.* New York: Penguin Books, 1971.

Ringer, Alexander L. *Arnold Schoenberg: The Composer as Jew.* Oxford: Clarendon Press; New York: Oxford University Press, 1990.

Roethel, Hans K., and Jean K. Benjamin. *Kandinsky: Catalogue Raisonné of the Oil Paintings.* 2 vols. Ithaca, N.Y.: Cornell University Press, 1982–84.

Rosen, Charles. *Arnold Schoenberg.* Chicago: University of Chicago Press, 1996.

Rosenthal, Marc. *Franz Marc.* Munich and New York: Prestel, 1989.

Schirn Kunsthalle. *Die Visionen des Arnold Schönberg: Jahre der Malerei.* Exh. cat. Frankfurt: Schirn Kunsthalle, 2002.

Schoenberg, Arnold. *Letters.* Ed. Erwin Stein. Trans. Eithne Wilkins and Ernst Kaiser. New York: St. Martin's Press, 1965.

———. *Style and Idea: Selected Writings of Arnold Schoenberg.* Ed. Leonard Stein. Trans. Leo Black. Berkeley and Los Angeles: University of California Press, 1975.

Shawn, Allen. *Arnold Schoenberg's Journey.* New York: Farrar, Straus and Giroux, 2002.

Solomon R. Guggenheim Museum. *Kandinsky in Munich, 1896–1914.* Exh. cat. New York: Solomon R. Guggenheim Foundation, 1982.

Stuckenschmidt, H. H. *Arnold Schoenberg: His Life, World and Work.* Trans. Humphrey Searle. New York: Schirmer Books, 1977.

Vriesen, Gustav. *August Macke.* Stuttgart: W. Kohlhammer, 1957.

Weiss, Peg. *Kandinsky in Munich: The Formative Jugendstil Years.* Princeton, N.J.: Princeton University Press, 1979.

Werkner, Patrick. *Austrian Expressionism: the Formative Years.* Trans. Nicholas T. Parsons. Palo Alto, Calif.: Society for the Promotion of Science and Scholarship, 1993.

Zaunschirm, Thomas, ed. *Arnold Schoenberg: Paintings and Drawings.* Klagenfurt: Ritter, 1991.

Zweite, Armin, ed. *Alexej Jawlensky, 1864–1941.* Exh. cat. Munich: Städtische Galerie im Lenbachhaus, 1983.

Illustration Credits

Numerals in **boldface** refer to pages.

ABBREVIATIONS

ASC	Arnold Schoenberg Center, Vienna
ARS	© 2003 Artists Rights Society, New York
BMP	© Belmont Music Publishers, Los Angeles
CNAC	CNAC/MNAM/Dist. Réunion des Musées Nationaux/Art Resource, N.Y.
GMJES	Gabriele Münter und Johannes Eichner Stiftung, Munich
LC	Library of Congress, Washington, D.C.
SGL	Städtische Galerie im Lenbachhaus, Munich
SRG	Solomon R. Guggenheim Museum, New York

Cover: SGL, ARS/ADAGP, Paris
Endpapers: ASC
Frontispiece: CNAC (left); ASC (right)
Back cover: ASC, ARS/VBK, Vienna

Wasserman Essay
16 ASC. **19** ASC, BMP. **21** From Arnold Schoenberg Center, *Schönberg, Kandinsky, Blauer Reiter und die Russische Avantgarde*, exh. cat. [*Journal of the Arnold Schoenberg Center* 1] (Vienna: Arnold Schoenberg Center, 2000). **22** Photograph by Claude Planch, CNAC, ARS/ADAGP, Paris. **23** CNAC, ARS/ADAGP, Paris. **25** Arnold Schoenberg Archives, Music Division, LC. **26** ASC, ARS/ADAGP, Paris. **27** GMJES, BMP. **28** ASC. **29** CNAC. **30** ASC, ARS/ADAGP, Paris. **31** Arnold Schoenberg Archives, Music Division, LC. **32** ASC, ARS/ADAGP, Paris (left); ASC (center); Arnold Schoenberg Archives, Music Division, LC (right). **33** ASC, ARS/VG Bild-Kunst, Bonn. **34** Arnold Schoenberg Archives, Music Division, LC. **35** From Arnold Schoenberg Center, *Schönberg, Kandinsky, Blauer Reiter und die Russische Avantgarde*.

Da Costa Meyer Essay
36 Arnold Schoenberg Archives, Music Division, LC. **38** ASC. **40** SGL, ARS/VG Bild-Kunst, Bonn. **41** ASC (top left, bottom left); photographs by Gabriele Münter, GMJES, ARS/VG Bild-Kunst, Bonn (top right, bottom right). **44** Museen der Stadt Wien. **45** © MUMOK, Museum Moderner Kunst Stiftung Ludwig Wien (top); ASC (bottom). **46** © Bettmann/CORBIS. **47** From Thomas Zaunschirm, ed., *Arnold Schoenberg: Paintings and Drawings* (Klagenfurt: Ritter, 1991), ARS/VBK, Vienna. **48** Leopold Museum–Privatstiftung, Vienna. **49** ASC, ARS/VBK, Vienna (top); Rheinisches Bildarchiv Köln (bottom). **51** Erich Lessing/Art Resource, N.Y., © 2003 The Munch Museum/The Munch-Ellingsen Group/ARS. **52** Digital image © 2003 The Museum of Modern Art, New York, ARS/ProLitteris, Zurich. **54** From G. Tobias Natter, ed., *Max Oppenheimer: 1885–1954*, exh. cat. (Vienna: Jüdisches Museum der Stadt Wien, 1994). **57** MAK–Austrian Museum of Applied Arts/Contemporary Art, Vienna, ARS/ProLitteris, Zurich. **59** The Jewish Museum, New York. **61** ASC.

Heller Essay
62 Photograph by Gabriele Münter, GMJES, ARS/VG Bild-Kunst, Bonn. **64** SRG, ARS/ADAGP, Paris. **65** GMJES. **66** Photograph by Bertrand Prevost, CNAC, ARS/ADAGP, Paris. **67–68** SGL, ARS/ADAGP, Paris. **69** Milwaukee Art Museum, ARS/VG Bild-Kunst, Bonn. **72** Rare Book and Special Collections Division, LC, ARS/ADAGP, Paris. **73** Saarland Museum, Saarbrücken. **74** ASC, ARS/ADAGP, Paris. **75** Photographs by Gabriele Münter, GMJES, ARS/VG Bild-Kunst, Bonn. **76** Rare Book and Special Collections Division, LC, ARS/ADAGP, Paris. **77** Rare Book and Special Collections Division, LC.

Dabrowski Essay
78 Photograph by Gabriele Münter, GMJES, ARS/VG Bild-Kunst, Bonn. **81** © 2003 Kunsthaus Zürich, all rights reserved. **85** State Tretyakov Gallery, Moscow, ARS/ADAGP, Paris (top); CNAC, ARS/ADAGP, Paris (bottom). **87** State Tretyakov Gallery, Moscow, ARS/ADAGP, Paris. **88** Photograph by Claude Planch, CNAC, ARS/ADAGP, Paris (top); CNAC, ARS/ADAGP, Paris (bottom). **89** ASC, ARS/ADAGP, Paris. **90** Private collection, ARS/ADAGP, Paris. **91** State Tretyakov Gallery, Moscow, ARS/ADAGP, Paris. **92** SRG, ARS/ADAGP, Paris. **93** Philadelphia Museum of Art, ARS/ADAGP, Paris.

Hailey Essay
94 ASC. **96** ASC. **97** ASC, BMP. **98** ASC. **99** ASC (top); ASC, BMP (bottom). **100** ASC, BMP. **101** ASC. **105** ASC. **107** ASC, BMP.

Plates
109 SGL, ARS/ADAGP, Paris. **110** SRG, ARS/ADAGP, Paris. **111** Yale University Art Gallery, ARS/ADAGP, Paris. **112** SRG, ARS/ADAGP, Paris. **113** SGL, ARS/ADAGP, Paris. **114** SGL, ARS/VG Bild-Kunst, Bonn. **115** Milwaukee Art Museum, ARS/VG Bild-Kunst, Bonn. **116** Private collection, ARS/VG Bild-Kunst, Bonn. **117–27** ASC, ARS/VBK, Vienna. **128** Private collection, ARS/VBK, Vienna. **129–33** ASC, ARS/VBK, Vienna. **134** Private collection, ARS/ADAGP, Paris. **135** State Hermitage Museum, St. Petersburg, ARS/ADAGP, Paris. **136** Collection Deutsche Bank, ARS/ADAGP, Paris. **137** Albright-Knox Art Gallery, Buffalo, New York, ARS/ADAGP, Paris. **138** SGL, ARS/ADAGP, Paris. **139** Philadelphia Museum of Art, ARS/ADAGP, Paris. **140** Sylvia and Ulrich Ströher Collection, Germany, ARS/VG Bild-Kunst, Bonn. **141** Photograph © The Israel Museum/by David Harris, Collection The Israel Museum, Jerusalem, ARS/VG Bild-Kunst, Bonn. **142** Photograph © Board of Trustees, National Gallery of Art, Washington, D.C., ARS/VG Bild-Kunst, Bonn. **143** Hanna Bekker vom Rath Collection, ARS/VG Bild-Kunst, Bonn. **144** ASC, ARS/VBK, Vienna. **145** Music Division, LC, ARS/VBK, Vienna. **146–47** ASC, ARS/VBK, Vienna. **148** SRG. **149** Albright-Knox Art Gallery, Buffalo, New York. **150** Albright-Knox Art Gallery, Buffalo, New York (top); SGL (bottom). **151** Westfälisches Landesmuseum für Kunst und Kulturgeschichte, Münster. **152** The Saint Louis Art Museum, ARS/VG Bild-Kunst, Bonn. **153** The Albert Bloch Foundation, Lawrence, Kansas. **154–55** Museen der Stadt Wien, ARS/VBK, Vienna. **156** ASC, ARS/VBK, Vienna. **157** University of Applied Arts Vienna Collection, ARS/VBK, Vienna. **158** ASC, ARS/VBK, Vienna. **159** Estate of Heinrich Jalowetz, courtesy Galerie St. Etienne, New York, ARS/VBK, Vienna. **160–63** ASC, ARS/VBK, Vienna.

Chronologies
165 ASC (left); GMJES (right). **166** ASC. **167** GMJES (left, center); photograph by Gabriele Münter, GMJES, ARS/VG Bild-Kunst, Bonn (right). **168** GMJES. **169** ASC. **170** GMJES. **171–72** ASC. **173** Centre Georges Pompidou, Photothèque des collections du MNAM/CCI, Paris, Bequest of Nina Kandinsky (top left, top right); Bauhaus-Archiv, Berlin (bottom left). **174** ASC (top); Centre Georges Pompidou, Photothèque des collections du MNAM/CCI, Paris, Bequest of Nina Kandinsky (bottom). **175** ASC (left); photograph by Hugo Erfurth, CNAC, ARS/VG Bild-Kunst, Bonn (right).

Program Notes for Compact Disc

All works are by Arnold Schoenberg.

The accompanying compact disc reproduces the program for the January 2, 1911, concert of Schoenberg's music in Munich, with the exception of the First String Quartet in D Minor, op. 7, which has been omitted because of space limitations. These pieces appear in the order in which they were performed at the concert. The CD also includes *Herzgewächse* (Heart's foliage), op. 20, which was written later in 1911; a facsimile of the score of this piece was reproduced in the *Blue Rider Almanac* (1912), edited by Wassily Kandinsky and Franz Marc.

Numerals in **boldface** refer to track numbers on the CD.

Second String Quartet in F-sharp Minor, op. 10 (1908)

1 I. *Moderato* (Moderate)
2 II. *Sehr rasch* (Very quick)
3 III. *Litanei* (Litany)
4 IV. *Entrückung* (Rapture)

Text by Stefan George

Benita Valente, soprano; Juilliard String Quartet (Robert Mann, violin; Earl Carlyss, violin; Samuel Rhodes, viola; Joel Krosnick, cello)

From *Schoenberg: The Expressionist Years, 1908–1920* (Sony Classical SMK 62020). Recorded in 1975.

Three Piano Pieces, op. 11 (1909)

5 1. *Mässig* (Moderate)
6 2. *Mässige Achtel* (Moderate eighth note)
7 3. *Bewegt* (Agitated)

Sarah Rothenberg, piano

From *Shadows and Fragments: Brahms and Schoenberg Piano Works, 1892–1911* (Arabesque Recordings Z6761). Recorded in 2000.

Lieder, op. 2 (1899)

8 No. 1, *Erwartung* (Expectation) (Text by Richard Dehmel)

Phyllis Bryn-Julson, soprano; Ursula Oppens, piano

From *Arnold Schönberg: Three Song Cycles* (Music and Arts Programs of America CD-4650). Recorded in 1990.

Lieder, op. 6 (1903–5)

9 No. 4, *Verlassen* (Forsaken) (Text by Hermann Conradi)
10 No. 6, *Am Wegrand* (By the roadside) (Text by John Henry Mackay)
11 No. 3, *Mädchenlied* (Maiden's song) (Text by Paul Remer)
12 No. 8, *Der Wanderer* (The wanderer) (Text by Friedrich Nietzsche)

Helen Vanni, mezzo-soprano; Glenn Gould, piano

From *The Glenn Gould Edition: Schoenberg Lieder* (Sony Music SM2K 52667). Recorded in 1968.

13 *Herzgewächse* (Heart's foliage), op. 20 (1911)

Text by Maurice Maeterlinck

Lucy Shelton, soprano; Sarah Rothenberg, celeste; James David Christie, harmonium; Susan Jolles, harp; Oliver Knussen, conductor

From *Arnold Schoenberg: Pierrot Lunaire, Op. 21; Herzgewächse, Op. 20* (Bridge Records BCD 9032). Recorded in 1991.

Compilation produced by Museum Music, Inc.
www.museummusic.com

Contributors

Magdalena Dabrowski is Research Curator at The Metropolitan Museum of Art, and was formerly Senior Curator in the Department of Drawings at The Museum of Modern Art. She is the author of *French Landscape: The Modern Vision, 1880–1920* (1999), *Kandinsky: Compositions* (1995), *Liubov Popova* (1991), *The Drawings of Philip Guston* (1988), and *Contrasts of Form: Geometric Abstract Art, 1910–1980* (1985).

Esther da Costa Meyer teaches in the Department of Art and Archaeology at Princeton University. Specializing in modern architecture, she has focused on issues of gender, urban pathology, and the interface between architecture and the other visual arts. Her book, *The Work of Antonio Sant'Elia*, appeared in 1995, followed by essays in *Assemblage*, *Modernism/Modernity*, *New German Critique*, and *Harvard Design Magazine*.

Christopher Hailey is Director of the Franz Schreker Foundation and the author of *Franz Schreker, 1878–1934: A Cultural Biography* (1993). He is also the coeditor of *Constructive Dissonance: Arnold Schoenberg and the Transformations of Twentieth-Century Culture* (1997) and *The Berg-Schoenberg Correspondence: Selected Letters* (1986). His score editions include Alban Berg's early songs and Schreker's dance pantomimes *Der Wind* and *Der Geburtstag der Infantin*.

Reinhold Heller is Professor and Chair of Art History and Professor of Germanic Studies at the University of Chicago. Among his many publications are *Confronting Identities in German Art, 1800–2000* (2003), *Gabriele Münter: The Years of Expressionism, 1903–1920* (1997), *Toulouse-Lautrec: The Soul of Montmartre* (1997), *Stark Impressions: Graphic Production in Germany, 1918–1933* (1993), *Munch: His Life and Work* (1984), and *The Art of Wilhelm Lehmbruck* (1972).

Fred Wasserman is Associate Curator at The Jewish Museum, New York. He was project director for *Entertaining America: Jews, Movies, and Broadcasting* as well as the reinstallation of the museum's permanent exhibition, *Culture and Continuity: The Jewish Journey*. He is the coauthor of *Becoming Visible: An Illustrated History of Lesbian and Gay Life in Twentieth-Century America* (1998) and *Ellis Island: An Illustrated History of the Immigrant Experience* (1991).

Index

Illustrations are indicated with numbers in italics.

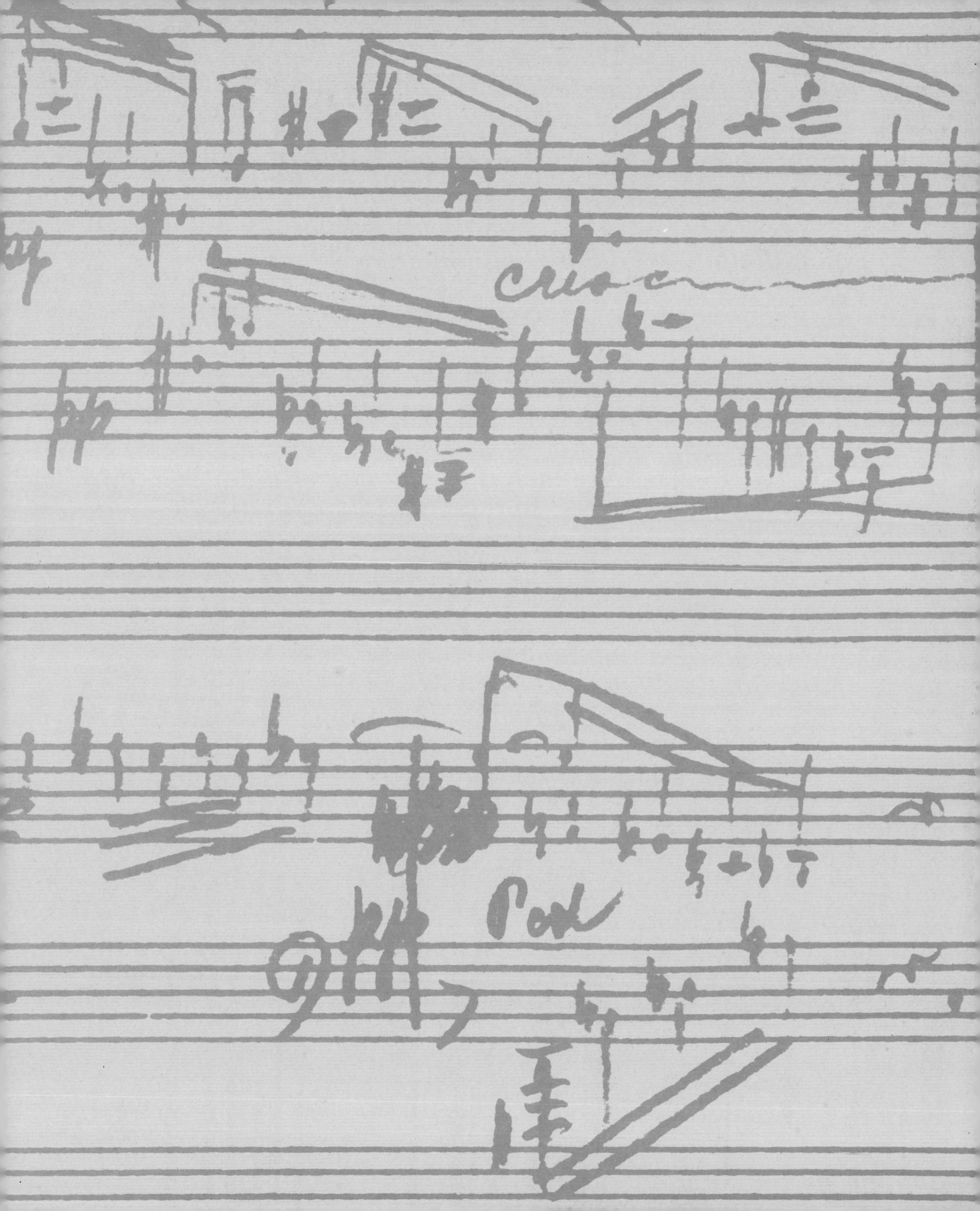
Cresc
Ped